TCP/IP

Running a Successful Network

Data Communications and Networks Series

Consulting Editor: Dr C. Smythe, Surrey University

Selected titles

X400 Message Handling: Standards, Interworking, Applications
  B. Plattner, C. Lanz, H. Lubich, M. Müller and T. Walter

Network Management: Problems, Standards and Strategies
  Franz-Joachim Kauffels

Token Ring: Principles, perspectives and strategies
  Hans-Georg Göhring and Franz-Joachim Kauffels

TCP/IP

Running a Successful Network

K. Washburn
J.T. Evans

Integralis Ltd, Reading

ADDISON-WESLEY
PUBLISHING
COMPANY

Wokingham, England · Reading, Massachusetts · Menlo Park, California · New York
Don Mills, Ontario · Amsterdam · Bonn · Sydney · Singapore
Tokyo · Madrid · San Juan · Milan · Paris · Mexico City · Seoul · Taipei

© 1993 Addison-Wesley Publishers Ltd.
© 1993 Addison-Wesley Publishing Company Inc.

Many of the designations used by manufacturers and sellers to distinguish their products are claimed as trademarks. Addison-Wesley has made every attempt to supply trademark information about manufacturers and their products mentioned in this book. A list of the trademark designations and their owners appears on p. x.

Cover designed by Chris Eley
and printed by The Riverside Printing Co. (Reading) Ltd.
Typeset by Meridian Phototypesetting Ltd, Pangbourne in 10/12 New Century Schoolbook, Futura and Melior.
Printed in Great Britain by T.J. Press Ltd., Padstow, Cornwall.

First printed 1993. Reprinted 1993.

British Library Cataloguing in Publication Data
A catalogue record for this book is available from the British Library

Library of Congress Cataloging in Publication Data applied for.

Dedication

To Maggie and Stella

Preface

Society, its government and commerce depend on accurate, reliable and convenient ways of exchanging information between individuals and organizations and across national boundaries. In the late 1980s, the success of computers and their interconnecting networks (particularly the personal computer and the local area network) completely changed the speed, accuracy and convenience of all manner of information transfer. The standards collectively known as TCP/IP, first developed to allow exchange of information between computers in the US government, defence and university research communities, have appeared in attractive, useful and widely available products for general commercial computing. With the increasing interest in the use of TCP/IP for general commercial applications, there is a need to know what TCP/IP provides, how to exploit its functionality, and what management and technical difficulties will be encountered.

This book is about the practical problems of installing, configuring and maintaining information systems based on the TCP/IP set of standards, from initial installation to on-going maintenance.

For a system to be successful and to retain that success over a long time requires frequent revision of initial assumptions; system designers must take account not only of technical, but also of social and organizational problems they will encounter. Successful systems grow and develop. They are used in ways and for purposes that the initial design probably did not predict. Once convenient and reliable operation is achieved, the users abandon and then lose the older, less convenient alternatives. The new system becomes part of the corporate infrastructure and day-to-day life, its value increases and any change in performance and availability can dramatically affect prosperity and well-being.

The planners and operators of any technology have responsibilities for its care and maintenance, if long-term viability is to be assured. In this book, we pass on our experience of designing, planning, installing and running large computer communications networks using TCP/IP, taking into account many of the factors that we have discovered can influence the short- and long-term success of computer networks.

Choosing Equipment

In a description of the practical issues, we will frequently point out that standards developers have included many features and facilities in the standards which are not yet generally implemented in available equipment. Equally, there are facilities in products which are not included in the standards. It is up to equipment users to recognize any gap between the potential of systems such as TCP/IP and the functionality of current products. In examining how improved systems would benefit their use of the technology, those with purchasing power can drive technology forward so that suppliers produce more advanced systems sooner. We will frequently emphasize the difference between the potential of the standards and recent practice.

How to use this book

The book is divided into three parts.

Part I describes the options and features of TCP/IP without discussing technology in detail. In particular, Part I is about the choices and decisions that must be made as any computer products which use TCP/IP for communications are introduced. It highlights key decisions which must be made early in the adoption of TCP/IP systems, if major upheaval and expense is to be avoided later. It shows how to make those decisions, and discusses the essential practical steps to producing reliable and flexible systems that are convenient both for commercial users and for system and network managers. We follow the development, expansion and day-to-day operations of the system, and outline how to maintain the performance of a TCP/IP system as it grows and is integrated into a corporation's infrastructure.

Part I is about 'what and how' not 'why'. It is for those who are content (for the moment at least) to work on the premise, 'if I don't need to change it and it is unlikely to cause trouble later, I don't need a detailed technological understanding'. For those configuring and managing small, unchanging TCP/IP networks, this information may be sufficient.

Part II describes the detailed technical standards behind TCP/IP systems, particularly where such technical detail leads to further choices which will influence the success of an installed system. Part II is about 'what else, why, what if, and what next'. It is intended for those who need to understand the detail of a protocol, the bits and bytes, in order to manage and maintain large and complex computer networks better. These are the people who may wish to take advantage of the most sophisticated features, who have a need to understand the 'why'. Equally, it is for those who seek knowledge out of technical interest.

Large networks often display problems and issues peculiar to their environment and configuration. Part II allows the more technically biased reader to determine the underlying limits of TCP/IP systems and to take action to ensure that systems, in particular, large systems, remain stable. It is concerned with tuning performance, achieving reliability, stability, and cost effectiveness through a detailed technical understanding which allows optimizing the foundations laid in Part I.

Part III is a collection of reference material and tables extracted from TCP/IP and local area network standards which can greatly simplify the configuration and management of TCP/IP systems.

Part I and Part II can be read in isolation, or in either order, according to interest and immediate need. Part III can be used as reference at any time. Part I will stand alone as a planning and implementation guide.

Acknowledgements

Many of the concepts, guidelines and drawings presented in this book were developed by the authors as part of their practical-based training activities on behalf of Integralis Ltd, Theale Reading, RG7 5AH, England. With the permission of the directors of Integralis, material has been included from the following Integralis training courses:

- Introduction to data communications technology

- Introduction to local area networks

- Practical TCP/IP

- Internetworking with bridges and routers

The authors wish to thank the directors of Integralis Ltd for their permission to include the material, for their support in its development and for their encouragement during the writing of this book.

That this book could be written in the first place is due to the foundations laid by V.A. Thomson and J.A. Robinson, who showed us the way.

It is also for researchers in the USA and worldwide who wrote informative and amusing, readable RFCs and showed that standardization does not have to read like OSI.

Kevin Washburn
Jim Evans

Theale, England
February 1993

Contents

PART I

The key implementation decisions

1

Introducing TCP/IP

In this introductory chapter we discuss what TCP/IP is and its background, and examine the need for such a protocol suite and its applications. Many of the basic concepts introduced here will be developed in later chapters. The subjects covered are:

- The need for internetworking
- OSI and TCP/IP initiatives
- TCP/IP as a communications architecture
- TCP/IP functionality
- Management choices
- The need for control
- The functions to be managed
- How organizational structure affects technology

The need for internetworking

It is some 13 years since the authors first began to work together on communications networks in a large commercial environment. In that early part of our careers, which of course predated readily available sophisticated systems like TCP/IP, we were first involved in the design and implementation of a large corporate terminal-based information network. The aims of our corporate network manager were expressed in three memorable phrases that appeared in many management presentations of the time:

- A single terminal on a desk
- One terminal per seated employee
- Total logical interconnectivity

The requirements were simple, if somewhat shrouded in the jargon of the day: employees should be able to access any information or system in the corporation (for which they had authority) from a single terminal on their own desk – they would not see the structure of the underlying communications medium; the terminal should become as important and widespread and as easy to use as the telephone; and the communications system that supported the terminals should be as reliable and responsive as our private telephone network.

Immediately, we were able to make some decisions based on the communications flows within the corporation rather than on the limitations of the technology. We needed any-to-any communications to move information reliably, we needed switching and we needed conversion systems that would allow access to different computers by any terminal type. As the number of terminals increased, it was also clear that we required a structured cabling system which would give an independent connection for each terminal, but which would greatly simplify installations and changes (Figure 1.1). The communications industry coined the terms 'local area network' and 'wide area network' to describe different aspects of this technology, but our organization had already seen the requirement for full interconnection of these two technologies as one integrated system. Certainly our data network users were not interested in the details of the technology as long as it delivered the data.

We thought of these requirements as just 'networking'. Since then, this level of integration has become known as 'internetworking'. In the late 1970s this was truly visionary for most commercial corporate environments.

The continued endurance of these statements is interesting. Despite the many advances of the 1980s, managers in Information Technology (IT) or of Management Information Systems (MIS) still have the same goals. But now the tool is the personal computer or workstation rather than a 'dumb terminal'. Data rates in common use in the 1990s were, in 1979, available only in research labs.

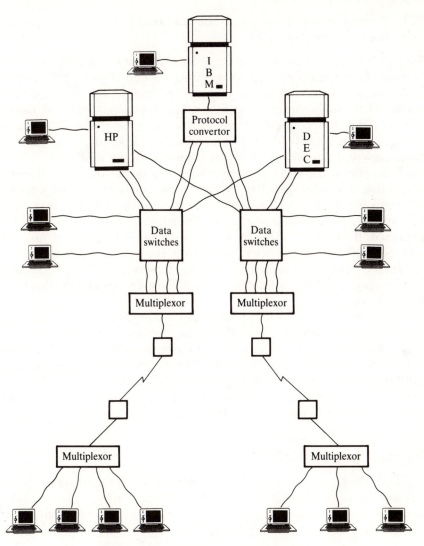

Figure 1.1 Terminal switching network.

Achieving the goals

If the goals described are to be achieved, three separate functions are required:

(1) The ability to move data anywhere in an organization with chosen reliability, security and performance.

(2) The correct interpretation of that data in a manner appropriate to the receiving equipment.

(3) Display of the interpreted information in an acceptable form for user consumption.

The requirement for communications transparency is often expressed by showing the communications network as a cloud (Figure 1.2). Network users are not interested in the technology that makes up the cloud, or indeed, where their communicating partner is located, only that the data is delivered reliably, in good time, and at acceptable cost. The network cloud can be surrounded by a second cloud which similarly disguises the technology and 'architecture' of the communicating machines. The two clouds represent the two key components of internetworking – intercommunication and interoperation. When these issues are solved, computer users can focus on using technology to further their businesses, rather than on the details of the machines, their locations or the way they are connected. If these technical details do become visible, system managers have perhaps failed the users. Creating the standards for these two clouds has, since 1977, been an aim of the International Organization for Standardization (ISO) with their Open Systems Interconnection (ISO OSI) initiative.

The third requirement, that of displaying data, is up to individual manufacturers and is one way they differentiate their products. In the early 1980s, OSI activity was perhaps strongest outside the USA. While ISO committees were developing the OSI protocols, the USA was developing in parallel, but with an interchange of ideas, an alternative set of techniques which became known as TCP/IP. These protocols became a US Department of Defense standard in 1983.

The popularity of TCP/IP

In recent years, knowledge of the capabilities of Transmission Control Protocol/Internet Protocol (TCP/IP) has spread far beyond the USA. IT managers in all types of organizations have begun to research its suitability as an internetworking technology. TCP/IP seems to be a ready-

Figure 1.2 Communications transparency.

made solution to the commercial information systems requirements of intercommunication and interoperation.

Many in the US government and research communities and many UNIX aficionados are already well versed in the vocabulary and configuration issues of this set of protocols. But for the newcomer to TCP/IP, the existing sources of information are, in many cases, written by developers apparently for developers. Most information is primarily technical with detailed descriptions of the bits, flags and fields of the protocols. Less information is given about the practical problems of implementing TCP/IP from scratch, in, for example, a commercial rather than a technical or research environment; here the skills and constraints may be very different. The information needed does exist, but you have to read a considerable quantity of material before finding what you need.

The first section of this book explains the commercial, organizational and technical issues that implementing TCP/IP raises. For the newcomer to TCP/IP, we present solutions where they exist. Where they are incomplete or do not exist, we try to offer alternatives or to highlight the limitations; it is to be hoped that equipment purchasers will explain their needs to suppliers in the manner that will best achieve the development of better products! The second section of this book develops the detailed technical aspects of the protocols, showing the implications of the bits, bytes and fields for the technical planners and implementors who must track down the difficult problems of interoperation and compatibility between different implementations.

TCP/IP emerges

When Berkeley Software Distribution released Berkeley UNIX 4.2BSD in September 1983, a comprehensive set of 'ready-made' communications protocols called TCP/IP became much more widely available and well-known than it had been before. This was not a coincidence; its inclusion in this release was funded by the US government. TCP/IP protocols are based on standards originally developed for the US government and US research community. With the release of UNIX 4.2BSD, these communications standards emerged from the confines of the US Department of Defense and the US university and research networks; TCP/IP became *the way* to interconnect UNIX systems. Berkeley UNIX 4.2BSD and subsequent releases spread quickly throughout the US university and commercial communities. As UNIX has achieved wide popularity as an 'open system', so the fame of TCP/IP has continued to spread. But TCP/IP is not, and never has been, narrowly confined to UNIX; it was developed to allow free interchange of data among all machines, independent of type, manufacturer, hardware or operating system.

In the late 1980s, TCP/IP received a further boost to its fortunes, when Sun Microsystems published the specification for Open Network Computing (ONC), often called the Network File System (NFS). NFS adds important functions to TCP/IP and is now very widely available and regarded as an integral part of the TCP/IP protocol suite. It is particularly valuable for the commercial implementor because of the simple user interfaces that it provides.

Cost-effective implementations of TCP/IP are now available for all types and sizes of machines from the largest mainframe to personal computers and workstations. This has brought TCP/IP and its capabilities to the attention of a very wide audience far beyond the initial US interest. Computer managers and users in commercial organizations throughout the world have begun to implement TCP/IP as a way of solving the problems of interworking between machines of different manufacture.

TCP/IP provides all the facilities for two computer systems to exchange information (intercommunication), interpret it properly, and present it in a format which can be understood by the local machine and its users (interoperation). NFS gives a simple and locally-familiar representation of a set of remote and possibly unfamiliar computer filing systems; like the original components of the TCP/IP suite, NFS is now available for many different computers.

OSI and TCP/IP initiatives

In 1977, ISO began to develop a communications architecture which would become an international standard, a set of communications protocols known as **open systems interconnection** (OSI). This initiative had the same general aims as TCP/IP – intercommunication and interoperation across different manufacturers' computing architectures – but unlike TCP/IP, in a way that met a published set of 'open' international standards. OSI now comprises many hundreds of standards, each of which has taken years to develop, agree and publish in its final ISO form. Regrettably, the best known aspect of OSI is still the OSI reference model and its seven layers (Figure 1.3), as the model itself is only a development aid to allow standards developers to produce the detailed communications standards within a consistent architectural framework.

In the standard which describes the reference model, OSI standards developers state that they will exclude any details which would be implementation dependent; the result is that while the standards have been kept 'pure', many details which would aid development of viable OSI products are excluded from the standards themselves. While some would argue that OSI is more rigorous in its standardization than TCP/IP, the OSI development process seems to have become enmeshed in procedures, weighed down by the difficulties of obtaining consensus in large committees and dogged by supplier politics. By confining OSI standards to abstract definitions in a complex vocabulary defined just for the purpose and then charging considerable sums for copies of those

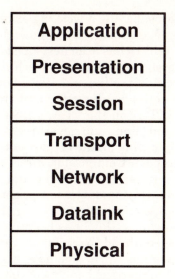

Figure 1.3   ISO OSI reference model.

standards, ISO committees have undoubtedly, if unintentionally, slowed the OSI development process and the delivery of useful conforming products.

With a more restricted geographic and technical scope, TCP/IP developers adopted a pragmatic approach. TCP/IP standardization was based on the Request for Comments (RFC), a flexible and fast standardization process using electronic mail to publish and exchange comments and ideas, and to update drafts. Developers often outlined parts of a standard in a familiar computer language, usually 'C' which, while not intended to be implemented directly, gave a very good starting point for an initial implementation.

TCP/IP standards are freely available on-line from a number of computer systems, originally without full drawings or graphics, but today with all the quality of a laser-printed, desktop-published document as PostScript files. If you must resort to paper and the postal service, the charge in the recent past has been a minimal $10 per copy. For manufacturers of communications and computing products, the contrast with OSI could not be more stark; it is just so much easier to obtain TCP/IP information than OSI. Standards were produced more quickly and they are written in a readable and comprehensible form by developers for developers.

The US government demanded TCP/IP for all systems, thereby ensuring every US government computer supplier provided it. They also funded universities to implement the standards. In the USA, such publicly funded work enters the public domain, and, if not of a military nature, is freely available to all citizens. While it may not be used directly for commercial purposes, having a working example in 'C' source code certainly assists future developments by commercial suppliers!

Neither OSI nor TCP/IP has been developed in isolation. There has been a considerable interchange of ideas and techniques, particularly evident in the changes in OSI since the mid-1980s with the development of the connectionless OSI suite. Nor have the OSI standards been ignored by suppliers. As with TCP/IP in the USA, universities have been busy developing OSI implementations and governments have, since the mid-1980s, required OSI-conforming products (particularly European governments through the European Commission directives). But this activity has not as yet created a general market demand and the same level of fully developed OSI computing products, except perhaps with the notable exception of X.25 network equipment.

The 'pump priming' of TCP/IP has been more successful and has ensured that it has moved ahead much faster than OSI. Governments and commercial organizations worldwide have waited patiently for OSI to become available and to reap the benefits of the promised flexibility of an international standard for computer communications and interoperation. Suffice it to say that the development of OSI has lagged considerably behind TCP/IP, despite support from a number of governments (including since 1985, the US government and Department of Defense).

When it comes to breaking down communications barriers between different computer suppliers, information systems managers in commercial companies now see TCP/IP as a fully functional, proven and low-cost alternative to open systems interconnection. OSI by comparison is still immature and almost unavailable. This may change in the mid-1990s, but the explosive interest in TCP/IP will, on the one hand, delay OSI implementation and, on the other, encourage it, as larger organizations come up against some of the known fundamental limitations of TCP/IP.

TCP/IP as a communications architecture

As with much of the specialist vocabulary which surrounds computers and telecommunications networks, the term TCP/IP will conjure up different concepts to different readers. TCP/IP is used as shorthand for a large set of standards with many different features and functions. The letters 'TCP/IP' stand for two communications protocols, Transmission Control Protocol (TCP) and Internet Protocol (IP). These were developed during the late 1970s and early 1980s as the key communications protocols for the US 'Internet', the collected set of interconnected communications networks (originally comprising ARPAnet, but now including NSFnet, and NYSERnet, and the Department of Defense Network among many others). Today these support the US government, Department of

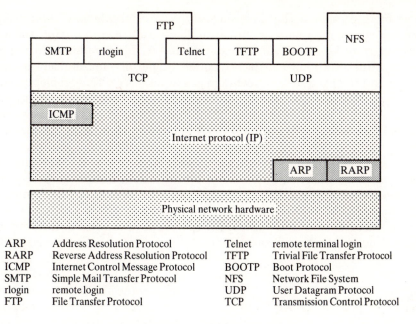

Figure 1.4   TCP/IP architecture.

Defense, US military, and the university, education and commercial organizations conduct research on behalf of those bodies. (Using the US Internet for commercial traffic between commercial organizations is not allowed.)

The two protocols, TCP and IP, are but two of the building blocks required for a complete communications 'architecture', but the term 'TCP/IP' is most often used as a **shorthand** term for the whole communications 'architecture' specified originally by the US Department of Defense. This architecture is a much bigger set of standards than just TCP and IP (Figure 1.4). We shall carry on this tradition and use 'TCP/IP' to mean the complete architecture, except where this will cause confusion.

Communications architectures have been developed by computer manufacturers since the mid-1970s. An architecture describes three facets of communications in an abstract way which is independent of particular hardware or technology. The three aspects are

(1) Data exchange (intercommunications)

(2) Data interpretation (interoperation)

(3) System management

Like the OSI reference model, communications architectures are described in layers, each layer providing its own functions but using the functions of the layer below. This layering decouples the functions of one layer from another so that layered architectures are flexible; their designers can respond to changes in technology and in application software without a major upheaval for existing users. The implementation and existing installations can be extended, hopefully indefinitely as new, often faster techniques and technologies become available. It is important to realize that the standards do not specify the interfaces seen by computer users. Though suppliers often base their implementations on a competitor's successful product, you must expect that user interfaces will differ in major or minor ways from supplier to supplier.

For TCP/IP, the architectural standards and the operational US Internet are controlled by the Internet Activities Board (IAB). The IAB devolves its responsibilities for development, operations and management to a number of subcommittees and working groups which it controls and to other commercial companies specializing in communications and computing research and consultancy.

TCP/IP – the complete suite

The two protocols, TCP and IP, describe only the communication aspects, the movement of data across a set of interconnected physical networks. The complete architecture must include standard mechanisms for interpreting and converting data for the common tasks that users of computers have come to expect. As these tasks sit on top of and depend on the communications protocols, they are sometimes called the Upper Layer Protocols (ULPs).

Historically, computer users have needed three major functions:

- File transfer (including some simple file management)
- Terminal access (virtual terminal protocols)
- Mail preparation and transfer

But in today's commercial environments other tasks have become equally important

- Resource sharing (files, printers, plotters)
- Diskless workstations
- Transaction processing
- Management
- Directory services
- Security

Those familiar with the resource-sharing Local Area Network (LAN) (such as Microsoft LAN Manager and Novell NetWare) will have seen the power of remote or distributed file and disk sharing and of peripheral sharing; for some companies, diskless workstations have a number of advantages.

In a complete, modern architecture, standard protocols are required for all these new distributed systems as well as for the proven minicomputer and mainframe-based architectures.

The TCP/IP protocol suite addresses these issues comprehensively. The standards are not static but are being added to at a steady rate. Current activities relate to new facilities in directory services at the application layer and improvements in routing and addressing mechanisms at the lower layers.

Upper layer protocols

Beginning with the well-known application layer protocols, File Transfer Protocol (FTP), Telnet (TCP/IPs virtual terminal protocol), and Simple Mail Transfer Protocol (SMTP), NFS adds a disk/file system resource-sharing capability, LPR deals with printing, the BOOT Protocol, (BOOTP) provides the basis for diskless workstation operation, and Simple Network Management Protocol (SNMP) is the Internet standard for management. As Figure 1.4 shows, TCP is complemented by the User Datagram Protocol (UDP). The differences between these are discussed in Chapter 11.

Lower layer protocols

IP is not the lowest level of the layered architecture. TCP/IP does not describe new standards for low-level communications but TCP/IP standards include descriptions of how IP operates over the commonly available long-distance and local physical (or link level) communications networks. These descriptions include many proprietary networks as well as CCITT and other international standard transmission mechanisms.

For long-distance operation over public telecommunications circuits, the standards include point-to-point leased and dial up, synchronous and asynchronous links, and X.25 connections. For local communications, Ethernet Version 2 (as specified by DEC, Intel and Xerox) is by far the most widely used. ISO/IEEE networks (ISO 8802.3, 8802.4 8802.5) and FDDI (ISO 9314) are also specified as are proprietary networks such as ARCNET.

Management issues and responsibilities

The information systems manager in a commercial organization must take a highly technical product like TCP/IP and turn it into a success for the company's commercial activities, so that the investment in equipment, software and training speeds up, improves accuracy and reduces the costs of business processes. This can be a long road to travel.

Adopting and using any new system presents managers with new issues and 'opportunities' (problems!). These centre on the technology, its standards, the supplier and the organization. Many questions must be asked about the capabilities of the basic technology itself, the capabilities of the supplier and about the organization that will use that technology. Managers attempt to map the features that are available onto the day-to-day operations of the company. Only when they achieve a good fit between the facilities and features of the basic system, the capabilities and support of suppliers and the requirements and practices of the company will the system add the highest value to the business.

In some business sectors, the application of new information technology is so revolutionary that rather than merely applying it to existing organizational structures, procedures and practices, those structures, procedures and practices are revised and simplified by it in a fundamental way.

Whatever the magnitude of the effect, there are two keys to success:

(1) Making the right choices – technological and organizational.

(2) Providing the correct training for technologists *and* for commercial users.

Choices

Standards for TCP/IP (or for that matter, OSI) specify only the facilities that should be available between two communicating machines. They do not specify (in general) how those facilities are delivered to the screens, keyboards, printers and disk systems of end users. There will often be one *de facto* way of supporting some features, but the details of that support will differ (in what can be annoying ways). It is this variety that allows suppliers to differentiate their products and attract particular market sectors to their interpretation of the 'best' user interface for a given purpose.

The early 1990s saw a departure from some of the traditional command-line, text-based TCP/IP implementations of UNIX, towards assistance for less computer-literate users through window-based 'point and click' interfaces.

The selection involves choosing:

● A product with the best user interfaces for our needs.

● The features of the product to use in practice (not all facilities will be appropriate).

- How to implement and control the user features.
- How to implement and control the internal technical features.

Flexibility and control

Suppliers sell features and flexibility. Many organizations adopt TCP/IP precisely because it covers such a broad range of function and options. But flexibility is a two-edged sword: it demands a degree of imposed control otherwise freedom becomes licence, flexibility becomes a snare.

Introducing the full functionality of a system as complex as TCP/IP over a short period of time to a large user population would be likely to fail, even if it were physically possible! Dividing up the problems and phasing the introduction across a number of departments is essential. Fortunately, the model presented by Figure 1.4 is in itself the guide to how to divide the problems into manageable pieces. It is this subdivision and structured approach to problem solving that guarantees success, particularly in a large organization where there may be hundreds, or even thousands of computers, each using TCP/IP.

Separating the management functions

The layering of TCP/IP as a communications architecture allows us to separate different functions, to consider them individually, and to simplify the management of the complex whole. This approach is valid whether we merely wish to describe the tasks to be carried out by one person for a small network or to divide up the management of a large, geographically diverse, corporate network for management by many different departments and individuals. In the latter complex case, we must ensure that *all aspects* of the technology are addressed, otherwise what should appear as one 'seamless' cooperating system will expose the managerial divisions to the users.

As we have seen, TCP/IP provides two complementary functions: *interoperation* in applications processors through the use of the upper layer protocols (FTP, Telnet, SMTP, NFS) and *intercommunication*, through the use of the IP protocol operating over a collection of physical communications networks, (LANs and point-to-point links). These two functions provide one possible division of responsibility: upper layer protocols operate only in personal workstations and shared mini- and mainframe computers; the internetworking protocols operate in all of these and in the routers/gateways that form the communications network. In a small implementation, one or two people are responsible for all aspects. In the larger network, the communications aspects are often implemented and managed by communications specialists. The applications are implemented and managed by business, computer system and programming specialists.

But this simple division of responsibility is a dangerous illusion. The application requires certain facilities and performance from the underlying communications networks. The communications networks must be planned with the application in mind; they must evolve with the changing use of applications and the demand that they impose. Consider two simple examples:

- The simplest change in the configuration files of a personal computer can have an unexpected impact on network load in resource-sharing systems such as NFS. An incorrect setting on 200 computers can make the difference between a system which performs well and one which is totally unsatisfactory.

- Application programmers today develop the applications to a standard network interface in the belief that the network will deliver everything in a short time. They often test the application on a lightly loaded, small, local area network and have no concept of how that application will perform in a more general environment. A simple change in the structure of a program can alter its loading on the network by a factor of 10 to 100.

Dividing communications architectures into layers has been very successful for the development of new low-level communications media and systems; it has been too successful at isolating the applications developers from the realities of available networks and the impact that their actions have upon them.

The upper layers of TCP/IP, the applications and their environment, must be managed and controlled not just from their interface to the user, but from their impact on communications. Unfortunately, this impact is often not well understood. When it is, we find that the controls and adjustments that are available require more intervention than is desirable and are not as obvious or instinctive as they should be.

A common aim of systems and network managers is to reduce costs while delivering good service; merely optimizing and reducing the costs of their own components is not likely to provide optimum performance of the whole system. Indeed, as expressed in Figure 1.5, squeezing costs in one area can have unexpected effects in other areas. Each group must have an understanding of how the actions that they take in pursuit of reduced costs impacts on the performance and spending of the other group. Communications and systems managers need to cooperate very closely to achieve an overall successful IT service.

In large installations the problem is even more complex, for the communications and applications management is subdivided further. Management of computer applications is usually divided in one (or more) of four ways:

Figure 1.5   Squeezing costs in one area.

- by department (a functional subdivision)
- by site (geographic subdivision)
- by manufacturer of computer system (technical subdivision)
- by computing function (FTP, SMTP, Telnet)

Communications functions are often split horizontally and vertically along the TCP/IP architectural model, by function and by technology into:

- Physical layer – building cabling
- Link layer – Ethernet, Token Ring, wide area circuits
- Network layer – Internet protocol (IP)

To this list should be added the transport layer; in TCP/IP the transport layer is TCP and UDP. Immediately there is a conflict of interest, for while these are quite definitely communications protocols and have the major impact on communications performance, they are only present in the host systems of TCP/IP, not in the traditional network components. If TCP/IP systems are to be successful, overcoming this territorial and organizational issue is key.

The design authority

Whatever the size of the organization and its networks, TCP/IP only operates correctly if the same high standards of configuration are used in every operational attached piece of equipment. This is easiest if the major design decisions are imposed by or agreed with a single (central) design authority which is educated to make the correct managerial and technical choices and then ensures their observance throughout the interconnected system. TCP/IP grew from a free culture of cooperating organizations and individuals with a collegiate and research ethos; overall standards and control came from the Internet Activities Board. The same degree of cooperation and control must be present in an operational commercial TCP/IP network. The control will normally come from somebody with the necessary technical and organizational authority.

Technical decisions

What technical decisions must be made? The complexity of the management problem depends on the anticipated size and growth rate of the overall system. Size, growth rate and corporate organization and culture must all be considered when the technical (and organizational) choices are taken during the planning and implementation processes. These choices may be conveniently considered in the layered way that the TCP/IP architecture suggests to us. The important technical decisions to be made centre around the following topics:

- The size of the problem
- Reliability
- Availability
- Budget and costs
- Local area networks to support TCP/IP
- Network addressing scheme (IP address space)
- Use of subnetwork addresses
- Router network and its routing protocols
- Domain name service
- Application layers, including their communications effects
- Overall system management and record keeping

These subjects are interdependent. The structure and geography of the organization determines the underlying communication requirements. This interacts with the layout of LANs. That layout predetermines the flexibility of network addressing, subnetwork addressing and the placement of routers.

Figure 1.6   Choosing the wrong combinations of technology.

Certain combinations of technology can at first sight appear to be compatible; the problems only become evident much later (Figure 1.6).

Subsequent chapters of Part I discuss each of the above as organizational, managerial and user issues without detailed technical description of the bits and bytes involved. Those discussions are deferred to Part II.

Choosing equipment

In a description of practical issues we frequently find that developers include many features and facilities in standards which are not yet generally implemented in available equipment.

Many descriptions of TCP/IP concentrate on the facilities that are available within the protocol and not on the features that can really be exploited by today's equipment. This is a moving target. Once network managers have determined what facilities they require they should produce a requirements specification for their suppliers, so they can determine what facilities are supported and the level of that support. Throughout the book we will give an indication of what is generally available, but that can be expected to change quite quickly. Readers must treat such statements as a trigger to ask the right questions of their suppliers to obtain the latest state of play.

Summary

In this chapter, we have introduced the components of TCP/IP which support interconnectivity and interoperability. We have discussed how technological influences affects and is affected by the size, growth rate, existing structures, culture and geography of the organization that deploys it.

The layered structure of the TCP/IP protocol suite suggests how we might divide up the management responsibilities, but it must be remembered that the technology must be treated as one integrated system if it is to operate successfully. Changes in one area cannot be made without considering the consequences for performance and costs in another.

Subsequent chapters in Part I discuss the parameters for success and the key managerial decisions that must be made on specific technical parameters if long-term success and stability is to be achieved with minimum effort.

2

Establishing the network foundation

The functions of an organization and the way in which it is structured directly affect its information flows and communications requirements. In this chapter we discuss the issues that must be considered when planning the networks that support TCP/IP. The topics covered are:

- Structures of the organization and its networks
- Features of the corporate network
- Laying out the local and wide area networks
- Estimating the network size
- Management choices
- LAN cabling
- Bridging and routing

Any distributed computer system is composed of two major components: the processors, which provide applications services to computer users; and the physical local and wide area networks and cable systems, which carry information between the sources of data (such as file servers) and the users of that data at workstations or personal computers. We shall discuss application questions later. First, we examine the local and wide area network implications of TCP/IP. This discussion cannot be completely divorced from a consideration of network addressing and of routing, for the three topics are interdependent. The structure of Local Area Network (LAN) and Wide Area Network (WAN) cables and the presence of bridges and routers change the TCP/IP addressing scheme. Computer systems on the same bridged LAN must be within the same addressing range. On either side of a router they are in different addressing ranges. Setting the right standards for the underlying LAN structure allows the design of TCP/IP to be right first time. It should be no surprise that addressing and routing are topics for the next two chapters.

For reliable and efficient operation, TCP/IP must operate over a stable platform of LAN cabling and components and wide area circuits. In this chapter, we consider how to design and implement that low-level infrastructure.

Planning the supporting network

The aim of TCP/IP network planning and design is to provide a communications infrastructure that meets the requirements of the organization with readily available equipment and skills. It must provide the correct level of performance for different functions within the organization, at different places, and at acceptable costs. In setting up a local and wide area structure for TCP/IP, the first task of the designer is to consider what each of these terms means for that situation. Each case is unique but the overall size of the organization and its network requirements will determine the complexity of the problems to be solved.

Size and growth rate

Whatever aspect of human communications you consider, it could be said that a measurement of success is often that the size and usage grows rapidly. As a result of experience in road network planning, this has become known as the 'motorway (or highway) effect'. If a system is useful, people change their travel habits and use the system in new ways that the planners never envisaged (Figure 2.1). Traffic grows to fill the space available. In an organization a successful network has been seen to grow at a rate which was totally unexpected and to expand rapidly to cover the company.

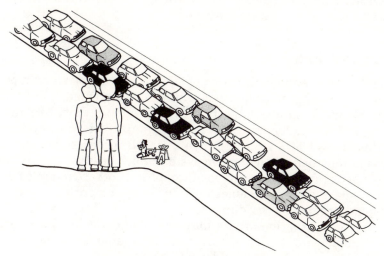

Figure 2.1 The motorway effect.

When planning a TCP/IP installation it is advisable to consider the initial size of the network and have some indication of maximum size and growth rate. This measure of size has two dimensions:

- The total number of attached ports, that is, computer and router connections to the network

- The geographic coverage

It is also important to consider in what ways the network could grow – by addition of devices on the same network or by connection to other TCP/IP installations. In the first case, all the issues are under the control of one organization; in the second, they may not be. The problems to be solved will be different in each case. Today's computer applications and systems are distributed on workstations and PCs throughout the sites and buildings where the computer users sit. Some types of change cannot be centrally managed and must be carried out at each machine. These changes are always difficult and labour-intensive, and hence costly. As far as possible, they must be predicted and eliminated.

These considerations can affect the detailed planning process of the LAN and WAN links, the planning of the address space and of the bridges and routers which interconnect LANs and sites. Planners will wish to determine solutions to the following questions. How many cable systems will there be? How can they be interconnected successfully? Will bridges suffice or are routers required? How should the address plan for the network evolve? Is there a requirement for the Domain Name Service? Is responsibility split or with one person or body? If it is split, is the division by function, by location, or by technology? Is there a need to split application management from communications management? Is there a need (in a large corporation) to split communications management into more than one subfunction?

Existing standards

In an attempt to avoid duplication of effort and perhaps more importantly to avoid choosing incompatible solutions to the same TCP/IP options and problems, it is quite important to determine if there are any other existing TCP/IP implementations in the organization. Some systems may hide their use of TCP/IP; the Banyan VINES resource-sharing LAN or any communications management system which uses the simple network management protocol are current examples. If other examples do exist and will share the same cables or TCP/IP equipment at any time, the developments must be coordinated.

In some situations there may already be a central authority for TCP/IP implementation which has set local standards for the use of TCP/IP. These standards should relate to:

- Addressing conventions
- Host-naming conventions
- Local area network
- Choice of equipment
- Choice of network software
- Configuration and management of the network
- Configuration and management of the applications

It is much easier if these standards can be used rather than starting from scratch.

Traffic flows and capacity

In planning the network layout and capacity it is important to know the volume of information which will be carried. At the simplest level, high-performance routes in the network must follow the high traffic flows in the organization. Faults on those major arterial routes will affect more users, so they, if any, may need to be protected against failure.

Judging future traffic flows is always one of the most difficult estimates in installing new TCP/IP systems. One of the great successes of modern software development techniques is to provide an effective barrier between the application developer and the underlying network. But it leaves the network planners with a major problem. Few people can relate the use of an application to the traffic it will generate.

Given the continued growth in workstation performance, existing LAN implementations already seem slow. For many commercial environments, a single physical LAN can support only 20 to 50 workstations and one or two file servers before the network must be partitioned with bridges or routers. The need for 100 Mbps Fiber Distributed Data Interface (FDDI) or even higher network speeds (1 Gbps – 10 Gbps) is evident, particularly for backbone networks and image systems, but the costs of such a system are not yet within the budgets of most network operators.

In the absence of such speeds, planners must ration the limited resource of normal speed LANs. They must understand how particular applications use the network and what the traffic flows between different user groups and applications processors are at different times of the day and business year. Key questions are:

- What will be the total volume of data on different parts of the network at the busiest time of the day? Is this traffic seasonal?

- How will the traffic grow with time, taking into account the changing and improving user perception of the network services and the increase in number of attached devices and a move towards more demanding applications?

- How is the traffic distributed among adjacent machines and to more remote machines?

Often the only way of obtaining such information is to measure the operation of real applications and extrapolate the results using spreadsheet or other modelling systems. Armed with the traffic information, and its growth, it is time to consider the network structure.

Network decisions

In a small, compact implementation of a few PCs and file servers in one building, the main issues and decisions centre on the choice of addresses (see Chapter 3) and on configuration and management of the computers. The network will be a few lengths of 'Thin Ethernet' cable or a simple Token Ring installation with, at most, one or two bridges to increase the total traffic capacity of the system. There are unlikely to be any routers. Implementation of the network is usually straightforward. In these small networks, one or two people make most of the decisions; they may also be responsible for carrying out the implementation and configuration.

Larger corporate networks often cover many sites and require long distance PTT-provided (Telco-provided) circuits to interconnect those sites. Rentals for such circuits can form a major portion of the cost which may increase with time[†]. Complex configuration of remote bridges and routers are required to ensure that these wide area circuits are used at optimum efficiency.

[†]In many countries the unit cost of intersite circuits has reduced considerably over the last 10 years, but the increase in capacity required for interconnected LANs has far outstripped the unit cost reductions.

Figure 2.2 Multiple protocols.

Networks are subject to hidden costs. Heavily loaded networks, where the traffic approaches the capacity of the cable, require more management time as systems are reconfigured and moved from cable to cable to reduce loading. Idiosyncrasies and limitations of the overall system and software faults always become apparent at high system loading. A heavily loaded network can also impose a load on application processors, reducing the amount of useful power available for end users.

Management decisions about networks centre on how to provide the right performance with chosen reliability to particular users and at acceptable cost. Options centre on the choice of technology for the cable, the interface cards and the bridges and routers that form the interconnection. These three components form the three lower layers of the OSI model. Cables are part of the OSI physical layer; LAN bridges operate medium access control, a part of the OSI data link layer; routers operate in the network layer. TCP/IP performance is not affected by the choice of cable as long as that cable can support the LAN technology at the normal operating speed in an error-free way. We shall not therefore discuss the issues of cabling further.

Link layer options

LAN cables and wide area circuits may be a shared resource, carrying not only TCP/IP data, but data from other applications and systems as well (Novell NetWare, IBM SNA, DECnet to name but a few examples). Transporting multiple protocols on one infrastructure increases the organizational and technical complexity. In these networks it is certain that the management of network resources, the infrastructure which carries data between application processors, will present as many difficulties as the management of applications themselves. A detailed discussion of these issues is beyond the scope of this book, but for those contemplating using TCP/IP in a multiprotocol environment, it is much easier for protocols to coexist peacefully if the number of options is reduced (Figure 2.2).

The first decision is what option to use for carrying information across the LAN cable that everyone colloquially calls Ethernet. Ethernet (even Version 2 Ethernet) is a different standard from ISO 8802.3[†] (IEEE 802.3). While the hardware is compatible for both systems, the frame content[‡] is not. Furthermore, Ethernet V2 is a *de facto* standard; IEEE 802.3 is the Open Systems standard which was adopted as the international standard by ISO.

TCP/IP on LANs predates these international standards, so the most common implementation by far for TCP/IP today is Ethernet V2; few manufacturers of TCP/IP yet offer IEEE 802.3/802.2 with the additional Sub Network Access Protocol (SNAP) software components required to support TCP/IP. For those who require TCP/IP to coexist with other OSI systems or intend an eventual move to full OSI, it *might be* more appropriate to use IEEE 802.3 as and when it becomes available.

The changeover to IEEE 802.3 encapsulation should not be undertaken lightly; the two standards can coexist on the same Ethernet cable, but they cannot directly interwork. Where both standards are in use, careful planning is required to be sure that all systems can see TCP/IP data in the form that they can recognize. Either the different systems must be segregated by frame type, or some device must selectively retransmit frames in the other format, effectively duplicating that traffic on the same cable and increasing the network loading. The technical aspects of IEEE 802.3 encapsulation are described in Chapter 10.

On Token Ring (IEEE 802.5) and FDDI (ISO 9314) networks there is no confusion; ISO standard frames are used exclusively with SNAP encapsulation carrying the Ethernet type field.

Structuring LAN interconnections

If data transfer rate were the only issue, directly attaching all computing resources to one extended 'local area' network of the highest possible speed without intervening bridges and routers would give the best pos-sible performance. This network would also be easier to manage than a complex hierarchical network with multiple speed Token Rings and Ethernets, bridges and routers. FDDI with its 100 Mbps capacity and 200 km circumference is a good choice. But that is to ignore cost, reliability and geography, which are also important considerations. Not only are the costs of such a solution unacceptable today to most organizations, but experience also suggests that faults on such a large single network topology, while quite rare, are more difficult to contain; faults when they do occur will affect more systems. Routers (and to a lesser extent bridges) limit the

---

[†]Rather than repeat the use of ISO and IEEE equivalent standards for LANs, we shall follow the practice of using the IEEE designations. These have been adopted verbatim for ISO OSI standards.

[‡]There are two standards for transmitting IP information on the cable that is commonly referred to as Ethernet. The first is accurately described as Ethernet Version 2; the second requires the lengthy description 'IEEE 802.3 + IEEE 802.2. + SNAP'. The detailed differences between these are left to Chapter 10.

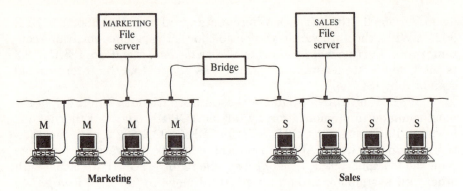

Figure 2.3 Location of servers.

effects of hardware and software faults to a small portion of a network.

While the costs of FDDI may not be attractive, the principle outlined above remains valid:

● For the best performance between two points, they should be joined together in the simplest way possible, as part of the same physical LAN using either copper or fibre optic cables or with a minimum number of bridges or routers.

Any device more complex than a simple repeater between two communicating stations has a measurable effect on performance; whether that effect is important to network users depends on the application and the underlying facilities of TCP/IP it uses. (TCP or UDP, see Chapter 12). To use analogies, sharing a single big pipe among many water company customers is always more efficient than having smaller pipes for a smaller number of customers. Larger aircraft are more economic per passenger mile provided that you can fill them. These analogies are not far removed from the arguments for single high-speed networks, though costs and marketing considerations may alter the practical realization of the theory!

Today's high-performance file servers, personal computers and workstations can easily fill a single Ethernet (10 Mbps) or Token Ring (4 Mbps) to capacity. For satisfactory operation the alternative to replacing the network with one of higher speed is to partition the overall system into small groups with a **common communications interest** (Figure 2.3); the smaller groups are interconnected into a wider any-to-any community using packet relays called bridges and routers. But the performance between these groups is always poorer than the performance within a group. The management of change will be more complex.

Immediately we have made the assumption – the largest proportion of network traffic is between users on the same physical cables. If it is not, then standard LAN applications developed during the late 1980s and early 1990s do not operate with maximum performance. LAN technology is based on the fact that servers, particularly application servers, are adjacent to their users.

The location of data upon which the applications operate is less critical, but many LAN systems download complete data files rather than extracting data and only transmitting what is necessary. While the location of data is less critical than applications software, high-speed LANs which can cover long distances may still be required (FDDI, Metropolitan Area Networks (MANs)). An alternative is to change the application to transmit processed data rather than raw data by moving towards distributed computing architectures rather than simple resource-sharing architectures.

Laying out LAN cables

Data flows tend to follow organization structure; a single department in an organization may not be located in one building and at one site. If everyone could share the same cable and there was still excess capacity, this would not be an issue. But where the cable is full and must be subdivided, how should we carry out that subdivision?

From some perspectives, LAN and WAN cables should be sub-divided and labelled according to the departments that use them, not according to the locations they serve. Bridges and routers should provide the links for the infrequent traffic between departments, not for the bulk of traffic within a department. In organizations where recovery of network costs is important, such decisions are politically important. If one department takes a disproportionate share of the network capacity and drives it to the next phase of expansion, it is much simpler to allocate and justify costs if the network is structured by department rather than by site.

In practice, networks laid out on organizational needs, rather than geography, are not intuitive to manage; training of maintenance staff is more difficult and configuration mistakes are more likely. Most organizations take the intuitive approach and provide an infrastructure firstly for the building and secondly for sites (Figure 2.4a). As traffic grows to fill that structure, it may be necessary to restructure on an organizational basis. But the technical principle remains:

- If optimum throughput is the aim, then try to connect directly the various subsections of a department within and between sites, to reduce the number of bridges and routers, and not to minimize the quantity of fibre, copper cable, and separate intersite circuits (Figure 2.4b).
- If optimum reliability and simplified management is the aim, limit the geographic coverage of a single physical LAN and partition the users with bridges and routers to limit the propagation of faults (Figure 2.4a).

The LAN planner needs a flexible set of tools to choose the layout of cabling and which systems are to communicate directly. Recent develop-

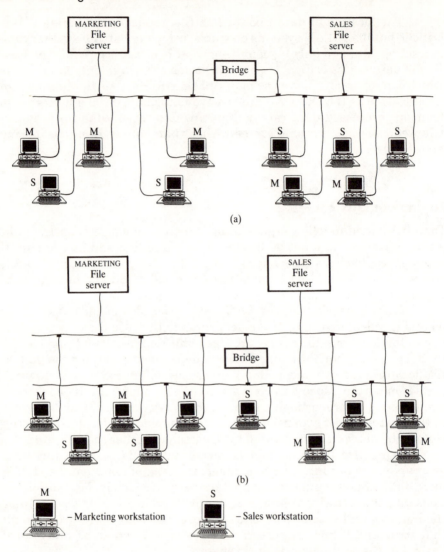

Figure 2.4 (a) Cabling organized by geography. (b) Cabling organized by department.

ments in Ethernet and Token Ring Hub technology allow the flexible creation of these groups of common interest within floor areas, between floors of a single building and across a single site using multiple copper or fibre optic backbones. It is worthwhile having a central point, a 'super hub' where the appropriate work areas can be joined into a single physical network with a common backbone fibre. Between geographically separated sites there is little option but to use remote bridges and routers. (Properly designed Token Ring and FDDI can have a degree of resilience to cable breaks.).

Splitting the network

Bridges and **routers** partition the network and improve performance for workstations on the same cable. The majority of network traffic should be local to the group of users and a small percentage (15–30%) should cross the bridges onto a backbone network which interconnects different user groups[†]. If this traffic split cannot be achieved, then the bridge is not used in the optimum way.

Splitting a network into small pools of users interconnected by routers and bridges is always a poor substitute for that single, reliable, large, high-speed network, for at any time a high proportion of the traffic is less than optimum. By adding bridges and routers to a network the cost per user, the administrative and the technical difficulties all increase and the reliability and performance between some remote portions of the network can fall to unacceptable levels. So why do it? In local area networks it is justified by the **containment of traffic** to physical networks which that traffic *must* traverse; this reduces the load on the local LAN segment and there is a dramatic improvement in performance for local traffic to local file servers. For long-distance wide-area interconnection, there must be a convertor between different link layer technologies.

The prime purpose of a bridge in a LAN is to *prevent* traffic flowing where it does not need to, rather than to allow traffic to flow where it will. Bridges filter traffic (Figure 2.5). In many networks, it is only a secondary function of the bridge to provide communications where none existed by translating to a different type of cable and extending the cable length limits of the basic LAN specification.

In network partitioning, routers have some advantages and some disadvantages over bridges. They have a more positive role to play. Routers relay only what they are specifically told to relay. They are part of the IP protocol and are designed to interconnect network technologies of different performance. Routers are particularly useful at matching the high speeds of LANs to the much lower speeds of intersite (wide area) communications circuits that are now available. On the other hand they have a higher cost and lower performance and require more careful management than bridges. Such is the importance of the router that we devote the whole of Chapter 5 to routers and their management.

Using bridges

Bridges filter traffic by Media Access Control (MAC) Address. They must examine each frame received on each port and build a table of frame source addresses with the port on which the frame was received. When

---

[†]Such 'rules of thumb' are not totally satisfactory, for the exact traffic distribution is dependent on the type of the application software and how it was designed to use communications facilities.

Figure 2.5 Bridges filter traffic.

the bridge learns that a source and destination are on the same port, it will not pass traffic for that destination to any other cable.

The important performance factors of bridges are:

- *Filtering rate* – the ability to examine frames for possible relaying.
- *Forwarding rate* – the ability to relay frames which have to be relayed.
- 'Routing' algorithm that allows bridges to be connected redundantly in parallel and in loops but prevents frames circulating round the loops.
- *Transit delay* – normally related to forwarding rate.
- Filter table size.
- Variations in performance with filter table occupancy.

Bridge filtering rate

Bridges now can filter at the theoretical maximum rate for Ethernet of 14 880 frames per second. Even in busy operational networks the offered traffic will not be this demanding, for this figure is based on all minimum-

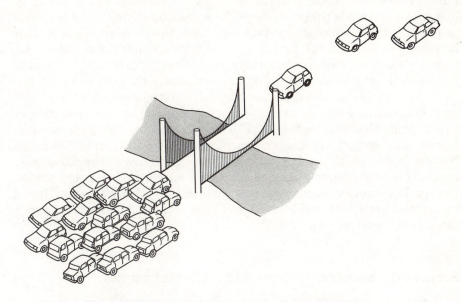

Figure 2.6 How bridges filter. Limited horizon.

sized frames. The true demand depends on the type of TCP/IP services in use. Networks used mainly for character-by-character TCP/IP Telnet terminal server traffic have a much higher number of small frames that those used for file transfer and NFS. The importance of a bridge operating at this theoretical maximum figure is not that it can examine that number of frames per second but that there is no limitation to the number of successive short frames that can be captured by the bridge, since it can capture at the maximum possible rate.

The frame rates on Token Ring systems are theoretically much higher than on Ethernet (20 000 fps on 4 Mbps and 80 000 fps on 16 Mbps Token Ring) but the overheads of TCP/IP mean that the absolute maximum practical frame rates are approximately 7700 and 31 000 respectively. Bridges for TCP/IP traffic could be chosen accordingly.

For multi-port hub bridges, one must ensure that each bridge port can examine all frames on every port simultaneously and that the specification does not just give some aggregate figure.

The limited horizon

A TCP/IP application working through a bridge has a limited horizon. A bridge isolates two cable segments so that systems have no knowledge of the traffic on the other cable, that is, on the other side of the bridge (Figure 2.6). A bridge is more likely to be unable to relay all traffic, not because it does not have the power, but because the output cable is continuously busy. Frames will queue in the bridge but bridges eventually throw away (discard) any frames that are older than about one second. Most low-level protocols – those which carry data over bridges – do not have any error correction or flow control. End stations may retransmit these lost frames from higher level software but, in an extreme case, this may just add to the network congestion that caused the problem in the first place.

It is up to the network manager to design the network so that traffic is distributed correctly and does not concentrate on one work area or in one bridge. Using a high-speed FDDI or Token Ring backbone or a hub bridge may complicate the design of the network. Traffic flows can become more critical, for they may arrive on the high-speed backbone successfully but focus on one work area where a number of key resources are located. High-performance resources, such as ONC (NFS) servers, should either be directly attached to the backbone or must be distributed on a number of feeder work area LANs.

Broadcasts, broadcast storms and multi-cast frames

TCP/IP protocols use two techniques which impact on the performance of a bridged network. They use **broadcast** and **multicast frames** for discovering the locations of resources and for communicating between systems which cooperate to provide a common service.

Multicast frames take capacity on the cable but are not processed by every station. They become a problem only on slower wide area bridged links. 'Slow' is a relative term; for today's LANs, 'slow' could be 256 kbps, 128 kbps or less.

Broadcast frames are much more detrimental to performance. They are generated by ARP, RARP, BOOTP, and RIP. Every system on an Ethernet or Token Ring network must process *every* broadcast frame. If the number of broadcast frames increases, the performance of every system will degrade noticeably. A frame takes some time to process, independent of its size. Each broadcast frame can reduce the performance of a PC by almost one normal data frame of 1000 to 1450 bytes. PCs slow down noticeably with 10 to 15 broadcast packets per second.

Bridges relay broadcast frames everywhere. To try to filter broadcasts is to destroy the possibility of any-to-any communication. So networks which are interlinked only with bridges reach a size where the percentage of broadcast traffic from all the devices is unacceptable. Unless the broadcast traffic can be reduced, it becomes impossible to manage the network or to grow it further successfully.

It has been known for in-house application programmers who do not appreciate the potential harmful effects to write applications using broadcasts. On more than one occasion, a complete LAN, including powerful minicomputers, has been brought to a standstill by a **broadcast**

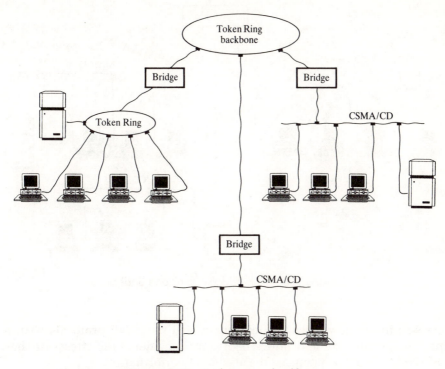

Figure 2.7 Bridging to a backbone.

storm of about 100 packets per second. Broadcast storms are sometimes attributed to Ethernet design limitations; it is often not realized that the broadcast storm is usually caused by a combination of bad software design and a poor bridged network structure of any type of LAN.

Bridging to a backbone

As an aid to structuring the distribution of data between work areas it is common practice to use a **backbone** LAN to carry the transit traffic. This backbone may be built with the same technology as the work area, though often on a more robust cable (Thick Ethernet, 10Base5, rather than Thin Ethernet, 10Base2, or Unshielded Twisted Pair, 10BaseT), or it may use a different technology (16 Mbps Token Ring or 100 Mbps FDDI).

This topology (Figure 2.7) places a minimum of two bridges in series between any two work areas. Unless application processors or file servers are directly attached to the backbone, the performance for demanding file transfer applications is affected by this double hop. This is most noticeable if the backbone is no faster than the work areas. Those applications using TCP as their transport layer will need an

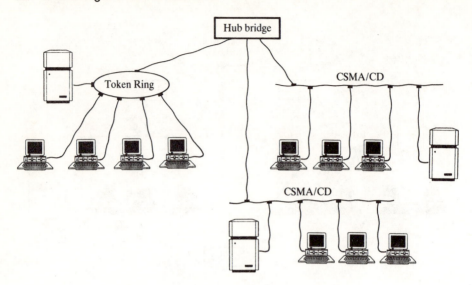

Figure 2.8 Hub bridge or multiport bridge.

increase in window size; applications which use UDP protocols with a small datagram size may suffer badly. We consider these effects further in Chapter 7 under a general discussion of performance.

Hub bridges

Hub and **multiport bridges** replace the backbone network with a single internal high-speed bus of greater speed than any **LAN**. This reduces the double hop effect but requires more extensive cabling and potentially reduces the backbone to a single point of failure (Figure 2.8).

Bridging different technologies

Using bridges to convert from one cable type to another but within a single access control method introduces no new issues – that is all Token Ring or all CSMA/CD. Bridging between networks with different access control methods from Token Ring to CSMA/CD or to FDDI Token Ring requires more careful planning, as the speeds of operation and hence the frame rate are different (Figure 2.9).

Contrary to popular belief, bridges between IEEE 802.5 Token Ring, ISO 9314 FDDI and IEEE 802.3 CSMA/CD networks are not transparent to protocol. Bridges must intercept the ARP/RARP protocols of TCP/IP and convert the MAC address representation. Depending on the bridge design this may affect delay and hence throughput. This conver-

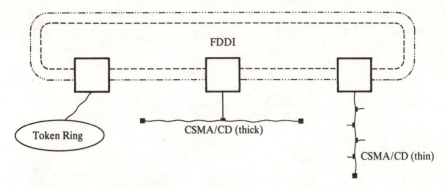

Figure 2.9 Bridging different technologies.

sion may limit the maximum number of frames which can be relayed. Do not assume that bridges will achieve the same performance when forwarding between two networks of different types as they do between networks of the same type.

Bridging to wide area links

Remote bridges operate in pairs to connect geographically separated sites over long-distance point-to-point links. The main issue is the large difference in speed between LAN technologies and the circuits which are generally available for this type of interconnection (Figure 2.10).

Circuit speeds

The cost of long-distance, high-speed digital services is still regarded by many as prohibitive. In large companies, with many computer users, the cost per user may be acceptable. Even so, few organizations can yet consider speeds above 2 Mbps. Outside the USA and UK many organizations find cost and availability of these circuits unacceptable and may be lim-

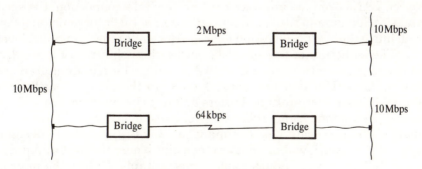

Figure 2.10 Remote bridge.

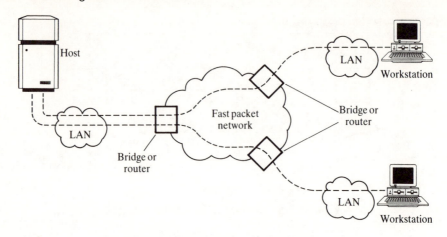

Figure 2.11   Frame relay backbone.

ited to 64 kbps or multiples of 64 kbps perhaps derived from the newer Integrated Services Digital Network (ISDN) services.

The time taken to send a typical TCP/IP datagram of 1024 bytes at 64 kbps is about 135 ms compared to 0.81 ms on a 10 Mbps network. Fortunately, TCP/IP Telnet and FTP were designed to be used in environments with long delays and have time-outs which can adjust to changes in network speed and loading. The performance of these slow network links for file transfers and a system such as NFS, which was designed for the LAN environment, may not be acceptable.

The speeds of wide area links are increasing and the unit costs are falling. By the mid-1990s, point-to-point speeds of 2, 8, 34, 45 and 51 Mbps will be more widely available on demand. But as applications developers continue to demand more capacity, the costs per user may not reduce.

The early 1990s saw the introduction of frame relay networks as a long-distance public or private network service. To the TCP/IP network manager, frame relay is a standard interface which remote bridges (or routers) can use to create multiple point-to-point long-distance links between LANs over one interface card. In this interconnection, the speed of the attachment and the speed and structure of the intervening network are all important to the delay and hence performance that can be achieved.

The structure of a frame relay network is shown in Figure 2.11. The frame relay network sends the LAN frames largely unaltered over the wide area. The structure looks similar to the bridged backbone of Figure 2.7. There are multiple buffers and hops between source and destination. In a public frame relay service, these delays are not under the control of the corporate network manager. Delays in a poorly designed frame relay network will build up to the point where the performance for certain TCP/IP-based applications is unacceptable. Unless the network planners know how the public network service is built, which is most unlikely, they cannot *predict* the performance that can be achieved by TCP/IP over that network. They can, however, measure the achieved performance and, for some applications, tune the TCP parameters for the desired effect. As with the bridging discussion above, those applications using TCP as their transport layer will need an increased window size. It will be possible to 'tune' the performance of these applications to meet most users' needs; applications which use UDP with a small datagram size will once again suffer.

Ethernet padding

The minimum frame size of Ethernet is 64 octets including overhead. This means that the minimum amount of data in a frame must be 46 octets and any frames which would be shorter are padded out to this minimum length. Some remote bridges which connect two Ethernets over point-to-point circuits remove this padding, which unnecessarily occupies expensive wide area capacity, but equally some implementations do not. In TCP/IP Telnet this could mean 22 unnecessary octets for each character a remote user types.

Broadcast and multicast packets are carried over all bridged WAN links and they often cannot be filtered.

'Routing' in bridges

In recent years, the use of the word 'routing' has been extended and applied to any mechanism which can determine and alter paths between end systems (hosts). Sophisticated filtering LAN bridges are often said to have routing features or routing capability. This type of routing does not use the network layer or IP address of TCP/IP, nor does it take account of the features of the 'best path' as requested by the communicating TCP/IP systems.

All IEEE LANs must ensure that all MAC frames arrive in the order they were transmitted and without duplication. Most systems therefore initially only allowed one path between source and destination. This precluded configurations with bridges in loops and in parallel. Such a limitation is unacceptable as a single failure can divide a network in two. The **spanning tree** and **source routing** algorithms incorporated in IEEE 802.1d overcome these limitations. For bridge routing, IEEE 802.1d has defined a mechanism called the transparent spanning tree algorithm which is particularly important for IEEE 802.3 (Ethernet) bridges.

Spanning tree is a disabling technique that suspends the activity of any bridge which provides a redundant path (Figure 2.12). Such bridges carry no traffic but come to life if the current active path fails. The

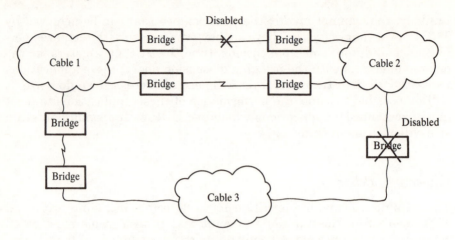

Figure 2.12 Spanning tree operation.

switch-over time is of the order of 15–30 seconds if the default configuration of bridges is not changed. This is slower than many computer users would wish but is faster than could be achieved by manual intervention. However, the technique is only fully satisfactory for on-site services. It is often not acceptable to have remote wide area links sitting idle. All the processing for the spanning tree algorithm is placed in the bridge and end systems are unaware of the spanning tree operation. Spanning tree bridges are therefore called **transparent bridges**.

For Token Ring networks a different mechanism referred to as **source routing** was adopted by the IEEE 802.5 committee, though it is not widely used outside IBM equipment. End systems must be modified to take an active part in setting up a route across redundant source routing bridges. IEEE 802.1d later adopted source routing as part of the IEEE bridge routing standards, though the detail is different from source routing as used by IBM.

An advantage of source routing (Figure 2.13) is that it allows multiple active routes between the source and destination cable systems, although one conversation will follow one route for its duration. The main disadvantage is that LAN driver software must be modified to add and remove source routing fields from the data frames. Attached workstations begin by discovering possible routes between source and destination using either a single route explorer frame or an all routes explorer frame. Transmission of the single route frame relies on the fact that a single stable spanning tree route has been set up either manually by the network managers or automatically by a spanning tree algorithm. Having discovered all available routes, end stations insert a list of bridges which are to be used into each frame they transmit. If the link fails, then an alternate route may be selected instantly from a list maintained in the workstation.

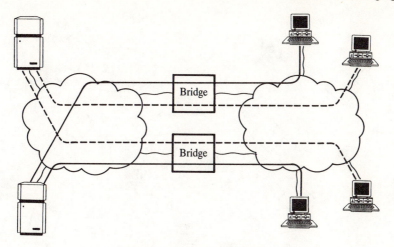

Figure 2.13   Source routing.

Source routing is only likely to be found with TCP/IP end systems on Token Ring. It is not normally used on Ethernet.

Before choosing a bridge, managers should check that the implementation is fully IEEE 802.1d compliant, and that interoperation of that implementation of spanning tree has been checked with any other implementation that is used in the network. They should also be aware of how the spanning tree algorithm operates, and how bridges determine if they are to be in the active topology. For effective operation, the spanning tree algorithm must be managed. This means that network managers must change the default configuration of their bridges.

In networks which use bridges between Token Ring and Ethernet, the network designers must have a plan of how the conversion between source routing and spanning tree is to take place in a consistent manner.

The limits of bridging

While these algorithms can have a place in smaller networks, spanning tree in particular is often not satisfactory for the larger network with WAN interconnections, since spanning tree disables otherwise useful routes. This is one reason why bridged networks can only grow to a limited size (Figure 2.14). Another is that the standards allow for only seven bridges in series.

But there is another limitation which we have already hinted at. Bridged networks, even when well structured, can grow to the point where the volume of broadcast and multicast traffic degrades performance, where widely varying loads on intermediate (backbone) networks affect performance because of packet loss, where spanning tree and

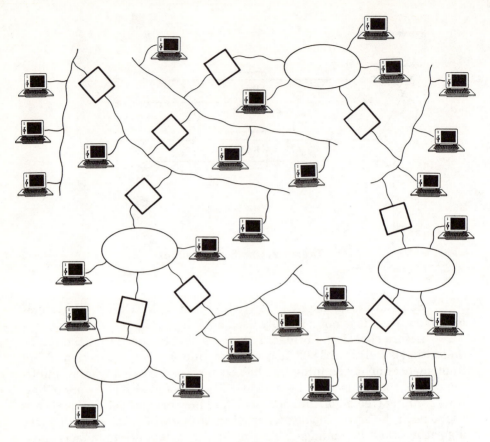

Figure 2.14 The limits of bridging.

source routing algorithms provide less than optimum routing and where the problems of conversion between Token Ring and CSMA/CD technologies are all too evident. The performance of the network in such circumstances is at best poor. Network users may see wide variations in both reliability and response. Uncontrolled congestion prevents the successful transmission of data. For some applications, the network may become unstable and unreliable.

Various authorities have tried to put a figure to the size of network that can be successfully managed with bridges alone. It depends on many factors other than technology. But many organizations find that when their network has a combination of many hundreds of interconnected devices, a few tens of servers and minicomputers, and ten to thirty bridges, the control of broadcast traffic can become impossible and the overall reliability and performance of the network decreases. The problems are made worse by having remote bridges with slow-speed links between sites.

In a poorly performing network, the network planner must carry out a more careful analysis of traffic volumes and flows and then take remedial action to alter network structure and the positioning of bridges to meet the corporate needs. If to these problems is added the possible inappropriate use of the network by badly designed software that propagates faults throughout the system, an alternative interconnection method that gives the network manager more control is required. Bridges do not normally limit the effects of excessive broadcast frames from poorly designed software. The router can provide the necessary control.

Using routers

In most communications architectures, routing is a network layer function, not the MAC or data link function performed by bridges. Network layer routing predates bridging; routers were in use in WANs before the link-level LAN bridge was introduced in the early 1980s by companies such as Sytek Inc. and by the Digital Equipment Corporation (which holds patents related to bridge algorithms).

During the mid and late 1980s, routing was eclipsed by an enthusiasm for bridging. It is only as the performance, stability and management limitations of large bridged networks using connectionless protocols have become apparent and the cost and performance of routers has improved, that routing has once again come to the fore in larger networks.

Routers do not represent a panacea for the problems of the network manager. Routers can usefully replace some bridges in a bridged internet which is already physically well structured; it is likely to be a waste of time and money to add routers to a network which is not well structured, or where the traffic flows are not understood and well managed.

Routers only operate properly if the network addressing structure is correct. We therefore delay a full discussion of router technology until after we have described how to plan an IP network address structure.

Summary

In this chapter we have discussed the factors that allow the LANs and WANs which support TCP/IP to be planned successfully. The key points are:

- The planning process begins by understanding the size and structure of the problem to be solved.
- That will be determined by the organization, its size, structure and communications flows.

- New TCP/IP installations should follow existing internal standards for TCP/IP installations so that any requirement for interconnection is straightforward.

- On Ethernet there is more than one encapsulation method. TCP/IP systems predate OSI standards and today use Ethernet encapsulation rather than full IEEE 802.3, IEEE 802.2 and SNAP. This may change by the mid 1990s.

- Bridges increase the capacity of a LAN by limiting traffic to cable segments where it needs to be.

- LANs interconnected with bridges must be carefully structured. It is up to the network planner to ensure that bridges do not discard large numbers of frames.

- Where different technologies such as Token Rings, FDDI and Ethernet are mixed in a true internetwork, the location of high traffic resources such as ONC NFS file servers requires detailed planning.

- Interconnecting LANs with wide area circuits requires careful consideration of intersite capacity. Today the interconnection speed is much less than the LAN speed and the data flows across those circuits must be adjusted accordingly.

- Technologies such as frame relay provide an alternative packet switching connection. TCP/IP protocols must be tuned to give optimum performance through these buffered networks.

- Some remote bridges may use wide area links inefficiently when relaying minimum size Ethernet frames.

- The bridge routing algorithms in bridged networks must be consistent.

- Broadcast frames limit the number of devices that can be connected together using bridges alone.

- Routers operating at the IP (network) layer of TCP/IP offer a solution to extending the LAN beyond the limits imposed by bridges and a more satisfactory method of interconnecting different local and wide area technologies.

3

Planning and managing IP addresses

Careful network planning is key to the long-term success of any networking technology, particularly for the larger installation. In the past, insufficient consideration has been given to planning the key parameter of IP addresses for TCP/IP. This leads to one of the commonest causes of escalating network support costs. In this chapter we discuss the following topics related to IP addressing:

- Different ways of addressing computers in a TCP/IP system
- Functions of the IP address
- Format of the IP address
- The need for a unique IP address
- The need for IP address registration
- The need for autonomous system numbers and registration
- How to choose a non-registered address
- Configuring IP addresses
- Organizational issues and IP address management
- The effects of moves and changes
- The need for record keeping

The focus of this chapter is how to plan and manage IP addresses. Implementors of TCP/IP must select, configure and manage IP addresses correctly. Selecting an IP addressing scheme is the first major decision the TCP/IP implementor must make.

Identifying a network connection

Connections to a TCP/IP network are often known to each other and to users in three different ways, all of which identify the same connection to the network but at different levels of TCP/IP:

- As names: in the **fully qualified host** and **domain** name

  vax1.integralis.com.uk

  Using the domain name scheme is often not considered early enough in the planning of commercial networks; users of larger networks will find it invaluable.

- As a group of four numbers separated by full stops. This is the **IP** or **network address** used by the IP layer of TCP/IP

  129.30.20.124

- On a shared LAN by its network interface card address the 48-bit **MAC address** (Medium Access Control address often called the physical address)

  02 60 8C 12 34 56

Why have three levels of address, since they all refer to the same connection to the TCP/IP Internet? The reason is that while at any one time these addresses identify the same location, over a period of time each may change for different reasons. The three types of address allow a degree of flexibility where none would exist if the functions were not separated:

- The host and domain name should remain unchanged for the longest time, for it is completely determined by the system designers and managers, though it will often change if there is a major change in machine location.

- The IP address may change due to network growth and reconfiguration, for example, if a machine is moved from one location in a building to another.

- The MAC address may change for similar growth or performance reasons, or because the network card is replaced following a card failure. The shortest lived address is likely to be the MAC address.

The fully qualified domain name is for 'human consumption' and consists of a set of identifiers, separated by full stops, which describe a computer in a hierarchical relationship to all others. For example:

machine.department.site.organization.org_type.country

Introducing flexibility brings with it the possibility of error and communications failure if the flexible functions are not managed and controlled correctly. The domain name system is described in Chapter 14. This chapter describes the management of the IP address space. MAC addresses are not normally separately managed in TCP/IP systems.

Planning the IP address space

To plan an IP addressing scheme you must have or acquire the following information:

- The maximum number of host ports that your organization could ever wish to interconnect. The whole of your organization is not just your particular department, but the whole organizational structure, if necessary, worldwide, which may at any time be interconnected.

- An understanding of the numbers of devices at each location and in each building on each site. Think big. Assume one address per member of staff in those buildings and leave some 25% spare.

- An understanding of the different departments, their geographic locations, and the likelihood that they will need to communicate. An estimate of the amount of information that is exchanged is useful but it has a very short-lived value.

- A knowledge of any other current users of TCP/IP and any standardization decisions that have been taken already

In a small organization of a few hundred people, getting this information is straightforward in comparison to a large corporation; but it is the large corporation that must have accurate figures and which must derive centralized standards that are adhered to everywhere.

Internet Protocol

The Internet Protocol (IP) may be described as the network layer protocol of TCP/IP. IP is operated and interpreted by each intermediate relay in an interconnected set of LANs and WANs which is using the TCP/IP protocol suite to communicate. Such a collection is often called an **internetwork** and the intermediate relays are routers. IP provides a best efforts delivery service based on a technique called **datagram transmission**; 'best efforts' and 'datagram' because no attempt is made (by IP) to recover any errors which may occur in transmission.

IP supports routing and relaying of information between communicating hosts (end devices) according to the Type (or quality) Of Service (TOS) they require. IP allows routing errors to be trapped and reported and their effects on system performance to be minimized. IP does not make assumptions about the underlying network of physical cables, LAN hardware (Ethernet, Token Ring or FDDI) or the point-to-point wide area links (PTT circuits).

IP addressing

The IP address is one component in the Internet protocol. The IP address is a number that uniquely identifies the *connection* of a host computer (or end system as OSI would call it) to a physical network as it communicates with other computers (or end systems). Hosts with more than one connection have a different IP address for each one. IP routers also have their own IP addresses for they can be the source and destination of IP datagrams.

The purpose of the IP address is twofold: to identify each connection to the internetwork in a way that is independent of the underlying physical network (LAN or WAN) technology, and to collect a group of connections together to simplify routing. Internetwork routers use IP addresses to make routing decisions.

The need for address management

IP addresses must be unique in the communicating internetwork. If not, communications will fail erratically. Since TCP/IP protocols do not directly provide any technical means by which IP addresses can be automatically made unique, it is up to network managers to configure and manage them correctly by traditional manual methods aided by database and network management technology.

About MAC addresses

Where TCP/IP systems are connected to a shared cable such as an Ethernet or Token Ring LAN, communication between stations must take place using MAC addresses, normally built into the network adapter card. Since the IP address is configured independently of the MAC address, it remains unchanged even if the network card fails and is replaced.

Every Ethernet or Token Ring card comes with a preconfigured 48-bit MAC address, its universally managed address. LAN standards also allow locally managed addresses; network cards can be loaded with a 48-bit address chosen by the network manager. Locally managed addresses are not normally used in TCP/IP systems. As IP addresses in TCP/IP must be controlled and managed, there is little value in adding a second layer of management by also configuring and controlling MAC addresses.

But the issue of MAC address management does not disappear completely from the TCP/IP story; some of the facilities of TCP/IP (such as the Boot Protocol, BOOTP) use the MAC address as a fixed reference point for obtaining other information. If you wish to use these features, you must at least have a record of the MAC address of each computer for which the facility will be used. These addresses appear as a reference point in look-up tables in information servers. But, as described above, the MAC address can change if the network card is replaced. In a large network, keeping an up-to-date record of MAC addresses and ensuring that all servers have the correct record can be time-consuming.

Some advanced star wiring systems have management facilities that can record the MAC address attached to each user drop cable (and can deny access if that LAN address changes to an unauthorized value). Such systems make it easier to record the location of particular MAC addresses.

Characteristics of the IP address

The IP address is a 32-bit number which must be unique in the internetwork. Devices which must have an IP address include every connection of each application processor and of each network router. As mentioned previously, computers with more than one network connection have a different IP address for each connection (Figure 3.1). In TCP/IP literature, such computers are referred to as **multihomed**. These connections are usually on different networks. This is the reason for sizing the network-by-network connections rather than the number of computers, though these numbers will often be very similar.

Unlike some other network addressing schemes, the IP address does not necessarily convey any information about geographic location. Given an IP address you can only deduce a management authority; that authority could manage one corporate network which in itself has global coverage and meshes with many other global networks. This has interesting implications for routing between two worldwide networks. Put another way, the IP addressing scheme is *not hierarchical* (unlike the telephone or telex network or for that matter the CCITT X.121 addressing scheme for the X.25 interface to public packet switched networks.

Network managers can choose to impose a geographic or organizational hierarchy on IP addresses (using subnet masks as described in Chapter 4) but this hierarchy is not a function of Internet standards.

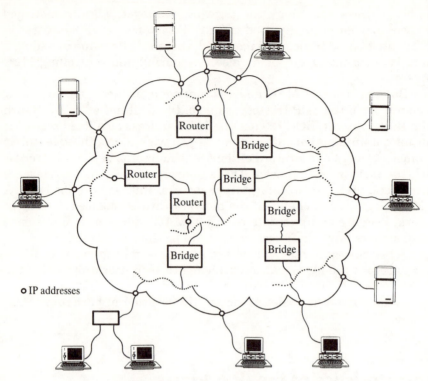

Figure 3.1 Allocation of IP addresses.

IP address format and components

The 32-bit IP address has two components (Figure 3.2): a **network number** (or network identifier) and a **host number** or host identifier. Some 'class bits' can be extracted from the network number, but trying to examine these on their own can lead to confusion. It is safer always to think of the network number as containing the class bits.

It is the network number which identifies the controlling organization and the port number which identifies the particular connection within the authority of that organization. The term 'host number' is historic and this name could cause confusion for, as we have seen, a multihomed host has more than one IP address and hence more than one host number. For reasons that will become apparent later, it would be unusual for two ports on the same machine to have the same network number.

Class bits + Network number	Host number

Figure 3.2 Format of the IP address.

Table 3.1   The limitations of each class of IP address.

Network class	Max. number of network numbers	Max. number of hosts on each network number
A	126	16 777 214
B	16 382	65 534
C	2 097 150	254
D	Not applicable – reserved for multicast systems	
E	Reserved for IAB use	

The terms **net id** and **host id** are in common usage for network number and host number.

Classes of address

IP addresses are divided into five address classes (A to E). It is important to understand that these divisions were conceived to ease the management of addresses by the Internet Activities Board (IAB); they have less immediate significance for the network manager.

The first three classes, A, B, C, are available for normal allocation and for host-to-host communications. Class D and class E addresses are not for general use; class D is reserved for special use by IAB designated protocols and class E is reserved for future use. One use of class D addresses is by routers, so network managers may encounter them while monitoring router protocols.

There are no practical distinctions in the way in which computer systems with class A, class B or class C addresses use those addresses. With some noted exceptions, which are discussed further below, any address from any class is equivalent for communications purposes. In principle, any host can communicate equally well using an address from any of these three classes. The distinguishing feature of each class of address is the number of network numbers and the number of host connections which each network number can support. The limitations of each class are shown in Table 3.1.

Most implementations give network managers full control over the IP addresses they allocate and configure into the equipment. It has been known for an implementation not to accept anything other than a class C address. There are situations where this could be unsatisfactory.

Network numbers and host numbers

The choice of network numbers is most important.

- Network connections with the same network number should communicate directly on the same physical LAN.

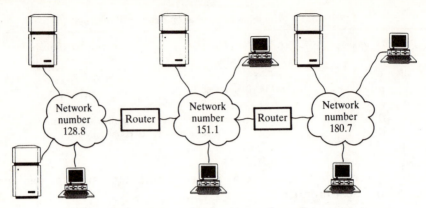

Figure 3.3 Choosing network numbers.

- Network connections with different network numbers do not communicate directly; they must use the services of a router. This router either is directly connected between the two LANs to which the hosts connect or it in turn knows of a router which can relay the message towards its ultimate destination (Figure 3.3). (The exact format of the IP address shown is explained in the next section.)

These factors determine the basic rules[†] for choosing network numbers and host numbers. They may alternatively be stated as:

- Computers or workstations separated only by bridges or repeaters will have the same network number.
- Computers or workstations separated by routers have different network numbers.

For the network implementor, the most important factor is that the choice of IP address for a particular host is affected by the presence of routers. The positioning of routers is determined by the exact geography of the underlying physical networks which connect computers, floors, buildings, sites and countries into a complete internetwork. As we saw in Chapter 2, it is also heavily influenced by organizational needs, traffic flows and traffic volume. The layout will change as the network grows and matures. If a bridge is replaced by a router, the network number on one side of the new router must change.

[†]Modifications to standard router operation can break these basic rules in both ways; stations either side of a router *can* have the same network number; stations on the same bridged LAN *can* have different network numbers. They are discussed as transparent routers and routing redirection in Chapter 16.

Table 3.2   IP address representation.

Dotted decimal	Dotted hexadecimal	C-style hexadecimal	Binary
44.123.110.224	2C.7B.6E.E0	0x2c7b6ee0	00101100011101101101110111011100000
129.6.48.100	81.06.30.64	0x81063064	10000001000001100011000001100100
128.240.1.109	80.F0.01.6D	0x80f0016d	10000000111100000000000101101101
192.33.33.109	C0.21.21.6D	0xc021216d	11000000001000010010000101101101

When combined with the limitations of Table 3.1, the maximum number of network connections that are likely to communicate within one network[†] (or organization) is therefore a key to determining which address class should be selected.

A TCP/IP addressing scheme evolves as the needs of users are better understood during the design process. Adding a TCP/IP addressing scheme to a LAN must take into account the existing layout of that LAN.

One factor is key. Network planners must attempt to design an addressing scheme that can remain substantially unchanged in a changing environment. This can best be achieved using subnetwork addressing (see Chapter 4).

Writing down the address

The convention is that the address is written down, or described to software, in **dotted decimal notation**. Each eight bits of the address (each **octet**) is converted to a decimal number in the range 0 to 255, and separated by a dot (.).

While the US standards initially specified 'dotted decimal notation' some computer staff are more at home with hexadecimal notation. **Dotted hexadecimal**[‡] (and UNIX or C-style hexadecimal) and **octal**[§] notations are sometimes used and will be accepted by some (though by no means all) implementations. Occasionally it is useful, if somewhat long-winded, to represent these numbers in binary. Some valid addresses are shown in Table 3.2. Leading zeros in each octet, which have no significance, need not be included. 128.1.0.9 is valid and more usual than 128.001.000.009, though this is also perfectly acceptable; however, 128.1.9 or 128...9 are not valid.

[†]As we will see in the next chapter, there is a mechanism for dividing one network number into subnetworks. In practice, hosts on either side of a router must be in different subnetworks rather than within different network numbers. However, if they do have different network numbers, they must communicate via one or more routers.

[‡]Counting in 16s, using the characters 0 to 9 and A to F.

[§]Counting in 8s, using the characters 0 to 7.

Table 3.3 Distinguishing the class of address.

Address class	Class bits	Number of network bits	First usable value	Last usable	Comment
A	0	7	1	126	Values 0 and 127 are reserved
B	10	14	128.1	191.254	
C	110	21	192.0.1	223.255.254	
D	1110	–	224.0.0.0	239.255.255.254	Not available for general use
E	1111	–	240.0.0.0	255.255.255.254	Not available for general use

Distinguishing the class of address

The five classes of address have already been mentioned. The class of address is determined by certain bits in the first eight bits, that is, in the first decimal number of the four (Table 3.3). The magnitude of the first number that defines the class of the address is given in the table.

There are two important features of this system:

(1) The division between one class and the next is always at an octet boundary. This simplifies finding the boundaries between the classes of address, since each decimal number represents one octet.

(2) When the network number is written down the 'class bits' are always included in the first octet, to ensure that the class of address and hence the true network number are unambiguous.

It is important that users of TCP/IP, planners and implementors should be fully familiar with the different classes of address and the limitations that they place on network growth. Many people new to the subject at first find the technique of dotted decimal notation a little eccentric. But it should become second nature to recognize the class of address, the network number, and the host id.

Compared to other network addressing schemes, the TCP/IP addressing range is quite limited. Current work in the IAB is investigating the options for extending the address range.

The IAB and network number registration

Since addresses in an internetwork must be unique, there has to be a registry which ensures that such a policy can be enforced.

TCP/IP was developed for use on the US Internet. This collection of networks is managed by many different authorities, with the IAB as overall design authority. In this environment of devolved management, the network number has two functions. First, since each IP address on the whole set of interconnected networks must be unique, the network number is used to identify one addressing authority (often called an autonomous system) responsible for issuing unique connection ids in that part of the address space. The second function is to support routing.

The IAB ensures that IP addresses on the Internet are unique, by registering and issuing network numbers to organizations that have reasons to connect to the Internet. Such organizations *do not choose* their own network number[†], it is issued to them. They agree to undertake certain network management responsibilities when they request an official IAB address allocation. They must then issue host ids so that they are unique within their own network number address space. If they fail to issue unique host numbers, only the services of that organization will be affected.

The IAB has devolved the clerical task of registering and issuing IP network numbers to the Internet Registry, part of the Internet Assigned Numbers Authority (IANA) which controls all numbers in the TCP/IP protocol suite, which must be managed if correct operation is to be guaranteed. The Internet Registry is operated by the Department of Defense Network Network Information Center (DDN NIC), now located in Chantilly, Virginia.

To register or not to register

For any commercial organization, applying to the NIC for a registered network number ensures that your IP addresses are unique in the whole world (of those who have similarly registered). But as Table 3.1 showed, the IP address space, other than class C addresses, is limited with only 16 408 'large' networks. Class C gives a further 2.1 million small networks. As worldwide interest in TCP/IP has grown, the address space is already under some pressure with over 50% of the class B address space already allocated and all the class A address space issued or reserved. There has to be good reason for allocating one or more registered class A or class B addresses from this finite resource.

In early 1992, the total number of hosts accessible from the Internet through the name service was 727 000. As not all registered addresses are connected to the Internet community, this is a very con-

---

[†]Those who have followed the text carefully may have noticed that an organization appears to require use of many network numbers if routers are to operate correctly. The IAB will issue at most a few different network numbers to one organization, which will not, on its own, apparently satisfy the requirements for a large router network. The alternative is subnetting of a single network number which is described fully in Chapter 4.

servative number. Growth is already on to the vertical portion of an exponential growth curve.

When should an organization apply for an IP address registration? At least one Request For Comment (RFC) recommends that all users of TCP/IP should register. We endorse that policy but the following gives guidance on which organizations *must* register, in decreasing order of importance:

- Any organization that connects to the worldwide Internet has no option; they must request a registered network number. These include organizations outside the USA which carry out work for the US government and wish to use TCP/IP for communications with the US Government in the course of that work. In general, such organizations already know of their responsibilities and have already registered.

- Any organization that wishes to communicate with a US parent organization which is itself connected to the Internet is advised to register. Accidental duplicate addresses advertised to the true Internet do not make the advertising organization popular with the US Network Operations Center.

- Organizations that have US subsidiaries or that acquire US subsidiaries which connect to the US Internet should consider registering.

- Large multinationals that wish to use TCP/IP for worldwide communications but which perhaps have limited control or knowledge of the activities of individual operating companies should consider registering.

For those who *do* register there are additional issues to resolve:

- Larger organizations, with many thousands of employees worldwide, will prefer a class B or class A address. All class A addresses are allocated or reserved; recent allocations have been to governments outside the USA. Class B addresses with 65 534 connections will become increasingly difficult to obtain.

- As we analyse the use of these IP addresses in TCP/IP, you will discover that the address space is consumed more quickly than might be expected; in practical networks, it often is not possible to use the available space efficiently. Large organizations will then require more than one class B address to satisfy their requirements.

- Smaller organizations who register will be encouraged to use one or more class C addresses. Unfortunately, class C addresses cannot have more than 254 connections on one bridged LAN. Today this number still seems small but as the network capacity demanded by an individual workstation increases with the general availability of 32-bit PCs operating at high clock speeds and of RISC computers, this limitation may become less important. Organizations may then be content to use multiple (registered) class C addresses.

Advantages and disadvantages of registering

The key advantage of registering is ensuring that as you use and extend TCP/IP to new applications, which may include communicating with external organizations using TCP/IP, your address and naming conventions are protected. If you are not registered and an address clash occurs in the future then the onus must be on the nonregistered organization to make changes.

For some organizations there is a disadvantage that if you connect to the Internet, your use of a registered address is recorded in the Assigned Numbers RFC together with a contact name who may be approached for network information. In an application for registration, the NIC requires details of two contacts, one for administrative and policy information, the other a technical contact for resolving technical problems associated with the network.

The NIC Assigned Numbers RFC, which is issued regularly, also records the identifier of the network. The NIC keeps records of the responsible organization and its name and address.

Those wishing to pursue registration further should contact the Network Information Center. Contact details are given in Appendix A.

Autonomous systems

An **autonomous system** (AS) is a collection of LANs and WANs and the interconnecting routers which are under the control of one management authority for configuration, addressing, naming and routing decisions. Decisions made within such an authority should not be visible to the rest of the interconnected Internet. Ideally, one commercial organization should form one autonomous system. The IAB also registers AS numbers which uniquely identify an autonomous system.

The concept of autonomous systems is extended in Internet to the Autonomous Confederation, a group of autonomous systems with a common interest which requires them to establish direct links to each other rather than route through the core Internet. The term auto-nomous confederation has a less clear value to commercial organizations unless they cannot achieve a single centralized control authority. This term seems to be falling into disuse with changes in Internet policy.

Autonomous system numbers

As well as registering a network number, commercial organizations should now register an AS number. The AS number is used by routers with the newer OSPF and BGP routing protocols to identify which AS is the source of routing information. This forms part of a low-level security facility.

Some organizations have registered more than one AS number. AS numbers can only distinguish 65 535 different organizations so, in due course, this could become another scarce resource, with the rapid growth in interest in internetworking with TCP/IP.

There may be managerial advantages in a large organization using several AS numbers to identify the authority responsible for configuring a particular device. This information can normally be derived from the network number.

How to choose your own network number

Our immediate recommendation is *don't*. *Do* apply for a registered address. But if you decide that registration is unnecessary, then *do* consider carefully which address you choose.

The maximum likely size of the network is the most important factor which will influence the choice of IP address class. Private self-contained networks may use any or many different network numbers, though there are good reasons to limit the range of network numbers used.

It is important to keep IP addresses unique in any internetwork of intercommunicating TCP/IP machines. As networks grow and develop and as TCP/IP is used to communicate with other external companies (for example for Electronic Data Interchange, EDI), this will become more difficult if the network number is not registered and a large number of network numbers are in use. An address is more likely to be unique if the network number is registered. If your organization does not fall into that group which should register, then to reduce the likelihood of an address duplication with another organization in the future you should:

- Avoid class A addresses, for they are all allocated to the largest networks to which everyone connects
- Do not copy examples given in manufacturers' handbooks, textbooks or sales literature.
- Avoid well-known addresses published in TCP/IP RFCs and other documentation.
- Do use one, or a limited number, of class B addresses at random in the higher part of the address range which will be allocated late in the day, or
- Do use a limited number of class C addresses chosen in a similar way.

If at some point you wish to undertake limited communications with a small number of organizations with which your addresses clash, then all is not lost. A router that performs address translation between the two networks will map a limited number of unused addresses from one network to the other. But the router must effectively isolate the address space of the two systems. Any-to-any communications are not possible.

Configuring the IP address

Every computer, workstation, personal computer, network router and network management station which 'speaks IP' must have a different IP address for each of its connections. The IP address is entered through the normal configuration management processes. IP addresses are usually represented and entered in dotted decimal notation; occasionally dotted hexadecimal notation is accepted. The address is usually stored in non-volatile memory, either RAM or on a disk file when available.

Diskless workstations often have no nonvolatile storage. They obtain their IP address across the network at start-up time using BOOTP or RARP.

Visiting each device to change the IP address is time-consuming, particularly in dispersed networks. BOOTP provides a mechanism for centralizing the distribution of IP addresses and other useful TCP/IP parameters, even for machines which do have storage. The key to distributing the correct IP address and other information via BOOTP is the MAC address of the interface card. It is then *essential* to record accurately the MAC address used by each machine on the network that uses the BOOTP service. This is excellent policy for fault diagnosis and security in any case, though it is often neglected.

In an operational network, IP addresses become recorded in distributed tables and in software in machines. While this is bad practice, it is unavoidable. Frequent wholesale changes to IP addresses must not occur, so preplanning is essential. Such changes are labour-intensive because of the widespread distribution of addresses; the change introduces errors and has unpredictable consequences for the integrity of operational applications and for the time taken to restore any-to-any communications.

Reserved IP addresses

Certain IP network numbers and host numbers are reserved for the use of particular aspects of TCP/IP communication. Not all these protocols are regularly used. If you configure a connection with a reserved IP address, the faults caused are likely to be obscure, apparently intermittent and difficult to isolate. Not all host software checks (or is even able to check under all circumstances) that the IP address it is requested to use is invalid.

The following addresses are reserved:

- Network number 127.X.X.X, where X.X.X is any set of numbers. This is used for a local software loopback test.[†]
- A network number of all 0s is classless and means 'my current network which I do not know the number of' – sometimes referred to as 'this network'.
- A network number of all 1s.
- Host number 0 is reserved to refer to a particular network number. For example, 192.0.0.1 is the first class C network address which could be allocated.
- Host number 'all 1s' is reserved to broadcast to all hosts on a specific network; it can only be used as a destination address.
- The full address 0.0.0.0 is reserved. It is used in two ways: as a source address when the host does not know its genuine address, for example during bootstrapping of a diskless workstation, and by routers in a list of addresses to advertise the default route, the route to all networks which are not explicitly listed. (It is not a source or destination address, merely an entry in a table.)
- The full address 255.255.255.255 is reserved as a destination address to mean 'broadcast to all hosts on my network'. 0.0.0.0 as a destination is an obsolete form of 255.255.255.255.

Further addresses become reserved when subnetworking is introduced. These are the more difficult to recognize. Subnetworking is discussed in Chapter 4.

IP addresses with routers and dial-up devices

Some older router implementations require that a point-to-point wide-area PTT or dial-up link between two LANs should be identified with its own unique IP network number with only two connections attached. In the larger network this is wasteful of the limited resource of IP network numbers. Check with your router manufacturer that the most modern techniques, which conserve network and subnetwork numbers, are used in their implementation.

[†]IAB standards say that any address beginning with 127. must not be transmitted across the physical interface and appear on the cable. Not all software implementations check and reject IP addresses beginning with 127 and some will transmit IP datagrams with that source or destination address. This has been known to cause networks to fail.

Common mistakes in choosing IP addresses

Common mistakes in choosing and managing IP addresses centre around the possibility of address duplication or using the wrong network number for the LAN to which the port is attached. This arises through the following:

- Not controlling the issuing of addresses (and subaddresses) centrally, or at a sufficiently high point in the organizational tree.
- Using the example in the software manufacturer's literature.
- Giving a supplier the responsibility of choosing and configuring an IP addressing scheme without understanding the overall needs of the organization.
- Copying the addresses from another part of the organization.
- Duplicating the address from the machine next door.
- Choosing an address from a nearby machine and modifying it slightly.
- Not fully understanding the concept of network and host (connection) number.
- Misunderstanding that workstations on the same LAN must use the same network number.
- Misunderstanding that stations either side of a router must have different network numbers.
- Using a reserved network number or host number.
- Failing to anticipate how and why IP addresses may change at a later date and avoiding that change.

The organizational structure and the IP address

Allocating TCP/IP addresses in larger companies raises political and organizational issues. If no scheme for address allocation has been developed and agreed, the first people to introduce TCP/IP may find themselves attempting to take addressing decisions on behalf of the whole organization, but without the necessary authority and influence to carry their decisions through.

If you are in that position, you either take up the challenge of agreeing the address structure for the whole organization or you take the pragmatic approach to make a local decision and trust that it will not cause problems with address clashes or major updates later. Be assured that it will. In a changing environment, this pragmatic decision will eventually rebound in increased catchback costs, for, even if address clashes do not occur, the address will change as routers are introduced in the growing network.

The second organizational issue of IP addressing is that IP addresses are entered into the software of applications computers. Network routers also use IP addresses to communicate among themselves and with host computers. In large networks, network routers and application processors may be controlled by different managements. The addressing authority must issue IP addresses, but they may not be welcome if they attempt to configure them in the larger mini and mainframe application processors. The central authority described in Chapter 1 must be able to enforce IP address configuration and even reconfiguration decisions equally on the owners and operators of host processors and network routers. Fortunately, once addresses have been allocated they should not change frequently, if the network has been well designed. But over the life of even a well-designed network, it is to be expected that some address reconfiguration will be necessary because of activities in another department.

Moves and changes

It is a feature of life in many organizations that staff move office location regularly. If their PC or workstation at the new location is in a different network number or subnetwork number, the IP address will change. This may have a consequential impact on other levels of TCP/IP, the domain name service, mail, and on other parameters of the machine's software (default router, BOOTP server, domain name server). These issues are fully explained in Chapter 18.

Record keeping

If TCP/IP management is to be successful, there must be records of each IP address and where, how, and by whom it is used. Some features of TCP/IP require a record of the Ethernet or Token Ring MAC address associated with the IP address. BOOTP supplies the IP address for a specific MAC address; domain name service supplies an IP address given the host domain name, or, given an IP address, will supply the host domain name.

To keep these records up to date requires proper clerical procedures, training of clerical staff and the correct vetting of entries by software, so that the task becomes routine. The aim of system managers must be to reduce the amount of skilled time consumed by such clerical activities.

The future of IP addresses

The IP addressing scheme appears to give access to over 2 100 000 networks with a total of 3720 million hosts. This seems a large number even given the number of PCs in use. Not all of them are yet using TCP/IP. But because of the strict divisions between network numbers and host numbers, the address space is now under considerable pressure. For example, an organization may have a class B address for 10 000 hosts and the other 55 000 host addresses are effectively lost to the Internet community.

Since 1990, the IAB has been investigating ways of modifying the addressing scheme to extend the addressing structure to identify 1 000 000 000 networks. The current views focus on reusing the address space in different parts of the Internet, that is, towards a more hierarchical system (based on AS numbers or administrative domains), or to extending the address to 64 bits. The extension of the address is unlikely as host software must change. Some of the new schemes are referred to as **supernetting**.

Another strong possibility is to change IP to the OSI Connectionless Network Protocol (CLNP).

While it is unclear what the outcome will be, there is a desire to confine the major changes to the main routers of the worldwide Internet. The changes are unlikely to affect a corporate network that is not connected to the Internet.

Subnetting

The network manager has a more immediate need however: to solve the issue of network numbering on either side of a router when only one network number can be used. The solution, introduced in 1985, is called **subnetwork addressing** and it is now standard on all TCP/IP equipment. This is such an important topic that the next chapter discusses it in detail.

Summary

Choosing whether to register a network number, choosing a network number, and planning and then controlling the IP addressing scheme for a TCP/IP internetwork are the most important initial managerial tasks. In large, multisite networks the management problem must be subdivided using different network numbers for different sites, for different buildings or even different floors. Network managers must establish and enforce the responsibilities for managing the different parts of the address space. Subnetworking, described in the next chapter, gives the network manager more local control of his or her portion of the IP address space.

The important points about IP addressing are:

- The IP address space must be correctly managed.

- Some organizations should apply for and be issued with a registered address from the DDN NIC.

- Where addresses are not registered, the whole IP address space is available for 'private' use but you should not use addresses quoted in suppliers' literature or given as examples in TCP/IP documentation.

- The IP address has two parts, a network number and a 'host' or connection number. The address is not hierarchical.

- The network number identifies a controlling organization, not the location of the network.

- Hosts will have a different IP address for each connection on the Internet. It is connections which are identified, not hosts.

- The class of address determines the maximum number of hosts which can share a single network number.

- Addresses should be unique in the interconnected network at all times.

- Do not allocate network 0.0.0.0 or 127.X.X.X.

- Do not allocate host id 0 or host id all 1s on any network number.

- Do keep accurate records of the use of IP addresses by each machine on the network, its location, who uses it and who controls its configuration.

- Do keep a record of all Ethernet or Token Ring addresses and their associated IP addresses, if you wish to use some of the features of TCP/IP such as BOOTP.

- Stations in a bridged LAN should have the same network number; stations on either side of a router should have different network numbers.

- IP addresses are stored on each workstation, computer or router in the network. They may also be used by software and stored in applications or in other parts of the TCP/IP protocol suite.

- Changes to the IP addressing scheme in the larger operational network could be difficult and expensive to implement.

- Moving a machine from one location (floor, building, site) to another may require a change in IP address.

4

Subnetworks and IP addresses

With the increase in the use of information technology, and hence in the number of attached computers in a typical corporate network, the strict class A, B and C divisions of the IP addressing scheme, as described so far, are too limiting. The solution introduced in the mid-1980s was subnetwork addressing or 'subnets'. In this chapter, we discuss what subnetwork addressing is and how it can be used to give the TCP/IP network planner much more control over the allocation and sizing of network numbers and subnetwork numbers. The topics considered are:

- The need for subnetwork addressing
- The structure and format of the subnetwork mask
- Managing subnetworks
- Configuring the subnetwork mask
- Creating hierarchical subnetwork address structures
- Using variable length subnetwork masks

If selecting an IP addressing scheme is the first major decision the TCP/IP implementor must make, the second parallel decision is how to subdivide an IP network number so that organizations can make efficient use of the available address space. It is often important to devolve management of IP addresses to local departments to give them more control of their own network implementation.

The IAB issues one or more full address spaces of class A, B, or C to an organization to allocate its own host ids. But network managers must be able to control the allocation not only of host numbers but also of network numbers if the standard TCP/IP mechanisms for using routers are to operate. These require that two stations on the same bridged LAN share the same network number; on either side of a router stations must have different network numbers. How can this be achieved if an organization has only one or a few network numbers available? The solution to this problem is **subnetworks** or subnetworking through the use of the **subnetwork mask**.

Subnetworking and the subnetwork mask

Subnetworking or **subnetting** increases the network manager's control over the address space and provides a mechanism for using routers when only one or a small number of full network numbers is available. The mechanism for creating subnetworks is the subnetwork mask, another 32-bit number which is allocated at the same time as the IP address.

Subnetworking divides the normal range of host ids (16 million for class A, 65 534 for class B and 254 for class C) into a number of subnetworks and a reduced number of hosts on each subnetwork. The product of these two numbers cannot exceed the original number of host ids. So, subnetting of class C addresses leads to a small number of networks with a very few host addresses on each. Some implementations may not allow subnetting of class C addresses, though it is sometimes used in research departments with high-performance RISC-based workstations where a few devices can saturate one LAN cable.

When should you use subnetting?

The simple answer is: 'Always plan for it even if you don't use it initially'. If an IP addressing scheme is planned without subnetwork addressing, then it is likely to be very labour-intensive to introduce it later, as a large percentage of addresses will change. Planning ahead is key. Most network implementors should plan their address space on the basis of subnetworks rather than multiple network numbers.

Small networks that will not use routers need not use subnetworking. Such networks are never likely to grow beyond a few physical

Table 4.1 The subnetwork mask.

	Binary	Dotted decimal
IP address	10000001.10000010.01001111.01010101	129.130.79.85
Subnet mask	11111111.11111111.11111000.00000000	255.255.248.0
Network id	10000001.10000010.01001000.00000000	129.130.72.0
Host id	00000000.00000000.00000111.01010101	0.0.7.85

LANs and up to 200 stations. Also, if you do not need to use a registered address and do not mind how many IP network numbers you use, then there is less impetus to use subnetwork addressing. However, careful use of subnetwork addressing, rather than multiple network numbers, will simplify future network growth and change, so it is highly recommended.

The subnetwork mask

All TCP/IP equipment which operates the network layer IP protocol, and hence has an IP address, must be capable of using subnetting and the subnetwork mask. The subnetwork mask is the 'number' under the network manager's control which determines how the subnetworks are structured. When two network numbers are compared to determine if a router must be used, they are compared after being 'filtered' by the subnetwork mask.

Inappropriate choice of the subnetwork mask can lead to great confusion when one tries to explain how routing will operate. The following description is a simple starting point. The interaction between routing and the subnetwork mask is discussed further in Chapters 5 and 16.

The subnetwork mask is a 32-bit number that allows a network manager to choose the number of subnets and hosts on each subnetwork. There are still certain strict limits imposed by the basic structure of class A, B and C addresses. There cannot be a greater number of connections than the basic address gives; in practice the total number of available connections is less due to inefficiencies in the way subnets can be allocated. What you gain is flexibility and control. By defining your own subnetworks you have some freedom to place routers for your own convenience without having to use different network numbers.

The rule, shown in Table 4.1, is simple:

- If there is a 1 in a bit position in the subnetwork mask, that bit forms part of the subnetwork number in this address space.
- If there is a 0 in a bit position in the subnetwork mask, that bit is part of the host (or connection) id.

Even if you do not choose to manage subnetwork addressing on your network, all equipment will still use the technique because it will generate

Table 4.2   The default subnet masks.

Address class	Default mask dotted decimal	Default mask dotted hex
Class A	255.0.0.0	FF.0.0.0
Class B	255.255.0.0	FF.FF.0.0
Class C	255.255.255.0	FF.FF.FF.0

default subnetwork masks that select the normal class A (8 bit), class B (16 bit) or class C (24 bit) network numbers. Once a piece of equipment is configured with its IP address it examines the 'class bits' to set the correct **default mask** automatically.

Subnetwork masks are represented in the same format as normal IP addresses: dotted decimal or hexadecimal. The three default subnet masks are shown in Table 4.2. The network manager takes control of the address space by changing 0s to 1s in the mask, which successively halves the number of hosts and doubles the number of subnets available. *It is strongly recommended that these 1s are added from the left of the address and that no intermediate 0 gaps remain.* This is sometimes referred to as a **mask of contiguous 1s**.

Subnetworks are used by routers. You may be able to work out how your routers will respond to a mask which is not contiguous, for example:

11111111.11111111.00011111.00000000

But have some thought for those who follow behind you, however. If you make a great success of this network, you will be promoted, but someone less able may be coming along behind! For the long-term viability of the network and the sanity of those who follow, do keep life as simple as possible!

The complete range of class B subnet options is shown in Appendix D. This shows the number of subnet bits, the resulting mask and the first and last usable host addresses on each subnetwork, together with the subnetwork broadcast address and the address that describes 'this subnetwork'.

Because the subnet bits are added from the left of a byte (the most significant bit) but are then represented in dotted decimal notation, the third octet has an unfamiliar pattern to it. These mystical numbers are formed as shown in Table 4.3.

Reserved subnet numbers

Understanding this subsection is only necessary for a complete understanding of the limitations in allocating subnet numbers; your sanity may be retained by skipping this section at first reading.

Table 4.3 How a mask octet is calculated.

Value of 3rd octet	How 3rd octet is calculated	Binary 'mask'
0	0	00000000
128	128	10000000
192	128+64	11000000
224	128+64+32	11100000
240	128+64+32+16	11110000
248	128+64+32+16+8	11111000
252	128+64+32+16+8+4	11111100
254	128+64+32+16+8+4+2	11111110
255	128+64+32+16+8+4+2+1	11111111

Subnetting is further complicated because a subnet of all 1s[†] is a broadcast to all subnets in this overall network number. A host id of 'all 1s' remains the broadcast to all hosts, either on a specific subnetwork or on all subnetworks in this network number. This makes the range of useful addresses (see Appendix D) more restricted than might have been thought. Because 'all 1s' is reserved, the first useful class B subnets are not 128.1.0.0 and 128.1.128.0 with a subnet mask of 255.255.128.0 or FF.FF.80.00 as might be expected. These addresses cannot be used, as 128.1.0.x refers to 'host x on this subnetwork' and 128.1.255.255 is 'broadcast to all subnetworks in the network 128.1.0.0'. 128.1.255.255 could also be 'broadcast to all hosts on the subnet 128.1.128.0'. The two conditions cannot be distinguished and therefore this subnet range is not used.

The first usable mask is the next mask of 255.255.192.0 or FF.FF.C0.0, giving four subnet values, but with only two usable subnetwork numbers of 128.1.64.0 and 128.1.128.0. While 128.1.192.0 at first seems usable, the address 128.1.255.255 again means 'broadcast to all hosts on all subnets in network number 128.1.0.0'. There is no separate way of defining a broadcast to all hosts on the single subnet 128.1.192.0. Any address 128.1.0.xxx refers to host xxx on 'this subnet' not on the specific subnet 128.1.0.0, so that subnet is also unusable. This is another reason why the IP address space is not, in practice, as large as might be thought.

When represented in dotted decimal, it can be difficult to recognize the broadcast to a single subnet.

[†]RFC1219 also states that subnet 0 must be reserved to mean 'this subnetwork'. This is not mentioned in the Internet Assigned Numbers RFC; it is not clear under what circumstances this would be used rather than a network number of 0. If subnet 0 must not be used, this reduces the number of subnetworks available in each range by two rather than one.

Keeping it simple – one value of subnet mask

Address management is much simpler if the same subnet mask is configured on all IP equipment that has the same network number. If more than one network number is available, different masks can be used with each number.

Before using different subnet masks at connections with the same network number, there are a number of implications for routing that must be fully understood for the particular manufacturer's equipment you have chosen to use. The use of different masks is not fully defined by today's standards.

Choosing a subnet mask

Moving the subnet mask boundary exchanges host numbers for subnet numbers. Hosts on different subnetworks cannot communicate directly; they must have an intervening router. So changing the subnet mask may equally be thought of as exchanging bridges for routers. Before choosing the subnet boundary, you must know:

- What is the largest subnetwork that you can successfully manage when it is interconnected with bridges alone?
- What are the cost, performance and management implications of using routers rather than bridges?

The first question implies that, as a network grows, bridges will be replaced by routers at strategic points and hence either addresses will change or the subnet mask will change on all equipment on either side of the new router.

The answers to these questions determine the upper and lower bounds to the maximum size of a single subnetwork. These decisions are important for, in an internetwork with a single subnet mask, *all subnetworks will have the same maximum size.* For initial simplicity, we just recommended that a single network number should use one subnet mask throughout the internetwork. In normal corporate networks, it is probable that there will be a few large subnetworks and a larger number of small networks. To optimize the use of the address space around the larger number of smaller networks, the larger networks may have to be subdivided into small subnetworks and interconnected by routers rather than bridges. As the price and performance of routers continues to improve, the performance and cost disadvantages of routers decrease, though the relative performance of bridges may be expected to improve in the same way. It may be appropriate to use more than one network

---

†We explain how to achieve subnetworks of different sizes below.

number with different subnet masks† to cater for different size and traffic requirements.

So, the power of subnetting is that it allows the network design authority a degree of flexibility in organizing the address space and in developing a router network to suit the organization. The issue is that this flexibility is not as great as managers of the larger corporate network would desire; they are restricted unless they can use multiple network numbers or different length subnet masks in different parts of the networks.

Subnetting a class B address

Most larger commercial networks use one or more class B addresses. (The principles of subnetting apply also to class C addresses; only the scale is different.)

The limits of a single class B address space are from 2 subnetworks of 16 382 hosts to 16 382 subnetworks of 2 hosts. It is likely that most managements will choose one of the following subdivisions of a class B network:

- 254 subnets of 254 hosts (quite small subnets)
- 126 subnets of 510 hosts
- 62 subnets of 1022 hosts
- 30 subnets of 2046 hosts (large subnets)

These figures produce an acceptable balance between the use of bridges and routers. It has been found that it becomes increasingly difficult to manage a large network comprised only of bridges. A network based only on routers is manageable but can be expensive. Subnet addressing, in the first option, 254 subnets of 254 hosts can be much easier to explain and manage.

If you do not use a registered address, a class A address gives a greater range of subnetworks and host numbers. In a class A address, there are then sufficient bits in a single network number to move towards a more geographic 'hierarchical address' allocation.

Configuring subnet masks

Subnet masks are entered into each device at the same time that its IP address is configured and are stored along with that address. In a large network, making any change to the subnet mask may involve visiting the equipment and manually changing the mask. Obviously, this is to be avoided, particularly in large, geographically spread networks. The boot protocol, BOOTP, allows the subnet mask and the IP address to be obtained from a central server. In Chapter 13, we describe how to distribute subnet masks and IP addresses using BOOTP.

If you do not provide a subnet mask, the installation software generates the default mask at the time you configure the IP address, by examining the class bits of the address you enter.

TCP/IP standards do not specify how particular parameters should be entered into machines, for they do not specify the user interface. Different TCP/IP implementations accept the subnet mask in different ways. These are:

- The full mask in dotted decimal (or hexadecimal) format,
- The number of bits or 'extension' bits in the mask.

A command of the form:

```
netmask = 255.255.224.0
```

allows you to enter the full subnet mask in dotted decimal format; such an entry may allow any dotted decimal number to be input, but remember it is incorrect to do other than extend the default subnet mask with contiguous 1s. For this reason an alternative (and preferred) representation is the 'number of 1s' in the mask, using a command like

```
subnetbits = 19
```

This example also produces a mask of 255.255.224.0 since the mask consists of $8+8+3$ ones. Yet another implementation expects the user to enter the *extra* number of bits added to the default mask. In such a case, for a class B address:

```
bits = 3
```

specifies the mask 255.255.224.0, since the default mask of 255.255.0.0 already has 16 ones.

Difficulties with a single mask

A single subnet mask and network number cannot satisfactorily span all the requirements of the larger corporation unless a class A address is used and the risk of an address clash is discounted. With a class B address, it is possible to have spare address capacity in some smaller subnetworks and to have exhausted address capacity in the large networks, but be unable to transfer the unused addresses. Without the flexibility of variable subnet masks, the network manager must either simply live with inefficient allocation of the address space or use more than one network number, possibly with a different subnet mask for each number. Using more than one network number has an impact on the operation of routers. This is discussed fully in Chapter 5.

Table 4.4   Hierarchical subnetting of a (nonregistered) class A address.

Network number	Site or location	Subnetwork or area	Host id
8 bits fixed	Variable width	Variable width	Variable width

Subnetworking with a single mask introduces a second level of hierarchy into IP address management. If available the use of variable subnet masks would allow a full hierarchical structure, doubling the number of subnets and halving the nodes for each bit added to the mask. Such a hierarchical structure is useful for a large corporate network, as illustrated in Table 4.4 for a nonregistered class A[†] address. The first level of division in IP addressing is the network number, the second level is the site or location and the third level is the area or subnetwork within that site. Each area has its contingent of attached hosts. A class A address gives the network planner 24 bits to divide into sites, areas and hosts with full flexibility as to where the boundaries should be, at least when the decision is made. Once deployed in equipment, the flexibility is reduced if not eliminated.

This technique can be used to overcome the problem of changing a bridge for a router, provided the addresses have been chosen correctly in the first instance. Using a router in the presence of subnets begins to bring local geography into play. If all addresses in one building are chosen from one of the subnet address ranges (see next section) and all those in another building are chosen from a second and correctly adjacent range then, merely by changing the subnet mask for the network, each area can be part of one or of two subnetworks, according to choice.

Consider the example of Figure 4.1. Two sites are initially connected by remote bridges using a 2 Mbps digital circuit. Two buildings on each site are connected by fibre optic links from the same bridge. All have the same network number, 191.250.0.0. But the distribution of addresses in the two sites and two buildings is such that by changing the subnet mask, the two sites and buildings within sites can become different subnetworks. At stage 1 the mask is the default of 255.255.0.0 and there is only one network, as required for a fully bridged LAN. In stage 2, by changing the mask to 255.255.240.0 no IP addresses need be altered when routers are introduced between the sites. A second change of the subnetwork mask to 255.255.252.0 places the buildings in different subnetworks (stage 3).

Grouping addresses together in this manner also assists with fault finding. When a fault is discovered, the IP address of the faulty equip-

---

[†]The technique applies equally to registered class A addresses but they are unobtainable.

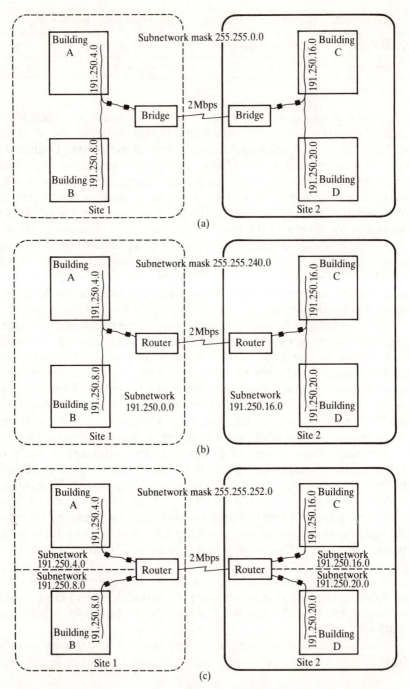

Figure 4.1 Planning routers using subnet addressing. (a) All one network. (b) Two subnetworks. (c) Four subnetworks.

ment immediately identifies the location of that equipment. If a number of devices in the same area are found to be faulty at the same time, it gives a good indication of where to begin looking for the fault.

Should traffic become unmanageable in a bridged LAN, the changes required to incorporate routing are simplified by subnetting. This is only possible because the upgrade is predicted and the addressing scheme is preplanned. The alternative is labour-intensive, with major changes to the IP addressing scheme required possibly simultaneously at different parts of the network, and having to take place outside normal working hours to avoid disruption.

The practice is rather different, however. By default each IP address and its corresponding subnet mask is configured at each attached workstation. Unless addresses and subnet masks can be managed and changed centrally, it is just as labour-intensive to change one bit of a subnet mask on each machine as it is to change a complete IP address. There is increasing justification for managing and distributing IP addresses and subnet masks centrally through the BOOTP.

A class B hierarchical network

The network number in an IP address does not contain any concept of a geographic location, only of a controlling authority. The IP addressing scheme is not hierarchical. But since the subnet portion of the address is totally under the control of the autonomous system manager, he or she can introduce a geographic component into the address if there is value in so doing.

The following is an example of what can be achieved within a single class B address. IP addresses can be allocated to different geographic sites, in blocks which are on a high-numbered binary boundary. Buildings within a site can be allocated on binary boundaries lower down the hierarchy, according to the number of host addresses they require.

For example, suppose Integralis Ltd has been allocated the class B addresses 191.250.0.0. They wish to cover up to 16 sites with a maximum of 4000 devices on a site. There are up to four large buildings on each site. By using a subnet mask of six extra bits, that is, a mask of 255.255.252.0, there are 64 networks (of which 62 are usable) each with 1022 hosts. The result is shown in Table 4.5. The progression of addresses seems perhaps strange, because the boundaries are determined by binary bit patterns which are then expressed in decimal. It is important that those who configure TCP/IP equipment are fully familiar with the addressing scheme and the subnet addressing scheme. They should be able to spot instantly any peculiarities in a chosen address. It is worthwhile spending some time in studying the examples given.

Table 4.5 A hierarchical class B network with a mask of 255.255.252.0.

Site	Building	Network number	First host	Last host	Comment
		191.250.0.0	191.250.1.1	191.250.3.254	Range not usable – seen as 'this subnetwork'
1	1		191.250.4.1	191.250.7.254	
	2		191.250.8.1	191.250.11.254	
	3		191.250.12.1	191.250.15.254	
2	1	191.250.16.0	191.250.16.1	191.250.19.254	
	2		191.250.20.1	191.250.23.254	
	3		191.250.24.1	191.250.27.254	
	4		191.250.28.1	191.250.31.254	
⋮	⋮	⋮	⋮	⋮	
⋮	⋮	⋮	⋮	⋮	
15	1	191.250.224.0	191.250.224.1	191.250.227.254	
	2		191.250.228.1	191.250.231.254	
	3		191.250.232.1	191.250.235.254	
	4		191.250.236.1	191.250.239.254	
16	1	191.250.240.0	191.250.240.1	191.250.243.254	
	2		191.250.244.1	191.250.247.254	
	3		191.250.248.1	191.250.251.254	
	–		191.250.252.1	191.250.254.254	Range not usable – seen as 'broadcast to all stations, this subnet

Such a scheme is wasteful of address space where not all sites are of equal size. But it introduces a true, hierarchical address space where certain bits designate a site, certain bits designate a building and other bits can specify a floor. Some further flexibility can be achieved with the correct combination of bridges and routers.

Note also the scheme is based on geography which may not exactly correspond with an organizational structure. Individual groups in the organization must accept that they are allocated a specific address by a central authority. With care it is possible to allocate a block of addresses, but meeting the needs of groups of widely different sizes may mean that strict geographic boundaries are infringed. Each time such guidelines are infringed it will complicate future changes.

Using a subnet mask of 255.255.255.0 for a class B network simplifies management at the expense of more routers. The third octet will indicate the site or building number directly with no confusion to boundaries.

Using different subnet masks

Using a single subnet mask can lead to exhaustion of part of the address space, while other parts may have spare capacity which cannot be transferred. In RFC 1219, P. Tsuchiya of Bellcore has suggested a technique which reduces these problems.

For this method to be successful, it requires an initial judgement of the maximum number of subnets and the maximum size of subnetworks. It also requires the use of **variable length subnet masks**[†] and of routers that understand, exchange and interpret variable length subnet masks. To date, the use of variable length subnet masks is still under discussion by the Internet Engineering Task Force[‡] (IETF); not all routers can be guaranteed to handle these in the same way.

The principles of the scheme are fairly simple, but the details could be difficult to implement in a real network with devolved management, unless there is close cooperation and a very good technical understanding of subnet masking.

The principle is that subnet numbers are allocated from the top of the mask boundary working downwards, while host ids are allocated from the bottom up. Some space is allocated between subnet bits and host bits for growth of either the number of subnetworks or the number of hosts. As the network develops this growth space can be allocated to hosts or to additional subnetworks as required. The procedure can become complex at the point an additional growth bit is allocated to either host or subnet; it requires a full understanding of the implications and careful coordination across different subnet addressing authorities in an organization. Those who require more detail should refer to RFC 1219.

Variable length subnet masks only work with routers that can exchange masks as part of their routing tables. This limits the choice of routing protocol and is discussed in Chapter 5. It may be impossible to broadcast throughout a number of subnets reliably if a variable length subnet mask is used.

Summary

Subnetting is an integral part of the IP addressing scheme. The two topics cannot be separated. In Chapter 3 we said that planning and then controlling the IP addressing scheme for a TCP/IP internetwork is the most important initial managerial task. In large multisite networks, the

---

[†]While the term 'variable length subnet masks' is frequently used, and we shall continue that use, the mask is always a fixed length of 32 bits – it is the number of contiguous 1s which varies.

[‡]The IETF is the committee of technical experts that has responsibility for the RFCs which are to become full IAB standards. They also vet all RFCs before general release.

management problem must be further subdivided using either different network numbers or different subnet numbers for different sites, for different buildings or even different floors. The preferred mechanism for local management of the IP addressing scheme is subnetting with the subnet mask.

The important points about subnetwork addressing are:

- Stations in a bridged LAN should have the same subnetwork number; stations on either side of a router should have different subnetwork numbers.

- Subnetting allows the network manager to create different 'network numbers' (actually subnet numbers) from one IAB network number.

- Subnetworks should be planned from the outset as an integral part of the IP addressing scheme.

- Subnet masks should be generated from the default subnet mask for the address class in use by adding contiguous 1s starting from the most significant bits.

- Subnetwork 0 or subnetwork all 1s must not be allocated for the particular subnet mask in use.

- Host id 0 or host id all 1s must not be allocated on any network or subnetwork.

- The subnetwork mask should be added to the records of each machine on the network.

- Subnetting can produce a hierarchical or geographic-based address structure.

- Subnetting can protect the network from IP address changes as routers are introduced in the larger growing network.

- The choice of subnet mask affects the ratio of bridges and routers in a network.

- Until the implications of doing otherwise are fully understood, the same subnet mask should be used with a single network number.

- Like IP addresses, subnet masks are stored on each workstation, computer or router in the network.

- The subnetwork mask is today an integral part of the IP addressing scheme; any changes, particularly in the larger operational network, could be difficult and expensive to implement.

- Moving a machine from one location (floor, building, site) to another may result in a change in IP address and its associated subnet mask

5

Routing

Routing, the feature within the TCP/IP protocol suite which allows the 'best' path between two communicating systems to be chosen for a given application, depends on the correct choice of equipment and routing software. In this chapter we examine the choices available and the decisions to be taken. The topics considered are:

- The need for routers
- What routing is
- Routers and IP
- Routing advantages
- Routers and the IP address
- Routing tables
- Choosing a routing protocol
- RIP, OSPF, integrated IS-IS, BGP, IGRP, Hello, EGP and GGP
- Configuring routers

The need for routers and their management

When designing and managing the IP internetwork, the router network is important to the overall stability and performance of any system based on TCP/IP. Particularly for larger networks of more than 200 devices, routers provide the network manager with more control over traffic flows and the containment of faults than does a network composed solely of bridges.

Routers (or **gateways** as they were originally called in TCP/IP literature) existed in TCP/IP networks before the simpler and lower cost bridge was introduced to LAN technology in the mid-1980s. In early commercial use of TCP/IP, UNIX systems were used as routers. UNIX systems are still delivered with routing software and any multihomed host can become a router. Indeed, if the default configuration of some UNIX implementations is not altered, any multihomed host will become a router!

Successful routing is complex and processor intensive. Current recommendations are that routers should be computers reserved for that purpose and not shared as application servers. Not only does this leave computing power for delivering applications, but it clearly also separates the two different functions of communications management and applications management, a division which, if not enforced, can lead to conflicts of interest.

Routers are programmed to interpret Internet protocols. They take an active role in TCP/IP networks and must be managed as part of the IP addressing scheme.

What is routing?

Routing (now appearing in some ISO standards as 'routeing') is the process by which two communicating stations 'find' and use the optimum (best) path across an internetwork of any complexity. The process has several components:

- Determining what paths are available.
- Selecting the 'best' path for a particular purpose.
- Using those paths to reach other systems.
- Adjusting the datagram formats to fit the underlying technology.

Routers and IP

The devices which perform routing based on IP addresses are (IP) routers. Historically, routers in TCP/IP have been called (IP) gateways, but since, in OSI, the terms 'router' and 'gateway' describe two different

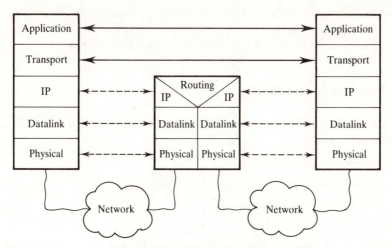

Figure 5.1   Routing with IP.

functions, we shall use the more modern term 'router' throughout, except where quoting an RFC standard which uses the word 'gateway'. Some recent TCP/IP literature has begun to use 'router' rather than 'gateway', but routing protocols are still referred to as gateway protocols in existing terms such as GGP, IGP, IGRP, EGP and even in the recent BGP. (These terms will be explained later.)

True network layer routing is performed in the IP layer of TCP/IP and uses the network number or subnetwork portion of the IP address to make routing decisions. The router relays IP datagrams between the IP layers of end systems (Figure 5.1).

Features of IP also allow routing decisions to be made on type of service, precedence, security and predefined routing options specified by the communicating partners. These predefined fixed routing options are called loose and strict source routing (see Chapter 11).

Routers must support **fragmentation**. This is the ability to subdivide received information into smaller units where this is required to match the underlying LAN technology. Fragmentation would occur when a router relayed an 8000 octet datagram from a 16 Mbps Token Ring to a 4 Mbps Token Ring which can only support 4472 octet frames. If each of the fragments was subsequently relayed to an ISO 8802.3 network with SNAP encapsulation it might be further fragmented into two 1492 octet frames and one shorter frame. Each fragment must have its own header, and after fragmentation the parts are treated as independent datagrams which can follow different paths. While fragmentation is normally invisible to the application programmer and application user, it can produce some bizarre effects for the network manager trying to optimize the use of limited resources. In general, repeated fragmentation in a network is undesirable because of the overhead of fragmentation in routers, the extra headers and the processing power for reassembly. Where options are available[†] they should be set to avoid fragmentation.

This is a level of functionality not available in bridges.

Routing advantages

Why use IP routing rather than the much simpler and less costly bridges? The key points are:

- Better choice of routes,
- Matching different link-level technologies,
- Resilience and control,
- Error reporting.

While these are features of the IP standards, not all end systems and commercial routers support them as yet. Indeed, it is only recently that support for Type of Service routing has become available in some commercial router products.

Modern routers are designed so that the routing complexity is contained within a relatively small number of powerful multiprocessor machines specifically designed for the task. Hosts use simpler methods to discover and use their nearest and best router for the communications task in hand. This leaves all the processing power in the host and workstation end systems for the task that they should really be doing, processing the users' data, not expending effort trying to be a good communications processor. Applications processes should be performed in machines chosen for that specific task; likewise network relaying and communications should be devolved to specialist processors designed for that intensive process.

Better choice of route

Routers, using the best modern routing protocols, can have multiple parallel operational links, can find any available alternative route and will share traffic across those paths according to criteria established by the network manager and by software in the communicating hosts.

Matching different link-level technologies

Long-distance (wide area) point-to-point links and the variety of ISO/IEEE LAN standards have very different performance and data transmission characteristics. It is not possible to disguise the detail of the

---

[†]To configure the maximum transfer unit, described below and in Chapter 11.

underlying technology from a bridge. A router is specifically designed to take account of the differences as it is made aware of maximum transfer units (related to frame data size) and can convert with fragmentation.

Resilience and control

Routers form an integral part of network layer protocols and network layer addressing. End systems (hosts) can choose one specific router to relay information. Routers will not relay MAC layer broadcast or multi-cast frames, unless those frames contain the correct network layer proto-col. They act as a barrier between network areas and prevent the propagation of certain types of faults (broadcast storms) from one area to another. Because routers understand the IP network layer protocol, they can discard information that is valid at the MAC layer but which is not operating correctly at the network layer. They protect against more com-plex software failures and poor software implementations that bridges assume are operating correctly.

Error reporting

Routers and hosts must use a protocol called the Internet Control Message Protocol (ICMP) to report and record error conditions and to try to control network congestion.

Routers and the link layer

While routers are network layer devices, they must encapsulate their net-work layer information in link layer frames. The issues of MAC layer encapsulation raised in Chapter 2 apply to routers. All manufacturers support DIX Ethernet; but it may be some time before SNAP encapsula-tion on ISO networks is widely available. For maximum flexibility, routers should be able to support either encapsulation, Ethernet or SNAP.

Routers and the IP address

Routers and end systems use the network number or subnetwork number to decide how to relay a particular IP packet (IP datagram). As described in Chapter 3, there is a very close correspondence between the network layout and structure (due to the geography of the organization) and the (subnetwork) address plan. Any change in the location of a host or workstation computer may mean that its IP address must change. (Its domain name may remain the same unless there is a major geographic change, as domain names often contain a geographic component.)

A connection on a router is an IP connection on the network number or subnetwork number to which it attaches. Every router port can be the source or destination of IP datagrams. It must have an IP address and a subnet mask that corresponds to the networks to which it connects. This is how a router knows which networks it is directly attached to. The router must be configured with IP addresses and subnet masks for each of its network connections. This is normally done through the hardware terminal port on the router chassis.

Workstations and dial-up TCP/IP

Workstations and PCs that dial in to a different TCP/IP network must have a valid IP address for the network they call into. There are two low-level protocols that support dial-in:

- Serial Line Internet Protocol (SLIP)
- Point-to-Point Protocol (PPP)

SLIP is a simple protocol which does not have the status of an IAB standard, though it is described in an RFC. SLIP does not allow the calling device to determine its IP address; it must be preconfigured. PPP is a more flexible protocol that has been accepted as a full IAB standard. Loosely based on ISO 7776 HDLC, PPP has a negotiation phase which allows a calling device to determine an acceptable IP address for that physical connection. The details of PPP are discussed in Chapter 10.

As these protocols are intended for use across slow-speed (less than 19 200 bps) dial-up links, versions providing compression both for TCP and IP headers and for user data are available.

Routers with point-to-point wide area circuits

A router can be the source and destination of IP datagrams, so each of its connections must have an IP address with the appropriate network number. Where two routers connect two LANs over a point-to-point PTT-provided circuit, some router implementations require that this single intermediate circuit has its own unique network or subnetwork number. This is unsatisfactory. In a large network it will consume considerable numbers of network or subnetwork ids; more recent router implementations do not require point-to-point circuits to be explicitly labelled.

It may be appropriate to use a different network number and subnet mask for these point-to-point links. The subnet mask can be 255.255.255.252, which leaves two usable addresses for each end of the link; the addresses would progress ending in 1 and 2, 5 and 6, 9 and 10, 13 and 14, 17 and 18.... Addresses ending in 0 and 3, 4 and 7, 8 and 11... cannot be used as they are the 'this network' and 'broadcast' identifiers for the subnet. A single class C address could be partitioned into 64

Table 5.1   Subnetting a class C address for point-to-point router connections.

Link no.	'A' end IP address	'B' end IP address	Comment
–	223.250.250.0		Not usable
1	223.250.250.1	223.250.250.2	
–	223.250.250.3		Not usable
2	223.250.250.5	223.250.250.6	
3	223.250.250.9	223.250.250.10	
4	223.250.250.13	223.250.250.14	
5	223.250.250.17	223.250.250.18	

subnets and thus support 64 point-to-point links. This is illustrated in Table 5.1.

When two routers from different manufacturers are connected together over point-to-point leased telephone company (PTT) circuits, there is no guarantee that they will work together unless both manufacturers have implemented the identical link-level protocols on the circuit. Even where two manufacturers claim to use the same protocol, the two routers may not interoperate when joined by a point-to-point link. If interoperability is important at this level, check with the manufacturers that it has been tested.

One acceptable wide area protocol for routers is PPP, though it is by no means universally supported. PPP is a low-level protocol that can be used by routers on point-to-point circuits; it is not a 'router protocol' or 'routing protocol'[†].

Routing tables

Every router contains a **routing table** of the network numbers (or subnetwork numbers) that it knows about. The table records which router connection(s) can be used to reach a particular network and some indication of the performance or cost of using that connection to reach that network number. Most TCP/IP routing is based on a knowledge of only the 'next hop' in the path to the destination network number and host. To use an analogy from the road network, routers do not keep a 'road map' of the complete network, rather they have a set of 'signposts' with 'distances' or 'speed limits'. At each 'crossroads' (the next router), the next signpost is consulted to find the direction of the shortest or fastest path there. Like the road network, occasionally something turns a road sign around; traffic then takes a less than optimum route, or may even go round in circles.

In the simplest and older routing protocols the measure of performance of a particular link is the number of hops (routers) that have to be

---

[†]A routing protocol allows routers to describe and exchange routing tables and updates.

traversed to get to the destination network. Such a simple measure can lead to the use of totally anomalous routes.

One routing option is **static routing**. This may be appropriate where the network is small or because network managers wish to enforce a fixed routing policy for security or operational reasons. Static routing tables are generated manually by the network manager and loaded into the router either through the control port or across network links. Such a procedure is error-prone and cannot give the best response to network and wide area link failures. It becomes increasingly difficult to manage as the numbers of networks and routers increases, and only a limited number of routes and alternative routes can be devised and managed successfully by hand.

It is unusual in a closed corporate TCP/IP environment to implement static table-based routing. It is more usual to allow the routers to operate a routing protocol or interior gateway protocol (IGP) which will update routing tables dynamically. Routers exchange information about network numbers they are aware of and of the performance of the routes to those networks, on a regular basis, using the routing protocol. These exchanges provide routing table updates as conditions change. So 'routing protocols' are used not to perform routing but to exchange information about available routes and, in some cases, about their performance. The skill in designing routing protocols is to ensure that changing conditions and routes are tracked quickly throughout the internet without producing temporary routing anomalies or using up all available (wide area) capacity with routers exchanging routing information rather than useful user data.

Choosing a routing protocol

The first function of a **routing protocol** is to provide information from one router to another about the network numbers and the subnetwork numbers that are known to it, combined with some measure of performance such as distance, throughput, transit delay, error rate, and cost. These measurements are known as (routing) **metrics**. Today TCP/IP supports Delay, Throughput and Reliability (DTR), where reliability indicates the desire for a low probability of datagram loss. (Remember that in datagram transmission there is no error correction.) Few routing protocols can support all metrics. Even fewer current computer applications attempt to specify the performance environment they wish to operate in. Much of the power in TCP/IP protocols is dormant and yet to be fully exploited by applications.

Routers do not usually measure and update the DTR metrics associated with a particular link or set of links; they are configured as static values by network managers. It has been found that dynamic load-measuring schemes can become unstable with traffic oscillating from one route to another and back again in response to rerouting from highly loaded links. TCP/IP documents discourage standards developers from devising dynamic load-balancing routing schemes.

Where variable length subnet masks are used, the routers must also exchange the network mask which they use to make a routing decision for a particular subnetwork. This itself depends on the choice of the routing protocol designed for the purpose. As described in Chapter 4, variable length subnetwork masks are important for hierarchical and efficient addressing in TCP/IP networks.

A routing protocol does not directly perform routing. It updates routing tables in routers so that they may perform routing. In the jargon of TCP/IP, a routing protocol 'advertises reachability information'. However, the performance information that is recorded in the routing table is dependent on the routing protocol for update; the basis of the router's choice of a particular route is completely determined by the ability of the routing protocol to convey that performance information.

Those implementing a TCP/IP-based internetwork have a wide choice of proven and newer routing protocols. Normally an Autonomous System (AS) manager will attempt to standardize on one routing protocol for use within the AS. This is referred to as the **Interior Gateway Protocol** (IGP) for that AS. So an IGP is a concept, not a single technical specification. In practice, many network managers find they must support several routing protocols simultaneously for reasons of flexibility and equipment compatibility.

Routing protocols are chosen on a number of criteria

- Availability from suppliers;
- Speed to adapt and find alternate routes round network failures;
- Conveying best route information according to service needs or performance;
- Support for active alternate and parallel routes to a destination network;
- Speed to resolve routing anomalies such as routing loops and 'black holes';
- Load imposed on networks and internetwork links by the routing protocol itself;
- Load imposed on host systems by the presence of the routing protocol;
- Load imposed on the routing processors by calculating the 'best routes';
- Scalability – change in routing performance and routing traffic with the size of the network;
- Security;

- Support for 'policy-based routing';
- Legal requirements.

Some routing decisions that would be legal between organizations in one country may be against PTT and government policy in another. Restrictions are diminishing in many countries, but equally the regulations are often very different from the substantially deregulated nature of communications in the USA and the UK. The available protocols are not necessarily sophisticated enough for this type of routing decision (nor would governments allow control of routing to be within the authority of corporate network managers). Network managers working under such restrictions should be aware that inappropriate interconnection and configuration of their networks to their trading partners' networks could mean that they unwittingly act as a carrier for transit traffic between third parties.

The oldest routing protocols only convey the distance between networks as the number of hops – the number of routers that the information passes through to get to the destination from that router. This is a very limited and unsatisfactory measurement, for it takes no account of the performance and changing load of a route.

The routing protocols available for TCP/IP routers and end systems are:

Routing Information Protocol (RIP)

Open Shortest Path First (OSPF)

Integrated Intermediate System to Intermediate System (IS–IS)

Border Gateway Protocol (BGP)

Interior Gateway Routing Protocol[†] (IGRP)

Hello

Exterior Gateway Protocol (EGP)

Gateway to Gateway Protocol (GGP)

The protocol in most common use is RIP, because of its widespread availability. It has some limitations for internets with more than a few networks. OSPF is a recent development which is set to become a full IAB standard. It has a number of advantages over RIP for the larger network. Integrated IS–IS is attractive for networks which must also support connectionless OSI protocols. It remains to be seen whether it will become widely available. While it is a well-developed standard, integrated IS–IS may suffer from the chicken-and-egg problem; there are no implementations available so there is no market, so no implementations are developed ....

[†]A Cisco proprietary protocol.

Detailed discussion of these routing protocols can be found in Chapter 16 in the technical section of the book.

Configuring routers

Many modern routers are easily configured from a management terminal through simple menu-driven commands. They key parameters to configure for IP routing are, for each connection:

- IP address,
- Subnet mask,
- Routing protocols to be enabled,
- Maximum transfer unit of the interface,
- 'Cost' of using that interface.

Summary

Routers provide the network designer with options not available from bridges. Because they operate at the IP layer, they block link-layer broadcast and multicast traffic. They can also prevent the propagation of some faults which bridges would pass.

Routers are better adapted to connecting different network technologies than bridges: through fragmentation they can adjust (downwards) to the maximum frame size available; through the error protocol, ICMP, they can slow the transmission from hosts, reduce network congestion or better match the speed difference between networks such as FDDI and Ethernet or between local and wide area links.

Routers base their routing decisions on the network portion of the IP address. Through sophisticated routing protocols, such as OSPF, routers exchange information about all possible paths. When a failure occurs they can quickly switch to a backup path. They can have multiple paths between any two networks and can use them simultaneously.

This is the functionality with which IP was designed and routers exploit the facilities.

6

TCP/IP upper layers, transport and application services

This chapter reviews, from a management perspective, the application level services that are usually supplied with the TCP/IP protocol suite. These services are discussed technically in Part II. To understand some of the management issues, it is also necessary to discuss the part played by the transport services that support these applications over the IP network which was described in Chapters 2 to 5. In this chapter, we describe the management issues of:

- UDP
- TCP
- NFS
- The X Window System
- Telnet
- FTP
- TFTP
- SMTP

The previous chapters highlighted the decisions to be made when choosing and setting up the equipment which forms the communications network of TCP/IP implementations. This chapter introduces the remaining components of the TCP/IP protocol suite: the transport layer, which interfaces to the underlying network, and the application layers, which support the services for the end users.

The TCP/IP standards leave each manufacturer considerable flexibility in how the standard upper layer communications services are presented to end users. The first products to the market will often provide basic functionality. As the market matures and feeds back ideas for improvements to developers, subsequent products will build more sophisticated user services onto the same basic standards. The size of the TCP/IP market expanded considerably in the early 1990s. The basic facilities described below may be quickly overtaken by more highly integrated solutions, many of which will be based on graphical interfaces and Windows.

The transport layers

The **transport layers** of a protocol are the first layers in most communications systems that operate in the host end systems only and are not used by the intermediate network equipment[†]. The transport layers allow multiple applications or users to share the same path between the same two machines; they provide a consistent interface to the applications and a mechanism for them to specify their communications requirements. As shown in Figure 6.1, the transport layer operates end to end whether the communication path is across a single network (interconnected with bridges) or across multiple networks interconnected with routers.

Today, most TCP/IP applications use one of two transport protocols, the **User Datagram Protocol** (UDP) and the **Transmission Control Protocol** (TCP). For applications which must operate over long-distance circuits, TCP is the protocol of choice, as it can be 'tuned' to provide better performance. This tuning process is described in Chapter 7. UDP has no alterable parameters.

UDP provides an unreliable service; there is no guarantee of message delivery. If the application requires absolute reliability, it must perform its own error checking and error correction. UDP is ideal for distribution of information which changes every few seconds – status reports for stock market screens or airport information systems for example. If one transmission is lost there will be another more up-to-date

---

[†]This strict interpretation of the OSI reference model is no longer valid. Transport layer relays, devised to connect different types of network systems, do implement the transport layer protocols in the network. OSI gateways also do so where the term gateway is used to mean a protocol conversion between dissimilar application systems rather than a router – the early TCP/IP usage.

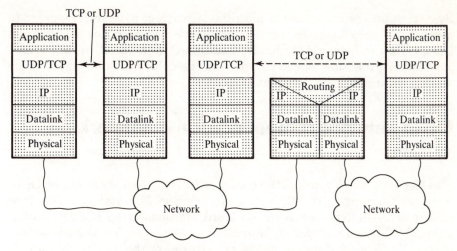

Figure 6.1 TCP/IP transport layers.

value transmitted in a few seconds. Unreliable datagram services can be 'broadcast' to many different destinations simultaneously, since the receiving systems can just listen, they do not need to reply.

On the other hand, TCP provides a reliable 'point-to-point' service and has facilities which improve performance over slower, wide area (PTT long-distance) circuits. TCP would be the choice for operating in a wide area environment. It was designed for point-to-point applications that must have reliability – file transfer, mail transfer and terminal access systems.

The transport protocol used by a particular application is usually fixed (at compile time) by the application developer. For the network operator, there is little opportunity to choose between UDP and TCP for a particular product. Further, because UDP involves less processing over-head and is perfectly adequate in a purely local LAN, many application programmers, who may not fully consider the implications for wide area telecommunications systems, choose UDP rather than the extra com-plexity (and hence larger processing overhead) of TCP. Alternatively, the application may be too restricted by a point-to-point connection for each conversation[†]. As a result, these applications have high throughput per-formance in a strictly local environment, but, as bridges, routers and slow-speed, long-distance circuits are introduced, the performance degrades quickly. If the path between two devices which use UDP includes multiple bridges, routers or multiple wide area links, the per-formance will be poor. We explore the reasons for this in Chapter 7.

[†]The Versatile Message Transport Protocol (VMTP) was developed for such applications. It provides the performance advantages of TCP for wide area operations, without imposing some of TCP's connection-oriented restrictions. VMTP is not widely used.

System planners may have to plan the location of network resources to avoid wide area links for certain applications which use UDP. Even though they may be able to justify and afford high-speed, multimegabit connections, the 'slow' speed of light and the delays in buffering of information will reduce the throughput of UDP.

Open network computing or the network file system

The Network File System (NFS), as it is still commonly known, or Open Network Computing (ONC), as its creator Sun Microsystems Inc. now calls it, is one of the more recent standard additions to the TCP/IP protocol suite. ONC was developed by Sun Microsystems Inc. for its high performance UNIX workstations and later released to the 'public domain' as three RFCs which describe the major protocol components. Recognizing the importance of the IBM PC, Sun also developed NFS software for the IBM PC, the PC-NFS client. This allows PCs to use UNIX workstations as remote file and print servers. NFS client and server software is now available for most computer systems.

NFS provides user services familiar to any user of a proprietary resource-sharing LAN such as NetWare, LAN Manager or Banyan VINES. Files, directories and peripherals on a remote NFS server are mapped to 'virtual' drives, directories or peripherals on the local system. For most purposes, these virtual drives and printers are indistinguishable from, and are used identically to, local resources. This is illustrated in Figure 6.2.

On a UNIX system, each remote directory appears as an additional directory off the main local directory structure. For a PC, with PC-NFS, the remote directories appear as additional disk drives. From the perspective of the commercial information systems manager, this is ideal, for unlike other TCP/IP applications described below, most business users require no new training to use NFS; they merely have access to more information with bigger disks and better printers.

But NFS can go beyond simple resource sharing. It provides the mechanism for true distributed computing, where processing power, not just data, is shared among networked machines. These client/server applications can reduce the load on busy networks significantly.

NFS management

The major management issues of NFS can be hidden from the users. These issues centre on the security and mapping of user identifiers and access rights between different operating systems. NFS works in conjunction with the Network Information Services (NIS), a distributed

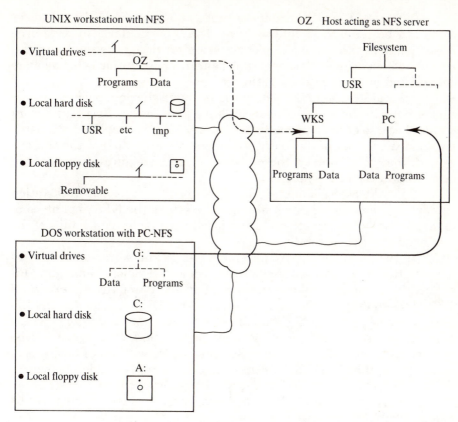

Figure 6.2 NFS representation of resources.

database system for NFS security which provides for centralized management of a highly distributed system. Technically, the tools have been provided by Sun; the administration of a large user population still requires careful organization, with the correct clerical procedures in place to ensure that security meets the requirements of the organization. It must not be so lax as to compromise data integrity and not so tight that no one can get work done. The technicalities of setting access rights on different NFS systems are discussed in Chapter 15. The organizational issues depend on local circumstances.

As always in a network environment, security of access from a PC represents a problem. Unless PCs have nonstandard hardware, most security barriers can be overcome by a proficient and determined attacker. The NFS suite uses an authentication program for PCs, the PC-NFS Daemon, running on a server to validate user access to the filing system. This provides a basic level of security. Some operational environments require additional security features. 'Secure NFS' addresses these issues by using Data Encryption Standard (DES) authentication techniques.

NFS uses the UDP transport protocol. Remote disk data transfer rates can be reduced significantly by delay, particularly in wide area links. There is at least one implementation providing the same services as NFS, which uses TCP transport. An alternative solution is to buy more servers and place them close to the users.

Where the main NFS activity is resource sharing, poor configuration options in the workstations can have a dramatic effect on network traffic. The use of print spoolers, temporary files, backup files, PC batch files and the format of the 'path' statement can all influence the traffic a workstation generates on the network. These configuration issues are developed in the next chapter.

To make NFS completely invisible to end users, each workstation should have a script or batch file which executes the NFS 'mount' commands to make the remote resources locally available. The details of the command line can be totally hidden.

In the past, memory requirements for PC network software have left too little of the available 640k to run some of the more demanding PC applications. Some implementations of PC-NFS require in excess of 130 kbytes to load a LAN card driver, the TCP/IP core software and the NFS client application. By reducing the number of file systems which may be mounted and by tuning other parameters, this figure can be reduced by a few kilobytes. As 80386 processors with large amounts of memory and the MS DOS 5.0 operating system replace older configurations and software, the PC memory will become less of a restriction. Where replacement cannot be considered, careful memory sizing will be required for NFS systems.

The X Window System

The **X Window System** was developed by Massachusetts Institute of Technology (MIT). It is a method of controlling an advance graphical 'windowed' interface. From the perspective of TCP/IP, the X Window System is a message protocol between an X server and an X client (Figure 6.3).

This protocol is described in RFC1013. Copyright remains with MIT, though permission is given to distribute the RFC document as long as the copyright is acknowledged. Other aspects of the X Window System, although not published as RFCs, are described in standards available from the X Consortium at MIT.

With the X Window System, the boundary between user interface, which is not normally defined, and the communications protocol may seem to been breached, but in fact it is intact. RFC1013 only describes the protocol between server and client. The style of the display is determined by other standards, typically the OSF/Motif display standard promoted

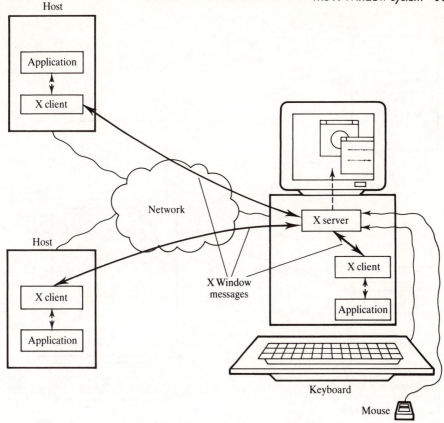

Figure 6.3   X Window protocol.

by the Open Software Foundation Inc. (which includes DEC, Hewlett-Packard and Microsoft) or Open Look from AT&T.

Unlike every other reference to client and server in TCP/IP, with X Window the server is normally at the user's workstation and the client, which generates the new drawing instructions, is at the application host. The X server operates the display terminal, drawing graphics objects and text in response to messages from the X client. The server must also report user actions such as keystrokes and mouse movements to any X clients that will be affected by them.

Since a window system may display output from many different applications and hosts simultaneously, each display should have a window manager, a special X client that supervises the construction of all the graphics objects on the screen (Figure 6.4). It is the window manager that implements the window style, or 'look and feel' as it has been called, of the display standard (OSF/Motif, Open Look or some other standard). More practically, it is the window manager that adds and controls the scroll bars, title line, move buttons, sizing, scaling and overlaying of

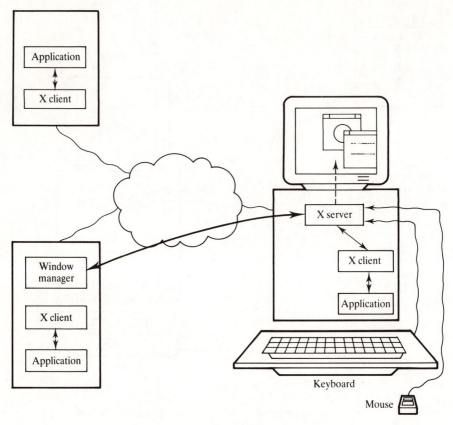

Figure 6.4   The X Window manager.

windows in response to user actions. Any graphical interface with the modifications to provide the correct software interface to the X server can act as a window manager for an X Window server. Microsoft Windows has been adapted for this role.

The X terminal

The X terminal is an X Window display station that implements the X server. It runs no user applications (X clients) locally. All display requests are received on the network connection. Extensions to the X user interface can provide for colour, image support and Display PostScript among others.

Some X terminals have been adapted to operate over dial-up modem links (using either the SLIP or PPP protocols described in Chapter 10). Since modem links are limited to 9600 bps or 14400 bps before compression, many suppliers offer some form of data compression for this type of connection. The result is a usable, if somewhat sluggish, display system provided that the dial-up link is carrying data for a single X terminal user. Where possible, higher speed lines should be used for X terminals. The increasing availability worldwide of ISDN 64 kbps 'dial-up' circuits will alleviate these restrictions.

Managing the X Window System

Graphics applications, particularly when bit-mapped graphics is involved, are demanding both of processing power and of communications capacity. The communications requirements will increase if the X server and window manager are not on the same workstation. The earliest X Window terminals operated with a remote, host-based window manager; the standards specifically provided for it. In this case, every user action, from a key press to a pointer (mouse) movement generates network traffic, with a large movement of the pointer potentially generating a stream of X protocol messages.

The X Window protocol uses TCP reliable connections between a server and its clients. Each TCP data segment sent may be individually acknowledged, almost doubling the expected traffic. If the protocol is confined to a LAN segment reserved for the purpose, this traffic is unlikely to be an issue. Where X systems cross bridges or routers between LANs or more particularly cross wide area lines, the traffic generated by particular actions should be measured for every X implementation being considered. The network capacity and layout should then be planned carefully to carry the expected traffic. Some of the more recent X terminal implementations use a local window manager, which removes a high proportion of the traffic from the network.

Tuning TCP may not improve the performance of an interactive protocol like X Windows as much as a bulk transfer protocol like FTP.

Telnet

Telnet is the virtual terminal protocol of TCP/IP. It operates over the TCP error-corrected transport layer. It provides the terminal service that was mentioned in the very first pages of this book – total terminal interconnectivity and interoperability.

Telnet gives terminal users the ability to log-on to many different 'Telnet hosts' from a single terminal on their desks. As shown in Figure 6.5, there are four ways of using Telnet. The terminal could be a simple 'dumb' terminal connected to a TCP/IP terminal server with a standard communications interface (V.24/V.28 or EIA232). Equally, that simple terminal could be a workstation or PC running a terminal emulator and connected to the same terminal server in the same way. A minicomputer

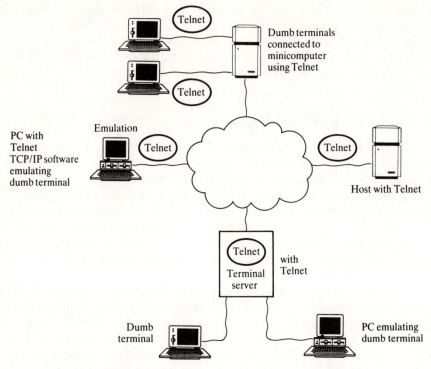

Figure 6.5 Telnet support for terminals.

can run Telnet software which provides the terminal server capability from within the minicomputer. Alternatively, a PC or other workstation could run a version of TCP/IP and a terminal emulator and connect directly to a LAN.

The Telnet service was one of the first to be provided in a standard way by the TCP/IP architecture. It delivers a similar service to that provided by the switching statistical multiplexers of the early to mid-1980s which provided many companies with their first example of flexible access to information.

The Telnet user interface

Telnet allows terminal or workstation users to gain access to a host system and to display host data on their screens. It is a remote terminal service; any terminal user must know how to operate the host system or host application from a terminal of that type. No attempt is made to map the user interface environments from one system to the other.

The Telnet service is most commonly used with ASCII asynchronous terminals such as the ANSI standard terminal or the DEC VT series. Most manufacturers of other terminal types have registered them with the Internet Assigned Numbers Authority (IANA) so that they can be identified to the Telnet protocol. That does not mean that a particular implementation of workstation Telnet will necessarily match the host software. Any-to-any protocol conversion is not necessarily a feature; systems which match must be carefully chosen.

The terminal server

The advantage of the Telnet terminal server is that it provides a low (capital) cost connection. But the interface often operates in asynchronous character-by-character mode; the terminal is strictly limited in its capabilities with little possibility of upgrading the service in the future.

Asynchronous interfaces can involve large management overheads. Cabling for the terminals may require only three wires, but for some terminal types and uses, it could be more. A structured cabling system with centrally located terminal servers can reduce management costs. At each interface, a number of parameters must be configured – speed, parity, flow control method and type of terminal (to ensure the correct control sequences are used). Unless a single standard for these parameters can be enforced throughout the organization, any apparent cost savings can be quickly swallowed up in increased management costs. This is particularly so in the larger installation, where the unit costs of supporting large numbers of terminal servers may not reduce with increasing size. Where terminal servers can be remotely configured from a central network management system, support costs may be more easily contained.

Configuring Telnet

One of the most difficult aspects of Telnet is ensuring that character and keyboard mappings are standardized across all systems. In a large organization, host configuration will be the responsibility of many different groups; the responsibility for terminal servers may also be devolved. But the workstation or terminal servers and hosts must be matched, particularly in their use of the backspace, delete and 'arrow' keys. A consistent policy is required across the organization. One of the responsibilities of technical management in an organization where many different systems run Telnet will be to standardize key mappings.

If every nationality used the same (US) keyboard with PCs, then there might be some possibility of consistency, but, when national keyboards and currency symbols are involved, that consistency may elude even the most vigorous attempts to introduce it. PC implementations of TCP/IP are famous for not being configured correctly. Trying to operate a remote system when keys marked '@' or '#' or '|' or '£' produce a different character on the screen can be quite demoralizing even for an experienced technical user. This situation is improving as US software developers recognize the international features of the IBM PC and include support for different national keyboards.

Many implementations of Telnet for workstations and PCs support IBM 3270 terminal operation intended for accessing IBM hosts (with an appropriate implementation of TCP/IP Telnet on the mainframe). Such a connection eliminates the need for IBM 317x cluster controllers. The support is likely to be limited to text only, but could include an emulation of 3278/9 colour terminals on PC colour screens with extended sizes of up to 32×80, 43×80 or 27×132 characters (model 3, 4 and 5). Where Telnet is used like this across different platforms, it may be impossible to map every key on one keyboard to a logical keystroke or combination on the other. At least one manufacturer includes the ASCII to EBCDIC translation table (PC to IBM character set translation) so that any modifications can be made by user management. As always, once a decision is made to change these defaults, continued local support will be essential throughout the life of the system. For keyboard mapping, the manufacturer's manuals should be kept to hand. 'Quick reference' keyboard templates permanently attached to each terminal may save a great deal of user frustration.

Most Telnet implementations allow the workstation user to open multiple connections simultaneously to different destination hosts. Terminal users may also 'escape' to the operating system (for example, a DOS shell) while still connected in Telnet. Depending on the operating system and program memory requirements, this allows other programs to be run. Some Telnet versions allow file transfer and Telnet to operate together. While this can provide a useful environment for computer development and maintenance staff, it is less useful as a general business tool, unless the mechanisms can be hidden from the commercial user by an in-house application.

Another feature of some PC Telnet implementations is the provision of a simple data transfer mechanism to which users can integrate their chosen terminal emulator package. (In a PC implementation, the soft-ware interface is often through software interrupt 14H.) The Telnet connection then replaces the PC's hardware communications port (COM1 for example). This means that any communications features of the emulator package can be used with Telnet. These could include support for nonstandard terminal types, graphics or colour support, and the use of a 'script' communications language to automate frequent communications tasks.

Where Type of Service routing is available in the network, Telnet may usefully use paths with low delay. Whether the Telnet implementation can be configured to select that type of service is a question to be asked of suppliers of the TCP/IP stack to be purchased. Such advanced facilities are increasingly available.

The place of Telnet in the 1990s

Even into the 1990s, a character mode terminal service can play an important role in commercial information systems, though it is beginning to look dated.

With the correct (text) menu-driven applications on the hosts, the data users can be protected from the command line of a particular operating system and can quickly navigate around complex commercial applications. Accessing text systems from one window in an X Window, Presentation Manager or Microsoft Windows environment with the ability to move data between applications easily, further enhances this traditional information systems environment. Delivering a text answer to an enquiry across a LAN in a fraction of a second, rather than in seconds across slow-speed links, brings a new perspective to such systems. Once the data is retrieved from the central resource, it can be massaged and presented in a graphical form at the workstation, if necessary.

But many factors dictate that for an increasing number of users, more transparent and sophisticated data retrieval and presentation are likely to be required.

File transfer protocol

The function of the **File Transfer Protocol** (FTP) is self-explanatory; it provides a means to move files from one computer system to another. So FTP usually only has a part to play on a workstation or host which has a local filing system, normally its own hard disk[†]. The FTP RFCs define the protocol which computers use to pass file transfer information between them, not how the user application or interface generates those commands.

As well as transferring files, FTP also provides facilities for managing files on remote systems; you can show or change the current disk directory, list the contents of that directory, delete files from the directory and rename files. While it is not part of the FTP standards, most systems also allow similar file management commands on the local system while connected to a remote computer. When FTP is running on a multitasking operating system, connections can be opened to different remote computers simultaneously; PC implementations often only allow a single remote connection.

FTP regards each file as a stream of bytes to be transferred. There is no concept of structured data or of opening a file to access individual records.

[†]There is no technical reason why this could not be a RAM drive or a floppy drive, though it is certainly less frequent in commercial operations.

The FTP user interface

The commands the user types while in FTP are not defined by the RFC standards. While most implementations are based on the interface of UNIX, there are significant differences between manufacturers' exact commands and in the facilities they provide. The normal UNIX implementation is character based, and is similar to entering commands at a DOS or UNIX prompt. It was designed in the early 1980s for use by computer 'professionals'. While the interface looks similar, not all commands are implemented in the same way, or at all, in every implementation. The exact format may also be subtly different. Each command typed by the user translates into a sequence of FTP protocol commands on the network. Since some FTP commands are mandatory and others are optional, there may be a mismatch between workstations and host. These differences in user interface and host and workstation implementation can be a source of user frustration.

Like Telnet, FTP is not an application that should be delivered to the untrained or casual user whose main activity is commerce rather than computing. Some FTP versions allow a sequence of FTP commands to be taken from a local file. Some user tasks could be reduced to a single command which would log-on to the remote machine and manipulate and transfer files without intervention. But this command file is often not a true 'program'; it cannot change its actions because of user input and it cannot recover from changing conditions or errors encountered from one run to the next. Its use must be limited to simple recurrent tasks. An alternative but more costly option is to develop a custom application which uses FTP as its underlying file transfer mechanism. The FTP standards still limit the type of actions available.

There are a number of FTP implementations which use Microsoft Windows or an X Window manager to present remote file systems and the FTP operations that are available in a familiar form of file and command selection boxes. This reduces the interface to simple mouse actions. This type of interface is provided by AIR for Windows as shown in Figure 6.6.

Configuring FTP

There are few options with implementations of FTP. A common trap for new users is that FTP is aware of two types of files: text (or ASCII) files and binary (or image) files. If not told otherwise, FTP assumes that it is transferring text files. When files are stored in different environments (IBM, VAX, UNIX and PCs), this may corrupt any file which is not text and where the transfer is between different types of computer. Often the file transfer type must be changed manually once the workstation is logged-on to the remote host.

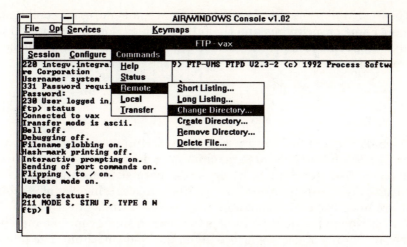

Figure 6.6 AIR for Windows FTP interface.

While almost any type of computer can act as a central file store for one other type of computer using FTP, file-naming conventions are a barrier to simple transfer among a range of different computer types. As an example, PCs use a name of eight characters with three character extensions name; other systems use any length of name and file version numbers that cannot be represented in the PC environment. Some implementations attempt to translate long names to DOS names in a predictable way using 'globbing'.

FTP uses the TCP transport layer for reliability. Optimizing TCP (Chapter 7) improves the throughput of FTP over wide area links.

Trivial file transfer protocol

The **Trivial File Transfer Protocol** (TFTP) is a simple program with mimimal facilities, designed to be implemented in permanent memory (PROM), so that diskless computers may perform their initial loading of an operating system. It is often used in conjunction with the boot protocol. It is not usual for it to be used for other purposes.

TFTP lacks the security features of FTP and it is normal to disable the TFTP server on hosts which do not provide a BOOTP service.

Simple mail transfer protocol

The **Simple Mail Transfer Protocol** (SMTP) provides the mechanisms for TCP/IP users to exchange mail messages. SMTP with Multipurpose Internet Mail Extension (MIME) now supports binary file attachments or enclosures. Mail users are identified by their mail address, a combination of their name or nickname and the fully qualified domain name of a particular host computer which receives and stores their mail. Some possible mail addresses are:

```
catherinej@integv.integralis.co.uk
medavies@eclecticsys.co.uk
registrar@nic.ddn.mil
```

SMTP client software uses simple techniques to send text mail often directly from the source machine to a destination machine over a TCP (error-free) connection, using ASCII data streams and commands. Alternatively, the destination mail address can contain a list of machines that are to be used for forwarding mail to the ultimate destination. The sophistication in the mail protocol is that only a single copy of a mail item is sent to a group of users who are all on the same machine. The protocol between the machines can indicate a number of different user names at that machine and check that they are recognized at the destination. Where a user is not recognized, three different actions are possible:

(1) The receiving machine may refuse the mail.

(2) The receiving machine may, if it knows where that user is located, offer to forward the mail towards the user, in which case no further action is required by the sender.

(3) The receiving machine may refuse the mail and, again, knowing a possible address for that user, may suggest an alternative address.

Mail may also be sent to a distribution list retained at the receiving machine. Where implemented, the sender can request an expansion of the mail list into individual mail names.

For SMTP to operate, each sender must be able to convert the host and domain name into an IP address. The network must use the domain name system, or each host must have a list of destination hosts in a hosts file to map the domain name to an address. An alternative is to deliver all mail to a gateway computer which can use the domain name service.

The simplicity of SMTP and its ready availability mean that it is frequently used as the gateway protocol between other proprietary mail systems, though in some instances X.400 has assumed this role.

Managing SMTP

Some of the organizational issues of SMTP arise because of the association of a person with a particular computer. Those computers are the **mail servers** of SMTP and they must always be available to receive mail. An individual workstation or PC is unlikely to make a satisfactory mail server as its availability cannot be guaranteed. A mail server is more likely to be a part-time task carried out by another server machine.

Building on SMTP protocols, some manufacturers have introduced the **mail relay** or mail store, which receives and stores mail on behalf of workstation users until they access the store using an SMTP client on their workstation. A workstation can be a satisfactory generator of SMTP mail, but it is a poor and inattentive recipient.

Staff who travel must be able to access the mail system they are registered on, for that is where their mailbox resides. Alternatively, a method of mail forwarding can be devised, but such features are beyond the SMTP itself and are implementation dependent.

If mail users change location permanently, their mail addresses may change. They will have to advise all their correspondents of that change. TCP/IP standards do not include a directory service to relate people to mail addresses (or for that matter to relate application servers to network addresses). Worldwide research into directory services has concentrated on perfecting and implementing the CCITT X.500 recommendations which are accepted as part of OSI. Indeed, the US Internet is said to be the biggest trial of X.500 directory services in the world. Several RFCs describe how X.500 is to be used on the Internet, and the adaption required to operate over TCP/IP protocols.

Another potential problem is that the name part of a mail address can in some implementations be case sensitive. The remainder of the domain name is not.

Summary

The TCP/IP protocol suite provides upper layer protocols which support the major computing requirements of most commercial users. The most recent additions, Open Network Computing or NFS and the X Window System are the two that are creating the most interest. As well as the communications environment these two provide consistent user interfaces across different platforms, with NFS mapping disk and other peripheral resources and X Windows complementing it for graphical displays. Because of the high network traffic these two applications can generate, they require more careful planning in a large installation.

The traditional applications of mail (SMTP), file transfer (FTP) and terminal access (Telnet) still have an important role in commercial systems. The text-based command line interfaces of the early 1980s have been improved with graphical 'front ends' that can isolate the inexperienced commercial user from the complexities of driving a system like FTP. Other in-house developments could provide further isolation, but any in-house development, other than simple configuration, is becoming unacceptable to many commercial IT managers.

7

System configuration and optimizing performance

This chapter is more technical than previous chapters, but continues to discuss the principle rather than the detail of any particular protocol: it considers technical aspects that can be skipped at first reading. In this chapter, we review the issues of configuration that affect system performance, both in the network and in the host end systems which provide user service.

The major topics of this chapter are:

- What is performance?
- Performance tuning and optimization
- Planning shared systems
- Measurement of network loading
- The effects of tuning
- Determining the changes required
- The effect of network buffers
- NFS retransmission timer
- Improving the bucket brigade delay
- Bridging Token Ring and Ethernet
- How applications load the network

This chapter is for those technical managers who wish to know how to get the most from their TCP/IP installation. It is about optimizing performance and identifying why systems do not deliver the expected performance. The discussion is more technical than in other chapters in Part I, but analogies are used extensively.

In modern resource-sharing systems or distributed computing systems, overall performance is dependent on network and host software and hardware configuration. The four components are interdependent in a complex way. Those managing the whole environment must cross traditional managerial boundaries to understand the complex interaction between application and network. Many organizations are not yet structured correctly to foster the cooperation necessary for success.

This section considers both network and application issues.

What is performance?

The term 'performance' in general conjures up the idea of speed and power from its use by the motor industry to describe sports models. In computing and communications too, the same is true; speed and power are the terms that prevail. Undoubtedly a high-performance computer system can deliver more useful work to more users than a low-performance one. But the term needs closer analysis: does a 70-seat bus full of passengers have the same performance on a road as 35 two-seater sports cars? In the transport world, probably not; in the computing world, where one system is centralized and the other is distributed, more detailed analysis is necessary. The centralized system may still have an attraction for some managers.

However, without the concept of value for money, pure speed is a poor measure of performance in networks. Is a system which has 99% of its users content with the service 99% of the time, performing better than one which has 95% of users content only 95% of the time? Probably yes, until you learn that the first is three times over budget and the second is within budget.

Performance tuning and optimization

The question then arises as to what is to be done to satisfy more users for more of the time without increasing the budget. This is where **performance tuning** and **optimization** have a role to play. By understanding the tuning parameters that are available in a particular system and managing them correctly, the performance can be improved and the life of a system extended, without incurring significant, if any, capital expenditure. Nothing is totally free however. Some of the expenditure will transfer from capital to revenue, as staff training and staff effort for system reconfiguration are now involved.

Tuning a network after installation is a long process because each alteration must be made at individual machines. A single change by itself may apparently have little effect. Taken together, a number of changes will lead to the required improvements. By understanding the tuning parameters at first installation, the system can be optimized at design time rather than involving a catchback, under pressure, when the user complaints reach an unacceptable level.

In general, however, performance and performance tuning involve designing and configuring a system to satisfy the computing and communications of the maximum number of users for a given amount of money. Where an existing installed base is involved, design options are restricted by that set of equipment.

Tuning can take two separate forms: changing soft parameters in communications and applications systems to alter throughput; and changing the location of network resources or altering the interconnection paths of resources to reduce the number of items between two communicating devices, so that traffic is localized and follows shorter, faster routes. The first is preferable, for it does not involve significant physical activity; in some TCP/IP systems only the second option is available for those applications that use UDP.

Planning shared systems

Communications systems should be planned with some service level in mind. The service level includes:

- The performance; that is, the time taken to deliver a certain quantity of data between two systems.

- The availability of the system; the time lost due to failures of the system, both planned and unplanned, due to faults. The frequency and duration of faults should be estimated.

As with any shared system, the performance varies depending on the activities of other users. Individual performance or service level can only be expressed as a statistical average based on **queuing theory**[†]. Given the average delay of a system, it is possible to estimate that 90% of transfers will be handled in less than a certain time based on the average, and similarly 95% of transfers will be completed in some higher figure. But all these measurements vary widely depending on how heavily loaded the system is.

[†]A detailed discussion is beyond the scope of this book.

As any system approaches 100% loading, over an extended period which is of interest to the users, and more particularly, a period which is of interest to the user protocols, then delays begin to vary dramatically and uncontrollably. Whether we are discussing the queues in a super-market, the traffic on your favourite orbital motorway system[†], or indeed a local or wide area network cable, once the load reaches 70% of full capacity (or less in some circumstances) it is time to consider the effects on system users and whether there is a requirement to reconfigure or upgrade. At 70% loading, the delay is some three times what it is on an unloaded network.

Most shared communications systems are designed on the premise that one user can take only a small portion of the resource. Where the user is a Telnet session and the resource is a 10 Mbps CSMA/CD network, this may be a valid assumption. Where the users are two RISC-based UNIX workstations processing CAD/CAM images, further analysis is almost certainly required. Equally a relatively small number of Telnet users can fill a 64 kbps wide area circuit.

With RISC-based file transfer systems, simple queuing theory breaks down because one user can fill, that is they can load to 100%, a 10 Mbps LAN for an extended period. If two terminals try to use the resource together, they will share it equally between them. This doubles the time for each to complete the task. If that is a doubling from 0.1 to 0.2 seconds, it is unlikely to be a problem for human operators; where it is a doubling from 5 to 10 seconds, a service that was previously acceptable can become unacceptable. As more of these high-performance users are added to a network, the individual performance degrades rapidly for each user, precisely because each one really wants the whole network pipe for themselves.

Measurement of network loading

When deciding how heavily loaded a system is, the measurement time is important. As discussed in Part II, some applications which use UDP transport have a fixed time-out of 700 ms. If the application does not get a reply to a request in that time, it resends the request. These applications also use a maximum number of retransmissions after which an error is reported to the user. With a retransmission count of 5, an error occurs if the application cannot communicate reliably for 3.5 seconds and during that time it will have retransmitted information four times; it is operating at an efficiency of 20% and loading the network possibly at the worst time. For these protocols, the loading that matters is that measured over tens of seconds, not over minutes or hours. This is particu-larly important where slow-speed WAN links are involved.

[†]London's M25 or the Los Angeles freeway system.

The effects of tuning

System tuning involves the two processes of changing software parameters and hardware layout to optimize performance. These two cannot
be totally separated; they interact in unpredictable ways. In some cases,
tuning a system can cause it to cross that boundary between demanding a small or large percentage of the total capacity and hence between
having little impact or a large impact on other users.

   Correcting an anomaly in one area may reveal a bottleneck in
another area. The bottleneck must be removed before the expected performance is achieved, but this in turn may reveal a third limitation.
Complex systems often have a number of closely related limitations, with
each one not evident until the previous one is removed. Put another way,
the reason that 100 users can share one LAN may be that each workstation is badly tuned and sharing the same overloaded NFS file server.
Tune the end systems and the file server or add a second file server and
the LAN may become the bottleneck. The two bottlenecks may be so close
together that it is not until both changes are made that any real benefit
is evident. If your favourite firm of consultants recommended one change
and then discovered after the event that a second change is necessary, it
is a courageous, or at least knowledgeable, network manager who accepts
the second recommendation.

   Another disadvantage of tuning one host system to give the maximum throughput on an unloaded network is that when the network
becomes loaded, the variation in response time is far greater and more
obvious. If performance is poor on a lightly loaded LAN, the relative
degradation on the loaded LAN will often be less and hence more acceptable. Computer users, like car users, are frequently more frustrated by
wide variations in speed than by a low but consistent speed.

Determining the changes required

The starting point for a study of the likely effects and requirements for
network optimization and tuning exercise can either be with the network
or with the hosts. A detailed knowledge of current network loading at
every point in the path between two systems that are underperforming
will show whether reconfiguring the hosts will help. If that loading
is generally light, the bottleneck is either in the protocols or in the end
system performance; it is less likely to be in network capacity if all links
are loaded to less than 50% over approximately 30 seconds at a time when
the response is unacceptable. In this case, the first consideration should
be to change software parameters to allow the systems to exchange
larger amounts of data in one transmission or to generate more transmissions per second. In either case this will immediately increase network loading!

If the network is already heavily loaded, the next question is whether the load is genuine user traffic or is due to retransmissions because of time-outs or errors. Here the statistics on application level (UDP) and TCP retransmissions collected by end systems are the starting point. Most modern TCP implementations have their own automatic time-out calculation which should not be altered. Lengthening the UDP time-outs may reduce the load on the network due to retransmissions[†] and produce a satisfactory service. This is likely to be a temporary respite except where the bottleneck is in a wide area link.

The technical argument is as follows. If 700 ms time-outs are occurring, then the systems are only exchanging one UDP datagram of up to 8 kbytes every 700 ms. In an NFS system, this amounts to 11.7 kbytes per second, low by today's standards. If frequent time-outs and hence retransmissions are occurring, it is more likely that an IP fragment of the UDP datagram is lost. If the reason for that loss cannot be corrected, assuming that it can easily be identified, then reducing the maximum size of the UDP datagram that the end systems can generate, from 8192 bytes to around 1400 bytes, may reduce the quantity of data retransmitted by a factor of 5. This will reduce the loading on the network and improve the throughput. Once the retransmission load is reduced, the network load is likely to remain high but it will all be useful activity!

If the high network load is not due to retransmissions, then altering end system speed and parameters will have a minimum effect on the end system performance. The only recourse is to increase the traffic capacity of the network by splitting the network with bridges and routers and reducing the number of devices on a shared cable. To return to the familiar analogy, a sports car on a heavily used motorway is limited by the performance of the vehicles in front. There is no point in increasing the engine size. More lanes are necessary[‡].

The effect of network buffers

Today's communications networks, including most of the link-layer protocols that support TCP/IP, work on the basis of buffering and relaying one complete frame of data. The unit of data transmission is the link-level frame. Each frame contains a frame check sequence to ensure that it has been transmitted correctly. To relay frames that are known to be in error is a waste of time, so only frames that are received correctly are relayed. This has the effect of building up the network end-to-end delay quite

---

[†]As discussed in Chapter 13, there are few technical reasons for decreasing default time-outs in systems. It is treating symptoms rather than the root cause and risks making the network unstable.

[‡]There is an alternative mechanism available in both transport systems. Charge more for using what has become a scarce and hence valuable resource. That is a political decision beyond the scope of this discussion.

Figure 7.1 Effects of network buffering.

quickly since the data cannot be sent on until it has been completely received. Figure 7.1 illustrates this as a sequence of buckets (the buffers) between a source and destination tank of liquid, the source and destination of data. The liquid cannot be poured out of one bucket into the next until it has all arrived from the previous bucket.

As long as the network buffering delay is much less than the transmission delay and processing time in an end system, the reduction in performance because of buffering is small. This small effect can be measured even on LAN systems where the path between systems contains only local bridges. For most medium-performance systems it causes a drop of between 4% and 30% but is unlikely to cause users any anxiety. It is most noticeable where there are multiple hops in a WAN across point-to-point links, across frame relay networks and X.25 systems. In some cases, the network planner has no control over the intermediate networks and cannot therefore commit to a definite performance. Protocols that use UDP are most affected; for those using TCP the system manager has the option to increase the window size.

NFS and the retransmission timer on wide area links

As NFS uses UDP transport and its applications are normally designed around high-speed LAN transfer, wide area circuits can have a major effect on performance. Even on a local circuit with minimum delay, the time to transmit a full Ethernet frame across a 64 kbps circuit is 190 ms. To send a full 8192 byte datagram in six frames takes over 1 s; immediately there is a configuration anomaly. The default timer for NFS retransmissions if no reply is received is 700 ms. As this default is less than 1 s, it ensures that when NFS data is sent across a 64 kbps wide area link, every 8192 byte datagram is always sent twice whether it is in error or not! Either the timer must be increased to around 2 seconds or the datagram size in the NFS end systems should be reduced to not greater than 3000 bytes. These figures assume that this system is the only user of the 64k bps link. Where there are other users, much higher timer figures or lower datagram sizes should be employed.

With the increased retry timer, this NFS system loads the 64 kbps link to about 97% or approaches 8000 bytes per second. If the datagram size is reduced to 1500 bytes, more requests are required and the throughput may drop to 88%.

The 'bucket brigade' effect of Figure 7.1 is most evident if a second remote link is added in series with the first. The time taken for the last of the 8192 byte datagram to arrive is increased by one maximum frame size or 190 ms. The throughput of the 64k link drops from 97% to 84%. If the frame size were only 1500 bytes to start with, each frame would be delayed by the same amount again for each bridge added; the throughput would drop to 50% for two bridges, 33% for three bridges and 25% for four bridges.

Where satellite circuits or intercontinental terrestrial circuits are used, the round trip delay due to the length of the path compared to the speed of light must be taken into account. As a satellite path has a round trip delay of over 0.5 s, it is unlikely to be satisfactory for UDP-based protocols.

Two facts are evident: too small a request size reduces efficiency, particularly in the wide area, but with too large a datagram size the probability of error increases to the point where retransmissions become too frequent – the network manager may have to tune each protocol for each possible route it could take. This is not satisfactory and in general it is not an option available in software. The latest version of NFS adjusts its time-out and data size dynamically to suit WAN delay characteristics.

Improving the bucket brigade delay

Remote bridges cannot improve the delay through the network as bridges must relay the received frame without modifying its size. On the other hand, routers have the ability to fragment. When a router fragments a low-level frame, the fragments travel more quickly across the network, as the buffers (the 'buckets') are smaller. Routers can improve the throughput across wide area links compared to remote bridges. More importantly, they adjust the fragment size automatically according to a configuration parameter, the Maximum Transfer Unit (MTU) with routers. The system manager does not have to adjust the end system configuration according to the path that will be used.

Bridging Token Ring and Ethernet – the MTU

Where bridges are used to link Token Ring to Ethernet, the larger maximum frame size of Token Ring cannot normally be used where hosts may wish to communicate with stations on the Ethernet. The frame size, or

MTU in TCP/IP terminology, is usually set and fixed for a particular interface. If it is set to the larger size for local communications within the Token Ring environment, any large frame which is sent across a bridge to the Ethernet will be discarded by the intervening bridge as being too large.

This can be an obscure fault to find as there are no error reports from bridges, though it may record some internal statistics. There are two solutions:

(1) Set the MTU for all Token Ring interfaces which could communicate with Ethernet to the Ethernet limit of 1500 octets.

(2) Use routers between the two environments.

There is a potential third solution; use source routing bridges on the Token Ring interfaces and appropriate bridges to convert between the two environments. Source routing can report the smallest MTU in a path between two systems, but it is not clear if IP software can make use of this information to vary the size of frame for each individual conversation. IP is normally given one fixed size of frame for an interface. Those using IP over Token Ring with source routing should ensure that the software can vary its frame size.

In due course, source routing drivers might become available for Ethernet systems, together with source routing bridges for Ethernet.

How applications load a network

In planning the larger TCP/IP networked systems, it is important to know what traffic is generated by each possible user transaction for typical commercial applications. Often this is dependent not on the TCP/IP standards, but on how the end user application uses the network. The only satisfactory method is to measure it for a particular set of user activities. Two different figures are required: frames per transaction and octets per transaction including all overhead. The first figure allows the loading on bridges and routers to be checked. The second allows the loading on LAN cables and WAN circuits to be estimated. Although no definitive figures can be given here, for they are implementation dependent, some guidelines are possible.

Telnet

The Telnet terminal service, described in Chapter 6 and with technical details in Chapter 12, provides a remote terminal service mostly for ANSI/VT-style terminal systems and their emulators. Originally, such terminals would have connected directly to minicomputers by V.24/EIA

232 interfaces. Each character typed by the user is sent individually to the host computer and the identical character is echoed back (remote echo) or produces some other output action. For example a Tab character input is likely to produce a command to reposition the cursor to a particular screen position or to move to the start of the next unprotected field.

When Telnet was produced for TCP/IP terminal systems, remote echo was retained for these networked terminals. Each time a key is struck, it generates a single TCP segment containing that one user character. This is echoed by the remote host in a return segment containing one character. (See Chapter 12). That echo normally carries an acknowledgement of the received character and the echo itself must be acknowledged by the originator. In the normal case, each character typed in a Telnet session generates three TCP segments of 40 or 41 octets of data. Where these are carried on Ethernet, they have a frame overhead of 18 octets and have 5 or 6 octets of padding to bring the frame to a minimum length of 64 octets. While this appears wasteful of Ethernet capacity, with 14 880 of these minimum-size frames available every second, there can be over 1000 two-fingered typists typing over a single cable before the cable reaches 70% loading. More important is the effect on a remote bridge or router.

Where Telnet is used over wide area circuits, the type of bridge used affects performance. Some remote bridges send the Ethernet frame unaltered including padding, some remove the padding and yet others compress either the TCP/IP headers or the whole frame. Compression increases the capacity of the wide area link. Compression algorithms can reduce the data transmitted by at least a factor of 2, doubling the capacity of a circuit. This can be most useful on long delay, high-cost international links.

If no compression is used, a 64 kbps remote bridged circuit is fully loaded by 90 typists typing at 2 characters per second. As a 64 kbps circuit is full duplex, half the typed traffic goes in one direction and the echo and acknowledge return in the other, as does any output from the host. The traffic flow is not symmetric. For text-based, full-screen data, a 64 kbps circuit can support about 480 kbytes per minute. Assuming a transaction or screenful of 1500 bytes, such a circuit will support 320 transactions per minute or between 50 and 100 active users depending on the type of application they are using.

Routers with compression, where available, are the most efficient method of remote interconnection for they will remove Ethernet padding.

Telnet uses TCP. The efficiency of transfer is improved in many implementations if the TCP window size is made large enough to allow one transaction to be sent without an intermediate acknowledgement. A window size of 2048 is more appropriate than 1024. There is no advantage in increasing beyond this for most text systems, though graphics output benefits from higher window sizes. This change does not produce an improvement noticeable by individual users at normal network loading.

At the limits, in the larger busy network, it reduces the network loading by reducing the number of acknowledgement segments.

Effects of host loading

We have on occasions observed that a host which is busy with application tasks is less efficient in its use of the network than the same host when normally loaded. For example, Telnet acknowledge segments are generated separately from the character echo. At the time when the host and the network are most heavily loaded, the host chooses to increase its load by 25%, taking four segments for each user character typed rather than three. The only solution here is to reduce the loading on the host, or to use a more efficient implementation of TCP/IP for that host.

Host buffering

Application hosts must devote sufficient buffers to handling network operations. In a UNIX environment, buffer performance is available through the *netstat -m* command. System managers should check that there are sufficient buffers of each size configured for reliable operation of the network software when the host is most heavily loaded.

In PC implementations, advanced configuration options allow the installer to choose between minimum memory (buffer) use, and maximum performance. PCs are often memory limited, but restricting the buffer available will reduce their performance and may impact traffic on the network. Where memory is available, it can usefully be given over to communications buffers.

File transfer protocol

FTP uses the TCP transport protocol. Since the highest performance file transfer must be able to stream data continuously, FTP operates most efficiently with the largest possible TCP window size. This is particularly true across wide area links where routers are not fragmenting the TCP segments generated by FTP. If the highest possible performance is required, then there is some advantage in setting the window size to release enough segments to fill all the buffers on the route. For example, if the standard MTU for the whole network is 1024 octets and there are three bridges in the path, a window size of 3072 should produce higher throughput than a window size of 1024, as three segments can then be in transit at the same time.

In general, the system manager does not know what the maximum number of bridges or routers will be. Also, it is the receiving workstation that controls the flow of data by advertising the size of buffers it is prepared to make available. When a user complains that the file transfer on a particular link is too low, it is their machine that should be reconfigured with more buffering to release data more quickly from the host.

Configuring NFS systems for performance

Because NFS presents an additional set of apparently local resources, it seems deceptively simple. Applications write to the normal interfaces for the disk or printer system locally and are redirected across the network to remote resources. Every access that should take place on the local resource is mapped into some network activity and duplicated at the remote resource.

The important management factors about resource-sharing systems using NFS from the system manager's point of view are:

- All processing and memory are local – disk and printers can be local or remote.

- Configuration choices apparently unconnected with networking can have a considerable effect on network load, for example, spool files and the program search 'path'.

- If resources are distributed around the network, data can transit the network several times between one buffering system and another before reaching its final destination.

- There is often inadequate or even no control over the size of frames used for particular purposes.

- It is often impossible to estimate the traffic that will be generated by a particular application except by measurement.

As an in-house application is developed, network planners should take measurements of the numbers of datagrams or segments and their sizes. Any anomalies should be fed back to developers for resolution. These figures can then be used to plan the network infrastructure that will be required to support a particular application.

These issues only arise when there is a resource limitation somewhere in the supporting network and the application does not perform as anticipated. It is then often found that applications are not using the network as expected or that a poorly designed application abuses local resources such as disks and printers. On a single user workstation, such abuse may go unnoticed as the application may just appear sluggish. Even in a shared minicomputer, such as a UNIX host, such abuse may never be fully uncovered, though it impacts more users. When the abuse is extended over the LAN, the effects on other systems is immediately noticed. Tracing the fault to a particular machine, application or even one user activity within an application can be much more difficult.

In what ways can an application 'abuse' the resources? This can arise because all remote resources appear to the operating system exactly

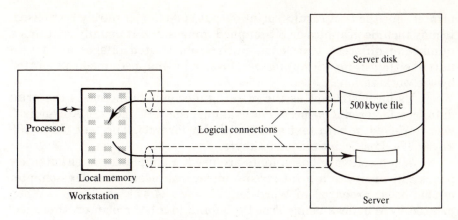

Figure 7.2 Copying a file.

as local resources. The network becomes an external extension of the computer's internal memory and peripheral buses. The following paragraphs give examples of the how a resource-sharing network such as NFS is used.

Copying a file

Consider Figure 7.2 which shows a workstation copying 500 kbyte of data file from one file to another on a remote file server. In a resource-sharing environment such as NFS, this generates in excess of 1 Mbyte of network traffic, a 500 k transfer between the file server and the workstation and a 500 k transfer from the workstation back to the file server. It occurs because the workstation treats the remote disk exactly as it would treat a local disk; each block of data to be copied is first loaded into the local memory and then written back to disk. This should not be regarded as abuse of the network, merely the normal operation of a resource-sharing system, but the traffic generated must be planned for. In a truly distributed computing system, the file server would copy the file locally – the network traffic would be minimal.

Printing and printer spool files

A major advantage of a system such as NFS is the ability to share a single high-performance, and hence costly, printer remotely across the network.

Remote printing can generate far greater network traffic than might at first be thought, particularly when the most modern printing methods are considered. It is likely that the shared printer is a laser printer. For the best results, print output is no longer purely text based. It may include graphics or bit-mapped images and it usually contains a number of different text fonts. Such sophisticated images are transmitted either in PostScript format, or as a bit-mapped image generated by the workstation.

Using PostScript as the printing mechanism increases the print data by a factor of 2 or more. For example, the RFC index of Appendix C was retrieved in both text and PostScript formats. The text file is 165 kbyte. The PostScript file is 303 kbyte.

When software-based fonts are used, a simple document of a few pages can turn into a print stream of several megabytes. This chapter of this book, prepared in Word for Windows is 41k characters. When printed by Windows using TrueType fonts to a laser printer, the 'spool file' is 4.5 Mbytes. This file is printed at about 1 page per minute or 3.65 kbyte s^{-1}.

If colour is used files may increase in size by a factor of 4 to 8. Software fonts can be loaded to a printer. But to ensure that the correct set of fonts is in place on a shared printer, each application may by default load the fonts to the printer for every new task, whether it is a one page memo or a fifty page report. As more people change to using these sophisticated techniques and wish to access systems scattered throughout an organization, network planning becomes more difficult.

A remote shared printer collects files to be printed in a print queue called the print **spool file**. To ensure that pages from one task or job are not interleaved with pages from another, each print task will only start printing when the last page is delivered to the print queue and the file for that task is closed†. Depending on the speed of the processor creating the task, the speed of the network and the speed of the printer, this can double the time taken to print a task compared to sending it to a locally attached printer. There are few options other than to use a faster printer or a faster processor or both. As always it is important to determine what the bottleneck is by connecting the printer to the processor locally and comparing the time to print there with the time taken to print across a network. The time taken to print across a lightly loaded network could be compared to the normal network. Another possible option is to split each print task into smaller parts, with the attendant issue that they may be interleaved with output from other print users.

Microsoft Windows uses a print spooler, Print Manager, to buffer data to disk. Where a printer cannot keep up with the applications (common even with a laser printer when bit-mapped images or software fonts are involved) this can free up the application for more work more quickly

---

†Ensuring that the file is properly closed is in itself an issue. This is discussed in Chapter 15.

than when Print Manager is not used. This print spool is in addition to that on the print queue. If both the printer and the Print Manager are remote resources, the print data may transit the network four times before it is printed. It should not normally be necessary to enable Print Manager with a remote spooled printer. For this reason, by default, Windows does not use Print Manager with a network printer.

If diskless workstations use Print Manager, the Print Manager spool files will be remote. The print data will transit the network twice even when printing locally.

While these figures may appear to generate high traffic, the load per printer is quite small. Except for very high performance printers using bit-mapped graphics, the load generated by one printer is likely to be insignificant. It is when a large number of systems share the same network and traffic must be reduced that consideration should be given to the load generated by printers, particularly if fonts are downloaded or software fonts are used.

The path statement

Operating systems maintain a list of disks and directories that are searched to find command files. In UNIX and MS-DOS this list is referred to as the **path**. If all disks are local, then users are unlikely to notice that the size and order of entries in the path command affect the performance of their application. When the resources are remote across a busy network and mapped to a number of different file servers, the length and order of entries in the path command may affect the performance of an application. More particularly, the order and length of items in the path command determine the number of network requests that are made by a workstation and hence the network load.

The network activity due to a path command can be reduced by ensuring that when an application is started, it is started from a batch command or script that sets the current directory to the main directory for the application, and that the path command is set up just for that application so that there are no redundant entries. The order of entries may make a difference; the most frequently used directories should come first. These will usually be the home directory and any data directories of the application. For a system using a remote copy of Word for Windows, a suitable path statement might be

```
G:\WINWORD;G:\WINDOWS;C:\MSDOS;C:\
```

The wrong way to set the path is to load one value that refers to every directory that the user of that workstation could ever wish to use. If the application is using a directory at the end of the list, it will search the complete path each time, generating many redundant datagrams. An unacceptable path for Word for Windows would be

```
E:\FRELANCE;F:\CAD;C:\MSDOS;C:\;G:\WINDOWS;G:\WINWORD
```

Backup files

Most workstation-based applications write timed backup files at intervals determined by a user-alterable parameter. For word processors and graphics packages, these files can amount to many hundreds of kilobytes where large documents are in preparation. The timed backup interval chosen is normally 5 or 10 minutes, though some users may reduce it. Where the default backup drive is a remote drive, these backup files create additional network traffic of little value. Again, should the drive be over remote links the performance of all users could be compromised.

The time interval between backups should be extended where network loading is an issue. End users should be prevented from changing the configuration.

Temporary files

Workstation applications also produce temporary files (*.tmp files in some PC applications) for their own housekeeping requirements. This includes paging sections of memory to disk when system memory is a limitation. It is less clear when and how often these files will change. Most applications provide a degree of control by providing an option to set the drive and directory where the files are stored. Where possible, such files should be stored locally rather than generating network traffic.

These temporary files are frequently found on disks as the aftermath of a system crash.

Swap files

The operating system itself may page applications or sections of applications to disk when memory is limited. Again, allowances must be made for this traffic and the impact of any delays on system performance. Local disk, where available, has advantages for some purposes.

PC batch files

How the MS-DOS operating system interfaces batch files to the disk is not a concern when those files are local. When a batch file contains labels and GOTO statements the operating system closes and reopens the batch file whenever a label is discovered; it then rereads the batch file from the beginning in case the label was a 'jump back'. If the batch file is common to a number of users and is held on central remote storage, this additional traffic must be planned for.

Diskless workstations

For a diskless workstation, all disk resources are remote! While this is an obvious statement the effects on the network may be less clear. Having removed the disk, it is not reasonable to reduce the amount of memory. With increased memory, some can be allocated to a local disk cache to reduce network load. In a multitasking or task-switching environment increased memory will reduce the amount of paging of applications to disk and the creation of temporary files.

Summary

The parameters discussed in this chapter all affect the overall performance of a distributed system using TCP/IP. They cross the traditional boundaries between system design, application management and communications configuration. They interact in unexpected ways to impact on what is seen as the network service, though many of the adjustments are in end systems and in user applications. System and communications managers must cross the same boundaries to achieve the best performance for the integrated system.

For many of the effects discussed, the impact of a single occurrence or instance is small. Taken together in a complex internetwork of hundreds of workstations and servers, these minor changes can increase the system throughput considerably. Tuning these parameters can delay the need for costly hardware upgrades and system partitioning.

In many commercial applications, a 4 Mbps Token Ring or a 10 Mbps Ethernet appears to be an infinite resource. For other users, the loading factors from modern application systems are already a constraint and are forcing the consideration of 100 Mbps FDDI not only for shared backbone systems but also right to the user's desk. Tuning gets the best from the installed base and can bridge the gap while other upgrades take place.

8

Request for comments

This chapter discusses the process by which TCP/IP has been standard-ized, the documents referred to as Request for Comments or RFC and standard or STD. We describe what that process was and has become, and the wealth of valuable information that is available through RFCs. You will learn how to obtain RFCs – through the Internet, by electronic mail, from bulletin boards and on paper from the Network Information Center. Topics covered are:

- RFCs – what they are
- What information is available
- How you obtain RFCs

The Request for Comments (RFC) was the original mechanism through which all standards related to TCP/IP were agreed and produced. An RFC is often also the standards document that results from that standardization process. However, not all RFCs describe formal standards. RFCs can fall into a number of categories:

(1) Formal standards, which are accepted by the IAB as full standards that must be implemented by equipment which attaches to the Internet. These documents are indicated as an 'IAB standard' in the IAB official standards list, which is itself an RFC (see Appendix E).

(2) Draft standards, formal standards which have not yet been fully evaluated and agreed.

(3) 'Informal' standards: techniques which were or are in common use but which, while solving a problem, are not considered the correct solution to be fully endorsed. (SLIP and RIP are two such protocols).

(4) Documents that clarify the meaning of early standards which perhaps were less rigorously defined and where implementors have produced incompatible equipment.

(5) Information and education about the Internet, its services and protocols (For Your Information (FYI) documents).

(6) Managerial and organizational documents: descriptions of the composition and responsibilities of the various bodies which control and develop the US Internet; descriptions of technical and managerial responsibilities for those sites attaching to the Internet.

(7) Discussion documents identifying and describing technical issues and limitations in the Internet architecture or in the existing protocols; issues which must be resolved if the latest networks and user applications are to be supported on the Internet.

It was this final category that gave the request for comments its apt name. RFCs are a rich source of education on how sophisticated computer systems are developed and on the present and past thinking about computer networks as seen by the developers in the US research communities and their colleagues worldwide.

Current RFCs

Appendix C contains an index of RFCs discussed in this book. These are listed in numerical order. At the end of each chapter in Part II is a list of the RFCs that are applicable to that chapter. In Appendix E, there is a list of the RFCs that are current IAB official protocol standards.

Numbering scheme

RFC documents are numbered RFC XXXX. At the time of writing, the latest RFCs issued have numbers in the high 1300s. There is no version number or issue number for the RFC itself. There may be a version number for the protocol or technique which is described, but if an update is required, a new RFC number is allocated. A reference in the RFC index indicates the RFC(s) which it replaces (obsoletes) or updates, or the RFC which has replaced it. In the RFC document itself, the heading gives the sequence of RFCs that refer to the standard, and the opening paragraphs give reasons for the replacement.

In March 1992 an additional reference, the STD, was introduced to identify the key protocol standards among the large number of RFCs which are purely informative. It was proposed that all IAB protocols which had reached the accepted status of IAB official standard should be identified with another designator, the STD. STD numbers will not change during the life-cycle of a protocol; however, the RFCs to which they refer will change as the protocol evolves and progresses following initial approval as an IAB official standard protocol. Some standard protocols require several RFCs to describe them fully.

The STD process is fully described in RFCs 1310 and 1311. When these RFCs were issued, there were 32 standard IAB protocols. Appendix E lists standards protocols from RFC 1311.

Style

For anyone who has tried to understand the functions of 'open' computer networks by studying ISO and CCITT documents, RFCs are a welcome breath of fresh air in a muggy room. The style of writing is totally different from the dry, formal documents of international standards. An RFC is often more like a well-written research report.

RFC writers take time to explain, in detail, the nature of the problem to be solved, the options that were considered, their relative advantages, the solution chosen and the reasons for that choice. Where complex techniques are involved, the standard solution may be explained in terms of a concise piece of C or Pascal source code. While it is frequently emphasized that this does not imply anything about the implementation of products, when a standard is expressed in this form rather than in prose it certainly helps developers produce a consistent interpretation.

The changing RFC process

A request for comments was originally precisely that: an incomplete discussion document available throughout the research community, and to which objections and suggestions for improvement were required and expected. When a consensus was reached on the technical questions, the agreed solution would become a 'standard' for the Internet. Anyone with access to this discussion could contribute their ideas.

The discussion form of RFC still does exist; anyone may submit a document for publication as an RFC. It is vetted for content by the IAB and for technical content by the appropriate research or engineering task force. However, those RFCs which are to become IAB approved protocols now go through a rigorous vetting procedure, the 'standards track'; maybe first as 'experimental', then as 'proposed standard' to 'draft standard', to 'standard'. For the most part, while comments are still invited, when RFCs become available to the public they are now much more mature, the result of considerable deliberation, and they are standards which could be implemented, not just first sketches. It is still possible for anyone to obtain the early working papers of the IETF, so this process is not carried out behind closed doors.

The standards track is not normally an issue for the commercial TCP/IP user. The details of an RFC will not usually be of interest until the standard is stable and is implemented in user equipment. However, in some circumstances, it may be important to know what work is in progress, for example to ensure that a supplier's development plans include the latest techniques.

RFC content

The process of moving towards a full protocol standard will result in multiple RFCs, having different numbers, with standard paragraphs which report the status of documentation, experience with implementations and work on standardizing the management of the equipment. It will include considerations like 'impact on the Internet' (traffic) and 'security architecture'.

Increased formality has arisen because of some equipment incompatibilities in the late 1980s and because of the considerable expansion in use of TCP/IP protocols. Unlike the current work in the OSI field, TCP/IP products have no formal conformance-testing procedures. Some products have failed to interwork immediately because their designers interpreted the standard differently. The more formal approach is intended to reduce the likelihood of a repetition of these problems.

This earlier lack of clarity was addressed in RFC 1122 and 1123. For Internet hosts, RFC 1122 describes the features of IP and TCP (the communications layers) that are mandatory or desirable and how specific events should be handled. RFC 1123 addresses the same issues for the application layers (Telnet, FTP, TFTP, SMTP, DNS and remote management). RFC 1009, Requirements for Internet Gateways, describes how routers should implement addressing, subnet addressing, some of the

Table 8.1   RFCs for OSPF

RFC	Subject	Date and size	Comment
1131	OSPF specification. Moy, J.	October, 1989; 107pp.	Obsoleted by RFC 1247
1245	OSPF protocol analysis Moy, J., ed.	July, 1991; 12pp.	
1246	Experience with the OSPF protocol. Moy, J., ed.	July, 1991; 31pp.	
1247	OSPF version 2. Moj, J.	July, 1991; 189pp.	Obsoletes RFC 1131
1248	OSPF version 2: Management Information Base. Baker, F.; Coltun, R.	July, 1991; 42pp.	Obsoleted by RFC 1252
1252	OSPF version 2: Management Information Base. Baker, F.; Coltun, R.	August, 1991; 42pp.	Obsoletes RFC 1248; obsoleted by RFC 1253
1253	OSPF version 2: Management Information Base. Baker, F.; Coltun, R.	August, 1991; 42pp.	

routing protocols and the ICMP error protocol. These documents represent the closest that TCP/IP has so far come to protocol implementation
conformance requirements. They should ensure that all recent host and
router implementations will interoperate correctly and to the highest
level of compatibility. Equipment purchasers should ensure that their
suppliers are aware of them.

The IAB standards track

As an example of the recent standards process, the IAB has defined how
new gateway (router) protocols will be approved (RFC 1264). The standards must be written with sufficient clarity that the standard alone is
sufficient for a successful implementation; a discussion with the authors
should not be necessary to interpret exact meanings. At least two independent implementations of the standard must be produced. When the
implementations are complete, interoperability tests are to be conducted
among the different implementations. All major features of the standard
must be tested for compatibility[†]. Any failure to interoperate in the
expected manner must be highlighted, implementations corrected and
the features retested. Where the failure to interoperate can be attributed

---

[†]This interoperability testing refers only to the interoperation of the protocol between
like devices; a conformance test never implies any endorsement of the product by the tester
or testing of the user or management interfaces or of the performance of an implementation.

to a lack of clarity in the standard, the text must be modified. Only when this process is complete can the RFC be adopted by the IAB as meeting the needs of the Internet community.

RFCs for the Open Shortest Path First (OSPF) routing protocol listed in the RFC index illustrate the above documentation procedures. The seven RFCs which refer to OSPF are listed in Table 8.1.

The initial published draft standard, RFC 1131, was used to produce three independent implementations and others derived from these. The implementors took part in three separate rounds of inter-operability testing. No major problems were found with the standard, though one minor change was made and a number of clarifications were added. The version 2 protocol standard (RFC 1247) was published in July 1991. This replaced the earlier version. To meet the IAB requirements, further documents were also issued; RFC 1246 describes the results of the tests; RFC 1245 analyses the protocol, its implementation issues for hardware, memory in routers, scalability, and traffic on networks; RFC 1248 introduces the Management Information Base (MIB) that is used with the Simple Network Management Protocol (SNMP). This was the first formal issue of an OSPF MIB and it appears to have elicited changes and extensions, for it was quickly replaced twice.

IAB official protocols

Periodically, the IAB updates the list of standard protocols and their status in an RFC entitled IAB Official Protocol Standards, (for example, RFC 1280, March 1992). Protocols with the status of 'standard' are allocated an STD reference number.

Equivalent MIL-STDs

The US Department of Defense also uses the same protocol standards, and while its standards book has not been updated recently, the following MIL-STDs identify the key protocols. The text format is different, but the protocols are technically identical to the original RFCs:

```
Internet Protocol (IP)        MIL-STD-1777    RFC 791
Transmission Control          MIL-STD-1778    RFC 793
   Protocol (TCP)
File Transfer Protocol        MIL-STD-1780    RFC 765
   (FTP)
Simple Mail Transfer          MIL-STD-1781    RFC 821
   Protocol (SMTP)
Telnet Protocol and           MIL-STD-1782    RFC 854
   Options (TELNET)
```

The current RFC for FTP is RFC 959. This is a later version than MIL-STD-1780. The IAB clarified the requirements of hosts and gateways in later RFCs (1122, 1123 and 1009). These must be considered when consulting the MIL-STD documents which predate those RFCs.

All these MIL-STDs are available as The Department of Defense Network Protocol Handbook (1985).

Conformance to RFCs

Manufacturers will sometimes describe their products in terms of the RFCs they implement. It is important for a prospective buyer to have at least a list of the current RFCs in numerical order and categorized by function.

RFCs such as 1009, 1122, and 1123 are important when incompatibilities arise. It is important to confirm, before purchasing products, that the clarifications of these 'conformance' standards have been incorporated. In the limits, if products do not behave as expected, it may be necessary to prove which of two devices does not meet the standard as laid down. Fortunately, such problems are becoming increasingly rare.

Obtaining RFCs

Of all the standards in the communications and computing industry, RFCs are the most easily obtained and most widely available. These documents are generally in the public domain and may be freely copied and circulated; many contain the phrase 'distribution unlimited'. Furthermore, they are prepared and stored electronically and are most often obtained and distributed by electronic mail, and bulletin board systems[†]. Some systems keep RFCs in a compressed or archived format. The correct decompression program must be obtained, often from the same source as the RFC itself.

Early RFCs were prepared in ASCII text format. They are available on a number of different Internet-attached databases and mail systems worldwide. These text files may be downloaded across the Internet and reformatted with a word processor (see Appendix B). Some of the protocol descriptions in these early RFCs reproduce sketch drawings using ASCII mathematical symbols. While the effect is not totally aesthetic, it is quite satisfactory for many purposes.

[†]In some organizations, obtaining any information from such sources is prohibited, as a virus might be unwittingly loaded. The RFC itself is not virus prone, since in the strictest sense this is not an executable program; however, where the RFC file is compressed it is important to check that the corresponding decompression program does not carry a virus.

Some of todays protocol specifications require more sophisticated drawings. Recent RFCs are also available as PostScript print files. These files, while large, give a quality equal to desktop publishing. The disadvantage to the user is that each file may be several megabytes long. They are also more expensive to transmit from mail systems over telephone or data networks, and mail system managers may object to megabyte files in someone's mailbox for any length of time. Mail and information system managers who might otherwise keep RFCs are likely to limit themselves to the text versions when disk space becomes a limitation. Even when storage compression techniques are used, RFCs can quickly consume disk space.

The following methods have been used by the authors to obtain copies of RFC documentation:

- The Department of Defense Network Protocol Standards (1985) Book [MIL-STD] is obtainable from the Network Information Center at Government Systems, Inc. Full contact details are in Appendix A.

- Individual RFCs can be ordered from the Network Information Center. The cost of these RFCs has been particularly attractive; a copying charge of $10 is payable for any size of RFC.

- Directly from a number of Internet information servers by 'anonymous FTP', for those who can access the Internet directly – not a common feature in commercial organizations outside the USA.

For those not connected directly to the Internet, those Internet servers can still be accessed by electronic mail. Many commercial information systems provide mail access to the Internet. Two that the authors have used are CIX (Compulink Information Exchange) and CompuServe Information Service (CIS).

As well as information servers in the USA there are a number of mirror sites on research networks around the world. Whether access to these networks is available for commercial use may depend on local policy and regulations. A complete statement of how to obtain RFCs is itself available from the Internet. This lists all primary and secondary sites around the world which officially hold Internet information. See Appendix B for the appropriate mail mechanism. Appendix B also shows the content of a message to request a number of RFCs from servers in the USA.

Mirror sites

A number of academic sites worldwide act as mirror sites for the storage of RFCs and other standards documents in the public domain. Some of these may be accessed by electronic mail.

By this method, three RFCs with a total text content of 251 kbyte or some 160 pages were obtained and printed in around one hour.

On-line systems

Some on-line information and bulletin board systems used by computer professionals hold copies of RFCs. This is often not an official service; moving RFCs from the official sources to these unofficial sources is likely to be an act of public service by an individual with access to both systems. Disk limitations can restrict the information to text versions only and may prevent the latest versions from being loaded quickly.

Summary

Access to up-to-date information in the still evolving world of TCP/IP is most important for technical specialists, developers, consultants and trainers. But there are times when everyone operating and maintaining TCP/IP networks will wish to have access to definitive source documents.

The ability to retrieve this information on-line and at acceptable cost is a key difference between TCP/IP and other communications architectures. As storage techniques and printing technology improve along with the world's communications infrastructure, it will be the work of moments to produce a desktop-published, quality standards document anywhere in the world for discussion about TCP/IP.

PART II

Technology and standards

Chapter 9   Introduction

Chapter 10 The physical and datalink layers

Chapter 11 Internet protocol

Chapter 12 Transport layer protocols

Chapter 13 Application layer services

Chapter 14 Working with names

Chapter 15 The network file system

Chapter 16 Routing IP

Chapter 17 Simple network management protocol

Chapter 18 Configuration and testing

Chapter 19 TCP/IP and the future

9

Introduction

Part II of this book is a detailed technical discussion of the components and protocols that make up a TCP/IP implementation. Before delving into the depths of the technology, this chapter discusses the growth of the successful network and offers some analogies to explain the performance problems that are likely to be encountered.

In this second part of the book, we consider the TCP/IP protocols and their configuration aspects in more detail. It is not always essential to understand the operation of a system in detail, but, if you do, you can get better performance, more efficiency and resolve problems more easily. We often compare a network to the motor car[†]. You can drive safely and quite adequately without knowing a thing about its workings, but when something goes wrong – it starts making an abnormal noise – a more detailed understanding of how the components operate allows you to judge how serious the problem is; whether to continue your journey, call out the rescue service or head for the nearest dealer to buy a new car.

Talking of cars brings to mind another analogy as to why we should understand a protocol in more depth. Suppose you stand on a motorway (freeway) bridge and watch vehicles passing below. You notice that the road is very busy; all lanes are full of fast-moving traffic. At first sight, you may believe this is all useful traffic and this transport system is working well. But you notice that occasionally traffic grinds to a halt and you might think, 'we need an extra lane on this stretch'. However, when you realize that there are many different types of vehicle and they each have different significance, you get another view; you start to understand what is really happening on your transport system.

How big are the lorries? Does the fact that there are only a few large lorries and many small vans indicate that whatever is being carried is being carried inefficiently? Could the goods being carried be handled more efficiently in larger lorries or some other transport system, by air, rail or canal? What does the presence of all the breakdown trucks indicate? They are adding to what initially seemed useful traffic, but they are probably towing away cars that had broken down. What about all these cars with just a driver? If this is a commuter route, can they be persuaded to form a car pool, or to use public transport? Would this save the need for that other lane, or at least postpone it? Adding an additional lane to an operational motorway is hugely expensive and, until the work is completed, tends to cause even more congestion. Planners sigh in disgust and say 'we told you so'.

Most of the above aspects apply to the life and operation of a network. Understanding the basic operation of a network protocol allows you to realize what is *really* happening on the transport system. We have seen a number of networks that *appeared* to have very high levels of traffic with users complaining about poor performance. Everyone was set to increase the capacity at great expense. On closer examination, the traffic was, in fact, generated by retransmissions due to high levels of errors. Correcting the problem on the network did not affect the level of traffic, but since it was now carrying useful data, not retransmissions, the effec-

---

[†]There are a huge number of useful analogies, one of the most important of which is the traffic jam!

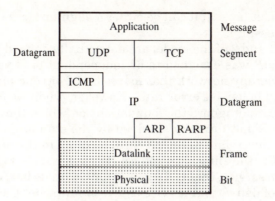

Figure 9.1 TCP/IP model.

tive throughput of the system increased significantly, and the cost and disruption of the upgrade was delayed. Of course, sometimes the planners just 'got it wrong' or it was never really planned in the first place or, returning to the analogy, some sharp salesman sold them the idea of motor transport and got them to build a country lane, when they really needed a four-lane highway. Alternatively, and more positively, perhaps no one really believed that the system would ever get that big!

So, in this part, we look in more depth at the workings of the TCP/IP protocol stack, starting at the lower physical layers and moving up to the application layer. We have also provided some of those useful bits of reference material that you often need, but can never find, when analysing TCP/IP systems.

Protocol layering

Communications protocols are described in layers. This divides up the huge problem of how to communicate data between two or more devices into smaller, manageable pieces which can be more easily understood. If the functionality of each layer can be described accurately, people can easily build systems that are totally compatible. The model resulting from combining the layers defined is often referred to as a **protocol stack**.

The TCP/IP protocol stack has been defined in this layered way and the definitions of how it should work are written down in RFCs. Each layer of the protocol stack has been carefully defined and developed over many years to provide a reliable and stable platform for implementation and for further development. In the following chapters, we will be considering the functions of each layer.

TCP/IP is a five-layered model (Figure 9.1), not seven-layered like the ISO OSI model. Figure 9.1 shows what the unit of information is at each layer; at layer 1 it is a **bit**, at layer 2 it is a **frame**, at layer 3 it is the **datagram**, at layer 4, it can be either a **segment** or a datagram, and at layer 5 a **message**.

Layers 1 and 2 of the model are not actually defined by the TCP/IP RFCs, as TCP/IP was designed to be independent of physical media. It can operate over any network that moves bits from one place to another with a reasonably low bit error rate[†]. However, when we come to install networks, we cannot ignore the foundations on which they are built just because they are not formally specified by the standards. We therefore discuss issues that relate to the physical medium in the next section.

Layer 3 is the Internet Protocol (IP) layer. This layer provides a basic datagram service, that is, IP moves data with its best effort but with no guarantee of delivery. A service called the Internet Control Message Protocol (ICMP) is normally provided within this layer. ICMP reports problems in the transmission of datagrams and allows systems to adapt to current conditions in a network. Also contained within the IP layer are the Address Resolution Protocol (ARP) and the Reverse Address Resolution Protocol (RARP). These are used for mapping IP addresses to MAC layer addresses.

At layer 4 there are two possible options, the User Datagram Protocol (UDP) and the Transmission Control Protocol (TCP):

- UDP just extends IP's connectionless datagram service to applications that do not require reliability – there are such things! UDP datagrams can be sent to a network without the overhead of creating and maintaining a connection. In some environments, this is more desirable.

- TCP provides a reliable service with error correction and flow control. The cost of providing a reliable service is more overhead in connection set-up and closedown, processing power for correcting errors and data transmission, but some applications need reliability irrespective of cost.

Connectionless protocols, like UDP, are used in a situation where a node wishes to send information quickly to a large number of destinations. This will often be a small amount of information and there will be a new better value coming along in a few seconds (for example, the time, users currently logged on, the stock market index). The most efficient way in a broadcast network is to send one packet with a destination address which is recognized by all nodes, so they all receive it. If this were attempted with a reliable connection-based point-to-point service like TCP, broadcasting would not be possible and a large number of packets would be generated in building a connection, sending the message and closing the

---

[†]This should be as low as possible, but better than 1 in 5×10^5 (end to end) to give a block error rate of 10% for standard IP datagrams of 576 octets on a wide area link. Today, there is rarely any reason why this should not be improved upon by a factor of 10.

connection to each node. This would take time, processing power and large amounts of bandwidth, possibly just to repeat the process 10 seconds later, because the value sent is now out of date.

Layer 5 of TCP/IP is the application layer. This layer provides services suitable for the different types of application that might wish to use the network. It does not provide the application itself, although the two are closely related. Examples are terminal connections (Telnet), electronic mail, the Simple Mail Transfer Protocol (SMTP) and the File Transfer Protocol (FTP).

Achieving compatibility

When we consider the functionality required to connect computers and their users together across a network, there are two basic areas that must be addressed to perform some useful task: moving data and interpreting it. The lower layers of the model deal with getting data on and off the cabling systems, and moving it between cabling systems and into computers, reliably if required; the higher layer of the protocol stack deals with getting information into a form that each end can understand.

As network developers and managers, lower layer compatibility is an obvious requirement and hits you between the eyes. It is clear that we must use the same kind of medium and physical connector to attach two systems together in a compatible way; you would have difficulty attaching an optical-fibre-connected device to a radio-system-connected device without a conversion box. Similar problems arise at the higher layer with data compatibility, but the effects are often at first less striking. At the higher layers there is a difficulty because different computers and operating systems deal with data in different ways. It is up to the higher levels of the protocol stack to smooth out these differences, so that information sent from an application on one computer still has the same meaning when it arrives at another. It is not just a matter of transporting data transparently across a network.

For example, some operating systems store numeric values with their most significant byte first (68000 architectures) and others with least significant byte first (80x86). If we passed a value in one form to a machine that used the other form the actual value would be misread: see Figure 9.2. The value 480 ($256 + 128 + 64 + 32$) is shown represented in both ways. If the value 480 were sent from the machine that uses Most Significant Byte (MSB) first to the machine that is Least Significant Byte (LSB) first, the LSB machine would read the value as 57345. This is only a simple example to illustrate the point; the issue gets more complex as we look at more complex data structures.

The requirement for modern communication systems is to consider all levels of the problem – true internetworking.

LS byte representation of
480 (80x86 machines)
11100000 00000001

MS byte representation of
480 (680xx machines)
00000001 11100000

Figure 9.2   The representation of numbers.

'Packet' formation

The previous paragraphs highlighted differences in information within a machine. Across a network, the structure of data is under the control of the protocol designer. How is information structured as it travels across a network?

Figure 9.3 shows two TCP/IP protocol stacks in two separate nodes A and B. An application in node A wishes to send data to node B. The application calls the application layer communications service on A. The application layer takes this data and adds some information, the Application Header (AH), to that data, which tells the remote application layer on B what to do with the data. The application communications layer passes this complete data unit, AH and its data, to the transport layer and instructs it to send data to node B. Transport adds its own Transport Layer Header (TH) and passes the new longer data unit,

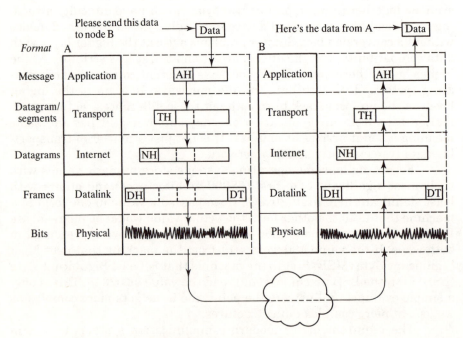

Figure 9.3   Building a frame.

a segment, to the network layer with instructions to pass it to node B. The network layer adds its own header, NH, and passes the new data unit†, a datagram, all down to the datalink layer. The datalink layer adds its own header and often some form of checksum at the end to form a frame and passes it to the physical layer. The physical layer converts the bits of the data into relevant signals for this type of medium and sends it on to the interface cable.

When node B's physical layer receives the signals from the medium, it translates the electrical signals back into bits and into the octets‡ of the frame sent by node A. It then passes it to the datalink layer which checks the checksum and then considers the information in the Datalink Header (DH) to ensure that this frame is for this node. If it is, then it removes the header and the trailer (DH and DT) and passes the information up to the network layer. The network layer considers NH to see what it needs to do with this datagram and, if destined for this machine, it passes it to the appropriate transport layer. The transport layer considers TH, removes it and passes the information to the application layer which again considers AH and passes the data to the correct application on node B.

In this way, data is sent between two computers. The headers added by each layer are messages between the equivalent layer in two machines (peer layers). We can consider each layer as sending information directly to its partner with instructions that relate to the information being carried. The layer is not concerned about how the information was carried, only that it is correct and what to do with it. Most of the header information is some form of addressing to ensure data reaches the correct computer and the relevant application in that computer.

TCP and OSI

In our training courses, we are often asked: how does TCP/IP relate to the OSI model? Or where does TCP/IP fit into the OSI model? First, let us look at the two models together (Figure 9.4). Quite clearly, OSI has more layers than TCP/IP, but if we consider the functionality of the layers, the bottom four layers are comparable. Up to layer 2, the models are compatible. OSI in layers 1 and 2 defines many different media systems that can be used, and TCP/IP was designed to be medium independent, so, in

---

†As we shall see, the network layer may split the segment into several datagrams to fit the underlying network technology.

‡A CCITT and OSI word meaning eight bits of information. Unlike a byte, there is no inference that these eight bits represent one character; they can be eight individual flags, or part of a 64-bit number or structure in between. We shall use the word octet rather than byte.

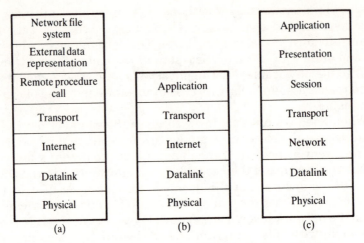

Figure 9.4 Comparing (a) NFS, (b) TCP/IP and (c) OSI.

principle, TCP/IP *should* run on any OSI standard system. In general, and with some careful thought to configuration details, this is also true in practice. It allows us to operate both protocols on the same media.

When we consider layers 3 and 4, the Internet and transport of TCP/IP and network and transport of OSI, OSI has a number of different options that can be used at these layers. However, there is a set of options in OSI that produces almost identical functionality to TCP/IP, comparable but not compatible. (This set is selected by the OSI profiles for US GOSIP or the connectionless suite within UK Government OSI profile (GOSIP).

Major differences occur at the application layer of TCP/IP. At this level, the OSI model separates into three layers, adding, most importantly the presentation layer. This is perhaps the most significant difference between the two protocol suites. The presentation layer of OSI deals with the problem mentioned above, that of unambiguously conveying and interpreting the full meaning of information between computers with very different architectures. In OSI, the power of these functions is far superior to traditional TCP/IP. With OSI it should be far easier to achieve compatibility and interoperability between different systems, though some would say at a significant reduction in performance.

One of the advantages of OSI, with its full presentation and File Transfer Access and Management (FTAM) application layer, is that it could replace the functions of a traditional Network Operating System (NOS) when transparently connecting different systems. A NOS, such as Novell's NetWare or Microsoft's LAN Manager, provides connectivity between computers by handling the access rights and sharing of programs and information. If a protocol stack like OSI provides transparency to a computer that has a multitasking operating system which, by definition, already has file-sharing and access rights, those file-sharing and access rights are already converted. When using such a full protocol stack to connect to such a system very little additional functionality is required.

This level of functionality has been provided in TCP/IP through the Sun Microsystems Inc. Network File System (NFS), more correctly termed Open Network Computing (ONC). The architecture of this system added an extra three layers on top of the transport layer of TCP/IP, giving a seven-layered model. NFS adds powerful functions to the traditional TCP/IP application layer[†].

So how does TCP/IP fit into the OSI model? The strict answer is that it does not. TCP and OSI are similar in certain aspects with similar aims, but they are clearly different in the way they operate. At one low level, they should co-exist, but they cannot interwork (without a gateway).

How does TCP/IP relate to OSI? There is a good match at layers 1 and 2, and a reasonable match at layers 3 and 4. At the higher layers, TCP/IP lacks a powerful presentation layer, making it more difficult to provide full transparency.

Summary

In this chapter, we introduced the layering of TCP/IP and compared it to OSI. We discussed why it is important to understand the detail of a protocol, for it allows us to ascertain exactly why a system is not performing as expected.

The rest of Part II considers each of the layers of TCP/IP in technical detail and points out the steps to take, the options to configure, and diagnostic techniques to use to optimize the performance of a TCP/IP installation.

[†]While NFS is discussed in this book for completeness, a companion volume in this series, *TCP/IP and NFS* by M. Santifaller, ISBN 0-201-54432-6, covers NFS in more detail.

10

The physical and datalink layers

The design of the TCP/IP protocol stack was intended to allow it to operate over any kind of communications system. To meet this requirement, features have been added to hide the various characteristics of these systems and allow the network layer (IP) to provide a unified view of all media to the transport layer[†]. We will explain some of the issues that relate to the most common medium types that TCP/IP uses.

In this chapter we will consider:

- Ethernet
- IEEE and ISO
- Token Ring
- FDDI
- SLIP
- PPP
- X.25
- ISDN
- Fast packet technology
- Bridging TCP/IP

[†]Normally the User Datagram Protocol (UDP) and the Transmission Control Protocol (TCP).

The TCP/IP Model

Figure 10.1 shows the TCP/IP model. We can see that the Internet Protocol (IP) provides the network layer that operates over the two lower layers, the datalink and physical layers. In this chapter, we will consider the makeup of these lower layers and issues that relate to their use by IP.

The different types of media can all be used for end-node connections or for interconnection to other networks, but certain architectures are more suited to supporting one type of operation than another. Applications programs sitting on the transport layer above the IP layer must not be concerned with the underlying communications medium. Achieving this transparency begins with the IP layer.

The most significant differences between communications systems are their performances and the number of connections they can support. The most difficult characteristic to hide is performance; the different media successfully used by TCP/IP can vary in speed from 1200 bps (bits per second) through to 100 000 000 bps.

Ethernet

Probably the most common medium over which TCP/IP systems operate is **Ethernet**. Ethernet is a coaxial-based bus cabling system developed jointly by the Digital Equipment Corporation, Intel Corporation and Xerox Corporation often collectively referred to as DIX. Ethernet uses baseband transmission techniques to transport data, and is available on two sizes of coaxial cable known as **thick-wire Ethernet** and **thin-wire Ethernet**. These two types of cable are both widely used throughout the world.

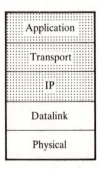

Figure 10.1 TCP/IP model.

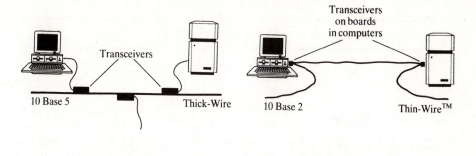

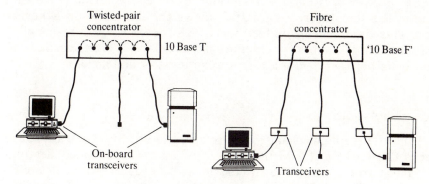

Figure 10.2 Ethernet topologies.

Ethernet topologies

Figure 10.2 shows the topologies available with Ethernet. Thick-wire Ethernet has better electrical characteristics than thin wire, so longer lengths are possible before signal regeneration is necessary. Thick-wire Ethernet can support up to 100 connections over 500 metres of cable. Special devices called **transceivers** provide a standard interface to the cabling system for computer connections. This interface is usually referred to as the **Attachment Unit Interface** (AUI). An AUI or transceiver cable connects the network interface card (LAN card) in the computer to the transceiver.

Thin-wire coaxial systems are simpler and therefore cheaper; many LAN cards have transceivers suitable for thin wire built into them.

Ethernet's significant advantage in the early days of LANs was its speed. Operating at 10 Mbps, it provided extremely fast response to the interactive terminal systems then in use. As computers and their networking hardware have become faster and have begun to exchange larger amounts of data, this speed of the network is often a limiting factor.

8 octets	6 octets	6 octets	2 octets	46–1500 octets	4 octets
Preamble	Destination address	Source address	Type	Data	CRC

Figure 10.3 Ethernet frame.

The Ethernet frame

The Ethernet specification defines the physical aspects of layer 1 and the services of layer 2. It details the format of the packet, usually called a frame at the link layer. Figure 10.3 shows the format of an Ethernet frame. This frame encapsulates the TCP/IP protocol and is responsible for transporting it across the cabling system to layer 2 of the destination device, whether that device is a router, gateway or end node.

MAC addressing

The Ethernet frame uses addresses referred to as physical or **Medium Access Control** (MAC) **addresses**[†]. MAC addresses labelled 'destination' and 'source' identify the specific network cards the frame is travelling between. These MAC addresses are 48 bits long and are fixed. They are configured into the hardware of network cards at manufacture, normally on programmable read-only memory. It is possible with some systems to configure the card to use a local address defined by the user, rather than the address that is held in PROM. MAC addresses are supposed to be unique, so that every network card ever manufactured can be addressed explicitly. This address is often referred to as a **unicast** address, an address specifying a single LAN card.

Cards attached to a LAN cable decode all frames transmitted on that cable medium, but the hardware of the LAN card will only accept and fully process frames with three kinds of MAC address. This reduces the processing load on the LAN card's workstation. The first kind is those frames with a destination address corresponding to their unicast MAC address. The other two MAC addresses which are accepted are **broadcast** and **multicast**.

A broadcast MAC address, which must only be used as a destination address, has all 48 bits set to binary 1 (hexadecimal FF FF FF FF FF FF). A frame that has the broadcast address in its destination field will be fully processed by all LAN cards on the same network[‡] and may be passed by the card to the workstation software. This type of frame is used when the sender does not know the destination MAC address of the node with which it is trying to communicate.

[†]We will refer to layer 2 addresses as MAC addresses.

[‡]A network consists of cabling, repeaters and bridges. Routers separate networks.

Table 10.1   Ethernet type fields.

Type	Protocol
0x0800	IP
0x0806	ARP
0x8035	RARP

Multicast addresses refer to groups of LAN cards that are co-operating or are related in some way. The LAN cards have to be configured to know that they are members of a particular multicast group. An example of a MAC multicast is when a message is sent to all LAN cards of a particular make. This technique is used by some proprietary systems to address frames to all of their associated LAN cards.

The type field

The **type** field identifies different protocols. A computer running multiple protocols can easily differentiate between them and pass the contents of frames to the relevant network layer software.

TCP/IP systems generally use three Ethernet type values as listed in Table 10.1. We shall consider each of these protocols in detail later. Ethernet type numbers are registered with IEEE to ensure that the use of a particular number is unique.

The cyclic redundancy check

At the end of the frame is a **Cyclic Redundancy Check** (CRC). This is a 32-bit value that is calculated from all the bits of the Ethernet frame and its contents, but ignoring the preamble and the CRC itself. The CRC is passed with the frame to the remote node, which performs the same calculation. If none of the bits is corrupted, the destination node should produce the same result as the original node. If the frame has been corrupted, the value calculated will be different from that in the frame. The LAN card hardware will then not pass the frame to the network layer.

The service provided by Ethernet

Ethernet provides a shared medium access system that can be used by many different protocols. Hardware to support it is widely available and it is generally well known and understood. The most significant characteristics are its transmission speed, medium access mechanism and, as a transmission mechanism for TCP/IP, its frame sizes.

The medium access mechanism used by Ethernet is **Carrier Sense Multiple Access with Collision Detection** (CSMA/CD). This allows nodes on the network to manage shared access to the cable, but it restricts the length of the cabling system and also the number of nodes that use it. These restrictions are physical aspects of the network and do not affect the protocols, so they are not specific to TCP/IP, but network planners must ensure that the physical design constraints are adhered to otherwise the basis upon which TCP/IP operates will be unstable.

The minimum and maximum frame sizes of Ethernet are 64 and 1518 octets. This includes all of the frame, apart from the preamble.

The maximum size limits the amount of data that can be transferred in one frame. Because of the frame header fields, the CRC and then the overhead of the IP and TCP or UDP higher layer protocols, the amount left for useful application data is less than 1518. The actual value depends on a number of factors. To give an example, the Ethernet frame overhead consists of 18 octets and the higher layer protocols often need 40 octets. That leaves 1460 octets (1518 − 40 − 18 = 1460) for application data.

The minimum size of 64 octets increases the overhead for transmitting small IP datagrams. All frames must be padded out to 64 octets if the protocol carried produces a shorter frame. To transfer a single byte of application data in the TCP/IP environment requires a pad of an extra 6 octets. The minimum frame would consist of typically the Ethernet frame overhead of 18 octets, 40 octets for the higher layer protocols and 1 for the application data, a total of 59. This requires Ethernet to pad out the frame with an extra 5 octets to reach 64 octets.

In later chapters, we shall describe how these fields are used by the TCP/IP protocols to achieve effective communication across a cabling system.

Configuration and management

Configuration of TCP/IP to operate over Ethernet is limited to selecting the maximum frame size available to TCP/IP and the number of buffers available for receiving datagrams. The maximum size will normally default to 1500, the Ethernet maximum having removed its 18-byte header. Choosing alternative values is discussed in Chapter 18.

IEEE and ISO systems

By adopting the IEEE standards for LANs which are based upon the OSI reference model, the ISO has defined a collection of access control methods, cabling systems and cable types that are international standards. Figure 10.4 shows the most common systems used today. IEEE 802.3 uses the CSMA/CD[†] mechanism for medium access control. IEEE 802.4

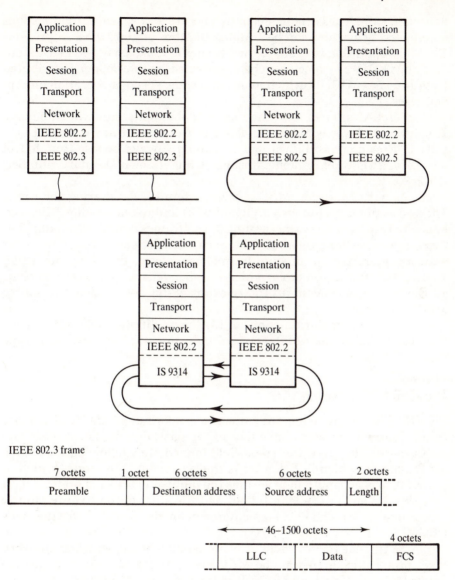

Figure 10.4   IEEE 802.3 frame and IEEE topology.

uses a token-passing mechanism on a bus, whereas IEEE 802.5 and fibre distributed data interface (IS9314) use a token-passing mechanism on a ring.

   Apart from the topology and numbers of connections that can be made to the different OSI media, their major differences are their speeds of transmission and the maximum sizes of frame they support. Like DIX

---

†CSMA/CD is the same mechanism for accessing the medium as used by DIX Ethernet.

Ethernet, CSMA/CD systems usually operate at a speed of 10 Mbps, but token passing systems can be 4 Mbps, 16 Mbps or 100 Mbps. At present, 100 Mbps operation is available on fibre optic cable using the FDDI standard, but FDDI is expected to be augmented by the Copper Distributed Data Interface (CDDI), which allows the same speed of operation on copper wires.

For LANs, layer 2 of the OSI model is split into two sublayers. The lower sublayer is MAC and above it, **Logical Link Control** (LLC). LLC is a common sublayer which should always be used on top of any ISO/IEEE LAN implementation. It has its own standard number, IEEE 802.2.

As with Ethernet, MAC is the mechanism for sharing the cable. The two common techniques are CSMA/CD and token passing. The original intention was that the content of the frames would be similar, but there are some fundamental differences which reduce the options for network planners in mixing technologies from the different IEEE standards. After a preamble, which is dependent on the access method, all the basic frames contain the relevant 48-bit destination and source MAC addresses.

One of the major functions of LLC[†] is to differentiate between the different types of network layer protocols, in a similar way to the type field of Ethernet.

The IEEE 802.3 frame

The IEEE 802.3 frame has the same general format as the DIX Ethernet frame. Many discussions have not, in the past, distinguished these two technologies. However, the 16-bit field immediately following the source MAC address, which in Ethernet is the type field, is the **length** field in IEEE 802.3. The length field verifies the number of octets of protocol data between the end of the length field and the start of the **Frame Check Sequence** (FCS). The FCS is calculated in an identical way to Ethernet's CRC.

As there is no type field, it is not possible to detect which network layer protocol is carried at the MAC layer. The MAC frame consists of only addresses, length and FCS. It is the function of LLC to separate the different network layer protocols.

Coexistence with DIX Ethernet

The IEEE 802.3 standard was based on DIX Ethernet, so IEEE 802.3 cabling and components today only have minor differences, thus allowing the two types to be used together.

[†]LLC has three variants called LLC1 to LLC3. Only LLC1 is likely to be used with TCP/IP.

IEEE has standardized more cabling types than DIX Ethernet. As IEEE 802.3 transceivers also support the AUI interface to any of these cabling systems, a LAN card supporting AUI can connect indirectly to any of the different media. Some LAN cards have the transceiver circuitry fabricated into their hardware so the cabling system can connect directly to them.

One cabling system can support both IEEE 802.3 and DIX Ethernet transmission simultaneously, though the two systems cannot interwork. A station receiving a valid frame examines the 16 bits following the source MAC address. If this value is less than 1501 (hex 0x05DD), the frame must be an IEEE 802.3 frame as that is the maximum allowed length; if this field is greater than 1501, these 16 bits are an Ethernet type field and the frame is processed accordingly. For this to work, there are no commonly used registered Ethernet types of less than 0x600.

IEEE 802.3 cable types

The common IEEE 802.3 cabling types are:

- Thick wire or 10Base5 using thick coaxial cable in a bus topology up to 500 metres per segment (often referred to as thick Ethernet).
- Thin wire or 10Base2 using thin RG58 coaxial cable in a bus or star topology up to 185 metres per segment (often referred to as thin-wire Ethernet).
- Twisted pair or 10BaseT using unshielded twisted pair cable (UTP or telephone cable) in a star topology up to 100 metres radius from a wiring concentrator or hub (often referred to as Ethernet on Twisted Pair (ETP)).

The IEEE 802.5 frame

A detailed explanation of IEEE 802.5 is beyond the scope of this book but we will give a brief summary of the relevant functions and options.

With token-passing a simple frame, called the **token**, is passed around the medium from node to node. If any node wishes to transmit, it can only do so when it 'holds the token', which means it has received the token and the token is flagged as being free. When a node receives the token it has a specified amount of time (token hold time) to transmit data.

Figure 10.5 shows the format of an IEEE 802.5 frame. A token consists of the **start delimiter**, **access control** and **end delimiter** fields. The functions of each field are:

Data frame	Octets
Start delimiter	1
Access control	1
Frame control	1
Destination address	6
Source address	6
Routing information	0–30
Information (data)	4–max
Frame checksum	4
End delimiter	1
Frame status	1

Token frame	Octets
Start delimiter	1
Access control	1
End delimiter	1

Figure 10.5 IEEE 802.5 frame.

- *Start delimiter*   The start delimiter provides synchronization with the incoming data.

- *Access control*   This field is used to manage token priority. Nodes on a Token Ring can operate at different priorities so certain nodes can be given higher priority to use the ring and hence get preferential treatment for throughput. A node can use reservation bits if it has lower priority than the token so that it may get a chance to transmit next time the token comes around.

  The access control field also contains the token bit (T) and the monitor bit (M). The token bit is 0 for a token and 1 for a data frame. When the node accepts the token to transmit a data frame, this field is changed from 0 to 1.

  A frame will rotate around the ring and back to the originator; the originator is responsible for removing its frame and releasing a free token. The M bit is used to ensure that frames are removed from the ring in the event that this sending node fails to remove the frame. One node on a Token Ring acts as a monitor to manage the protocol. As frames go through the monitor the M bit is set to 1. The frame should be removed by the sender; if not, it will return to the monitor with the M bit set at 1. In this case the monitor will remove the frame from the ring and pass on a free token.

- *Frame control*   This field has two subfields within it. One is used to distinguish between token management frames and those carrying data. The second is used for LLC service call priority.

Table 10.2   The longest 802.5 frame header.

Field	Octets
MAC header	15
Routing information	30
LLC†	4
SNAP†	5
MAC trailer	6
Total	60

†Covered later in this chapter.

- *Destination and source MAC addresses*   These are the MAC addresses as discussed for IEEE 802.3 and Ethernet.

- *Routing information*   Token Ring systems can use a mechanism called source routing for determining the path to take through a multiple path bridged network. The routing information field carries a path in each frame indicating the route to the relevant bridges and networks. This field can be from 0 octets, when not using source routing, to 30 octets long.

- *Information*   LLC and its data field.

- *Frame checksequence*   A 32-bit frame check sequence.

- *End delimiter*   A special non-data pattern to define the end of the frame.

- *Frame status*   A special octet which is two identical nibbles (4-bit quantities) with two flags, A and C. Flag A is used by a receiver to indicate that it has recognized that the frame was for itself and the C flag is used by a receiver to indicate that it has copied the frame into memory.

  It is possible for a node that is short of resource to recognize a frame but not able to copy it. In this case, A would be set but not C. The nibbles are duplicated as this field is not protected by the FCS and so is unreliable. This field is not used by the protocol, but is for management purposes, to build statistics of resource problems.

The most significant factor of IEEE 802.5 for TCP/IP systems is the maximum amount of data that can be transmitted in a frame. Unlike CSMA/CD, this is not fixed, as the Token Hold Timer (THT) is configurable and alters the size of the maximum frame. Normally the THT is around 8 ms, so for a 4 Mbps transmission rate it is possible to transmit a frame which is 36 000 bits or 4500 (36 000/8) octets.

As shown in Table 10.2, the longest header, including a full routing information field, will be 60 octets long. Subtracting these 60 octets from 4500, leaves 4440 octets for TCP/IP headers and data.

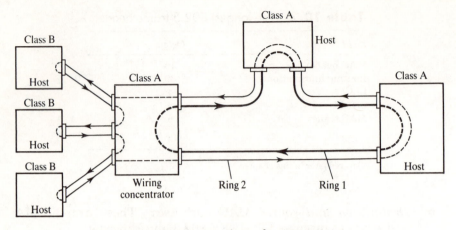

Figure 10.6 Topology of an FDDI ring.

The IS9314 FDDI frame

FDDI is based on the token-passing standards used in IEEE 802.5, but with a few adaptations to suit fibre and to build a highly reliable dual ring mechanism.

Figure 10.6 shows the physical architecture of FDDI which consists of a dual ring system with class A devices that attach to both rings and class B systems that only connect to a single ring. If the ring fails between two class A systems, they are able to loop the working part of the ring back on itself, so the system turns into a single ring, and remains operable.

The major benefits of FDDI are the distances that it can cover and its high speed: nodes can be up to 2 km apart with a perimeter of 200 km; it operates at 100 Mbps. FDDI makes an ideal backbone networking system because of its performance and the characteristics of fibre.

The maximum frame size of FDDI is 4500 octets and the normal FDDI header is shown in Table 10.3 with a size of 32 octets. It is recommended that 148 bytes are allocated for header fields to allow for future expansion, giving a recommended maximum IP frame of 4352 octets.

Table 10.3 Normal FDDI header.

Field	Octets
MAC header	16
LLC[†]	4
SNAP[†]	5
MAC trailer	7 (approx.)
Total	32

[†]Covered later in this chapter.

The FDDI frame is similar to the IEEE 802.5 frame but has a few differences to cater for the medium and its speed of operation. FDDI uses a special encoding mechanism called 4B/5B which encodes each 4 bits of data into a 5-bit 'symbol' for transmission. Not all combinations of five bits need be used; some are invalid and others are used to mark the beginning and end of a data frame. These symbols are transmitted at 125 Mbps so the 'normal' data rate is 100 Mbps. This makes it easy to recover the system clock and is more efficient than the encoding system used on Ethernet or Token Ring. Because of this mechanism, transmissions are considered in 4-bit quantities which make up each symbol.

The function of each field is as follows:

- *Preamble*   This is a special sequence used to synchronize the incoming frame with the receiver clock – 16 symbols.

- *Start delimiter*   The start delimiter indicates the beginning of the frame – 2 symbols.

- *Frame control*   This field has a number of functions based on the flags used within it. It has the bit format CLFFZZZ, where C indicates whether the frame is synchronous or asynchronous (a basic priority scheme), L indicates whether 16- or 48-bit addresses[†] are used, FF is used to distinguish between MAC or LLC frames and ZZZ defines the type of MAC frame.

- *Destination and source MAC addresses*   These are the MAC addresses as discussed for IEEE 802.3 and Ethernet.

- *Routing information*   Token Ring systems can use a mechanism called source routing for determining the path to take through a multiple path bridged network. The routing information field carries a path indicating the route to the relevant bridges and networks in each frame. This field can be from 0 octets, when not using source routing, to 30 octets long.

- *Information*   LLC and its data field.

- *Frame check sequence*   A 32-bit frame check sequence – 8 symbols.

- *End delimiter*   A special non-data transmission to define the end of the frame – can be 1 or 2 symbols.

- *Frame Status*   A special field which is three or more symbols. The first three symbols are used to indicate the flags E, A and C respectively. Flag A is used by a receiver to indicate that it recognized that the frame was for itself and the C flag is used by a receiver to indicate that it has copied the frame. E is used to flag a frame which was in error. It is possible for a node that is short of resource to recognize a frame is for itself, but not be able to copy it to

---

[†]16-bit addresses were never widely used in IEEE LANs.

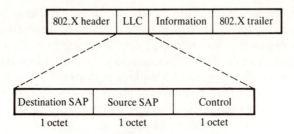

Figure 10.7 LLC in an IEEE frame.

memory, hence A would be set but not C. The symbols are duplicated as this field is not protected by the FCS and so is unreliable. This field is not used by the protocol but for management purposes, to build statistics of resource problems.

FDDI is included in OSI standards and is used with IEEE 802.2 LLC as described in the next section. A version of FDDI has been designed for use over copper cabling instead of fibre CDDI. Both of these standards are likely to become more popular as the need for higher speed transmission increases.

Logical link control, IEEE 802.2

The LLC layer provides a compatible interface, irrespective of the MAC layer used, so this interface remains consistent no matter what type of cabling system is used – Token Ring, FDDI or CSMA/CD.

LLC is responsible for passing incoming packets to the appropriate network layer protocol. Its variants are LLC1 to LLC3. LLC1 (logical link control, type 1, connectionless) is the only variant likely to be found with TCP/IP systems. Connectionless systems use datagrams – transmissions that are not acknowledged – so the sender does not know definitely whether the frame arrived or not. Error correction is the responsibility of a higher layer. This is the best match for TCP/IP's requirements.

LLC carries two more 8-bit addresses (Figure 10.7), the destination and source **Service Access Points** (SAPs). Since SAPs define a protocol, and protocols cannot talk to a protocol of a different type, these numbers are usually the same. To make sure systems do not interfere with each other, SAPs are registered with ISO. For example, there is a SAP defined for the ARPANET Internet Protocol (06). In principle, this would allow IP to operate over an OSI cabling system, but the recommended way of using TCP/IP protocols over OSI LLC is through use of the **SubNetwork Access Protocol** (SNAP). This uses the SAP 0xAA. SNAP is fully described later in this chapter.

While not necessary for supporting IP and ARP, all implementations of LLC are required to support IEEE 802.2 standard class 1 service.

This requires support for Unnumbered Information (UI) commands, eXchange IDentification (XID) commands and responses, and TEST link (TEST) commands and responses. The third octet of LLC, the control field, is used to differentiate between these different types of frame.

The UI frame is key, for it carries data for the higher layer protocols. A UI frame has an LLC control field of 0x03 (3 decimal).

When either an XID or a TEST command is received, a response must be returned with the destination and source addresses, and the DSAP and SSAP swapped. The XID command or response has an LLC1 control field value of 0xAF (175 decimal) if poll is off or 0xBF (191 decimal) if poll is on. There is no significance to the poll or final bit in the LLC control field. In a UI frame it is always off or 0, but in XID and TEST it can be either on (1) or off (0).

A command frame is identified with the high-order bit of the SSAP address set to 0. Response frames have the high-order bit of the SSAP address set to 1.

The TEST command or response has an LLC control field value of 0xE3 (227 decimal) if poll is off or 0xF3 (243 decimal) if poll is on. TEST response frames should echo the information field received in the corresponding TEST command frame. TEST is used to perform loopback tests to check the path between two LLC entities.

XID response frames should include an 802.2 XID information field of 0x810100 indicating class 1 (connectionless) service (type 1). There is no specific usage of XID defined in the standards, merely suggestions.

The service provided by IEEE LANs

The service provided by IEEE 802.X/IEEE 802.2 is similar to that of Ethernet. They all provide a transparent network system for TCP/IP.

Token Ring systems, although quite different in their operation to CSMA/CD systems, show similar characteristics at the top of the LLC layer. The main differences are their speeds of operation and maximum and minimum frame sizes.

Token Ring operates at two different speeds, 4 Mbps and 16Mbps. The maximum frame size on these systems can be altered but is normally 4000 octets on 4 Mbps Token Ring and 8000 octets on 16 Mbps Token Ring. Having such large maximum frame sizes makes them suitable for file transfer, as it reduces the number of frames required, therefore reducing the overhead and providing better performance.

FDDI operates at 100Mbps, much faster than other current systems. Its maximum frame size is still restricted to around 4000 octets. Because of its characteristics and cost it is generally used as a backbone technology at present, but the copper version of this system, CDDI, could well bring these speeds to the desktop.

Configuration and management issues

There are no specific configuration options for TCP/IP to operate success-fully over these IEEE systems other than to consider the need for the SNAP. But systems using SNAP cannot directly interwork with those on DIX Ethernet using the Ethernet type field. Conversion is required, either in a bridge or a router. At present, few bridges can convert DIX Ethernet to SNAP; suitably configured routers would handle the situa-tion as a matter of course, but the demand for SNAP encapsulation on 802.3/802.2 will have to increase before they become more generally available.

When TCP/IP runs on CSMA/CD LANs which are bridged to token passing LANs, the bridge must carry out the correct conversions. This is discussed below.

SNAP

Initially, TCP/IP was used almost exclusively with DIX Ethernet LANs, but with the widespread availability of Token Ring and increasing use of FDDI, it is now a common requirement to use TCP/IP with IEEE-compli-ant cabling systems. IEEE networks must be able to support TCP/IP in a standard way.

As already described, IEEE/ISO LANs distinguish different network layer protocols by the SAP. SAP addresses are registered by ISO; half the space has been reserved for up to 63 ISO protocols and the other half for another 63 proprietary protocols from the rest of the world. This very limited address space is unsatisfactory. A SAP of 0x06 is regis-tered for the IP but in practice TCP/IP implementations use the alterna-tive SNAP.

SNAP is a convergence protocol designed to allow any non-OSI pro-tocol which has a type defined for DIX Ethernet to operate over an OSI datalink layer. So SNAP overcomes the restricted number of SAPs avail-able and allows any proprietary protocol to use IEEE LANs in a standard way. The SAP 0xAA has been allocated to SNAP. The format of SNAP is shown in Figure 10.8. The SNAP header immediately follows the LLC fields and is five octets long.

As well as the Ethernet type field, SNAP also provides a **Protocol ID**, which is important where different vendors' versions of a protocol are not compatible but use the same Ethernet type value. This is common with XNS systems, but not an issue with TCP/IP where the vendor field should be all zeros.

The example in Figure 10.9 shows a computer that can support OSI, XNS and TCP/IP stacks through the use of SNAP. This architecture can use a true OSI conformant medium, while allowing the use of non-OSI conformant protocols above it. The SNAP header of 5 octets further

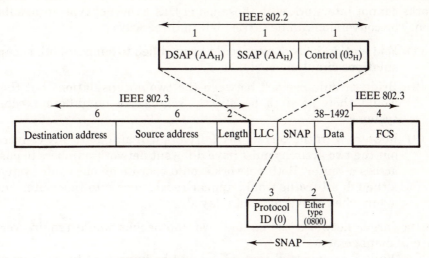

Figure 10.8 SNAP frame format.

reduces the amount of higher level data which can be carried in an 802.3 frame to 1492 octets (1500 minus 3 for LLC minus 5 for SNAP).

As SNAP operates over LLC, it can be used on any OSI/IEEE LAN medium to transport TCP/IP protocols. SNAP is also used to carry TCP/IP on frame relay systems.

Few implementations of TCP/IP for CSMA/CD networks yet support SNAP, though it is the standard on Token Ring, FDDI and frame

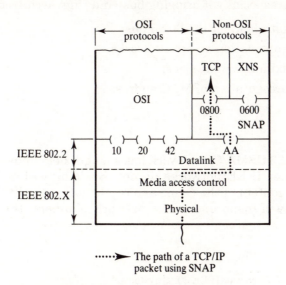

Figure 10.9 SNAP architecture.

relay. Systems using SNAP encapsulation on IEEE 802.3 CSMA/CD networks cannot interwork with those using DIX Ethernet type encapsulation. The conversion can be carried out in three ways:

(1) End station LAN drivers could be modified to support both encapsulations simultaneously.

(2) Bridges could convert between the two encapsulations but they would then have to be strictly segregated on different cable systems.

(3) Routers with the correct LAN drivers will automatically convert, but the two systems must have different network numbers to pass across a router. Both networks could operate on one cable system although all traffic would appear twice, once into the router and again when converted and relayed.

In the larger network, the second two approaches would require very careful management.

While it is expected that SNAP will be important to those using TCP/IP with the intention of migrating to OSI, great care will be needed during the transition phase to ensure that any-to-any communication is maintained.

Bridging TCP/IP

Bridging between IEEE LANs is often promoted as transparent to any protocol above the MAC layer, so one might expect no particular issues with TCP/IP. There are, however, four important differences that need consideration, especially if bridging bus[†] and ring[‡] architectures:

(1) the length field for the 802.3 bus,

(2) the encapsulation on bus networks,

(3) the maximum frame sizes,

(4) the representation of MAC addresses.

Length field

The IEEE 802.3 CSMA/CD network has a length field immediately before the LLC. Other IEEE networks do not. Bridging will at least involve changing the content of the frame and recalculating the FCS. This action will be totally transparent to the network planners; the other issues will not.

[†]This could be Ethernet or IEEE 802.3 systems.

[‡]This could be Token Ring (IEEE 802.5) or FDDI (IS9314).

Encapsulation

The issue of encapsulation on bus networks (IEEE 802.3 + IEEE 802.2 + SNAP or DIX Ethernet) was covered above, but it too affects frame size.

Frame size

A bridge cannot change the higher level protocol content of a frame so it is unable to fragment (split) frames. If a frame which should be relayed is larger than the outgoing medium can support, the bridge must discard the frame. There is no mechanism within the protocol to notify the sender; the frame disappears almost without trace, except that a 'number of frames discarded counter' in the bridge will increment.

IEEE 802.3 is so closely modelled on DIX Ethernet that when bridging bus to bus one might expect there to be no particular problems. But if SNAP increases in popularity and a bridge is used to convert DIX Ethernet to SNAP protocol, then a maximum length Ethernet frame of 1500 octets of data cannot be converted; it must be discarded. The maximum data size in an IEEE 802.3 + 802.2 + SNAP frame is only 1492 octets. These two systems cannot communicate through a bridge unless the Ethernet station reduces its frame size.

The same type of problem will occur with ring-to-ring bridging, if the rings have different maximum frame sizes and spanning tree bridges are used. With ring-to-ring bridges using source routing instead of spanning tree, there is a mechanism for the end stations to detect the shortest allowed maximum frame size on any particular route. Hence the end stations should be able to adapt their transmissions to suit different connections.

For TCP/IP, the transmitted frame size is determined by the **Maximum Transfer Unit**[†] (MTU) set in the driver software for the LAN interface. It is possible on most TCP/IP implementations to modify the MTU to match the number of data octets carried by the link layer protocol. Setting the MTUs of each interface on a Token Ring 1492 will prevent its frames from being too large for bridging to IEEE 802.3. However, this reduction will limit the efficiency of connections between nodes on Token Ring.

Representation of MAC addresses

The IEEE 802.1 committee defined how IEEE LANs should represent 48-bit MAC addresses as a bit stream on the cable, but IEEE 802.3 and 802.5 committees chose to represent these addresses in different ways higher up the protocol stack. IEEE 802.3 defines MAC addresses as having each

---

[†]The concept of Maximum Transfer Unit is explained further in the next chapter.

octet LSbit first but IEEE 802.5 and FDDI represent MAC addresses MSbit first. This presents bridge manufacturers with one of their most difficult problems and it has a direct impact on bridging TCP/IP between CSMA/CD bus and Token Ring architectures.

Bridges connecting bus and ring architectures must reverse the bits in each octet of a MAC address so that they are correctly represented to each network. This would be simpler if all information in the frame required reversal, but data octets go through unaltered[†]. Most bridges now deal with this issue quite adequately; it means they have to manipulate the frame and change the FCS. A bridge between a Token Ring and CSMA/CD is now complicated and, by strict definition, it is breaking the rules of bridging; a bridge is supposed to pass frame content through unaltered.

The real difficulty occurs when a MAC address has to be represented in the data field of a frame. This occurs in TCP/IP address look-up protocols such as ARP and RARP (see Chapter 11). When a sender uses ARP to request the MAC address of a node across a bridge, it will be given that MAC address in the format of the network the receiving node is located on. As the ARP response returns a MAC address in the data field of a LAN frame, if the two stations are on networks which use different MAC representations (one on a ring, the other on a bus), the address will be reversed, because data in the frame goes through unchanged. If the node requesting the ARP then attempts to use this MAC address, it will fail to get a response. (For a complete example see Chapter 11).

To get around this problem, bridges connecting ring and bus architectures detect ARP (and RARP) packets and modify the MAC addresses in the ARP's data field so that they are correctly represented. The bridge is programmed to recognize the ARP protocol and to modify the MAC address in the data field. This is beyond the definition of a true IEEE 802.1 bridge.

While most Token Ring to Ethernet bridges support this conversion for TCP/IP, some do not. The situation is further confused with FDDI. While this represents data and MAC addresses in the same way as IEEE 802.5, RFC 1188 proposes that TCP/IP nodes on FDDI should do the necessary conversion themselves, leaving the bridge transparent. For the unwary network developer, bridging TCP/IP from ring to bus architectures has some potential pitfalls, though many bridge manufacturers have now attempted to address the issue.

Where a ring or bus system is used solely as a backbone without any hosts on it and is connected to distribution areas of the opposite architecture through the same type of bridge, the problem will not occur. Here the MAC address reversal will occur an even number of times and hence cancel out. This issue will only cause difficulty if the originating and desti-

---

[†]A hardware designer would complain that this description is inaccurate. It is how it appears to software.

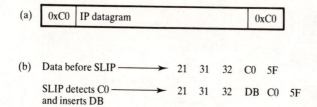

Figure 10.10   (a) SLIP frame format. (b) Escape insertion where datagram has 0xC0 within.

nation nodes are located on opposing cabling architectures, ring and bus.
This problem of MAC addresses only applies to **bridged** ring and bus networks. Where these are connected by a router, the significance of the MAC address is restricted to each side of the router independently so the problem does not occur.

Serial line Internet protocol

In some situations, it is advantageous to use asynchronous serial lines to carry TCP/IP protocols, either by dialup modems, by modems on private wires, through an asynchronous network or by a direct-wired connection between two computers. The simple non-standard[†] **Serial Line Internet Protocol** (SLIP) defines how this can be done.

The service provided by SLIP

SLIP provides a point-to-point connection between two devices for the transmission of IP datagrams. The devices can be two computers or a computer and a router. It can be used to great advantage for remote access to a TCP/IP network or a simple connection between two machines.
The name 'serial line IP' could be confusing in that it suggests the IP layer is different from normal IP, but this is not the case. The IP layer remains the same as for any other medium; SLIP defines a method of framing used to carry IP over asynchronous lines.

SLIP frame format

SLIP defines two special characters referred to as SLIP END and SLIP ESC (escape). SLIP END is a character of value 0xC0 and SLIP ESC is 0xDB. Datagrams sent using SLIP are framed by SLIP END characters as shown in Figure 10.10. If a data octet within a frame has the same

---

[†]SLIP is a *de facto* standard not an Internet standard, even though it is defined in RFC 1055.

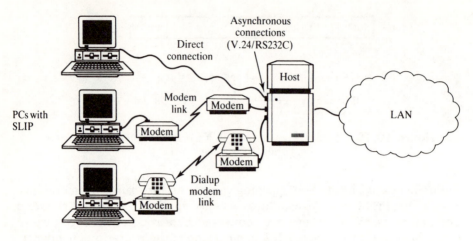

Figure 10.11 SLIP functionality.

value as SLIP END, a two octet sequence of SLIP ESC and 0xDC is sent instead. If a data octet has the value of SLIP ESC, the two octets SLIP ESC and 0xDD are sent instead. The remote end then translates these two octet codes back to the original octet.

Figure 10.11 shows possible SLIP connections to a host using V.24 (RS232C). In this diagram PCs have been connected to the central host, but these could be any computer able to operate TCP/IP and SLIP. The host is also shown connected to a LAN, as it could be used as a router to allow the PCs to connect through to other services on that LAN.

Normal parameters for an asynchronous line apply to this protocol – speed in bits per second, parity and stop bits. As the data in the IP header could be of any octet value 0x00 to 0xFF, it would not be practical to use SLIP through buffered communications systems that use special characters for control purposes. A typical example would be the use of XON/XOFF (0x11, 0x13) for flow control. XON/XOFF is frequently enabled on terminal servers, PADs and multiplexor systems to control the flow of data and prevent data loss. SLIP requires a port configuration of 8 data bits, no parity, and EIA or hardware flow control, so that all 8 bits are available for the transmission of any octet value.

SLIP is a very simple protocol that does not provide any protection against line errors and frame corruption. It relies on the higher layer protocols for this. Some higher layer protocols which operate over UDP (such as NFS), normally rely on the datalink layer to detect errors, so the performance of these can be affected badly by corrupted frames. On error-prone communications lines, SLIP would not be satisfactory.

As asynchronous lines normally only operate at up to 19 200 bps, SLIP is going to be slow. Data compression can dramatically improve throughput, especially where dialup lines are used at 2400 bps.

Configuration and management issues

SLIP connections need two IP addresses with the same network number at both ends of the link. A SLIP connection is treated as a network that has only two nodes.

There are no significant differences between configuring a SLIP connection or an Ethernet connection apart from loading the appropriate SLIP software drivers. SLIP is unable to determine its IP addresses dynamically; they must be loaded manually when the system is configured. This is seen as a significant limitation, particularly where a user is dialling into different networks using different routers. As each router would have a different IP network address, the computer must be configured with a different IP address each time.

In true TCP/IP fashion, the higher layer protocols will not recognize the difference between SLIP and other interfaces, apart from performance.

Point-to-point protocol

The **Point-to-Point Protocol** (PPP) is another datalink protocol that allows IP to be carried over serial lines. PPP overcomes a number of the limitations of SLIP. PPP has been designed to operate over both asynchronous (start/stop) connections and bit-oriented synchronous systems.

This protocol provides more than just a simple connection between hosts. It also defines several management and testing functions to deal with line quality, option negotiation and the setup of IP addresses. The standards suggest how data compression can be used to improve performance.

The service provided by PPP

PPP provides a point-to-point connection between two TCP/IP systems for the transfer of IP datagrams. These datagrams can carry any of the higher layer protocols (discussed later). PPP can operate over virtually any serial link interface. The only limitation is that it requires a full duplex connection. It does not need serial interface control signals, but the standard recommends that they can be used to help improve performance. There is no restriction on the line speed used with PPP. RFC 1171 states that it is capable of operating over any Data Terminal Equipment (DTE)/Data Communications Equipment (DCE) interface, either asynchronous (character-based) or bit-oriented synchronous.

PPP is based on the HDLC standards of ISO, as adopted by the CCITT for X.25 systems. This allows it to operate with standard bit-oriented hardware. It cannot connect to any other HDLC-based standard.

Flag 01111110	Address 11111111	Control 00000011	Protocol 16 bits	Information	FCS 16 bits	Flag 01111110

Figure 10.12 PPP frame format.

The PPP frame

The frame format is shown in Figure 10.12. The address field is all 1s and the control octet contains the value 0x03, the UI control field indicating a connectionless protocol.

The **protocol field** defines the protocol carried by this frame, which for TCP/IP systems would be:

Link Control Protocol	0xC021
Network Control Protocol	0x8021
Internet Protocol	0x0021

For IP, the NCP is called the **Internet Protocol Control Protocol** (IPCP) with a protocol field of 0x8021. Other values assigned for the protocol field allow other protocols, including XNS, Novell's IPX, AppleTalk, and DECnet to share one PPP link.

Synchronous HDLC datalink protocols detect the end of a frame by recognizing the flag sequence 0x7E. Special techniques, often known as 'zero bit insertion' or 'bit stuffing', must be employed to prevent a data pattern that has the same bit pattern as the flag from being misinterpreted as the end of the frame. It would be difficult to use the same tecniques on asynchronous lines so an **octet insertion** principle is used instead.

The octet insertion principle is based on use of an escape character 0x7d. If a data octet has the same value as the flag 0x7E, or an octet

Example 1 (data same as escape character)

Data	0x7D		0 1 1 1 1 1 0 1
Complement bit 6			0 1 0 1 1 1 0 1
Add escape 0x7D	0 1 1 1 1 1 0 1	0 1 0 1 1 1 0 1
Data transmitted	0x7D	0x5D

Example 2 (data is less than 0x20)

Data	0x01		0 0 0 0 0 0 0 1
Complement bit 6			0 0 1 0 0 0 0 1
Add escape 0x7D	0 1 1 1 1 1 0 1	0 0 1 0 0 0 0 1
Data transmitted	0x7D	0x21

Example 3 (data same as flag)

Data	0x7E		0 1 1 1 1 1 1 0
Complement bit 6			0 1 0 1 1 1 1 0
Add escape 0x7D	0 1 1 1 1 1 0 1	0 1 0 1 1 1 1 0
Data transmitted	0x7D	0x5E

Figure 10.13 Octet insertion with PPP on asynchronous lines.

containing a value of less than 0x20 is seen, 0x7d is placed in front of it and the original octet has its sixth bit complemented. At the receiver the 0x7d is removed and the sixth bit returned to normal. Figure 10.13 shows some examples.

Values of less than 0x20 represent ASCII control characters, so they are modified to prevent any misinterpretation by the communications link. Examples are flow control characters, XON and XOFF (0x11 and 0x13). If these octets are transmitted into an asynchronous communications link they can disable or enable transmission at the wrong times, possibly causing loss of data and, at worst, total and irrevocable lockup of the link.

To initiate a connection, the Link Control Protocol (LCP) is used. It can test the quality of serial lines and then negotiate options for link establishment. The basic services provided by LCP are link establishment, link termination and link maintenance. It is intended that before a link is established the LCP will test its suitability for operation. However, a mechanism for performing this test is only hinted at and not explicitly defined. It is suggested that the LCP echo-request, echo-reply protocol is a method of testing a link.

After LCP establishes a connection through the use of the configure-request frame, IPCP comes into operation. It is responsible for handling the IP modules at each end of the serial link and will deal with negotiation of the IP addresses and the compression technique to be used. Once the connection is finished, LCP is used again to close the link with the terminate-link frame.

PPP can multiplex data from many sources, which makes it practical for high-speed connections between bridges or routers. RFC 1220 describes how PPP can be used for remote bridging. Because of the protocol field, it can be used to carry other protocols simultaneously with IP on the same point-to-point circuit.

One of PPP's strengths is its ability to configure a connection to a remote network dynamically. The LCP within PPP is responsible for selecting an appropriate IP address and testing that the link is usable.

Where PPP is used to interconnect bridges or routers from different manufacturers it is important to check the level of compatibility and interoperability. Careful testing is advised if mixing different vendors' equipment.

For the connection of a host to a remote network over a switched service, the major issue may be preventing unauthorized access. These issues are outside the scope of physical and datalink layers.

X.25

X.25 is a network interface defined for accessing packet-switched public data networks. There are many national and international networks that

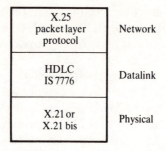

Figure 10.14 X.25 architecture.

provide this interface, making it a useful mechanism for interconnecting LANs. With this wide availability, it is not surprising that there is an RFC describing how IP datagrams should be carried over X.25 interfaces.

As shown in Figure 10.14, X.25 defines three layers: layer 1, physical (usually X.21 or X.21bis – V.24); layer 2, datalink (usually HDLC LAPB); and at layer 3, the network layer, the X.25 Packet Layer Protocol (X.25 PLP). Layer 1 deals with physical connections, bit representation, timing and control signals. Layer 2 provides the basic point-to-point connection between the terminal and the X.25 network. It defines the basic HDLC frame and how it provides reliability with error correction and flow control. Layer 3 gives X.25 its strength. It provides a switched service like the telephone network for multiplexing up to 4095 logical connections at a time over one link-level connection. In support of TCP/IP this allows a single X.25 interface to have connections to different destinations concurrently, that is, to appear as multiple point-to-point circuits.

The service provided by X.25

An X.25 network, a packet switched public data network using X.25 for example, provides switched virtual circuits – reliable, error-free, flow-controlled, point-to-point connections between two interfaces. Equipment with the appropriate X.25 interfaces can access remote networks transparently. With X.25's wide availability and coverage, it is common for it to be used to interconnect TCP/IP systems.

How TCP/IP uses X.25

The X.25 network provides a simple transport service for IP datagrams. When TCP/IP systems connect over X.25 they make no new assumptions about the underlying service; the fact that an X.25 connection is already error corrected is ignored. In fact, the IP layer is totally unaware that it

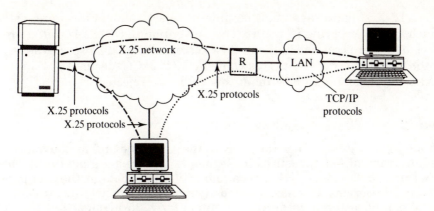

Figure 10.15 X.25 provides connections to hosts on different networks.

is operating over X.25. It sees a single X.25 interface and the logical channels as it would multiple point-to-point links (Figure 10.15).

Because of the incompatibilities between the two systems, the equipment that connects a TCP/IP protocol stack with an X.25-based system is often referred to as a gateway. Gateways are normally regarded as protocol converters, but this gateway does not convert the protocol; it merely puts IP on top of X.25 and maps the IP network number to an X.25 destination address (NUA). The three layers of X.25 sit where the two layers of PPP (for example) would sit. An alternatively way of looking at this is that the network layer has two sublayers, X.25 PLP as the lower sublayer and IP as the upper sublayer (Table 10.4).

An IP gateway for X.25 should translate the destination IP address into a relevant X.25 **Network User Address** (NUA). If no connection exists to that destination, it must establish the connection to a remote gateway. IP datagrams can then begin flowing between the two systems. Some gateways can open multiple **virtual circuits** between the same two interfaces to increase the traffic-carrying capacity (but this is only useful where capacity is limited by an X.25 packet level window size that cannot be increased). TCP/IP is ideally suited to using these multiple circuits, for it will re-order from IP datagrams which are received out of order.

Table 10.4 IP and its use of X.25.

Layer	Protocol
Network b	IP
Network a	X.25 PLP
Link	HDLC
Physical	V.24

IP X.25 gateways must be able to reject random incoming calls which are not carrying IP traffic. The convention in CCITT is that a protocol identifier is carried in the first two octets of the Call User Data Field in the Call Request Packet. This value for IP is 0xCC (decimal 204) in the first octet. Incoming calls without this value are rejected.

Reducing X.25 public network charges

Public X.25 systems often charge by connection time and by the amount of data transmitted, measured in 'segments', where a segment may contain from 1 to 64 octets. If there is a connection-time charge, the user pays for any idle periods. It is also more costly if packets are not filled to capacity. When choosing a gateway (or router) for X.25 it important that it closes idle connections after a timeout period which can be set by the network manager. It will re-establish them when IP data begins to flow again.

X.25 systems, by default, transfer data in 128 byte packets. Through configuration, or negotiation with the exchange equipment at call request time, this may be increased to 1024 or 4096 octets. IP, by convention, must support a minimum datagram size of 576 octets, that is, the MTU of all underlying networks should be at least 576 octets. If this cannot be achieved, there is a loss of efficiency as the 20 octet IP header must be copied into each smaller IP datagram. If no other action were taken, each 128 octet X.25 packet would contain a 20 octet IP header and only 108 octets of higher layer protocol data; hardly an efficient use of resources. The solution for IP is to use X.25's M-bit, the more data bit, and advertise the X.25 network as having an MTU of 576. If packet sizes larger than 512 can be negotiated, the MTU can be increased without the use of the M-bit.

In an X.25 packet, when the M-bit is one, it indicates that this packet is one of a sequence that are somehow related. The last packet in a sequence has the M-bit set to zero. IP X.25 gateways use the M-bit to relate 'fragments' of a 576 octet IP datagram. As shown in Figure 10.16, the first packet contains 20 octets of IP header and 108 octets of the datagram, the next three packets contain a full 128 octets from the datagram and the last contains 84 octets.

Configuration and management issues

The following parameters will need to be configured on X.25 gateways for IP or on routers that offer X.25 support for IP:

- tables for mapping between X.121 addresses (X.25 NUAs) and IP network numbers or subnetwork numbers with subnetwork masks for each network;
- the time-out after which the X.25 call will be cleared if no traffic flows;

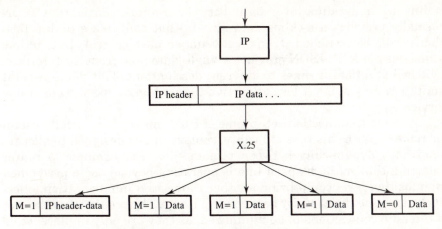

Figure 10.16 Use of the M-bit in X.25.

- setting the MTU, enabling the use of the M-bit and negotiating packet sizes with the X.25 network where available;
- ensuring that the protocol identifier of 204 is set in the call user data field.

Applications which generate UDP broadcasts between networks will prevent the idle timer from operating. Where connect time is charged, this is a costly item.

Traditionally, X.25 has been used for file transfer and terminal applications similar to TCP/IP's FTP and Telnet. Public network performance is often in the range from hundreds to thousands of bits per second. Tariffs are often set accordingly. Those intending to use public X.25 networks for general TCP/IP LAN interconnection should conduct careful pilot trials to check that this performance and the tariffs are acceptable. More modern TCP/IP applications using UDP as the transport protocol may operate satisfactorily. This could include ONC.

Integrated Services Digital Network

The **Integrated Services Digital Network** (ISDN) is comprised of a number of different standards and facilities. In this section we confine the discussion to Basic Rate ISDN. Later sections look at the more recent fast packet technologies which are being developed as part of ISDN standards.

There are currently no RFCs which define the use of ISDN switched service connections for carrying TCP/IP. It is expected that with wide acceptance of the ISDN standard for public networks, ISDN basic rate switched services will be used for transporting TCP/IP protocols, mainly as a datalink-level path between routers. Basic rate ISDN normally provides a 64 kbps data stream that can, like a dialup telephone call, be switched dynamically under user control. But, unlike frame relay or X.25, ISDN provides a single 'data pipe' from one interface, switched at different times to different destinations. This point-to-point limitation may make it less attractive than a higher speed frame relay service.

The fast connection setup time of ISDN makes it especially useful for routers. With this type of facility, routers can be designed to allocate bandwidth dynamically between remote sites. For example, a router detecting that its high-speed line is operating beyond some predefined high loading level could bring another connection into operation, effectively doubling the capacity between two LANs. This would allow the cost of intersite connections to be minimized, as they are only in place while they are needed, often for the busiest hour in the morning and afternoon. Such systems can 'peak-lop' transmission costs.

This feature of transmission on demand may also be used to back up failed leased point-to-point circuits. When a failure is detected the routers will re-establish the path via ISDN in a time scale which, for TCP/IP, will not lose any connections or user data. The users should experience only a few seconds pause in activity while the failure is recognized and the alternative ISDN route is brought into operation.

It is too early to discuss specific detail of how ISDN will be used with TCP/IP systems, but as it provides medium speed, transparent, point-to-point connections, it will integrate well into existing bridge and router technology using a protocol like PPP once the ISDN call setup is complete.

The management of routers with ISDN connections is likely to be similar to X.25 connections so the following parameters must be configured on routers using ISDN to support IP:

- tables for mapping between ISDN network numbers (telephone numbers) and IP network numbers or subnetwork numbers with subnetwork masks for each network;
- the time-out after which the ISDN call will be cleared if no IP traffic flows;
- setting the MTU;
- ensuring that the correct link layer protocol is set once the connection is established.

Fast packet systems

Like X.25, the fast packet standards are interface standards for connection to public (or private) WANs. Interface standards do not describe how networks should operate internally, only how to connect to those networks.

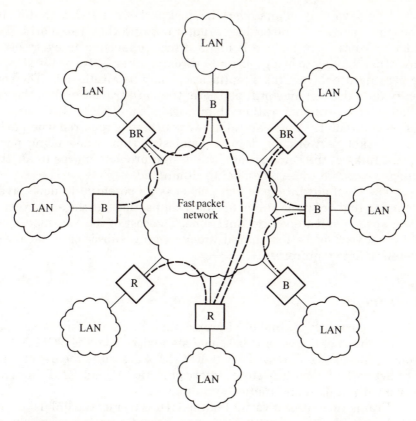

Figure 10.17   Bridging and routing using fast packet technology.

Fast packet is a general term which is used to describe two very different technologies known as **frame relay** and **cell relay**. While they have some similarities, the performances that can be achieved, and the applications which they support, are different. For example, cell relay will support voice systems due to its more consistent delay characteristics, whereas frame relay is less suitable for voice as its delays are more variable.

For a single physical interface (connection), both systems provide multiple data streams to separate remote interfaces. As shown in Figure 10.17, a bridge or router with the correct hardware and link-level software need only have a single connection to a fast packet network to communicate with multiple destinations simultaneously through virtual circuits. If the intervening network is correctly designed, it creates an illusion of multiple point-to-point links directly from one bridge or router to another. A bridge or router with a single high-speed fast packet interface is similar to a multiport remote bridge or router.

The advantage of an underlying fast packet network is that it simplifies the structure of the bridge or router network that it supports. Each bridge or router can believe it has a direct connection to every other, rather than having to bridge or route through other LANs or WANs with the attendant delays. This simplification may be an illusion. The complexity (and delays) may still be there; they are transferred to the fast packet service supplier rather than within the TCP/IP LAN and its bridges and routers. More careful network design is required when using a fast packet network for data transmission than when using point-to-point links of the same speed. The design problem moves to another management area rather than being eliminated.

The chief advantage of fast packet is its potential to make available much higher speed public network connections at the same cost as slower speed point-to-point connections. The cost of the core high-speed public network is better shared among many subscribers each with different traffic requirements.

Frame relay

There are currently a number of proprietary standards for frame relay, although much of the work is based on standards from the CCITT Q.922 recommendations and ANSI T1.618. RFC 1294 describes the use of frame relay networks for multiprotocol interconnection including IP interconnection with bridges and routers simultaneously.

Frame relay uses a variant of the HDLC frame, the link layer protocol (ISO IS7776) used with X.25. Any equipment which can operate X.25 can, in principle, be reprogrammed to support frame relay instead. The same hardware can handle much more data with frame relay standards than it does with X.25, so frame relay techniques are rapidly gaining in popularity with suppliers of private and public network equipment.

Frame relay networks are so-called because the network can carry the link-level protocol (frame) from any other type of LAN or WAN. The frame is carried transparently inside the modified HDLC frame of the frame relay network. Some frame relay networks send the frame exactly as received, others use their own form of fragmentation (see Chapter 11) to improve the 'bucket brigade' delay. For most implementations the header consists of two octets and contains the fields shown in Figure 10.18. Some networks allow a longer header of three or four octets. This allows more connections to be identified across the interface. We will confine this discussion to the two octet header:

- *DLCI – 10 bits*   Datalink connection identifier, a 10-bit number uniquely identifying the virtual circuit (connection) to which this frame belongs.
- *C/R – 1 bit*   A command/response bit.

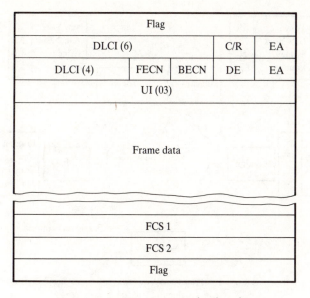

Flag				
DLCI (6)			C/R	EA
DLCI (4)	FECN	BECN	DE	EA
UI (03)				
Frame data				
FCS 1				
FCS 2				
Flag				

Figure 10.18   Frame relay header.

- *EA – 2 bits*   The extended address markers, 0 in the first octet and 1 in the second octet to indicate the end of the header.
- *FECN – 1 bit*   Forward explicit congestion notification.
- *BECN – 1 bit*   Backward explicit congestion notification.
- *DE – 1 bit*   Discard eligibility.

The FECN, BECN and DE flags are described below.

The frame begins and ends with a normal HDLC flag[†] with the end flag preceded by a 16-bit FCS used to detect frame transmission errors. Frames with an invalid FCS are discarded.

The DLCI identifies one of 1024 virtual circuits on an interface; it determines to which remote port and remote DLCI the frame will be delivered. The DLCI is used for routing within the frame relay network. The DLCI has a significance only at the local interface. As illustrated in Figure 10.19, the DLCIs are usually different at the two ends of the connection.

Frame relay networks do not today support broadcast or multicast. In the first releases of frame relay systems, the mapping between DLCIs

---

[†]HDLC flags delineate a frame by appearing at the beginning and end of a frame; the pattern of an HDLC flag is 0x7E.

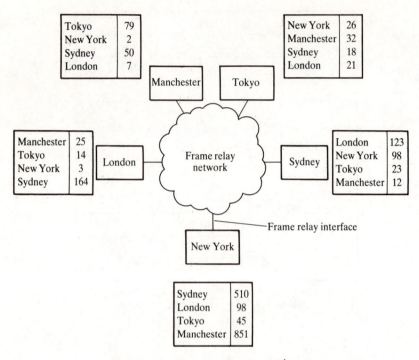

Figure 10.19 Connections and DLCIs.

and the remote nodes is agreed when you subscribe to a public service or when the network manager sets up the private frame relay network. Most current implementations do not include a mechanism for the DTE, the 'user equipment', to set up the connection dynamically (though this is a function within ISDN standards). Frame relay systems today provide Permanent Virtual Circuits (PVCs), in imitation of point-to-point leased lines, not Switched Virtual Circuits as X.25.

The service provided by frame relay

Frame relay is so called because it relays the basic user frame as it is presented. If a 16 Mbps Token Ring network has an MTU of 8000 octets in a frame, the frame relay network will transmit frames of that size. (There is a maximum recommended frame for current frame relay implementations of 8192 octets but older systems used fragmentation and had a basic frame size of 262 octets.)

The frame relay service is sometimes referred to as connection oriented, for it supports virtual circuits, multiple data streams identified by the DLCI. These generally follow fixed routes and will not be delivered out of order or duplicated. However, unlike X.25, there is no error correction or reliable flow control in this network. Any frame with an FCS error will be discarded with no notification. If network congestion occurs, the network is entitled to discard frames. This is the same service that bridges and point-to-point links normally provide, so frame relay is a suitable mechanism for supporting TCP/IP transmission with bridges and routers, provided the intervening frame relay network is designed to have low rates of congestion and packet loss.

In a private frame relay network, these design parameters are under the control of the one company using and providing the service, though the control may be under different management. With a public network, congestion control is outside the end user's authority, but in a properly configured large public network, where the shared resources are of higher overall capacity, congestion should be less likely to occur.

Frame formats for frame relay networks

Either bridges or routers may encapsulate their data in a **frame relay frame**. One interface may process both bridge and router frames simultaneously (a **brouter**).

The carrying of either router data (the network layer) or bridged data (the MAC layer) within a frame relay frame is identified by the **Network Layer Protocol Identifier** (NLPID) which immediately follows the UI control field. The NLPID concept is described in an ISO Technical Report (ISO/IEC TR 9577) and NLPID values are registered with ISO. If the NLPID has a value 0x80, SNAP follows as shown in Figure 10.20. SNAP can be used with an NLPID as well as after a link layer protocol identifier such as SAP.

When the frame relay frame carries bridge data, the SNAP header does not indicate an Ethernet type field. Instead, it contains an organization identifier for the IEEE 802.1 committee that standardized bridges and a two octet code indicating which type of network or medium the frame came from (802.3, 802.4, 802.5, 802.6, FDDI or a spanning tree bridge).

When the frame relay frame carries IP (router data) the NLPID has a value of 0xCC, indicating that IP follows immediately (Figure 10.21). An alternative and incompatible way of carrying IP is to use SNAP – an NLPID of 0x80, followed by SNAP, followed by an Ethernet type of 0x800 and IP. This second method is discouraged as it has a higher overhead.

Since frame relay is a multiplexed protocol, routers (or hosts) using TCP/IP over frame relay interfaces must have a mechanism to determine the DLCI that should be used. A protocol called Inverse ARP (INARP) has been developed for this.

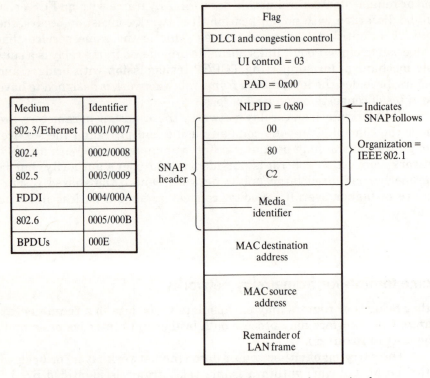

Medium	Identifier
802.3/Ethernet	0001/0007
802.4	0002/0008
802.5	0003/0009
FDDI	0004/000A
802.6	0005/000B
BPDUs	000E

Figure 10.20 SNAP and bridged data within a frame relay frame.

Why is it 'fast'?

Frame relay technology is 'fast' in comparison to older X.25 public networks, but not necessarily fast in terms of the requirements of a LAN designer and implementor. The term 'fast' in fast packet can be justified by the higher interface speeds than normal X.25 packet networks and the reduction of switching time in each switching node.

Frame relay interface speeds range from 64 kbps to 2 Mbps, though special hardware will extend the upper range to 34 Mbps. These speeds begin where standard X.25 stops. Public telecommunications operators are introducing services with access speeds between 64 kbps and 1 Mbps. These speeds are likely to prove too low for the more demanding remote TCP/IP applications. Frame relay networks still introduce delay.

The processing power needed to switch a frame relay frame is small compared to standard X.25. Frame relay switching uses only the DLCI at link level, not a logical channel identifier at packet level. There is no lower level error correction or flow control. There is no packet level with its associated flow control for each virtual circuit. These features of X.25 allowed a public network operator to deliver a reliable error-free ser-

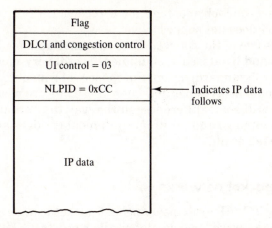

Figure 10.21   Router data within a frame relay frame.

vice over the error-prone analogue lines of the mid-1970s. In the 1990s, many public telecommunications systems are already installed on fibre optic systems where the interval between errors can be measured in days on the best routes. The overhead of X.25 error correction and flow control cannot be justified, hence the lightweight frame relay service.

Congestion control in frame relay networks

As mentioned, an overloaded frame relay network will discard frames (as will an overloaded bridged network). To reduce the rate of frame loss, the frame relay header format provides three bits for **congestion control** Forward Explicit Congestion Notification (FECN) Backward Explicit Congestion Notification (BECN) and Discard Eligible (DE).

There is some discussion among standards makers as to how networks should use these flags; many current frame relay implementations ignore them. Using the DE bit, a DTE can indicate a preference that if frames are to be discarded, those with DE set should be dropped before those with DE clear, but it remains a preference. At the limits, the network may drop any frame.

RFC 1294 currently makes no recommendation of how these bits are to be used. In TCP/IP it would be appropriate to clear DE (that is, not to be discarded) for those IP frames with a high reliability TOS or a high precedence (see Chapter 11).

The FECN and BECN bits are set by the network to advise the receiving (forward) and sending (backward) nodes that the network is about to begin (or has begun) to discard frames on that connection. These bits correspond rather well with the ICMP source quench message. In future, routers with frame relay interfaces could be expected to interpret these bits in the same way as ICMP source quench messages, if necessary relaying a source quench message for a received FECN/BECN frame. Again, RFC 1294 does not suggest this.

The exact use of the congestion control mechanisms by public network operators and by attached equipment is still very much in the preliminary stages of standardization. Purchasers of frame relay equipment and services should ascertain exactly how these bits are used by each system. There are still some differences in the way they are used by different networks (switches) and terminal equipment (bridges and routers), if they are supported at all.

Delay in fast packet networks

When designing TCP/IP systems using fast packet frame relay, planners should focus on the word 'packet', not on the word 'fast'. The terminology can disguise the important fact that the delay across any packet network will never be less than twice the delay of a point-to-point leased circuit of the same speed as the access lines; it will often be more, perhaps considerably more. This delay is referred to as **network latency**. The reasons are exactly those highlighted in Chapter 7, where we discussed the bucket brigade delay effect. A switch should not decide where to send the information until it has examined the end of the frame (FCS) to be sure that the frame has been correctly received[†].

On a point-to-point leased circuit only the final destination must wait for the FCS; on a fast packet frame relay network each switch normally waits for the FCS, so the delay across the network increases for each network hop.

This network latency significantly affects the performance of internetworks using bridges or routers with frame relay interfaces.

Configuration and management issues

On a bridge or router, a frame relay interface replaces a number of individual interfaces each carrying point-to-point connections. For a connection of a given speed, the throughput of that frame relay interface will be less than a point-to-point circuit. The advantage comes from exchanging a number of heavily loaded point-to-point circuits, for example at 64 kbps, for one much higher speed frame relay access to a shared network with very high speed internal lines. Since not all traffic from all network users peaks at the same time, there are considerable benefits to the network supplier. It is the 'large pipe' – one user can only have a small impact on

---

[†]There is no apparent value in beginning to relay information that may be in error: if the error occurred in the DLCI, the information would be transmitted to the wrong destination; if the output line speed is higher than the input line speed, you could run out of input data and would then have to abort the frame and begin retransmitting. Some switches will take a risk on FCS and will check on speed mismatching to reduce network latency

the overall service. The public network operator can then provide a high-speed connection at much lower cost than dedicated high speed point-to-point connections. It is the responsibility of the network designer to ensure that they use higher speed connections to compensate for the greater delay (network latency) compared to point-to-point circuits. They themselves may benefit from aggregating several slow-speed lines into one high-speed interface. Where multiple 64 kbps are replaced, speeds between 128 kbps and 2 Mbps may be more appropriate. If 2 Mbps circuits are in use, careful traffic analysis is required to determine what should be provided.

Fast packet interfaces are available for remote bridges or TCP/IP routers. The interface is multiplexed, so the access speed must be sufficient to process all anticipated traffic on all virtual circuits. If it is not, congestion will result and congestion control will operate if the equipment is programmed to use it.

A network which is operating without congestion control in its busiest periods is overconfigured and probably not operating at maximum efficiency. But once congestion begins, the service will deteriorate rapidly if traffic increases further. Congestion control in a growing network is a sign of the requirement for some rapid remedial action. Once congestion control leads on to frequent IP datagram loss in a fast packet network (or point-to-point router-based network), the service and performance levels seen by end users will degrade rapidly if the network is allowed to grow further.

Setting up frame relay bridges

In addition to the normal configuration of any LAN bridge, the network implementor must:

- Agree the allocation of DLCIs with the network supplier for the interface at each end of a virtual circuit.
- Configure the DLCIs into the bridge software so that only they are used to generate broadcasts and build filtering tables.
- Set the discard eligible operation for broadcast and multicast frames (if supported).

Setting up frame relay routers

Each virtual circuit is seen by the IP layer as a direct point-to-point link to a remote IP network number. Once the DLCIs are agreed, as for a bridge, the network manager must set up:

- The relationship between DLCI and network number. As with any other circuit, each DLCI will have its own subnet mask.

- The association of TOS and precedence bits with discard eligibility (where supported).
- The use of any FECN/BECN bits with ICMP, where supported.
- The use of any routing protocols across a particular interface.

Tariffs for frame relay services

Many network suppliers are introducing frame relay services specifically for remote LAN interconnection. The service can be offered potentially at a much lower initial cost than dedicated point-to-point links. A single high-speed connection to the network can support multiple remote destinations. The network user can choose the access speed, and hence cost, to meet the traffic needs of an individual site.

Most public network services are being introduced with a flat-rate fixed tariff dependent on access speed rather than the volume of data transmitted. This is perhaps fortunate. Estimating traffic volume requires the detailed knowledge of protocol operation; as discussed in Chapter 7, this can often only be determined by measuring and scaling the results. Few network planners have the time or the detailed knowledge to know what volume of traffic will be generated in what period of time by particular network implementations. While such information is very useful when designing and sizing a stable network, it is essential where public network tariffs and charges depend on traffic volume!

Cell relay

Also referred to as **Asynchronous Transfer Mode** (ATM), cell relay is a more complicated technology than frame relay. It has been developed for very high speed operation on the Synchronous Optical Network (Sonet) standards as part of the Broadband ISDN (B-ISDN) initiatives by CCITT and ANSI. Cell relay will operate at speeds from 2 to 600 Mbps, with the initial design aim for speeds of 155 Mbps for public network operators.

Rather than encapsulating the data protocol frame from the LAN exactly as received, in a cell relay interface the frame is fragmented into standard size small packets or 'cells' of 53 octets, each containing 48 octets of data from the original frame and 5 octets of control information. This reduces the network latency (to around 53 bytes at the access speed). Together with the very high data speeds, this standard size reduces the variations in delay; all frames are exactly the same size so they can be 'packed together' in an optimum fashion. The network is much less likely to reach saturation when the internal speeds are 150–600 Mbps.

Some of the same issues that concern frame relay are still to be resolved: call setup and signalling, flow control and congestion management. The standards may also have to be adapted to lower speed operation for private network use.

Cell relay systems are expected to become available by 1993/1994 and will provide an alternative fast packet mechanism for transporting TCP/IP data.

Switched multimegabit data service and IEEE 802.6

The Switched Multimegabit Data Service (SMDS) is based on the IEEE 802.6 metropolitan area network Distributed Queue Dual Bus (DQDB) standard. IEEE 802.6 is the technological standard. SMDS is a public network service based on that standard. It is particularly advanced in the USA, but is now being piloted in a number of other countries.

SMDS provides a high-speed packet-switched connectionless datagram service on demand between geographically separated locations. Like a LAN, it has high throughput and low delay and supports individual and multicast addressing (although not broadcast as it is a public service!). The addressing allows the creation of closed user groups or a virtual private network over the service.

RFC 1209 describes how IP data is carried on this service for use by one organization in such a virtual private network for end systems and routers directly connected to the SMDS. It does not discuss how such a bearer service should be used by bridges. Neither does it discuss the issues of using the service for IP between different organizations.

The protocol layering with IEEE 802.6 and SMDS is exactly the same as the other IEEE networks: the IEEE 802.6 medium access control, 802.2 LLC type 1 with a DSAP and SSAP of 0xAA indicating SNAP. SNAP will have an organization code of 0x000000 indicating that the Ethernet type follows. The Ethernet type will distinguish the IP, ARP and RARP protocols. The format is as Figure 10.8, though the headers for the lowest layer, IEEE 802.6 are different.

An IEEE 802.6 frame has a maximum size of 9180 octets of IP data excluding the LLC and SNAP headers. It uses a 64-bit address field.

Because SMDS does not support broadcast, a multicast SMDS address allocated to the closed user group must be assigned to carry any broadcast traffic from the TCP/IP stack. A second address may be required for the multicast traffic of the TCP/IP stack. These assignments must be agreed with the network provider and configured into all the affected interfaces.

Relevant RFCs

877   Standard for the transmission of IP datagrams over (X.25) public data networks

894   Standard for the transmission of IP datagrams over Ethernet networks

895   Standard for the transmission of IP datagrams over experimental Ethernet networks

1042   Standard for the transmission of IP datagrams over IEEE 802 networks

1055   Non-standard for transmission of IP datagrams over serial lines: SLIP

1088   Standard for the transmission of IP datagrams over NetBIOS networks

1132   Standard for the transmission of 802.2 packets over IPX networks

1144   Compressing TCP/IP headers for low-speed serial links

1171   Point-to-point protocol for the transmission of multiprotocol datagrams over point-to-point links

1172   Point-to-point protocol (PPP) initial configuration options

1188   A proposed standard for the transmission of IP datagrams over FDDI networks

1201   Transmitting IP traffic over ARCNET networks

1209   Transmission of IP datagrams over the SMDS service

1220   Point-to-point protocol extensions for bridging

1294   Multiprotocol interconnect over frame relay

Summary

TCP/IP can run on many different types of media and little configuration is required to deal with them. MAC address connection can be dynamic on networks that support broadcast through use of the ARP protocol; on point-to-point networks end node addresses may need to be configured into the software.

The major factors to consider when operating TCP/IP on the different media systems are frame compatibility, throughput and frame sizes.

11

Internet protocol

This chapter studies the network layer of the TCP/IP protocol family, the Internet Protocol (IP). IP provides the basis for transporting all the higher layer TCP/IP protocols over all physical networks. Understanding the fields used in the IP header helps you to appreciate the facilities that IP supports and some of the configuration requirements for TCP/IP systems.

In this chapter you will learn:

- The format of the IP datagram
- The facilities provided by IP
- The Type of Service options used by IP
- About fragmentation and how it is performed
- The basis of IP routing
- The need for certain configuration options relating to IP
- How the address resolution protocol works
- How the reverse address resolution protocol works
- ICMP and its use for network management

The Internet Protocol (IP) is the underpinning protocol for the TCP/IP stack. IP is the layer 3 or network component of the TCP/IP model, providing functions for transferring information between devices across any combination of underlying relay networks. The basic functions provided at the network layer deal with conveying data to the correct machine on the correct physical network; to put it another way, routing is performed in this layer.

IP is described as a 'connectionless datagram service'. Datagrams are packets of information that can be destined for one, many or all stations; they can have unique, multicast or broadcast destination addresses. There is no requirement for the intended recipient or recipients to acknowledge whether the datagram was received. No error correction takes place at this level and the reliability of the service is solely dependent on the basic error performance of the underlying networks. The service is connectionless because there is no call or virtual circuit set up before data transmission begins; each datagram contains all information needed to route it with the right performance.

In a connectionless datagram service each datagram is regarded as complete. There is no concept of a sequence of datagrams making up a message. The datagram service does not have to keep datagrams in the same order as they were sent. If important, a receiving station must allow for information arriving in the wrong order and for duplicate datagrams because they were retransmitted by the sender.

As IP is connectionless, no specific route is defined between two communicating nodes, so datagrams travelling between them can travel along different routes and possibly reach their destination in a different order than they were sent. But this is very flexible: because datagrams do not have to establish a connection along a fixed route they can easily be re-routed with little switching delay if there is a network failure.

One of the major functions of the IP layer is to make it unnecessary for higher layer protocols to understand anything about the physical capabilities of the media supporting them. IP provides a barrier between the physical layers discussed in the previous chapter and the next layer up, the transport protocols. This is important for application developers writing programs on top of the transport layer, as they need not produce variations to cater for different types of media.

The facilities of IP

For datagrams, the basic facilities of IP deal with **addressing**, **fragmentation** and obtaining a suitable **Type of Service**. There are some powerful network management and security options available, but today these are rarely used.

As was discussed in detail in Chapter 3, IP encodes the network number as part of the IP address; some protocols (XNS, IPX) have a com-

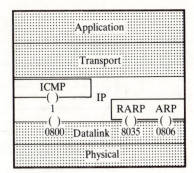

Figure 11.1   The IP architecture.

pletely separate field for a network number which they call the network address. As mentioned in Chapters 3 and 5, the network number in IP addressing is used to determine how to route the datagram.

The IP address uniquely identifies an individual connection on a particular network number in a standard way which is completely independent of the technology of that network connection. The underlying datalink address could be the MAC address of a LAN card or an X.121 address on an X.25 network.

Often shown within the IP layer (Figure 11.1) are three other protocols that are needed with some types of media. They are:

(1)   The Address Resolution Protocol (ARP)

(2)   The Reverse Address Resolution Protocol (RARP)

(3)   The Internet Control Message Protocol (ICMP)

All of these will be covered in detail in this chapter. ARP and RARP are shown at the bottom of the IP layer because they do not use IP and are recognized as separate protocols by the datalink layer supporting them. ICMP is shown at the top of the IP layer as it is transported across a network in IP datagrams. The IP layer recognizes ICMP datagrams by the protocol value of 1, which is also shown.

Encapsulation

Both the header and data field of the IP datagram become the data field of the datalink frame of whichever network they happen to be on. This is called **encapsulation** or, sometimes, **enveloping**. The IP datagram data field contains headers of the higher layer protocols and ultimately, end user information; IP itself encapsulates the higher layer protocols. An example is shown in Figure 11.2. This shows IP being encapsulated in both an Ethernet and an IEEE 802.3 frame.

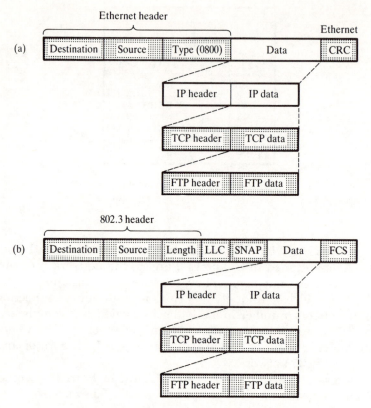

Figure 11.2 IP in: (a) Ethernet and (b) IEEE 802.3 frames.

Fragmentation, reassembly and the maximum transfer unit

One of the issues in hiding physical layer restrictions from the transport layer is to conceal the limited amount of data that can be sent in datalink frames. The IP layer has to give the impression of having no restriction on the amount of data that can be transmitted at one time. In principle, the higher layer protocols can send a datagram of whatever size they prefer. IP has to split datagrams that are larger than the medium can manage into fragments and reassemble them at the remote node as if they were a single datagram. The process is predictably called **fragmentation and reassembly**. For example, IEEE 802.3 and Ethernet systems have maximum data sizes of 1492 and 1500 octets respectively. The limit for IEEE 802.5 frames is not defined, but in practice it is usually no greater than 8192 octets. The packets used in an X.25 system are often no greater than 128 octets in size[†].

[†]Because of the way IP is carried within X.25, the 128 octet limit of X.25 may be invisible to IP as described in Chapter 10.

This size limit seen by IP is known as the **Maximum Transfer Unit** (MTU). In some, but not all, TCP/IP implementations, this value can be adjusted for each interface. It is not normally necessary to do so unless bridging different LAN technologies (ring and bus). To the higher layer protocols, this size limitation is invisible, as IP will take the data supplied to it and fragment it into smaller datagrams as necessary.

IP addressing

The mechanism for choosing an IP addressing scheme was thoroughly explored in Chapter 3. The fundamental purpose of the IP address is to provide an addressing scheme that is completely independent of physical network type. The same addressing structure is used independent of any medium, hardware and software used for layers 1 and 2. So from an application programmer's or user's perspective the addressing scheme is always the same.

As with telephone systems, even though some of them are electronic and others are electromechanical with completely different designs, the addressing scheme, the phone number, remains the same. We, as users, need not recognize that the destination is on a different type of system; it is not necessary to have different procedures for each system. Because the addressing scheme remains consistent and is part of a CCITT[†] 'international standard', the system type is transparent to users and application developers.

Normally, an IP address is allocated to a network connection when the TCP/IP software is installed. The address is configured to represent a particular network number and unique host connection on that network. If more than one connection is made to a computer, a different IP address is required for each one.

Type of Service

In an attempt to provide a 'better' service, the IP header has a number of flags, the **Type of Service** (TOS) bits, that allow software to request different types of performance for a datagram: low delay, high throughput high reliability and low cost (Figure 11.3). In this context, high reliability means that there should be a lower than normal probability that the datagram will be discarded because of either congestion or a transmission error.

When a higher layer protocol requests a particular TOS from IP, the relevant flags are set in the IP headers of the datagrams; routers that process these datagrams are expected to attempt to provide paths through the network that satisfy the options requested[‡].

[†]International Telephone and Telegraph Consultative Committee.
[‡]Only the most recent routers honour type of service routing.

Vers	IHL	Type of Service		Total length	
Identification			Flags	Fragment offset	
Time		Protocol	Header checksum		
Source IP address					
Destination IP address					
Options					Padding
Data					
⋮					

Figure 11.3.   IP datagram format.

It would be unusual for all three options to be valid and required at the same time. Their characteristics tend to be mutually exclusive. It is normal to set only one of these bits, but it is not unknown for a TCP/IP implementation to request all three services together – however, that is simply not playing fair. Protocols which support interactive traffic need low delay, as a user's performance is affected directly by long delays. Large data transfers that involve long blocks of information require high throughput. Higher layer protocols that provide datagram services should request high reliability. For standard TCP/IP applications, the recommended TOS for Telnet is low delay; for FTP it is low delay for the control connection and high throughput for the data connection (see Chapter 13).

A user or network manager does not normally have access to the TOS values; they are preset by developers when they build TCP/IP software. If you are developing your own application package it is possible to set your own values.

As more flexible implementations of TCP/IP become available, it may be worth checking to see which products support TOS, if this is seen as important for system performance. Remember, however, that it is only routers that can take decisions on these TOS bits. TOS is only important in internetworks which have routers and then only if those routers support TOS routing! Some diagnostic tools do allow TOS to be set for testing purposes for example, to verify that routers do make use of them.

The IP datagram

The IP datagram is shown in Figure 11.3 and, as is standard for TCP/IP systems, is shown as 32 bits wide. When transmitted to a network the transmission order is from top left to bottom right. This transmission order is called **network byte order** and applies to all TCP/IP-related diagrams. Since numbers are always represented with the most significant components on the left, all TCP/IP numbers are transmitted most significant octet first. This is most important when decoding any TCP/IP information on a protocol analyser.

We will now describe the fields in the header in order:

- *Version – 4 bits*   This field indicates the version of the IP protocol so incompatibility can be discovered. The current version is 4.

- *Internet header length – 4 bits*   This field indicates the length of the header in 32 bit words so the beginning of data can easily be found if any options are present. It is normally 5, which indicates no options are used.

- *Type of Service – 8 bits*   This field holds the flags used for TOS and precedence. The first three bits are used to indicate one of eight levels of Precedence. This allows an IP node to designate certain datagrams as having higher priority than others. Some routers ignore these flags.

    The D-flag requests a low delay connection. If there is a path to a network that a router understands to be lower delay than others, it will be selected. Interactive traffic using remote echo could request this service.

    The T-bit signifies a requirement for high throughput. Again, a router should attempt to provide a route supplying this service.

    The R-bit requests high reliability, meaning there is a lower probability of the datagram being discarded. Some newer routing protocols are now setting the R-bit.

    A recent RFC adds the C-bit which requests a route with a lower cost.

    The last bit is unused.

- *Total length – 16 bits*   The total length of the IP datagram measured in octets including the header and data. The size of the data area is computed from the total length field and the IHL field.

    As this field is 16 bits, it means the maximum datagram size is 65 535 octets, which is very much larger than most physical networks support. (When a datagram is fragmented, this value indicates the new size of the fragment, not the size of the original datagram, so 16 bits is generous.)

- *Identification – 16 bits*   This is an integer value used to help identify all fragments of a datagram. This field should be unique for each new datagram sent by a host and is often simply incremented.

    It is important not to think of this id as a sequence number. Since the IP service is connectionless, there is no concept of a sequence of datagrams, and since that IP service may be supporting several different transport layer 'conversations', there is not necessarily a correlation between the values of id and the order of datagrams sent over a particular conversation with another node. This concept will be developed more fully in the following section covering fragmentation.

- *Flags – 3 bits*   The two low-order bits are used as flags to control fragmentation. The low-order bit, if zero, indicates the last fragment of a datagram, and hence is sometimes referred to as the more flag or MF bit. The middle bit is used to indicate that the datagram should not be fragmented, the **do not fragment flag** or DF bit. The high-order bit is unused. See the following section covering fragmentation for more details on usage of these bits.

- *Fragment offset – 13 bits*   This field is used with fragmented datagrams to indicate the position that the data in this fragment occupies in the original message. It is measured in 8-octet units, so fragments must be built in 8-octet units; the minimum fragment size is 8 octets of data, not including the IP header (which is 20 octets without options), or the datalink header field. See the following section covering fragmentation for use of this field.

- *Time to live – 8 bits*   The Time To Live (TTL) field is set by the datagram sender and is decremented by routers as the datagram passes through them. If this action reduces the TTL to 0 the datagram is discarded rather than relayed. This prevents datagrams that get routed in a loop from circulating forever. A router should never receive a datagram that has TTL set to 0.

  This TTL value may be configured in some implementations of TCP/IP software and its value can be important. If the value of this field is set too small, it is possible that datagrams may not reach the remotest parts of a large network; set too big and datagrams could travel unnecessarily in a routing loop creating inordinate amounts of traffic. The recommended value is 32, but it is not uncommon to find systems that are set to the maximum possible value of 255 or low values of 3 or 4.

- *Protocol – 8 bits*   The protocol field indicates the transport layer protocol carried by this datagram. It tells the IP layer which transport layer to pass this datagram to. The normal values for this field are:

17	UDP
6	TCP
1	ICMP
8	EGP
89	OSPF

- *Header checksum – 16 bits*   The IP header checksum is interesting in that the checksum only protects its header and thus does

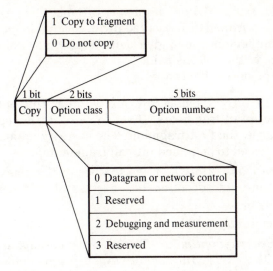

Figure 11.4 Measurement and security options.

not protect the data it carries. The main reason for this is that the checksum must be recalculated every time it passes through a router, for the value TTL, flags and fragment offset may change. If the data was also included in the checksum, it would take longer to calculate and hence delay the datagram further.

The checksum is a simple calculation. It is based upon taking the header as 16-bit integers, adding them together using 1s complement and taking the 1s complement of the result.

Some systems which work over error-detected networks do not set the header checksum. It is then all 0s.

- *Source IP address – 32 bits*   The source IP address.

- *Destination IP address – 32 bits*   The destination IP address.

- *Data – variable*   This includes the headers of higher layer protocols and sometimes user's data.

- *Padding – variable*   This field represents 0s used to pad the header out to a 32-bit word boundary so that the IHL can correctly point to the start of the data when the variable length options are present.

- *Options*   The options field supports debugging, measurement and security facilities. There can be multiple options in a single datagram, each with the format shown in Figure 11.4. These options are normally used in diagnostic datagrams sent in such as a way as to be echoed back by the remote node, otherwise the sender cannot obtain the results!

In some TCP/IP implementations, the setting of these options is within a utility called **ping**, covered in more detail later. Other implementations give neither user nor network manager interface to the options field.

The option fields are:

− *Copy (1 bit)*   Used to indicate whether this option has to be placed in all fragments. If set to zero (0) this option will only appear in the first fragment. The security options for example would need to be copied into all fragments.

− *Option class (2 bits)*   Used to specify the class of an option. The time stamp option has a class of 2, otherwise class is usually 0.

− *Option numbers (5 bits)*

Security: option 2   The security options are assigned by the US Defense Intelligence Agency and define a datagram as ranging from unclassified to top secret. This allows a router to detect datagrams that are carrying sensitive information and prevent them from leaving a secure environment. These features have not had wide usage in commercial TCP/IP implementations.

Time stamp – option 4   This option allows a datagram to be sent through the network and gather time stamps from each router it passes through. This can be used to assess delay and its variations within the router network. (The clocks in all routers must be synchronized, or time differentials used.)

Loose source route: option 3   This is another management option that allows a datagram to be directed through a particular set of routers using a predefined list of IP addresses of routers which must be visited in sequence. A loose source route allows other routers to be used in between those defined in this list of routers.

Record route: option 7   This datagram option causes each router to place its IP address in the datagram option field as the datagram travels through the network. This list is used to ascertain the path datagrams are using to reach a particular host or router. The datagram has to have enough space allocated in it to store the number of IP addresses it finds. This has to be allowed for by a developer when creating an application that uses this option.

Strict source route: option 9   Similar to loose source route except that only the routers defined in the list can be used, no others. If the datagram cannot be routed, an ICMP error message should result (see below).

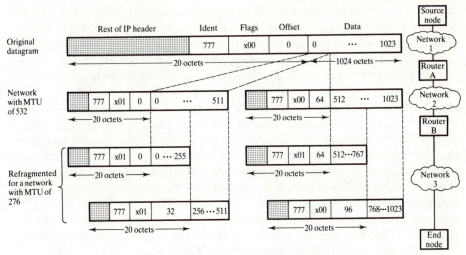

Figure 11.5 Fragmentation: the datagram has been fragmented twice.

Fragmentation and reassembly

We have already used the term 'fragmentation' in explaining how IP is carried over X.25. Fragmentation has a strict meaning in TCP/IP. It is the process used by IP to reduce the size of datagrams that are too large to be transported over a specific medium. Fragments must not exceed the network interface MTU.

IP reduces the size of a large datagram by splitting the data field into suitably small parts. The IP header has to be transported with every fragment for them to be routed correctly, so the size of the datagram can only be changed by reducing the amount of data.

All fragments carry the 32-bit identification number of the original datagram. This is used to identify fragments of the original datagram when reassembling them at the receiving node. Once a datagram has been fragmented, it will not be reassembled until it reaches the final destination end node. Attempts to reassemble a datagram before the destination could be troubled by two problems. First, in a multiple path network, it is possible that fragments will take different paths; an intermediate node will not see all of them so it cannot reassemble the complete datagram. Secondly, to reassemble at an intermediate (router) node would require that node to collect all fragments before forwarding the whole datagram. This would cause unnecessary delay, just to find that the datagram has to be fragmented again further along the path.

Figure 11.5 shows an example of a datagram being fragmented. The IP header is shown shaded and in front of the identification, flags and fragment offset fields. This is not true in practice; it is only shown this way to ease the explanation. The figure also shows a network configuration that would require a datagram to be fragmented. Network 1 has an MTU of 1200, network 2 has MTU of 532 and network 3 has MTU of 276. (These numbers are purely for illustration and are not representative of real networks.) Initially, the datagram has 1024 octets of data when transmitted onto network 1. For router A, the IP layer driving network 2 knows that network 2 has an MTU of only 532 and fragments the datagram into two datagrams each with 512 octets of data. The 20-octet IP header takes the maximum data at the datalink layer to be 532 octets, the MTU for this system. (The frames on the networks will be larger as they include the datalink header but the MTU only refers to the amount of data a datalink can carry in one frame). The fragment offset of the first fragment will be 0, indicating its position in the original datagram. The fragment offset in the second fragment will be 512/8, or 64, as the 13-bit fragment offset field indicates the position in units of 8 octets. The **more bit** in the first fragment will be 1 for there are more fragments to come; in the second it will be 0, as this is the last fragment.

When the fragments arrive at the next router they have to be fragmented again. As can be seen from Figure 11.5, the process is straightforward. The fragments are split again, with the **more flag** set to 1 in all but the current last fragment. The fragment offset indicates how the pieces fit together in the overall jigsaw which is the original datagram.

Using the fragment offset, the original datagram can be reassembled, even if the fragments arrive out of order. Fragments arriving out of order are impossible in the network shown, but in a large multipath network it is quite conceivable. The end node starts a timer that is used to determine the maximum time the node will wait for all fragments to arrive, usually about 30 seconds. If any fragment fails to arrive within this fragment reassembly time-out, the complete datagram is discarded and since the service is connectionless no attempt is made by IP to recover the situation, though an ICMP error message may be generated.

Some systems do not have the power necessary to reassemble fragments. This, at one time, would have been the case with a diskless workstation that has a simple bootstrap program in PROM. Where this is known by an originator, although there is nothing in TCP/IP protocols that would allow a sender to determine this, the do not fragment (DF) bit in the fragmentation flags can be set to advise any intervening routers that this datagram must not undergo fragmentation. If fragmentation is required, the datagram will be discarded and an ICMP (discussed later) error message returned to the sender.

Management issues

From the above description, it might be thought that fragmentation is only an issue on networks with routers, particularly on WANs. But fragmentation can, and does, occur on LAN-only networks. Fragmentation can take place within the originating node before the datagram reaches the LAN. Then the loss of a single fragment which causes the complete datagram to be discarded can become a very serious problem, even on some LAN-only systems. For example, in many implementations, the NFS protocol attempts to send datagrams that are 8192 bytes long, (where the total transfer is more that 8192 bytes). Consider the impact of this on an Ethernet network that has an MTU of 1024 octets[†].

The IP layer in the source node will realize that the datagram is too large for a single frame and will fragment it into eight full datagrams plus one smaller datagram[‡]. If any one of these datagrams does not reach its destination, the complete 8192 bytes has to be transmitted again. The effect of this is to increase the load on the network for a given amount of data with a longer time to transfer it. This phenomenon can cause the performance of a network to degrade significantly and rapidly. In the worst case, it can cause a 'black hole' effect where network analysers show very high network activity but the users are not seeing much data delivered: all the activity is retransmissions. A runaway effect (a packet meltdown) has occurred at a high load where fragments are lost due to resource limitations, which causes them to be resent, which causes more fragments to be lost....

Why should frames be discarded on a LAN? The error rate on a LAN is supposed to be very low. This statement makes a number of assumptions:

- The LAN cabling system must be properly installed and within the cable design limits. Where unshielded twisted-pair cable is used, the electrical noise level must be low.

- There must be no frame loss due to resource limitations in LAN hardware and software.

These assumptions are often not met in practice.

A discussion of error rates on cabling systems is beyond the scope of this book, but resource limitations can occur in three ways:

(1) In receiving workstations, because they have a much lower performance than the file server which is feeding them;

(2) In networks with a high number of short broadcast frames which detract from the performance of receiving workstations;

(3) In bridges, which cannot forward frames, either because of insufficient forwarding rate or because of output congestion.

When a high-performance workstation sends a series of fragmented datagrams, it can stream them onto a quiet network at the maximum speed

---

[†]The MTU of Ethernet is normally 1500 and of IEEE 802.3, 1492.
[‡]The 20-octet IP header makes the total datagram size at the IP layer 8212 octets.

that the network specification allows. The receiving interface, in an end workstation, a bridge, or a router, must be able to receive all of these frames successfully. If it drops[†] any one frame, a fragment is lost and all are retransmitted, often only to be lost again, until other activity on the network splits up the fragments. We have observed this effect between a UNIX RISC-based NFS file server and a 286 PC with an 8-bit Ethernet card. As a connectionless system offers no flow control, it is important that two devices communicating on the same cable are reasonably well matched. The Ethernet card must have sufficient memory to take all frames which contain the fragments of one datagram.

As explained elsewhere, this problem is made worse by a high level of broadcast traffic on the medium, for every LAN card will process all broadcasts.

In Chapter 2, we emphasized the need for bridges with the highest possible filtering and forwarding rates and for a good network structure which maps the data flows within an organization. The reasons should now be clearer! Bridges can be real performance bottlenecks for TCP/IP systems if they lead to the loss of fragments.

Setting the MTU

Some systems have an option to set the MTU for a particular network interface. It will normally default to the recommended maximum for that network. IAB standards for TCP/IP recommend that all networks supporting TCP/IP have an MTU of at least 576 octets. This means they can forward a higher level data field of 512 octets and still have room for the transport and IP headers with some options. All common networks meet this requirement, including X.25 by using the M-bit as described in Chapter 10.

An MTU should be set for the maximum size possible on the local medium, unless for some reason another network is unable to support such large frames and the interconnection between the two networks cannot support fragmentation. An example is a bridge between Token Ring and CSMA/CD LANs. The Token Ring would normally operate with an MTU of 4000 octets, but if such a frame were to be sent across the bridge to a CSMA/CD system, that bridge would discard the datagram, as a bridge operating at the MAC layer cannot fragment. By reducing the MTU on the Token Ring to, say, 1024 or 1492, all frames will fit the Ethernet or IEEE 802.3 system. However, the MTU cannot be adjusted

---

[†]On CSMA/CD networks the sender has no notification that this has happened, though the receiving LAN card should record a receiver overrun. One advantage of Token Ring networks is that the sender does know there is a problem – the address-recognized bit at the end of the returned frame will be set but the frame-copied bit will be clear. Whether any use is made of this information is up to the protocol designer and the network manager. It is usually ignored!

for each path, so for reliable any-to-any operation, all nodes on the Token Ring would have to use the reduced MTU. Communications within the Token Ring then operate less efficiently, as all high-level datagrams would always fragment down to 1024 or 1492.

For these and other reasons it can be argued that it is better to use routers between Token Ring and CSMA/CD networks. The routers will automatically deal with fragmentation when it is necessary.

IP traces

The following shows actual traces of the IP protocol taken from an operational network. In this example we show an Ethernet frame in hexadecimal without the preamble or the CRC. The table beneath the frame shown in hexadecimal gives a breakdown of the fields in the frame and their values. For a further explanation of the format of these examples see Appendix F.

As IP is a datagram service there is no interplay between both ends at this level. IP is shown as the area which is unshaded. This example is part of a session between two hosts, IP address 30.0.0.1 and 30.0.0.99. The headers for Ethernet and TCP are shown in this example for completeness only. Later chapters in this book detail TCP operation.

Note that the IP headers for each node are independent. The values of ID increment with respect to each IP address, not each datagram.

Frame 1

```
0260  8C0A  C49D  AA00  0400  0104  0800  4508     .`..D.*.......E.
0028  0B6E  0000  3C06  36F7  1E00  0063  1E00     .(.n...6w...c..
0001  0014  0C17  180C  CD95  0000  0AA0  5010     ........M.... P.
0000  7704  0000  0000  0000  0000                 ..w.........
```

Datalink:	Dest MAC:	02608C 0AC49D	Source MAC:	AA0004 000104	Type(Length):	0800
IP:	Version:	4	IHL:	5	Type of service:	08 (Thruput)
	Length:	0028	ID:	0B6E	FLAGS:	0
	Offset:	0	Time to Live:	60	Protocol:	06
	Checksum:	36F7	Source IP:	30.0.0.99	Dest IP:	30.0.0.1
TCP:	Source Port:	FTP(0014)	Dest Port:	0C17	Sequence:	180CCD95
	Acknowledge:	00000AA0	Offset:	5	Code:	10(ACK)
	Window:	0	Checksum:	7704		

Frame 2

```
AA00  0400  0104  0260  8C0A  C49D  0800  4500     *......`..D...E.
003D  0097  0000  FF06  7EC0  1E00  0001  1E00     .=......~@......
0063  1A57  0015  0000  17BA  1245  BC31  5018     .c.W.....:.EP.
0400  47C1  0000  504F  5254  2033  302C  302C     ..GA..PORT 30,0,
302C  312C  342C  3235  320D  0A                   0,1,4,252..
```

Translation:

Datalink:	Dest MAC:	AA0004 000104	Source MAC:	02608C 0AC49D	Type(Length):	0800
IP:	Version:	4	IHL:	5	Type of service:	00
	Length:	003D	ID:	0097	FLAGS:	0
	Offset:	0	Time to Live:	255	Protocol:	06
	Checksum:	7EC0	Source IP:	30.0.0.1	Dest IP:	30.0.0.99
TCP:	Source Port:	1A57	Dest Port:	FTP(0015)	Sequence:	000017BA
	Acknowledge:	1245BC31	Offset:	5	Code:	18(Push)
	Window:	0400	Checksum:	47C1		

Frame 3

0260	8C0A	C49D	AA00	0400	0104	0800	4500
003B	0B6F	0000	3C06	36EB	1E00	0063	1E00
0001	0015	1A57	1245	BC31	0000	17CF	5018
07C5	8931	0000	3230	3020	436F	6D6D	616E
6420	6F6B	6179	2E0D	0A			

```
.`..D.*.......E.
.;.o...6k...c..
.....W.E...OP.
.E.1..200Command
okay...
```

Translation:

Datalink:	Dest MAC:	02608C 0AC49D	Source MAC:	AA0004 000104	Type(Length):	0800
IP:	Version:	4	IHL:	5	Type of service:	00
	Length:	003B	ID:	0B6F	FLAGS:	0
	Offset:	0	Time to Live:	60	Protocol:	06
	Checksum:	36EB	Source IP:	30.0.0.99	Dest IP:	30.0.0.1
TCP:	Source Port:	FTP(0015)	Dest Port:	1A57	Sequence:	1245BC31
	Acknowledge:	000017CF	Offset:	5	Code:	18(Push)
	Window:	1989	Checksum:	8931		

Frame 4

AA00	0400	0104	0260	8C0A	C49D	0800	4500
0028	0098	0000	FF06	7ED4	1E00	0001	1E00
0063	1A57	0015	0000	17CF	1245	BC44	5010
0400	6EAC	0000	504F	5254	2033		

```
*......`..D...E.
.(......~T.....
.c.W.....O.E.
..n,..PORT 3
```

Translation:

Datalink:	Dest MAC:	AA0004 000104	Source MAC:	02608C 0AC49D	Type(Length):	0800
IP:	Version:	4	IHL:	5	Type of service:	00
	Length:	0028	ID:	0098	FLAGS:	0
	Offset:	0	Time to Live:	255	Protocol:	06
	Checksum:	7ED4	Source IP:	30.0.0.1	Dest IP:	30.0.0.99
TCP:	Source Port:	1A57	Dest Port:	FTP(0015)	Sequence:	000017CF
	Acknowledge:	1245BC44	Offset:	5	Code:	18(Push)
	Window:	0400	Checksum:	6EAC		

Address resolution protocol

As we have discussed in Chapter 10, LAN cards send and receive frames based on their MAC addresses. They can only respond to frames with broadcast, a recognized multicast or their own unicast address in the destination field.

TCP/IP uses IP addresses that are defined by the network manager at installation time; they are associated with the network layer of the protocol stack and have no direct relation to the MAC address.

All TCP/IP communications begin with the IP address. If we wish to connect to a remote computer we must know its IP address but we do not need to know its MAC address. End-to-end communication takes place with the IP address but hop-to-hop communication uses the MAC address. For efficient network operation, the MAC layer requires the unicast MAC address of the next MAC layer in the chain of hops between source IP address and destination IP address.

Early TCP/IP systems had to have a manually configured table which related MAC and IP address so that a frame could be unicast to the correct destination. Today, the **Address Resolution Protocol** (ARP) relates IP and MAC address but only on media that support broadcasts. Each node maintains a cache, called the **ARP cache**, of IP entries against their MAC addresses. When IP is requested to send a datagram to another IP address, it first looks in the ARP cache to find the corresponding MAC address that the datalink layer should use for the datagram. If there is no entry, it then attempts to find the MAC address from the IP address, using ARP.

To do this, ARP sends an **ARP request** datagram to all LAN cards, using the MAC broadcast address (0xFFFF_FFFF_FFFF). ARP uses its own Ethernet type 0x0806 for these requests, so they are passed to the ARP software in all nodes within a broadcast area. The ARP request carries the IP address corresponding to the required MAC address. All cards on a network read this request datagram and any that discover a match between their IP address and the requested IP address reply with an ARP response. If a response is received, the answer is entered in the ARP cache for future use; if none is received within a few seconds, the request is repeated. (The ARP might have been discarded due to a transmission error or bridge congestion.) To reduce the need for ARP broadcasts, a node responding to ARP requests will itself copy the IP and MAC address mapping of the source of the request in its own ARP cache. As the two systems are likely to communicate further, this removes the need for a second ARP in the reverse direction at some later time as it already knows the MAC address for that return IP address.

The ARP cache is often kept until the equipment is reset or powered off. With some TCP/IP implementations ARP cache entries have a time-out. If the entry is not used for a period, often of 15 minutes, that entry is deleted. Other systems provide an automatic refresh timer. An ARP is performed every 15 minutes to make sure the cache is up to date. Since MAC addresses usually only change when a piece of equipment is faulty or moved this seems of more limited value.

Some products allow you to view and alter the ARP cache and to change these timer values. This can be a useful diagnostic tool. It lists which hosts a node has communicated with. Where a system has failed, a card has been changed and the ARP cache contains an outdated value, the mapping can be altered. The MAC to IP address translation can be predefined for hosts that are not able to use ARP.

Frame header	ARP/RARP message

Hardware		Protocol
HLEN	PLEN	Operation
Sender HA (octets 0–3)		
Sender HA (octets 4–5)		Sender IA (octets 0–1)
Sender IA (octets 2–3)		Target HA (octets 0–1)
Target HA (octets 2–5)		
Target IA (octets 0–3)		

Figure 11.6 ARP datagram format.

ARP datagrams are not passed through routers, as a router operates at the IP layer and will not relay MAC broadcast traffic; routers create a useful buffer between broadcast domains. This enables routers to prevent broadcast traffic from flooding all networks in a system.

ARP format

The format of the ARP datagram is shown in Figure 11.6. It is simple and was designed to be generic; it is not used only for TCP/IP or for any one particular type of network. Its only restriction is that the medium must have the ability to send broadcast frames.

ARP operates directly over datalink and therefore is only encapsulated in the datalink frame. This requires it to have its own Ethernet type field of 0x0806 so that datalink can distinguish it from other incoming frames.

The fields of the ARP datagram are as follows:

- *Hardware* This field indicates the type of network hardware this datagram was generated on. Valid types are:

Type	Description
1	Ethernet (10 Mbps)
2	Experimental Ethernet (3 Mbps)
3	Amateur radio AX.25[†]
4	Proteon ProNET Token Ring
5	Chaos

[†]It may seem surprising to find amateur radio with its own reserved allocation. Radio amateurs have experimented with TCP/IP over the low speeds and poor error performance of packet radio links. In the best traditions of the hobby, a number of modifications to improve TCP/IP performance over these links have been adopted in mainstream TCP/IP standards.

    6   IEEE 802 networks
    7   ARCNET
    8   Hyperchannel
    9   Lanstar
    10   Autonet short address
    11   LocalTalk
    12   LocalNet (IBM PCNet or Sytek Inc. LocalNet)

- *Protocol* This field indicates which protocol requested this action. The values used in this field are the same as the Ethernet type field in the Ethernet frame. This is 0x0800 for IP.

- *HLEN* This indicates the length of the hardware addresses in octets. Normally a value of 6 for IEEE LAN MAC addresses.

- *PLEN* This indicates the length of network layer addresses in octets, normally a value of 4 for IP.

- *Operation* This field has a value 1 for an ARP request or 2 for an ARP response. This field is used by RARP with 3 for a RARP request and 4 for a RARP response (RARP is covered later in this chapter).

- *Addresses* Sender hardware address (the source MAC address); source IP address; target hardware address (the destination MAC address); destination IP address.

ARP in operation

Figure 11.7 shows an example of ARP in operation. The node with IP address 128.128.0.3 and with MAC address 0x02608121343 has been requested by its IP layer to find the MAC address of the node with IP address 128.128.0.1. First, 128.128.0.3 sends a broadcast ARP request which will be received by the ARP software on all nodes in that network. 128.128.0.1 will recognize its address in the request and return an ARP response but using the MAC address of the incoming ARP request. The ARP response will be processed and quickly discarded by the LAN cards of all other nodes on the network as it is a unicast frame with the wrong destination address.

ARP requesters trust the response they get. There is normally no check that a single MAC address is responding on behalf of many IP addresses. This leaves the way open to some useful extensions to ARP, but also the way open for security abuses.

Fault management and ARP

ARP can produce some challenging faults for the network diagnostics teams. What happens when IP addresses are duplicated? How does ARP behave in a large bridged network, particularly one with remote bridges and relatively slow-speed links?

(a)

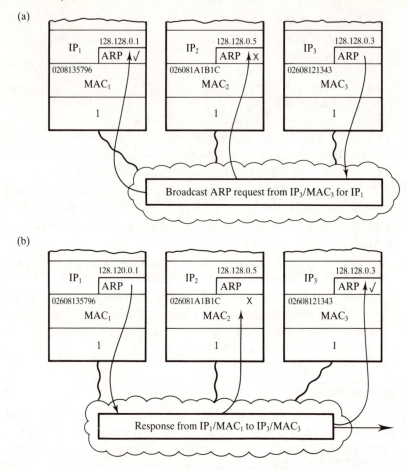

(b)

Figure 11.7 The ARP process. (a) ARP request. (b) ARP response. Note the layers which are involved in each transaction.

ARP with duplicated IP addresses

Of course, this will never happen in your network, because well-managed networks (like yours) do not have duplicated IP addresses. IP addresses must be unique, but what happens when they are not? It is useful to examine the operation of ARP when two nodes on the same bridged LAN have identical IP addresses, for example 142.1.32.99. We will refer to the two nodes as node A and node B.

Consider a scenario where two client systems connect to the same host. If they both connect to the same host, the effect they have on a host's ARP cache is the most significant issue; the resulting effect on the users of node A and node B is technically of great interest but frustrating and puzzling to the users and network troubleshooters alike!

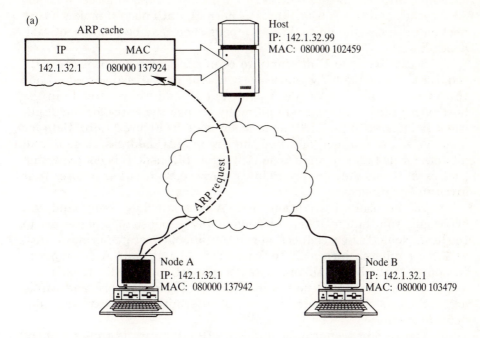

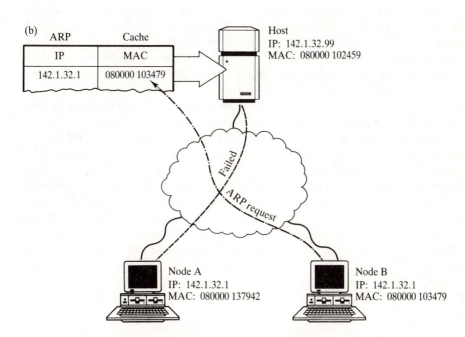

Figure 11.8 The effect of duplicate IP addresses on an ARP cache.

First, node A connects to the host and performs an ARP request to exchange MAC addresses with it (Figure 11.8a). Both ends set up their ARP caches and the session starts as normal, until node B makes a connection to that same host. What happens then may be implementation dependent.

Secondly, node B attempts to connect. It also performs an ARP request to exchange MAC addresses with the host. Because node B has the same IP address as node A, and that IP address is already in the host's ARP cache, the host will normally change the entry for the duplicated IP address to the MAC address for node B (Figure 11.8b). Data for node A's connection will now find the wrong MAC address, node B, and all data for node A will go to node B in error. But node B is not expecting that data; it matches no higher layer protocol, so it either ignores it or gives an error message.

To the user's frustration, node A is meanwhile 'hung' and will eventually time out, as it is not receiving any response to its messages to the host. Node B's new connection will continue to operate normally until at some point the increasingly frustrated user at node A attempts to reconnect to the host, causing node B's connection to fail! If these users are at widely separated points in a large bridged network and rarely access the same host, the problem will be intermittent and extremely difficult to diagnose.

The second scenario for duplicate IP addresses is where a client system, such as a PC, is given the same address as a host system. This will manifest itself as some users not being able to access the host service on a permanent or intermittent basis. Whether this problem appears consistently or intermittently depends on the architecture of the network, whether routers and bridges are involved and the different types of computers and software in use, as timing of the ARP requests and responses could affect the results.

As with the previous scenario we will refer to the computers concerned as node A, node B and the host. In this case though, node B and the host have the same IP address, and node A is different. In this scenario, when node A attempts to connect to the host and performs an ARP request to obtain the MAC address of the host, it may obtain the MAC address of node B instead, as they will both reply. Which one is accepted depends on the implementation of the protocol stack involved. If node A accepts the MAC address for node B instead of that for the host, it will fail to connect, as node B is unlikely to have the appropriate servers running on it. On another attempt it may be possible that node A gets the correct ARP from the host and hence connects. If node B is a PC, it is likely that it will be turned off when the user is not around, and therefore there will be times when this problem seems to go away. Whenever the PC is turned on the problem returns.

There is a third scenario. In this situation two host machines are given the same IP address. In this case, client machines can access dif-

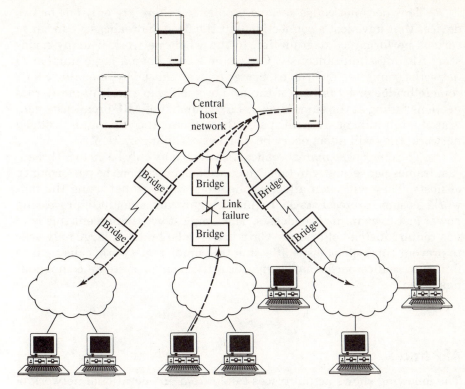

Figure 11.9 ARP on a bridged network showing the rebroadcast ARP frames for one connection.

ferent machines on different occasions and either will not be able to log in or will not be able to find the applications or data they thought they had saved. This is less likely to happen as host machines are not normally as abundant as client machines, and host addressing should be managed more carefully and be less likely to change.

With most client systems, it is quite possible for users to modify their IP addresses and cause the problems considered in these scenarios. The solution is simple. Do not allow IP addresses to be duplicated. This statement is more difficult to put into practice!

ARP after link failures

A problem can be caused by ARP when applications using a reliable service suffer a link failure. Most TCP/IP stacks will attempt to recover from the failure by retransmitting the lost datagrams a number of times and, where possible, expecting to be rerouted around the failure. Should all these attempts fail, the protocol stack will often revert to transmitting ARP broadcasts to see if the connection can be recovered from the lowest level (Figure 11.9).

This does not cause serious problems if there are only one or two devices that have lost a connection, but the flood of broadcasts can cause serious performance degradation to the whole network if many nodes start ARPing simultaneously. On systems that have a large number of networks connected by bridges, bridge failure, caused by line failure on a remote bridge or by failure of the bridge itself, can result in many connections failing at the same time. A large number of ARP broadcasts generated simultaneously will pass throughout the complete bridged network; they will affect every host on every cabling system.

The effect of so many broadcasts, which may only be 40 to 80 broadcast frames per second, can have an enormous impact on the performance of hosts. They will even affect applications that are not using the network, as some protocol stacks require a significant amount of processing power just to examine broadcasts. The simplest way to prevent this is to use routers instead of bridges. Care needs to be taken in large networks to prevent this type of issue affecting the complete network, causing it to fail or to reduce performance significantly because a single component has failed.

ARP traces

The following shows actual traces taken from an operational network of the ARP protocol. In this example we show Ethernet frames in hexadecimal without the preamble or the CRC. The table beneath the frame shown in hexadecimal gives a breakdown of the fields in the frame and their values. For a further explanation of the format of these examples see Appendix F.

In this example, we see IP node 30.0.0.1 starting a connection for the first time with IP address 30.0.0.99. Frame 1 shows the ARP broadcast from 30.0.0.1 with an ARP destination MAC set to all zeroes which is responded to in frame 2 with an ARP response with all fields complete.

Frame 1

```
FFFF   FFFF   FFFF   0260   8C0A   C49D   0806   0001        ........`..D.....
0800   0604   0001   0260   8C0A   C49D   1E00   0001        ........`..D.....
0000   0000   0000   1E00   0063   0000   0000   0000        .........c......
0000   0000   0000   0000   0000   0000                      ............
```

Datalink:	Dest MAC:	FFFFFFFFFFFF	Source MAC:	02608C 0AC49D	Type(Length):	0806
ARP:	Hardware:	0001	Protocol:	0800	HLEN:	06
	PLEN:	04	Operation:	01	(ARP request)	
	Source IP:	30.0.0.1	Source MAC:	02608C 0AC49D		
	Dest IP:	30.0.0.99	Dest MAC:	000000000000		

Frame 2

```
0260   8C0A   C49D   AA00   0400   0104   0806   0001      .`..D.*.........
0800   0604   0002   AA00   0400   0104   1E00   0063      .......*........c
0260   8C0A   C49D   1E00   0001   0000   0000   0000      .`..D...........
0000   0000   0000   0000   0000   0000                    ............
```

Datalink:	Dest MAC:	02608C 0AC49D	Source MAC:	AA0004 000104	Type(Length):	0806
ARP:	Hardware:	0001	Protocol:	0800	HLEN:	06
	PLEN:	04	Operation:	02	(ARP response)	
	Source IP:	30.0.0.99	Source MAC:	AA0004 000104		
	Dest IP:	30.0.0.1	Dest MAC:	02608C 0AC49D		

Reverse address resolution protocol

The **Reverse Address Resolution Protocol** (RARP) is intended for use with devices that cannot store their IP address, usually diskless workstations. Not surprisingly, RARP performs the reverse action to ARP: given the MAC address, what is the corresponding IP address? A requesting node supplies the MAC address in the RARP request.

RARP, like ARP, operates directly over the datalink layer and hence has an Ethernet type number of 0x8035 assigned to it so it can be distinguished from IP, ARP and any other protocols on a network. Nodes acting as RARP servers that find a match for the MAC address in their RARP tables will reply with the corresponding IP address in a RARP response. This system requires that at least one server is present and that the server has a table defining which IP addresses should be used by each MAC address.

The format of datagram is the same as ARP but in the operation field it uses 3 for a request and 4 for a response. When a RARP request is made, the originator only knows its own MAC address so that is the only field it can fill in. The response will normally have all fields filled in, defining the IP address the requester should use and often the IP and MAC address of the RARP server, although this is not necessary.

Although RARP fulfils its original intentions, it has several limitations in practice and has been largely superseded by the Boot Protocol (BOOTP). BOOTP is capable of operating through routers and provides more useful information than RARP when booting diskless workstations.

ARP and bridging

A bridge that connects the same type of cabling system together will transfer data transparently and hence gives no cause for concern. Problems occur when different types of media, such as IEEE 802.3 and

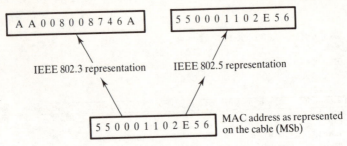

Figure 11.10 MAC addresses in different IEEE LANs.

IEEE 802.5, are bridged together. The issue is based upon the inconsistent standards of representation of MAC address for IEEE LANs (Figure 11.10).

The problem is that IEEE 802.3 (CSMA/CD) and IEEE 802.5 (Token Ring) or IS9314 (FDDI) media systems represent MAC addresses with different bit significance in each octet. The IEEE 802.1 standard which defines the address structure is the same for all, so the addresses in frames on the medium are identical, but when represented by the network hardware to the layers above they are different. This only causes problems when MAC addresses are passed between devices above the datalink layer, as with ARP. Figure 11.11 illustrates this problem. It shows a bus connected to a ring. To simplify the diagram, the MAC addresses used are only 8 bits long. In practice, they are 48 bits. 128.128.0.1 is connected to an IEEE 802.3 system and has a MAC address of 0xAA or 10101010 (in IEEE 802.3 representation). When the address is used on the 802.3 cable, the bits are swapped around by the hardware, so it appears as 01010101 or 0x55, so the lowest level hardware is looking for a bit stream that is 0x55.

The node on the ring network has a MAC address of 0x33 or 00110011, which is how it will appear on 802.5 and FDDI networks. 128.128.0.1 is about to attempt to connect to 128.128.0.3 for the first time and so will use ARP to obtain the MAC address of 128.128.0.3. 128.128.0.1 broadcasts an ARP searching for 128.128.0.3 which will be passed by the bridge to the ring. 128.128.0.3 will recognize its IP address. It replies to the ARP request with an ARP response, using the MAC address found in the hardware address field of the incoming request, giving its MAC address as 0x33 in the relevant field for its hardware address. From the ring, the response will return to a MAC address of 0xAA. 128.128.0.1 does not recognize itself as 0xAA but as 0x55, so the ARP response is ignored by the hardware in 128.128.0.1.

To get around this problem, bridges have to detect ARP frames and modify the addresses in the fields called hardware address of the request or response, so that they are appropriate for the destination network.

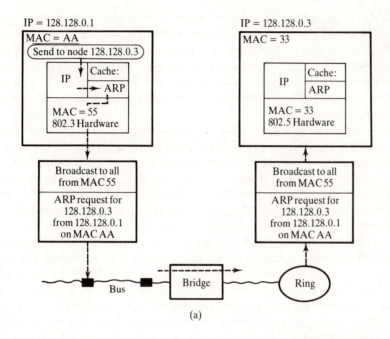

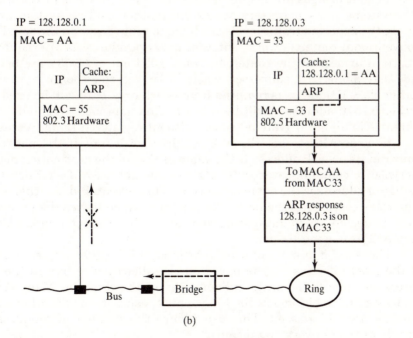

Figure 11.11   Bridging rings and buses. (a) ARP request for 128.128.0.3.
(b) ARP response to the wrong MAC.

Proxy ARP

Proxy ARP is a technique used by some IP routers. It was developed early in the life of TCP/IP as one solution to the problem of inefficient use of the IP address space. Today, with the availability of bridges and the almost universal use of subnetwork addresses, its use is limited. But proxy ARP is still supported by many routers and it can, in some smaller installations, allow routers to be used without planning a full subnetwork addressing scheme.

As a network grows, a point is reached where no more nodes can be added to the existing medium because of physical limitations. To expand the network a separate physical cabling system has to be added. In the early days of IP, before bridges and subnetwork addressing, the only way that two cabling systems could be connected was with a router with a separate network number on either port, assuming repeaters were inadequate because traffic filtering was also required. This was wasteful if only a small number of IP addresses had been used from the original range[†].

As an example, assume a company has a class B registered address 130.1.0.0. They use Ethernet and wish to connect 2048 hosts using TCP/IP. The class B address provides them with 65 534 possible node addresses on their network. As their cabling system is Ethernet, they can only have 1024 nodes on a single cabling segment before they use a bridge or router (but bridges are not yet available). Since they need to support 2048 systems, it is necessary to install another cabling system and, because the expected traffic levels are high, to route between the two. For a conventional router to work, different network addresses are required on both interfaces of the router, but only 1024 out of 65 534 are being used, leaving 64 510 addresses wasted. To get the router to work, another class B address is required from which only 1024 will be used so another 64 510 addresses will be wasted. This approach is usually unacceptable in all but private networks without registered IP addresses.

IP uses ARP to get the MAC address of a unit if the network number in its own IP address is the same as that of the destination node; otherwise it communicates with a router or gateway. To reduce the wastage of addresses the same network number is required at either side of the relay connecting the networks together, which leaves the problem of how to decide which datagrams to direct to the other cabling system. Proxy ARP is one mechanism.

There are a number of ways that proxy ARP can be implemented, but the most effective way is based on the allocation of bits in the IP address to identify separate subnetworks of the original. Many ARP broadcasts can be blocked at the relay; only broadcasts for the other subnetworks need be passed. This can reduce the number of broadcasts throughout the network significantly.

[†]The solution today is subnetwork addressing, the subject of Chapter 4.

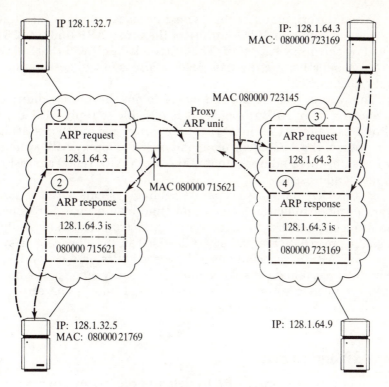

Figure 11.12   Proxy ARP.

The only devices that have to recognize which bits are used to identify separate networks are the proxy ARP units. Of course, the network
manager has to ensure that the correct address range is allocated appro-
priately. For example, the first four bits of the host part of the IP address
could be allocated to identify separate subnetworks[†]. In Figure 11.12 the
first four bits of the host part of the network address are used to define
subnetworks giving 14 usable subnetworks; subnet 0 and subnet 15
should not be used. When an ARP request is received on interface 1, the
proxy ARP relay device examines the bits in the node address to see if
those allocated to another subnetwork have been used. If so, the broadcast is relayed onto interface 2, but with the source MAC address of the
proxy ARP unit on interface 2. When a reply is received, an ARP response
is sent back to the originator on interface 1 giving the MAC address of the
proxy ARP unit on interface 1, instead of that of the true MAC address
destination node. The proxy ARP unit caches the MAC address of the
ARP reply from the source and destination nodes together with the interface they are on.

[†]While this scheme seems very like the subnetwork addressing scheme discussed fully
in Chapter 4, there is no subnetwork mask and the end nodes are not aware of any address
structuring.

When the originator sends its next datagram on interface 1, it will contain the destination MAC address of the proxy ARP unit, so it will be accepted by the proxy ARP unit. The proxy ARP unit will then relay it to interface 2, substituting the true MAC address of the destination node from its ARP cache.

This works because the end nodes do not check the validity of the MAC address in an ARP response. It is possible to reply with any valid MAC address and act as a surrogate or proxy for another station. An examination of the ARP cache of an end node in a proxy ARP system will show the same MAC address (that of the proxy ARP relay) against many different IP addresses.

Proxy ARP allows two separate cabling systems with the same IP network number to be connected other than by a bridge. It regenerates frames from one network to another and filters traffic, as frames only pass through the proxy ARP unit if they are destined for the other cabling system.

Proxy ARP is especially useful if some nodes on a network cannot support Internet standard subnetting. The disadvantage is the management effort needed to ensure that the subnet addressing structure is enforced on the separate cabling systems.

Proxy ARP and routers

Some routers operate proxy ARP by default even if they are not aware of a subnetting scheme described above. If such a router intercepts an ARP request and recognizes that the destination requested is on a different network or subnetwork, it will reply to the ARP giving its own MAC address. It will then use its normal routing mechanisms to relay datagrams to that destination IP address.

This can only happen when a misconfigured workstation believes it is on the same network as another station, but the router sees the network addressing structure differently. In other words, there is an addressing fault as two devices have different views of the IP addressing scheme. The most likely cause is that the subnetwork masks are different in the end station and in the router. The router is aware of a network structure which is not apparent to the end system.

Internet subnets

Subnetting or subnetwork addressing today provides the standard mechanism for locally managing IP addresses efficiently. The structure of subnetworks is not understood from outside an autonomous system, where the whole address space appears as one IAB-defined class A, B, or C network.

The topic of subnetwork addressing, including its technical aspects, was fully explored in Chapter 4.

Internet control message protocol

Even though IP is a datagram service and there is no guarantee of information delivery, the **Internet Control Message Protocol** (ICMP), is provided within IP which generates error messages to help the IP layer give a better 'best efforts delivery service'. For the network manager, ICMP provides some useful diagnostics about network operation.

RFCs for IP say that ICMP must be supported, but the level of support varies, often limited to not generating an error when an ICMP datagram is received. Not all products support ICMP to the level required of a sophisticated TCP/IP implementation. ICMP requests may not be fully acted upon.

ICMP uses IP datagrams to carry its messages back and forth between relevant nodes. ICMP error messages are generated by a node recognizing there is a transmission problem and they are sent back to the originating address of the datagram that caused the problem. The originating address will usually be a host or end system. The generator of ICMP could be the ultimate destination node or an intermediate router. Routers and hosts can both be the source of ICMP datagrams.

Figure 11.13 shows the basic format of the ICMP message encapsulated in an IP datagram and the different messages possible. ICMP has its own IP protocol number (1) so the IP layer knows when it receives

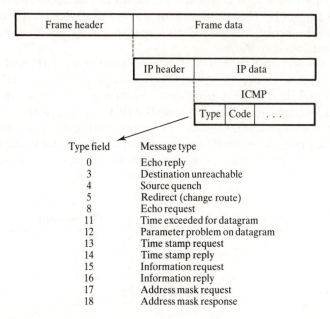

Type field	Message type
0	Echo reply
3	Destination unreachable
4	Source quench
5	Redirect (change route)
8	Echo request
11	Time exceeded for datagram
12	Parameter problem on datagram
13	Time stamp request
14	Time stamp reply
15	Information request
16	Information reply
17	Address mask request
18	Address mask response

Figure 11.13   ICMP encapsulated in IP and its type values.

them. Even though ICMP uses the IP layer, it is considered as being wholly within IP, because it does not necessarily provide any service to the layers above.

Since IP messages are carried in IP they may be discarded and fail to arrive for the same reasons as any IP datagram. It is worth noting that to maintain stability, ICMP messages are not generated about ICMP messages that themselves cause errors. Also, they are not generated about problems with IP fragments, unless it is the first one (fragment offset = 0).

The basic format of an ICMP datagram is shown in Figure 11.14, but the fields vary slightly depending on the type being used. The type field indicates the relevant ICMP message and the code field is used to provide more detailed information. The checksum, if used, is required because IP does not protect its data with a checksum. When operating over a physical network which has a frame check sequence the ICMP checksum may be 0, meaning 'not calculated'.

ICMP types 0 and 8 – echo

The most common ICMP messages when used for diagnostic purposes are type 0 and type 8. These are generated by the utility program widely known as 'ping'. Ping sends ICMP type 8 datagrams to a node and expects an ICMP type 0 reply, returning the data sent in the request (Figure 11.15).

The identifier and sequence numbers are used to identify these datagrams uniquely. If data is sent in the optional data field it must be returned in the reply. Varying data sizes on a ping are used to test for data transmission problems.

Earlier we said that ICMP is contained within IP and does not provide a service to layers above. How can ping generate ICMP echo requests if ICMP does not provide a service to the application ping? A ping implementation does not use ICMP to generate the request; it merely mimics what ICMP would do as a program that operates over the IP layer. Ping generates an IP datagram with a data field that equates to an ICMP echo request, that is, with a protocol number of 1 and the first

Type	Code	Checksum
Context specific		
Context specific		
Context specific		

Figure 11.14 Basic ICMP header.

Type	Code	Checksum
Identifier		Sequence number
Optional data		
...		

Figure 11.15   ICMP echo datagram format.

octet of data being 8, an ICMP type of echo request. It then adds the rest of the fields including the data pattern that it expects to be echoed.

ICMP type 3 – destination unreachable

If a router is unable to deliver a datagram, it can return the destination unreachable ICMP datagram to indicate why. The code field is used to identify the cause of failure. The Internet header plus 64 bits of the datagram prefix are used to identify uniquely the datagram which caused the problem (Figure 11.16).

The values provided in the code field help pinpoint the reason the datagram failed to arrive at its destination. The circumstances under which they will occur need some clarification:

● *Network unreachable*   The network specified in the IP address cannot be found. The IP address used should be checked or there is a fault in the routing tables of the intervening routers.

Type	Code	Checksum
Unused (must be 0)		
Internet header + 64 bits of datagram prefix		
...		

Code Value	Meaning
0	Network unreachable
1	Host unreachable
2	Protocol unreachable
3	Port unreachable
4	Fragmentation needed and the do not fragment bit set
5	Source route failed

Figure 11.16   Code values for destination unreachable.

This error message is only generated by a router. The point at which the fault occurred can be ascertained from the source address in the IP header that carried the ICMP message. This is the router that identified the fault.

- *Host unreachable* Unlike network unreachable, the datagram which caused the problem reached a router that is directly connected to the destination network, but, when the router tried to deliver the datagram, it could not communicate with the host. Probably the ARP failed on the first datagram. The host is down, or otherwise unavailable, perhaps because that IP address does not exist.

  This error message is only generated by a router. The point at which the fault occurred can again be ascertained from the source address in the IP header that carried the ICMP message. This is the router that identified the fault.

- *Protocol unreachable* In this case, the datagram reached the destination host, but the particular protocol carried in the IP datagram was not available. This would be rare, but is possible if the configuration of the remote machine is incorrect.

  The protocols normally carried by IP are mainly UDP, TCP, EGP or OSPF (see Figure 11.3 for more details). If one of these well-used protocols produces a protocol unreachable message for a particular host computer, the protocols which are operational should be checked. On UNIX systems, those protocols to be made operational on system startup are normally defined in a configuration file called *protocols*. This should be checked.

- *Port unreachable* This message from a host indicates that the particular application layer service on the remote host to which a connection is being established is not available. On hosts, individual application services are enabled and disabled at startup through a configuration file, usually called *inetd.conf*. This file should be checked to see if the service is available. Even if the name is present, be aware that a # in the left margin usually comments out the line and prevents that application from being automatically started.

- *Fragmentation needed and the do not fragment bit set* This message would normally come from a router, indicating that it needs to fragment the datagram, but is instructed not to by the do not fragment (DF) bit in the flags field of the IP header.

  This fault should be uncommon. DF is normally only used on diskless workstations booting via TFTP. TFTP only has 512 octets of user data. Why has this bit been set and why does the datagram need to be fragmented? Are the MTU's set correctly? All networks are supposed to be able to transport 576 octet datagrams without fragmentation.

If there are no faults with the network configuration and if these datagrams do have to pass across a router, then it cannot be this one!

- *Source route failed* The management options in IP allow an IP datagram to carry a source route definition that identifies the complete path, based on the router addresses the IP datagram should take. This error message indicates that the datagram referred to failed to complete the route.

  The point of failure will be the router that generated the ICMP message, again identified by the source IP address in the ICMP IP header. What was the next hop in the list of routers requested in the source route option? For some reason this router was not available from the router that detected the fault.

ICMP type 4, code 0 – source quench

The format of the source quench datagram is the same as that for destination unreachable shown in Figure 11.16 but with a type of 4 and a code of 0. One of the most useful ICMP diagnostic messages, source quench gives a router or a host the ability to request that a source of datagrams slows down. While an imperfect form of flow control, it is the only form that can limit congestion within an IP internetwork, for IP is a connectionless system. We believe that larger router networks will not be stable unless source quench is generally available.

Source quench will occur if a node is running low on buffer resources and is unable to process datagrams quickly enough. A good example is a router which is having difficulty passing datagrams from one network to another; it can use source quench to reduce the rate of datagrams sent to it and hence prevent data loss. Equally, the host can interpret source quench as: 'if you do not slow down, your datagrams will be discarded'.

RFC 1009 states that all routers must include code for generating source quench each time they discard a datagram and preferably before. But an issue with source quench is that not all host implementations will reduce traffic when seeing source quench. The standards do not indicate how much to slow down. If the source does not slow down enough, another datagram will be lost and the request repeated. Once a node stops receiving source quench datagrams, it is allowed to increase its rate of transmission gradually.

Even if this type of ICMP datagram is not obeyed by a host system, its regular presence in an operational network is an indication that there is a resource problem at the unit which originated the source quench request. If it is occurring at an increasing frequency in a growing network, remedial action is required to remove the bottleneck before end user performance suffers.

(a)

Type	Code	Checksum
Internet address of a more suitable router		
Internet header + 64 bits of datagram prefix		
...		

(b) *Code Value*   *Meaning*

    0   Redirect datagrams to go to that network
    1   Redirect datagrams to reach that host
    2   Redirect datagrams for that network with that TOS
    3   Redirect datagrams for that host with that TOS

Figure 11.17   (a) Format of the route change request message. (b) Code values used by route change request.

ICMP type 5 – route change request

The route change request is a function used only by routers. A router that knows that it is not the optimum router for a particular destination uses the relevant field of a route change request (Figure 11.17) to suggest a more suitable router to the originator, the source IP address of a datagram.

To ensure continuity of the data flow, the router also sends the datagram which caused the error message directly to the router that it believes has access to the better route.

Some host implementations of TCP/IP ignore the redirect messages. Because the router relays them to the start of the better path, overall the datagrams between this source and destination will follow a near optimum route, but the number of datagrams transmitted on the first cable system will double for this conversation, reducing throughput and increasing traffic.

The regular presence of ICMP route change request messages indicates that some optimization may be required on a system, or it could be that software needs upgrading. It could also be that the default gateway address configured into certain host systems is not targeting the most appropriate router (see Chapter 16).

ICMP type 11 – time exceeded for datagram

The format of this message is the same as destination unreachable. The time exceeded for datagram message is sent in one of two situations.

From routers, it is used to indicate that the Time To Live (TTL) value in the IP header has been decremented to 0. In this case it will have a code value of 0, so the datagram has been discarded before reaching its

Type	Code	Checksum
Pointer	Unused (must be 0)	
Internet header + 64 bits of datagram prefix		
...		

Figure 11.18   Format of ICMP parameter problem message.

destination. This would most probably indicate that the original setting of TTL is not suitable for the number of routing hops this datagram needs to take or that there has been a failure in the network which is causing inordinate length routes to be used. Whichever it happens to be, it should be investigated to find out what is causing this message.

From an end node, the other use of this message, with a code value of 1, is to indicate that an attempt to recreate the original datagram by the reassembly of fragments failed. Time-out on reassembly should not be regarded as too serious unless it happens frequently, in which case investigation is needed to detect what is happening to the fragments: what routers and datalinks are involved? Are fragments delayed beyond the 30 second reassembly timer or are they corrupted? Is an underpowered bridge discarding them?

ICMP type 12 – parameter problem message

This message probably indicates that a wrong argument has been used with an option field in the IP header, but more seriously it could refer to an error in the implementation of IP. It indicates that there is a value in the header that cannot be understood. This message is not sent unless the datagram has been discarded. The pointer field indicates the position of the octet position of the suspect field, that is, 1 refers to the TOS field and 20 refers to the first option octet in the IP header (Figure 11.18).

ICMP types 13 and 14 – time stamp request and reply

This message is used to obtain the time from the clock in a distant machine. The requester sends message type 13 and the destination replies with message type 14. The originate time stamp is filled in immediately before the datagram is sent, the receive time stamp immediately on receipt of the request and the transmit time stamp immediately before the reply is sent back to the originator (Figure 11.19).

This message can be used to gather performance statistics of connections to a host or to synchronize clocks in hosts; it is rarely used today. Later RFCs suggest that ICMP should be used primarily to report network problems or routing changes and for ping.

Type	Code	Checksum
Identifier		Sequence
Originate time stamp		
Receive time stamp		
Transmit time stamp		

Figure 11.19 Format of time stamp request/reply.

ICMP types 15 and 16 – information request

This message is used to obtain the network number the requesting host is on if it is not known. The addresses used in the IP header will have a value of 0, often referred to as 'this network', which will be filled in correctly by the destination and returned (Figure 11.20).

This mechanism can be used with dial-in systems that use SLIP as a method of allocating appropriate network addresses for each end of the link.

ICMP types 17 and 18 – address mask request

This function can be used in conjunction with subnet addressing to allow a node to discover the subnet mask of the network it is connected to. The node can either send the request to a known address, probably a router, or broadcast the request to the network. The reply will be directed back, if the node knows its address, or broadcast if not.

Type	Code	Checksum
Identifier		Sequence

Figure 11.20 Format of ICMP information request message.

Type	Code	Checksum
Identifier		Sequence
Address mask		

Figure 11.21 Address mask request.

The subnet mask is entered in the address mask field of the reply (Figure 11.21).

Management issues

In descriptions of TCP/IP, the power of ICMP is often ignored as it does not provide a direct service to the end user or the manager of a system. But ICMP messages provide an invaluable source of error reporting, performance information and diagnostic loopback tests for network planners and maintainers alike.

Unfortunately, the detail of the messages is not generally recorded in the equipment that receives them. Although these ICMP messages are sent across the network, they are rarely passed on to the system user who will be unaware that an ICMP message has been received. Most systems keep **statistics counters** of the number and types of each ICMP message received, but the source address and the other details of the IP header are not recorded. Loss of the source address reduces the value of the statistics considerably. These statistics are retrieved either by a console command (netstat -s in UNIX systems) or across the network by SNMP.

Some ICMP messages provide supplementary information in their code field that indicates in significant detail the reason a datagram failed to reach its destination. To an engineer analysing problems on a complex network, ICMP messages, once understood, will often explain the problem completely. In light of this, it is well worth understanding the use of ICMP messages. They can save hours searching for a solution to an obscure (or not so obscure!) problem, as ICMP can narrow down the search by pointing accurately to where to start.

Some TCP/IP applications allow ICMP messages to be viewed by operating in 'debug' mode. But by far the best way of reliably gathering this information is with a **network analyser**. This is an extremely useful tool for the maintainer of a larger network and while the more sophisticated ones are high cost, it may repay the investment quickly once the organization begins to depend on the network resource. Unfortunately, a network analyser cannot be used after the event or remotely. It must be attached to a point on the network where the ICMP message is passing. Infrequent but important events will require the dedication of an expensive unit permanently.

ICMP errors also raise organizational issues. Where data flows across organizational boundaries, an ICMP message may be generated by a piece of equipment under one management control, directed at an end system under a second management control and report a problem about resource availability in a third management area. It may be monitored on its path by any number of managements in between. Once management is aware of this it can set up the necessary procedures to resolve the problem. That is all part of the challenge of running a large inter-network.

ICMP traces

The following is a protocol trace of ping, the ICMP echo. In this example we show Ethernet frames in hexadecimal without the preamble or the CRC. The table beneath the frame gives a breakdown of the fields in the frame and their values. For a further explanation of the format of these examples see Appendix F.

This example shows IP node 30.0.0.1 pinging IP node 30.0.0.99. In this implementation of ping the data transmitted is an incremental count so is different in each frame sent.

Frame 1

```
AA00   0400   0104   0260   8C0A   C49D   0800   4500      *......`..D...E.
005C   0047   0000   FF01   7EF6   1E00   0001   1E00      .\.G....~v......
0063   0800   D7DE   0000   0001   0101   0101   0101      .c..W^.........
0101   0101   0101   0101   0101   0101   0101   0101      ...............
0101   0101   0101   0101   0101   0101   0101   0101      ...............
0101   0101   0101   0101   0101   0101   0101   0101      ...............
0101   0101   0101   0101   0101                           .........
```

Datalink:	Dest MAC:	AA0004 000104	Source MAC:	02608C 0AC49D	Type(Length):	0800
IP:	Version:	4	IHL:	5	Type of service:	00
	Length:	005C	ID:	0047	FLAGS:	0
	Offset:	00	Time to live:	FF	Protocol:	01
	Checksum:	7EF6	Source IP:	30.0.0.1	Dest IP:	30.0.0.99
ICMP:	Type:	08	Code:	0	Checksum:	D7DE
	Identifier:	0000	Sequence:	0001	Data:	0101......

Frame 2

```
0260   8C0A   C49D   AA00   0400   0104   0800   4500      .`..D.*.......E.
005C   0C00   0000   3C01   363E   1E00   0063   1E00      .\.....6...c..
0001   0000   DFDE   0000   0001   0101   0101   0101      ...._^.........
0101   0101   0101   0101   0101   0101   0101   0101      ...............
0101   0101   0101   0101   0101   0101   0101   0101      ...............
0101   0101   0101   0101   0101   0101   0101   0101      ...............
0101   0101   0101   0101   0101                           .........
```

Datalink:	Dest MAC:	02608C 0AC49D	Source MAC:	AA0004 000104	Type(Length):	0800
IP:	Version:	4	IHL:	5	Type of service:	00
	Length:	005C	ID:	0C00	FLAGS:	0
	Offset:	00	Time to live:	3C	Protocol:	01
	Checksum:	363E	Source IP:	30.0.0.1	Dest IP:	30.0.0.99
ICMP:	Type:	00	Code:	0	Checksum:	DFDE
	Identifier:	0000	Sequence:	0001	Data:	0101......

Frame 3

```
AA00  0400  0104  0260  8C0A  C49D  0800  4500    *......`..D...E.
005C  0048  0000  FF01  7EF5  1E00  0001  1E00    .\.H....~u......
0063  0800  B7BD  0000  0002  0202  0202  0202    .c..7=..........
0202  0202  0202  0202  0202  0202  0202  0202    ................
0202  0202  0202  0202  0202  0202  0202  0202    ................
0202  0202  0202  0202  0202  0202  0202  0202    ................
0202  0202  0202  0202  0202                       .........
```

Datalink:	Dest MAC:	AA0004 000104	Source MAC:	02608C 0AC49D	Type(Length):	0800
IP:	Version:	4	IHL:	5	Type of service:	00
	Length:	005C	ID:	0048	FLAGS:	0
	Offset:	00	Time to live:	FF	Protocol:	01
	Checksum:	7EF5	Source IP:	30.0.0.1	Dest IP:	30.0.0.99
ICMP:	Type:	08	Code:	0	Checksum:	B7BD
	Identifier:	0000	Sequence:	0002	Data:	0202......

Frame 4

```
0260  8C0A  C49D  AA00  0400  0104  0800  4500    .`..D.*.......E.
005C  0C01  0000  3C01  363D  1E00  0063  1E00    .\.....6=...c..
0001  0000  BFBD  0000  0002  0202  0202  0202    ....?=..........
0202  0202  0202  0202  0202  0202  0202  0202    ................
0202  0202  0202  0202  0202  0202  0202  0202    ................
0202  0202  0202  0202  0202  0202  0202  0202    ................
0202  0202  0202  0202  0202                       .........
```

Datalink:	Dest MAC:	02608C 0AC49D	Source MAC:	AA0004 000104	Type(Length):	0800
IP:	Version:	4	IHL:	5	Type of service:	00
	Length:	005C	ID:	0C01	FLAGS:	0
	Offset:	00	Time to live:	3C	Protocol:	01
	Checksum:	363D	Source IP:	30.0.0.1	Dest IP:	30.0.0.99
ICMP:	Type:	0	Code:	0	Checksum:	BFBD
	Identifier:	0000	Sequence:	0002	Data:	0202......

Trailer encapsulation

Some systems can be configured to allow Ethernet to carry IP and TCP
data as **trailer encapsulation**. This mechanism was designed for
4.2BSD UNIX systems as a method of improving performance. Trailer
encapsulation allowed the data to come before the headers in the datagrams. This mapped the data structures in UNIX memory that represented the data and so made it easier to manipulate the datagrams once
they were loaded into receiving memory. This is because it is easier and
more efficient in software to append headers to the end of data using
pointer logic than to insert headers in front of the data which requires
repeated buffer-to-buffer copying. This system has the opposite effect to
that intended on a host which does not have the same architecture as the

Format

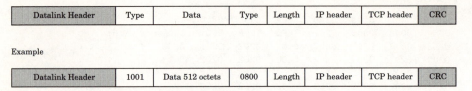

Example

Figure 11.22   Trailer encapsulation method.

original UNIX 4.2BSD hosts; for example it may have different ways of storing numbers in memory. The performance of such a host will degrade when using trailer encapsulation.

Trailer encapsulation has two Ethernet type values allocated to it, 0x1001 and 0x1002. With trailer encapsulation the data is sent in 512 byte blocks. An Ethernet type of 0x1001 identifies one 512 byte block and 1002 identifies two 512 byte blocks. The format is shown in Figure 11.22.

For two nodes to communicate using trailer encapsulation they must both support it. This is normally activated on each network interface through use of the command that initializes that interface, such as *ifconfig* in UNIX.

Relevant RFCs

760	Internet Protocol (IP)
777	Internet Control Message Protocol (ICMP) [1]
781	A specification for the Internet Protocol IP time stamp option
791	Internet Protocol (IP)
777	Internet Control Message Protocol (ICMP) [2]
796	Address Resolution Protocol
815	IP datagram reassembly algorithms
893	Trailer encapsulation
894	A standard for the transmission of IP datagrams over Ethernet networks
903	A Reverse Address Resolution Protocol
948	Two methods for the transmission of IP datagrams over IEEE 802 networks
1025	TCP and IP back off
1063	IP MTU discovery options
1071	Computing the Internet checksum
1141	Incremental updating of the Internet checksum
1154	Encoding header field for Internet messages

Summary

In this chapter, we have explored the facilities provided by IP, ARP, RARP and ICMP, all of which provide the ability to transport datagrams through a network and to report on their progress.

IP is the core protocol that allows TCP/IP systems to operate efficiently in local and wide area environments. IP itself is a datagram protocol; it is unreliable and no reliability is added at this level.

ICMP is provided to improve the probability that datagrams reach their destinations reliably by reducing the rate of discard through source quench and by changing routes dynamically if necessary through route change requests. As it is not connection oriented, IP can easily redirect individual or whole groups of datagrams dynamically when network link failures or performance changes within the system require it, always assuming there are redundant paths. These changes are carried out in a manner that is transparent to higher layer protocols and more importantly, the user.

Through IP and its associated protocols, an interface is provided for higher layer protocols that is consistent, irrespective of the type of medium that is used below, be it a low-speed serial link or high-speed LAN. The only feature IP cannot hide is the performance of the underlying system; throughput will vary and therefore it cannot provide total transparency for the user application. It is up to the network manager to ensure that the facilities available to IP allow it to meet the application performance expectations of the user.

There is little to configure within IP, mainly the IP address itself and possibly a subnet mask or changes to the MTU. ICMP provides an invaluable source of diagnostic information to allow the network developer to plan network extensions and the maintainer to resolve the most complex problems.

12

Transport layer protocols

IP provides a transparent interface to media and an addressing mechanism to reach other nodes. These services need to be enhanced to enable datagrams to be directed to the appropriate application layer services and to provide reliable stream services for those applications that need it. The services are provided at this layer by the transport protocols, the User Datagram Protocol (UDP) and the Transmission Control Protocol (TCP).

In this chapter we will cover:

- The services provided by UDP
- The services provided by TCP
- How reliability is achieved
- Ports
- Sockets
- The relevant configuration options

So far we have considered the frames of the datalink layer and the datagrams of the IP layer. The IP data is encapsulated by the IP datagram, which is in turn encapsulated by the frame. At the transport layer, there are two separate options, UDP and TCP (Figure 12.1). Depending on what type of service is required by the user's application, one of these protocols is carried in the data field of the IP datagram.

Once information has been transferred to the correct machine by IP, it then has to be passed to the relevant application-level service on that machine. Multiplexing and demultiplexing data from many applications to and from the IP layer and directing data to the correct application is one of the responsibilities of the transport layer. Providing an error-free and flow-controlled (connection-oriented) datastream service or merely passing on the connectionless services of IP to the correct application are also dealt with at this layer.

The **User Datagram Protocol** (UDP) provides a connectionless unreliable service. It allows data to be transmitted to a machine or group of machines without the need to establish a connection. Single datagrams are sent to a remote node without any requirement for responses to indicate that the datagram has arrived. In certain environments this is the most efficient way to operate. Application services such as TFTP and NFS use this mode of transport. Where broadcast is required it may be the only option available.

The **Transmission Control Protocol** (TCP) provides a connection-oriented service. A connection is like a data pipe that runs between just two points. There is no broadcast or multicast facility with TCP. TCP has all the features necessary to provide a reliable service between two computers. In achieving reliability, it adds a significant amount of overhead to manage acknowledgements, flow control, timers and connection management facilities. It has more overhead than UDP in terms of both the processing power required and the size of the network headers it uses. Applications that require the services are Telnet and FTP.

Ports

Both UDP and TCP use port addressing to deliver information to the relevant application layer services. A port is a 16-bit address of which a number of well-known ports have been defined within a range of 0 to 255 (Figure 12.2). In other words, port numbers have been allocated for the most common application layer services, such as Telnet and FTP. If application developers create a program to work over UDP or TCP, they have to define which port they wish to use; to ensure that this number is unique on a particular machine it should at least be a value outside the reserved range of well-known ports.

There is a dynamic alternative to this fixed binding of ports. NFS uses a service known as the **portmapper**, which allows new ports to be

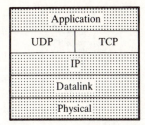

Figure 12.1 UDP and TCP.

defined and registered dynamically or the port used by a particular service to be discovered on request. We discuss the portmapper fully in Chapter 15.

For a full range of the well-known ports, see Appendix G.

Sockets

The term **socket** is frequently used in conjunction with TCP/IP. It is a fairly simple but important concept. The socket is a concatenation of the IP address and the port number. As the IP address, is, in principle unique to a node, assuming all nodes use registered IP addresses, and the port is unique on a node, the socket gives a unique identification of an application layer service. Because the socket reference is unique, both UDP and TCP include the IP address and port number in their checksum calculation. This is to ensure that a datagram arriving at the wrong host will not be accepted by the transport layer of that host even though that port, if it is well known, is likely to exist[†].

Most application layer services allow multiple sessions and thus need to be able to differentiate between these sessions to ensure that data is sent back to the appropriate computer. For example, a number of people are likely to be connected to the same host using Telnet (port 23), so all of them would be using the same Telnet port for access. One way to differentiate between different sessions might be to consider which IP address the datagrams came from, but it is possible that two users from the same host might be connected to one application. In this case, it would be extremely difficult to tell them apart.

To solve this problem, well-known port numbers are only used by server application layer services. Client programs select a unique port number that has not already been used on their machine. In this way, even if two sessions are set up to the same server host from the one client

---

[†]It is conceivable that an IP header could have its IP address corrupted and might therefore arrive at the wrong machine. If the IP checksum is ignored it will be passed to the transport layer where the port will be examined.

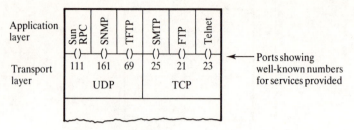

Figure 12.2   Ports used with UDP and TCP.

host, it is easy to use the source socket to differentiate between the two sessions, as they will always be unique. Application services transmit back to the source socket and this is one reason why both the source IP address and the source port are included in all communications between two machines.

A few services that operate on a peer-to-peer basis use the same port number for transmission and reception. These tend to be routing and management functions that have no need to differentiate between ports when returning messages.

User datagram protocol

UDP adds little to the underlying datagram service of IP, other than dealing with the problem of passing data to the correct application layer service. It does this by the source and destination port fields in its header. The block of data which UDP passes to IP, consisting of the UDP header and application layer data, is also referred to as a datagram. Figure 12.3 shows the fields added by UDP. They are:

- *Source port*   The port number of the application layer service the datagram came from.
- *Destination port*   The port number of the application layer service the datagram is intended for.
- *Length*   The length of the UDP datagram.
- *Checksum*   A checksum to protect the data carried by UDP.

0	16	31
Source port	Destination port	
Length	UDP checksum	
Data		

Figure 12.3   UDP header fields.

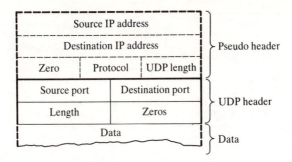

Figure 12.4 The UDP checksum is based on the pseudo header as well as the UDP header.

The checksum is fairly basic. It is calculated from the 16-bit 1s complement of the 1s complement sum of all 16-bit words in the header and user data, like IP. What is unusual about this checksum is that not only does it consider the UDP fields, but it also includes what is referred to as a **pseudo header** based upon certain fields from the IP layer, to ensure that the calculation considers the socket and not just the port (Figure 12.4).

Some products allow the maximum size of a UDP datagram to be configured. This would be necessary if some component of the system were unable to receive large datagrams, but would be unusual. Reducing the **Maximum Datagram Size** (MDS) reduces the amount of memory required by UDP from the host but also reduces the performance of services using UDP. It is unusual to need to change this from default values.

Transmission control protocol

TCP adds reliability to IP and, like UDP, also provides application layer addressing through the use of ports. TCP is a connection-oriented protocol; not only is it reliable, but before transmission can commence from one machine to another, a connection must be opened. When transmission finishes, the connection is closed.

The block of data which TCP passes to IP, consisting of the TCP header and application layer data, is usually called a **segment**.

Adding reliability requires a number of facilities:

- error detection and correction
- flow control
- resequencing
- removing duplicate segments

Error detection and correction deals with the possibility of segments being corrupted by the medium or lower layers of software. Flow control

Source port			Destination port	
Sequence number				
Acknowledgement number				
Data offset	Reserved	Code	Window	
Checksum			Urgent pointer	
Options				Padding
Data				
⋮				

Figure 12.5   TCP header.

is used to prevent a transmitter over-running a receiver owing to resource limitations. Resequencing is required because the underlying IP layer can deliver datagrams, carrying TCP segments, in any order; this happens when successive datagrams use different routes. Duplicate segments can occur because of the error-recovery mechanisms used by TCP.

TCP adds all these facilities by:

- using sequence numbers to identify data;
- positive acknowledgements of data received in the correct sequence;
- retransmission of segments which have not been acknowledged within a (variable) time limit.

The exact mechanisms will be discussed in detail below.

The TCP header

To provide the functions outlined above, the TCP header (Figure 12.5) is a lot more complex, with more fields than UDP. Like UDP, and for the same reasons, the header includes the source and destination ports to identify the application. Most of the remaining fields add reliability and deal with connection control:

- *Sequence number – 32 bits* With most protocols that use sequence numbers for error control, the sequence numbers count segments[†] as they are transmitted and received. But with TCP, the sequence numbers count *octets* within the transmission stream. The sequence number in the header of a segment identifies the position in the overall data stream of the first data octet in that segment.

[†]Segment is a TCP term for the unit of tranmission at this transport layer. The equivalent term in other protocols is often 'packet' or 'frame'.

On connection setup, new sequence numbers are agreed by both nodes and the connection starts. For system integrity after a machine crash, new sequence numbers do not start at zero.

If IP never delivered datagrams in a different order from that in which they were transmitted, data would always arrive in sequence and sequence numbers would increase smoothly. The sequence number allows TCP to slot a segment into the correct position in the data stream, even if IP delivers data out of order.

The sequence number is 32 bits, so that even on the fastest links the time taken for the same value of the counter to be valid again is very long[†]. This means that any segment received with the same sequence number as one already acknowledged can only be a duplicate, and due to the error correction process. Duplicates are allowed and are discarded without any action.

- *Acknowledgement number – 32 bits* The acknowledgement number acknowledges correct receipt of all octets up to the acknowledgement number −1. When a data sender receives a new value, it can dispose of data which was held for possible re-transmission. The acknowledgement number is only valid if the ACK flag is set.

  Acknowledgement numbers are responses to the correct receipt of sequence numbers and in-sequence data from the remote end. An acknowledgement number contains the (sequence) number of the next octet in its received data stream that the sender will pass to its application (with the octet 'zero' numbered with the sequence numbers which were exchanged at connection setup). Thus, the acknowledgement number is one greater than the octet number of the last in-sequence octet received. It is therefore the same as the sequence number that will be in the next segment of immediately useful data.

  In TCP, it is possible to have sent a number of segments that have been received correctly but have not been acknowledged, because the critical segment, which is the next in sequence, has failed to arrive. Either it is delayed, because it was routed via a slow path, or it was discarded by IP. The acknowledgement number cannot advance until this missing piece of the jigsaw is provided through retransmission on the retransmission timer. This is discussed in the section on error correction and retransmission time-out later in this chapter.

- *Data offset* This measures the offset to the start of the application data field in 32 bit words. The normal value is 5 (20 octet header) when no options are used.

[†]For 2Mbps continuous transmission, it takes 9.5 hours to transmit 2^{32} octets!

- *Flags* The flags are used to indicate the validity of other fields and for connection control. There are six separate flags:

  - *URG* This indicates that the urgent pointer field is valid. This field points to an octet in the data field which is the end of urgent data. Urgent data is not considered as part of the normal data stream and should be processed before any other data. This operation is used in instances where a message has to be passed across the network to the application, even if some mechanism is preventing normal data from doing so. It can be used to interrupt programs.

  - *ACK* This flag indicates that the acknowledge field is valid, which is on most segments. The acknowledge field is normally only invalid on connection setup, before each node has been able to determine which sequence and acknowledge values to use. The value in the acknowledge field may not have changed between segments, so although the field is valid it may not acknowledge new data.

  - *PSH* The push flag causes the remote TCP layer to pass this segment immediately to the application layer. TCP would normally hold on to the data from incoming segments and pass them to the application layer in larger buffers to reduce processing overheads, but in some situations, such as character-by-character terminal operation, this must not happen, even if only one octet of data has been received.

  - *RST* The reset flag is used when all else fails. It indicates that an error has occurred and the connection should be forcibly closed (or, if sent as a reply to a connection open request, that the request is being rejected).

  - *SYN* The synchronize flag is used at the beginning of connection setup between two nodes. At this stage neither end knows what acknowledge number to use. A connection setup consists of a two-way exchange of segments with the SYN flag set, each of which is acknowledged in a segment with the ACK flag set. Data transfer can then commence. This is covered in more detail later in this chapter.

  - *FIN* The FIN flag is used to terminate connections. When one end of a connection has no more data to send, it sends a segment with the FIN flag set. When both ends of a connection have sent the FIN flag, the connection is closed.

- *Window – 16 bit* The window advertises the amount of buffer space this node has allocated to this connection. The other node must not send more unacknowledged data than the buffer space indicated.

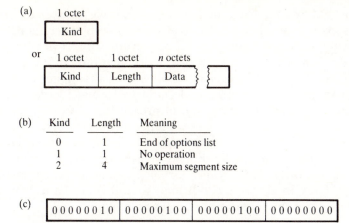

Figure 12.6 (a) Options format. (b) Options. (c) Example.

- *Checksum – 16 bit* The TCP checksum is a basic check on the header and data. It is calculated in the same fashion as that in UDP, from the 16-bit 1s complement of the 1s complement sum of all 16-bit words in the header and data.

- *Urgent pointer – 16 bit* The value in this field points to the end of data in the data field that is considered as urgent and requires immediate attention. This field is only valid if the URG flag is set.

- *Options – variable length* There is only one option normally used with TCP, which is **Maximum Segment Size** (MSS). It tells the destination TCP layer the maximum size of the segment (including the TCP header) which should be sent.

  The format of this option is shown in Figure 12.6. Kind 2 is the MSS option; kinds 0 and 1 are end-of-option list and no operation, respectively. The length field indicates the length in octets of the complete option, that is, it includes the kind and length fields.

- *Padding* If the options field is valid, padding ensures that the data starts on a 32-bit boundary, so that the data offset may correctly point to it.

In some implementations of TCP, MSS can be configured to set the maximum size of segment accepted by a node. This will normally be set to the maximum value possible to reduce the overhead of smaller segments. Some hardware may be restricted in the size of frames that it can receive and hence needs this value setting so that TCP will not allow the options parameters to exceed the abilities of the hardware.

The decision as to the size of MSS is quite complex. In a system which includes routers, they are required to support an MTU of at least 576 octets, allowing a maximum MSS of 556. (576 minus the minimum

IP header of 20 octets.) Smaller segments will give quicker response but create far greater overhead on the network, thereby decreasing efficiency, especially in routed connections. Large frames improve efficiency, but increase delay due to the time taken to fill each buffer. If a path in the network has a tendency to corrupt frames then the bigger they are, the more likely they are to be corrupted. So large frames increase the likelihood of larger retransmissions and of processing power in routers and hosts being taken up with fragmentation and re-assembly.

With the improvements in WAN technology, error rates are signifiicantly reduced, so the likelihood of lost or corrupt frames is also reduced significantly. This allows larger maximum-size segments to be configured. Only in extreme conditions should there be a need to alter these values from the maximum size possible.

TCP in action

To explain the operation of the features of TCP, we will consider the phases of a TCP connection. We will look at a connection setup between two nodes, 128.1.0.1 and 128.1.0.9, where 128.1.0.1 will establish a connection with 128.1.0.9.

The connection setup phase

The setup of a TCP connection is initiated through a request from the application layer of a node. In Figure 12.7, we consider node 128.1.0.1 requesting a connection to IP address 128.1.0.9. TCP then sends a segment to IP that has the SYN flag set, a value in the sequence number field (921) and the ACK flag not set, which denotes that this is the initial segment of a connection. At this stage, when the segment is passed to the IP layer, if the IP layer does not have an entry for IP address 128.1.0.9 in its ARP cache, it will submit an ARP request to obtain the MAC address of node 128.1.0.9. Once the MAC address has been acquired, the segment is transmitted as an IP datagram.

Node 128.1.0.9 will respond with a similar segment that has the SYN flag set, the ACK flag set and with its own sequence number (302). In the acknowledge field, there will be a value that is one greater than the sequence number sent by the node 128.1.0.1 (921 + 1 = 922).This segment is acknowledging that 128.1.0.9 received the sequence number from node 128.1.0.1 and is proposing its own sequence number.

Node 128.1.0.1 will acknowledge that it has received node 128.1.0.9's response by sending a second segment that only has the ACK flag set and with a value in the acknowledge field that is one greater than the sequence number sent by node 128.1.0.9 (302 + 1 = 303).

A TCP connection is now established; both ends have exchanged sequence numbers and are now ready to send data.

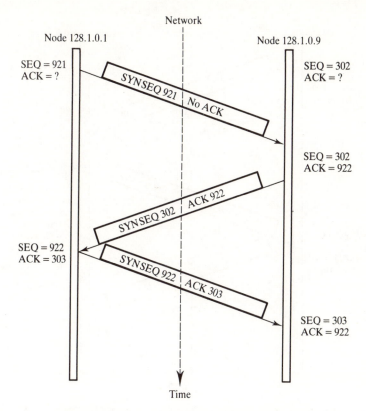

Network

Node 128.1.0.1

Node 128.1.0.9

SEQ = 921
ACK = ?

SEQ = 302
ACK = ?

SYN SEQ 921 | No ACK

SEQ = 302
ACK = 922

SYN SEQ 302 | ACK 922

SEQ = 922
ACK = 303

SYN SEQ 922 | ACK 303

SEQ = 303
ACK = 922

Time

Figure 12.7   Connections setup phase of TCP.

The data phase

As node 128.1.0.1 sends data to node 128.1.0.9, the sequence number in the segment points to the first octet of data carried and the response from node 128.1.0.9 should have an acknowledge number that is one greater than the sequence number received plus the number of octets carried, that is, the acknowledge number indicates which octet 128.1.0.9 expects to see next.

If the application is a terminal emulation service that requires character echo from the application at the remote end (node 128.1.0.9), the segments will also have the PSH flag set. This will prevent the TCP layer in either node 128.1.0.1 or 128.1.0.9 from holding on to the data and will force them to pass it immediately across the network and to the application layer so that characters can be echoed as quickly as possible.

This continues until all data is sent. Acknowledgements are only returned if there was data in the last segment received, otherwise the protocol waits for the next data to be sent. **Keep-alive** segments sent by some protocols, to test that a connection is still in place, are not normally used as they generate traffic that is not necessary for most systems.

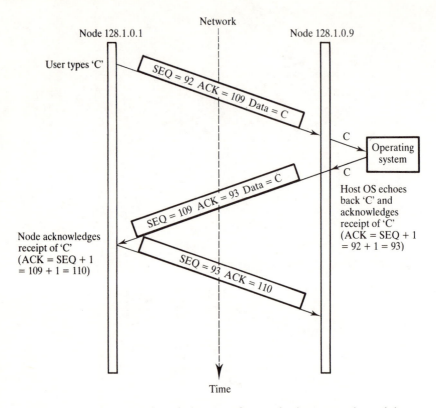

Figure 12.8 TCP acknowledgements for simple character echo with host.

As every segment has the same format, for either the transmission of data or control, TCP can acknowledge data from a remote node and carry outbound data in the same segment. TCP can be very efficient in the number of segments it uses. For a terminal connection using Telnet with character echo[†] from the remote host, TCP often requires just three segments for each character typed.

Figure 12.8 gives a simple example of TCP when a terminal connection such as Telnet is operating with a host in echo back mode. Characters typed by the user have to be passed to the computer and back to the screen to be displayed. They traverse the network twice between the user hitting the key and the character being displayed.

In this example the user has typed the character C, which is sent across the network with a sequence number of 92. The operating system echoes back the character and in the same frame the TCP protocol

---

[†]Character echo is used by most interactive systems. When a character is typed, it is not displayed on the local display until it has been sent back from the remote host. This gives the remote host the ability to decide what it wants to display in response to any character. In the early days of computing, it was used as an error-checking method.

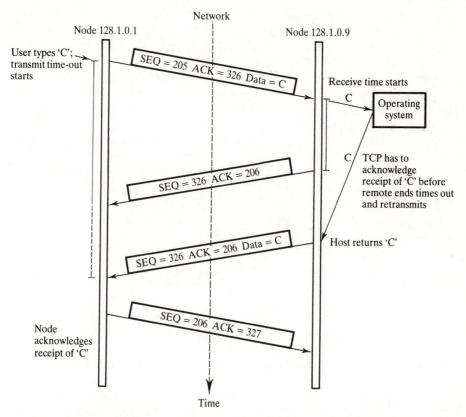

Figure 12.9 Four packets per character due to host delays.

acknowledges receipt of C from 128.1.0.1. Node 128.1.0.1 then has to acknowledge receipt of the character from 128.1.0.9, so an acknowledge segment is returned but with no data, the acknowledge field being set one beyond the sequence number received, as there is one character.

With systems that use remote echo, it is possible for more than three segments to be generated for each character typed, if the destination computer is under heavy load. This happens because each segment carrying a character must be acknowledged within a certain time, otherwise a retransmission will occur. If the application host is not ready to return its response within that time-out period it will generate a segment without the echoed character, but with an acknowledgement of the incoming segment. When the application is ready to echo the character back to the sender, it will send another segment and should receive an acknowledgement back from the terminal user's computer. In these circumstances, four segments are generated (Figure 12.9).

The impact of applications that use remote character echo in this way is worth careful consideration. Each segment has a TCP header, an

IP header and the single typed character, making 41 octets in all, and is carried in a datalink frame. On Ethernet, each frame must be a minimum size of 64 octets[†], which means that for the three or four segments sent for each character typed by a user, either 192 (64×3) or 256 (64×4) octets are transmitted between source and destination, depending on the load of the remote computer. So, when the application computer is put under load, it causes four packets per character typed and that puts a further load on the computer generating the extra acknowledgement. Network traffic for this application is increased by up to 33%, because the computer is loaded. The only way to reduce the overhead caused by this problem is to remove the resource bottleneck in the host computer, which may require a larger computer; it is likely that a computer causing this problem is slow performing its normal tasks as well.

A host which is under heavy load will often send responses in multiple segments, even though a single frame could support the amount of data to be carried. This happens because communications software usually runs at high priority and builds output frames on a timer. On a busy machine, the application is unable to assemble all the information required before the timer runs out.

While remote echo operation can be acceptable on purely local LANs with a capacity of 7000 to 14 000 frames per second, the traffic generated must be carefully considered when planning a WAN with remote bridges or routers. If each character typed generates three or four frames, this must be taken into account when sizing the speed of the intersite circuits. For example, the capacity of a 64 kbps circuit is about 120 minimum-size Ethernet frames per second (in each direction). If each user types two characters per second on average (20 words per minute – even today, computer users are often not trained typists), each may generate four frames in each direction. The line will be saturated in both directions by just 30 active users[‡]. This simplistic view does not take into account the purpose of all this typing, which is usually to request a computer-generated screen of information. Applications must be modelled individually and the traffic they generate considered at each point in the network. Traffic has two parameters: the number of bits per second required and the number of frames or packets per second. Bottlenecks are more likely in wide area links.

A spreadsheet model of the operation of a particular protocol is a very useful tool. While it cannot model the dynamics of user operation and the performance of the data sources, it can give a good indication of whether a particular design has any chance of working.

[†]As the Ethernet frame overhead is 18 octets, each frame carrying a single typed character will be padded by 5 octets ($18 + 41 + 5 = 64$). IEEE 802.3 frames will not require padding as LLC and SNAP add 8 octets, making a frame with a minimum TCP segment of 67 octets ($18 + 8 + 41 = 67$).

[‡]Bridges with a good data compression algorithm might help, but it must not extend the round trip delay to the point where users object to the delayed echo.

The amount of traffic than can be produced by TCP may appear high, but it is can be less than other protocols.

The final phase

In the final phase, when one end has decided to close the connection, the FIN flag is used. For an interactive terminal connection, the user will most probably log out of their application and the application will tell the TCP layer to close the connection. This causes the application node to send a segment with the FIN flag set. The FIN flag tells the terminal node that there is no more data to send. The terminal node responds with a segment with ACK (to acknowledge the FIN) and its own FIN flag set. The connection is not regarded as closed completely until both ends have sent a segment with the FIN flags set and possibly acknowledged that the FIN segments were received. However, if segments are lost at this late stage, the connection will be regarded as closed after a short time-out. In practice, either end may initiate the graceful closing of a connection with FIN.

In Figure 12.10 the user has finished work so has typed 'logout' to close the connection. This message is sent to the operating system that releases the connection which needs to be closed. Note also that the data 'logout' is acknowledged as any other data. The host then closes the connection by indicating to the TCP stack that the connection is to be closed. That causes the TCP software to send a frame with the FIN code value set. If 128.1.0.1 decides it has also finished and it has no further data to send, it will return an acknowledge and a FIN which will instruct 128.1.0.9 that the connection is complete.

Error correction and retransmission time-out

TCP provides the error correction for those TCP/IP applications that require it. The TCP/IP architecture leaves error correction to this transport level because it wishes to make no assumptions about the error-correction capabilities of the underlying networks. Since it then has to do error correction for certain applications, why not just do it once in the end nodes at the transport layer? This means that all error correction in TCP/IP is assumed to be end to end[†] and not hop to hop, unlike some networks, such as implementations of X.25[‡].

[†]If TCP operates over an error-corrected network like X.25, it just sees a system which is substantially error free and which has occasional sudden changes in delay as the error-correction mechanisms operate.

[‡]Unlike X.25 developers, TCP/IP developers were able to take a much higher level view of the application performance required, rather than just designing a data transmission network level service that had to deliver to the public certain guarantees of performance.

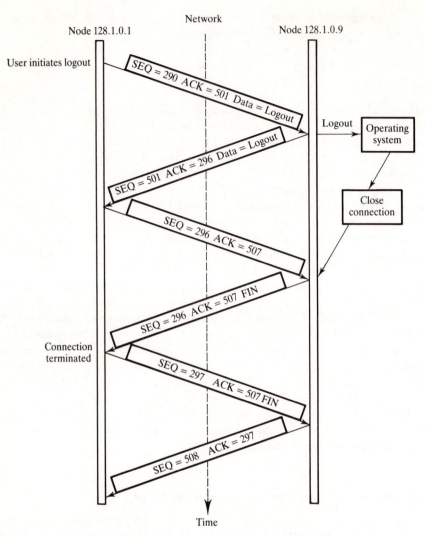

Figure 12.10   Closedown phase of a TCP connection.

There is an interesting management side-effect to this decision. While no assumption is made about the error performance of underlying networks, if that performance is not good, any single error will mean that a TCP segment is retransmitted end to end on every link. In an X.25 network, it would have been transmitted just on the one link in error. Indeed, the error-correction mechanism used by TCP works best when it is only occasionally required. Fortunately, the error rates on wide area circuits have improved considerably with the introduction of fibre optic transmission systems, so the decision by TCP/IP designers is justified.

TCP error-correction uses one simple mechanism: if an acknowledgement has not been received for any particular segment sequence number within a certain time-out value, the segment is resent. This is the *only* mechanism for error recovery. Unlike some other error-correction methods, there is no way that a receiver can force the retransmission from a particular point, partly because there is no concept of retransmitting data when it is out of sequence. The receiver must await the expiry of the timer at the sender.

Because segments are only acknowledged when in sequence, it is probable that once the time-out operates, a series of segments (if the value of the window size and MSS allows more than one segment to be acknowledged) will be retransmitted. It is also possible in some implementations that resending a single segment will cause a number of outstanding segments to be acknowledged. The TCP standard can accommodate both mechanisms. What happens in practice depends on how adventurous the designer of the implementation has been.

In Figure 12.11, a number of TCP segments have been transmitted because the window size last advertised to 128.1.0.1 allowed that amount of data to be sent. The segment with sequence number 39 did not succeed in reaching the destination even though a later segment (sequence number 49) did. TCP does not acknowledge the segment with sequence number 49 as it has not yet received all intermediate data. This causes the retransmission timer started for the segment with sequence number 39 to mature, causing the segment to be retransmitted.

In Figure 12.12, the loss of an acknowledge segment does not require any further action, as the segment following the lost acknowledge got through, which implies that all data from sequence number 72 up to and including the data in the segment with sequence number 170 has arrived at 128.1.0.9.

The value of the retransmission time-out is critical. It depends on the round trip delay or Round Trip Time (RTT) on the path in use. LANs will acknowledge in 20–100 ms; wide area connections over slow-speed satellite circuits could take many seconds. It is difficult to know the delay characteristics of networks in advance, and they can vary by a factor of 10 during the life of a connection, depending on route and loading. This makes it almost impossible to decide on one time-out value for this retransmit timer. If the time-out is set too low, it will expire before the acknowledge returns, causing the segment to be sent again unnecessarily, and increasing the traffic. If the value is set too high, it causes long delays waiting for the time-out to mature before a retransmission can be sent, so the loss of one segment will significantly decrease throughput.

Modern implementations of TCP have a technique which can deal with this wide variation in possible RTTs. To solve the problem, all implementations of TCP are now supposed to use a mechanism that works out the average delay of a connection and adds a threshold above that delay to deal with variations. A dynamic time-out allows a connection to change

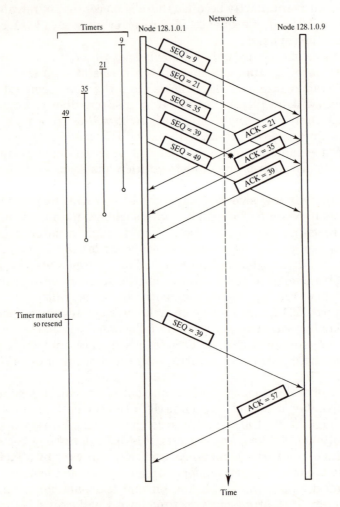

Figure 12.11 A segment carrying data failing to arrive.

its value to suit the immediate circumstances and helps build a robust protocol. It minimizes the number of unnecessary retransmissions while reducing the dead time when retransmission could have begun.

There are a number of issues about how this dynamic timer should be implemented. One of the most powerful techniques was developed for use on packet radio networks by Phil Karn, KA9Q. It accurately assesses the RTT regardless of lost segments. This mechanism has now been

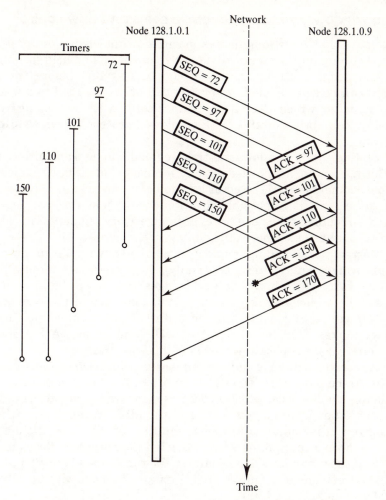

Figure 12.12 Acknowledge segment failing to arrive.

adopted by some commercial implementations of TCP/IP. Until this algorithm was introduced, it was found that some techniques would lock into a mode of reliably sending everything twice!

In TCP implementations a number of variants of the retransmission algorithm are used, so it is important to understand the basis of time-out algorithms and their stability under heavy load and high segment loss.

Even today, not all implementations of TCP/IP use dynamic time-out algorithms. Some have fixed timers and others have timers that can be configured. In some implementations different timer values can be set for each host in a table. None of these is as satisfactory as the dynamic timer unless the network topology is very simple.

Sliding windows, window advertisements and flow control

In networks that have long delays, positive acknowledge protocols can decrease throughput dramatically; each segment can be held up waiting for acknowledgements to travel through the system before the next segment can be sent. A medium or link can only be loaded to a fraction of its capacity, which decreases dramatically with increasing round trip delay. To improve on this, TCP employs a process known as **sliding windows**.

Sliding windows allows multiple segments to be transmitted without waiting for an acknowledgement for each individual segment. If multiple segments are received at a node before an acknowledgement is ready to be sent, it is possible to acknowledge just the last segment received, so reducing the need to acknowledge every segment. This allows higher throughput and more efficient use of the bandwidth.

Correct use of sliding windows is particularly important on paths through bridges and routers, especially where there are remote links. Even on a LAN which has only local bridges, delays will build up in the buffers of the bridges. Setting the correct window size will restore performance almost to that achievable on a direct cable connection. Sliding windows makes TCP (as opposed to UDP and other LAN protocols) particularly good at operating over long-distance WANs.

A receiver will have limited buffer space for each connection, so a limit has to be put on the amount of information that can be sent. This limit is the window size, which in TCP is measured in octets. There is a relationship between window size, and the MSS. When a new window size is given, it is usually an integral multiple of the MSS (though that integer is often 1 in systems with restricted memory, PCs for example). The size of these windows is normally in the range of 1024 to 4096, which is only between one and four segments on an Ethernet with an MSS set to 1024 and an MTU of 1500.

A data receiver advertises a window size in each TCP segment it sends. When the unacknowledged data is the same as the advertised window size, no more information is sent until an acknowledgement is received which advertises a new window size of at least one maximum segment.

The window advertised in each segment is a useful monitor when performance difficulties are being encountered. If the window values are often low or reach zero in the middle of data transfer, a device does not have enough memory allocated to buffers. Performance is likely to be improved if the relevant buffers can be increased.

A receiver may validly reduce the window size to zero to stop the flow of data completely, that is, to invoke flow control. It is only permissible to reduce the window as it is used up by valid data on this connection. A receiver cannot reduce a previously advertised window which has not been filled with data.

Telnet uses flow control: when the keys <CTRL> and s are typed at the same time on a keyboard, it stops any further information from being displayed on the screen of that terminal. <CTRL> and s generate ASCII character DC3 or XOFF. In this event, a Telnet terminal server operating over TCP has to stop the remote host from transmitting to prevent the terminal server buffers overflowing, otherwise data will be lost. As data continues to be received and to fill the previously advertised window, TCP sends segments with reducing window sizes until the window size finally reaches zero. If the flow of data is re-enabled with <CTRL> and q together (ASCII character DC1 or XON), the data will start to flow to the terminal again, buffers will be released and segments to the remote host will indicate the increasing terminal server window size.

For efficiency, a newly advertised window must always be at least one maximum segment.

In Figure 12.13, the example shows a connection where the buffers are filling up on 128.1.0.9 so the window has shrunk to 200 octets and then to 0. When 128.1.0.9 has been able to deal with the data it received, effectively clearing its receive buffers, it re-advertises a window of 1024, so data starts to flow again.

Configuration issues

There are not usually many parameters that can be modified at this level and there are none required for UDP at all, but some implementations allow certain TCP parameters to be set.

Connection time-out

This is the time to spend attempting to establish a connection with a computer. Changing this value affects the amount of time it will take to fail if the connection to a host is not possible.

Retransmission time-out

This is the time to wait between the retransmission of TCP segments. Modern implementations really should not leave this as a network manager's option!

This can be a difficult value to assess. One way is to use the ping utility, as it often displays the round trip delay to a host. If this utility is run for an extended time covering the busiest period on the system, the maximum delay seen could be taken as a reference and then used with some margin added. The margin would depend on the scatter in the values, but a factor of between 1.5 and 2 would be normal.

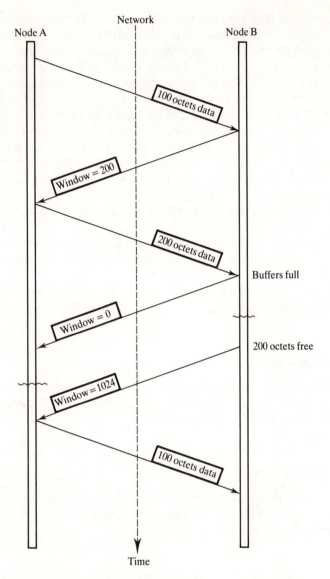

Figure 12.13 Window advertisements in TCP.

The maximum segment size

This is the maximum size of a TCP segment allowed. Probably the most sensible value for this field is the maximum size that prevents fragmentation from occurring across the most commonly used connection from that host. For operation in LAN-only environments, 1024 is a common figure.

Receive window

This is the maximum size of receive window that should be advertised. It should normally be a multiple of the MSS[†]. Where memory is a limitation, it will often be one or two maximum segments.

Setting a larger window size is the way to improve the performance of a TCP connection through bridges and routers. For example, in a route with two local bridges, maximum performance will be achieved when the receiver window is three times the MSS of the transmitter. As one segment is received by the end system, a second is being received by the second bridge. Just as the third segment, which exhausts the window, is received by the first bridge, an acknowledge is generated, which releases the window for further transmission.

Different calculations apply where there is a mixture of high- and low-speed local and wide area facilities.

Well-known ports used with TCP and UDP

Decimal	Keyword	Description
0	Reserved	
1	TCPMUX	TCP port service multiplexor
5	RJE	Remote job entry
7	ECHO	Echo
9	Discard	Discard
11	Users	Active users
13	Daytime	Daytime
17	Quote	Quote of the day
19	CHARGEN	Character generator
20	FTP-data	File transfer [default data]
21	FTP	File transfer [control]
23	Telnet	Telnet
25	SMTP	Simple mail transfer
247-255	Reserved	

For a complete list, see Appendix G.

TCP traces

The following shows actual traces taken from an operational network of the TCP protocol. In this example we show Ethernet frames in hexadecimal, without the preamble or the CRC. The table beneath the frame

---

[†]MSS refers to transmission and window size refers to receiving. There is no real connection between them. If all systems are set with a similar MSS (1024) and a maximum window which is a small multiple (2,3,4) of that, they can all make efficient use of the network resources.

gives a breakdown of the fields in the frame and their values. For a further explanation of the format of these examples, see Appendix F. For completeness the datalink and IP information is shown shaded.

This example shows the initial three segments sent to initiate a TCP session. It shows the three segments required to synchronize the sequence and acknowledgement numbers.

Frame 1

```
AA00   0400   0104   0260   8C0A   C49D   0800   4500      *......`..D...E.
002C   0002   0000   FF06   7F66   1E00   0001   1E00      .,......f......
0063   19CB   0017   0000   3E38   0000   0000   6002      .c.K....8...`.
0400   015D   0000   0204   0400   0000                    ...]........
```

Datalink:	Dest MAC:	AA0004 000104	Source MAC:	02608C 0AC49D	Type(Length):	0800
IP:	Version:	4	IHL:	5	Type of service:	00
	Length:	002C	ID:	0002	Flags:	0
	Offset:	0	Time to live:	255	Protocol:	06
	Checksum:	7F66	Source IP:	30.0.0.1	Dest IP:	30.0.0.99
TCP:	Source port:	19CB	Dest port:	Telnet(0017)	Sequence:	00003E38
	Acknowledge:	None	Offset:	6	Code:	02(Syn)
	Window:	0400	Checksum:	015D	TCP options:	Max Seg 1024

Frame 2

```
0260   8C0A   C49D   AA00   0400   0104   0800   4500      .`..D.*.......E.
002C   0B0B   0000   3C06   375E   1E00   0063   1E00      .,......7^...c..
0001   0017   19CB   11E7   39AD   0000   3E39   6012      .....K.g9-..9`.
0400   B5B7   0000   0204   0400   0000                    ..57........
```

Datalink:	Dest MAC:	02608C 0AC49D	Source MAC:	AA0004 000104	Type(Length):	0800
IP:	Version:	4	IHL:	5	Type of service:	00
	Length:	002C	ID:	0B0B	Flags:	0
	Offset:	0	Time to live:	60	Protocol:	06
	Checksum:	375E	Source IP:	30.0.0.99	Dest IP:	30.0.0.1
TCP:	Source port:	Telnet(0017)	Dest port:	19CB	Sequence:	11E739AD
	Acknowledge:	00003E39	Offset:	6	Code:	12(Syn,Ack)
	Window:	0400	Checksum:	B5B7	TCP options:	Max Seg 1024

Frame 3

```
AA00   0400   0104   0260   8C0A   C49D   0800   4500      *......`..D...E.
0028   0003   0000   FF06   7F69   1E00   0001   1E00      .(.......i......
0063   19CB   0017   0000   3E39   11E7   39AE   5018      .c.K....9.g9.P.
0400   CBB8   0000   0001   0800   0604                    ..K8........
```

Datalink:	Dest MAC:	AA0004 000104	Source MAC:	02608C 0AC49D	Type(Length):	0800
IP:	Version:	4	IHL:	5	Type of service:	00
	Length:	002C	ID:	0002	Flags:	0
	Offset:	0	Time to live:	255	Protocol:	06
	Checksum:	7F69	Source IP:	30.0.0.1	Dest IP:	30.0.0.99
TCP:	Source port:	19CB	Dest port:	Telnet(0017)	Sequence:	00003E39
	Acknowledge:	11E739AE	Offset:	5	Code:	18(Push/Ack)
	Window:	0400	Checksum:	CBB8	TCP options:	None

The following f'ur frames ($n-3$ to n) signify the end of the session. The user types 'logout' to the host which signals the host to close the connection. This is initiated by the host sending a segment with the FIN flag set (frame $n-3$). The workstation acknowledges receipt of the FIN segment and then sends its own FIN segment (frame $n-1$) which is acknowledged by the host with segment n. The disconnection is complete. It is interesting to note that the workstation could have used a single frame instead of $n-2$ and $n-1$ to acknowledge the FIN and send its own FIN; for some reason this implementation of TCP/IP does not.

Frame n – 3

```
0260   8C0A   C49D   AA00   0400   0104   0800   4500      .`..D.*.......E.
0028   0B54   0000   3C06   3719   1E00   0063   1E00      .(.T...7...c..
0001   0017   19CB   11E7   4256   0000   3E62   5019      .....K.gBV..bP.
0001   C6E5   0000   0000   0000   0000                    ..Fe........
```

Datalink:	Dest MAC:	02608C 0AC49D	Source MAC:	AA0004 000104	Type(Length):	0800
IP:	Version:	4	IHL:	5	Type of service:	00
	Length:	0028	ID:	0B54	Flags:	0
	Offset:	0	Time to live:	60	Protocol:	06
	Checksum:	3719	Source IP:	30.0.0.99	Dest IP:	30.0.0.1
TCP:	Source port:	Telnet(0017)	Dest port:	19CB	Sequence:	11E74256
	Acknowledge:	00003E62	Offset:	5	Code:	19(Push,Fin)
	Window:	0001	Checksum:	C6E5	TCP options:	None

Frame n – 2

```
AA00   0400   0104   0260   8C0A   C49D   0800   4500      *......`..D...E.
0028   006D   0000   FF06   7EFF   1E00   0001   1E00      .(.m....~......
0063   19CB   0017   0000   3E62   11E7   4257   5010      .c.K....b.gBWP.
0400   C2EE   0000   0000   0000   0000                    ...........
```

Datalink:	Dest MAC:	AA0004 000104	Source MAC:	02608C 0AC49D	Type(Length):	0800
IP:	Version:	4	IHL:	5	Type of service:	00
	Length:	28	ID:	006D	Flags:	0
	Offset:	0	Time to live:	255	Protocol:	06
	Checksum:	7EFF	Source IP:	30.0.0.1	Dest IP:	30.0.0.99
TCP:	Source port:	19CB	Dest port:	Telnet(0017)	Sequence:	00003E62
	Acknowledge:	11E74257	Offset:	5	Code:	10(Ack)
	Window:	0400	Checksum:	C2EE	TCP options:	None

Frame n – 1

```
AA00   0400   0104   0260   8C0A   C49D   0800   4500      *......`..D...E.
0028   006E   0000   FF06   7EFE   1E00   0001   1E00      .(.n....~~......
0063   19CB   0017   0000   3E62   11E7   4257   5019      .c.K....b.gBWP.
0400   C2E5   0000   0000   0000   0000                    ...........
```

Datalink:	Dest MAC:	AA0004 000104	Source MAC:	02608C 0AC49D	Type(Length):	0800
IP:	Version:	4	IHL:	5	Type of service:	00
	Length:	0028	ID:	006E	Flags:	0
	Offset:	0	Time to live:	255	Protocol:	06
	Checksum:	7EFE	Source IP:	30.0.0.1	Dest IP:	30.0.0.99
TCP:	Source port:	19CB	Dest port:	Telnet(0017)	Sequence:	00003E62
	Acknowledge:	11E74257	Offset:	5	Code:	19(Push/Fin)
	Window:	0400	Checksum:	C2E5	TCP options:	None

Frame n

```
0260    8C0A    C49D    AA00    0400    0104    0800    4500      .`..D.*.......E.
0028    0B55    0000    3C06    3718    1E00    0063    1E00      .(.U...7....c..
0001    0017    19CB    11E7    4257    0000    3E63    5010      .....K.gBW..cP.
0000    C6ED    0000    0000    0000    0000                      ..Fm........
```

Datalink:	Dest MAC:	02608C 0AC49D	Source MAC:	AA0004 000104	Type(Length):	0800
IP:	Version:	4	IHL:	5	Type of service:	00
	Length:	0028	ID:	0B55	Flags:	0
	Offset:	0	Time to live:	60	Protocol:	06
	Checksum:	3718	Source IP:	30.0.0.99	Dest IP:	30.0.0.1
TCP:	Source port:	Telnet(0017)	Dest port:	19CB	Sequence:	11E74257
	Acknowledge:	00003E63	Offset:	5	Code:	12(Ack)
	Window:	0000	Checksum:	C6ED	TCP options:	Max Seg 1024

Relevant RFCs

675   Transmission control protocol [1]
700   A protocol experiment
721   Out-of-band control signals in a host-to-host protocol
761   Transmission control protocol [2]
768   User datagram protocol
793   Transmission control protocol [3]
794   Pre-emption
814   Name, address, ports and routes
816   Fault isolation and recovery
817   Modularity and efficiency in protocol implementation
872   TCP on a LAN
879   The TCP maximum segment size and related topics
889   Internet delay experiments
896   Congestion control in TCP/IP networks
964   Some problems with the specification of the military standard transmission control protocol
983   ISO transport on TCP
1072   TCP extensions for long-delay paths
1078   TCP port service multiplexer
1106   TCP big window option
1144   Compressing TCP/IP headers for low-speed serial links

Summary

UDP and TCP provide the transport layer protocols of the TCP/IP protocol stack. UDP provides a datagram service adding only the necessary port addressing to define which application layer protocol data should be sent to. TCP, as well as providing application layer addressing, provides a reliable stream. Because TCP uses a windowing technique, it works efficiently on most media systems and it provides a flow control mechanism by way of its window advertising process.

Connections through the TCP/IP protocol stack are uniquely defined with sockets, which are a concatenation of the IP address and a port number. The more popular well-known applications, usually server software, use commonly defined well-known port numbers. Client software uses port numbers that are unique to their host and have not already been used by some other application on that host. This allows their connections to be described explicitly.

Setting the correct maximum segment size and maximum window size will dramatically improve TCP performance over buffered networks. For UDP it is possible to alter the maximum datagram size if necessary.

13

Application layer services

In the TCP/IP architecture, the application layer is responsible for interfacing between end-user applications and the transport layer services; the application service is *not* the end-user application, it merely interfaces that application to the communications network. There are several application layer services to suit the many different types of applications. There are also a few useful management utilities. For example, Telnet is a service to support terminal type activities, the File Transfer Protocol (FTP) suits file transfer type applications and the Simple Mail Transfer Protocol (SMTP) deals with mail applications. In this chapter we will look at the major services available and explain their operation.

Topics covered in this chapter are:

- Client/server
- Telnet
- FTP
- SMTP
- R commands
- NetBIOS
- TFTP
- BOOTP
- The X Window System
- Socket library
- Line printer services

Client/server

TCP/IP application layer services are often referred to as having a **client/server** relationship (Figure 13.1). This means an application layer service consists of two complementary parts, one on each of the two nodes exchanging information. The originator of a connection is called the **client** and the receiver the **server**.

A server application layer service waits for incoming connections or **requests**. Client services make connections or requests to servers as required. Once the connection[†] is agreed and opened, clients make requests and servers give **responses** or replies to those requests. Servers do not initiate a transaction. Server software cannot communicate directly with server software and client software cannot communicate with client software. So, to establish connections and transfer information, there must be both client and server software operating at the application layer.

Since the application server is software, a computer with an operating system that supports multitasking (OS/2, UNIX or VMS for example) can have many different types of server and client software running at the same time. So, these multitasking computers can manage multiple connections into their services and make outgoing connections to other computer services in what appears externally to be a peer-to-peer fashion, but is based on a client/server architecture for each conversation.

Therefore two different pieces of software are required to enable communication. For example, if you were using a Telnet terminal, both the local computer you were using and the remote computer you were communicating with would require Telnet, but you require Telnet client and the host end requires the Telnet server. This is true for FTP, TFTP and BOOTP; in fact most TCP/IP services operate this way.

Because of the close UNIX relationship with TCP/IP, the server software is usually referred to as a **daemon**, so the Telnet server is usually called **telnetd** (pronounced 'telnet-dee'), meaning the Telnet daemon, and the FTP server is called **ftpd** and so on. For a connection to work between two nodes, one must have Telnet and the other telnetd, or one must have FTP and the other ftpd. Table 13.1 lists client/server software modules.

Telnet

Before the PC became so common, users would connect to a computer using a dumb terminal. The terminal provided a keyboard and screen to display output from programs that ran on the computer – so-called inter-

---

[†]Connections need only be established in a connection-oriented environment. Connectionless systems just send requests and responses.

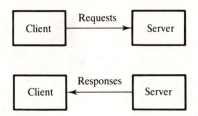

Figure 13.1 Client/server architecture.

active working. Computer data networks grew as users wished to access many computers without having a separate connection to each. Telnet was designed to provide this service, allowing users to access all computers that were connected to the 'network'. The remote host would appear to them, from their local host, as though they were attached directly to it. They would use standard commands on their local machine to access any type of computer.

Telnet is a terminal access application layer interface. It provides terminal access support for dumb terminals communicating with remote hosts. These terminals can connect in three ways:

(1) real terminals connected to TCP/IP Telnet 'terminal servers'

(2) real terminals directly connected to hosts running TCP/IP

(3) PCs running both terminal emulation and TCP/IP software

The standard for the Telnet service does not provide terminal emulation in its own right. In practice, this is only apparent to programmers, as the command telnet for end users usually causes terminal emulation to be invoked on top of the standard client Telnet service.

The role of Telnet

The main functionality that Telnet aims to provide is compatibility between computer systems so that client-end applications can gain terminal access to a remote server-end host without having prior know-

Table 13.1 The client/server software modules.

Client	Server	Port	Description
Telnet	telnetd	23	Terminal access services
FTP	ftpd	20/21	File transfer services
TFTP	tftpd	69	Remote boot services
LPR (721-731)	lpd	515	Remote print services
SMTP	smtpd	25	Electronic mail services
rlogin	rlogind	513	Remote login services

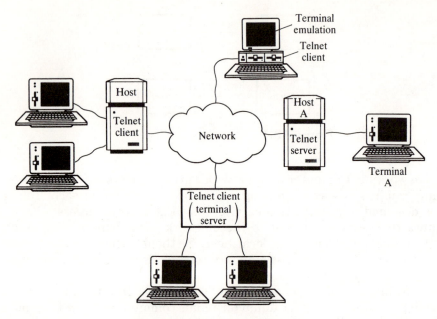

Figure 13.2 Telnet architecture.

ledge of how to support any particular terminal type. The specific use is to allow remote terminals to connect to an application server host, maybe through an intermediate computer, and appear as if they are terminals directly connected to that host.

The service the user sees is the terminal service of the remote host. Once connected, they are validated by userids and passwords and then are allowed access to authorized applications. The remote service is represented in the best possible fashion on their local terminal screen. They must know how to operate a terminal for the computer they access; no attempt is made to map two different computing command environments, only to translate the different keyboard and display mechanics to generate those commands and display the results.

The Telnet server has to make a connecting Telnet client appear like any other terminal user to its host operating system by activating all the necessary validation programs and creating an environment for each logical connection made to it. Once a user logs out from the Telnet server's host computer, it is also responsible for terminating the logical connection that was in place across the network.

In Figure 13.2, all users are able to access host A with the same functionality as if they were directly connected to the host as, for example, is terminal A. For such a connection to appear to the host as if it is a directly attached terminal, a reliable transport layer is required, so Telnet normally operates over TCP.

The environment of Telnet

Telnet was designed for an environment of many different terminal types, computer architectures and operating systems – a 'heterogeneous' environment. Many types of real terminal must be supported. No assumptions should be made about what type of terminal will wish to communicate with which type of host. Even though many terminals operate to the same basic character sets (ASCII), their enhanced features are incompatible.

Telnet attempts to match terminal and host systems. When a terminal first makes a connection, the protocols start by assuming that the terminal is the most basic type possible: a terminal that has a keyboard, produces line-by-line print output, uses local echo and uses the ASCII character set with a few simple control characters, such as carriage return, line feed, and form feed. This is a definition of the old TTY terminal (Teletype). This basic definition is referred to as the **Network Virtual Terminal** (NVT). Irrespective of how sophisticated the real terminal is, at initial connection time it is no grander than the NVT. As an NVT, all terminals can communicate with most types of host computer†; it is the basic level of compatibility between most terminals and computers.

Starting from this basic level of communication, Telnet provides a standard mechanism for agreeing the functionality of the real terminal and how it is to be used with this application. This process is referred to as **Telnet negotiation**. Before describing this in detail, we must know how Telnet distinguishes information that is flowing between the end users and their applications from control information that is to be interpreted by the client and server of Telnet itself.

Exchanging Telnet control information

In layered communications protocols, exchanging control information between peer layers at the two ends of a link would usually be by messages specifically reserved for the purpose and identified by a layer header, in this case the application layer header. Telnet does not have an application header as such. Rather, to communicate between the client and server, it uses special control commands that are inserted into the user data field of TCP and hence carried to the remote Telnet application layer service.

To explain how control information is carried, we can consider the handling of the < Break > key. Pressing the < Break > key is often used to interrupt processes on a computer by attracting the attention of the

---

†Some computers assume a full-screen or forms-based system and cannot work well with TTYs. Many applications can only be successfully operated from a full-screen terminal.

operating system. If we consider <Break> in the asynchronous ASCII V.24/EIA232 environment, it is not a character; it does not have an 8-bit code allocated to it. Hitting the <Break> key causes a binary 0 (high) signal to be placed on the transmit line of a terminal for at least 200 milliseconds. As a character on a line running at 9600 bits per second only lasts for around 1 millisecond, this is an abnormal signal state. It is not practical to use the same kind of approach to send a <Break> signal across shared media such as dedicated point-to-point lines or a LAN. The <Break> has to be encoded and transmitted in a standard message across the network. This is one of the functions of Telnet.

Telnet reserves a character which it inserts in the data stream when transmitting to the remote Telnet application layer to indicate that it is sending special control sequences. This character is decimal 255 or hexadecimal 0xFF. It is referred to as IAC meaning 'interpret as command'. Following IAC will be one of the commands shown in Table 13.2.

For example, if a user presses the <Break> key, the Telnet client will send IAC,BRK or 255,243 (decimal) in a TCP segment that will be received by the appropriate host. The Telnet server software, on receiving IAC,BRK, will translate it into an action that is allocated to <Break> in that operating system, for example to cause an interrupt to the relevant application program. Telnet only provides the mechanism to send the <Break>; what it means when it arrives at the server outside the specification.

Having described the function of IAC, we can now look at how it is used in more detail.

Telnet negotiation

To take advantage of the more sophisticated features that the real terminal may have available and which the host may also be able to understand, Telnet performs negotiation, a process of building up terminal capability beyond the very basic NVT. It uses a special set of commands, IAC DO, IAC DON'T, IAC WILL, IAC WON'T (Table 13.2), as a conversational way of negotiating the facilities that both terminal and host can support. Some of these can be further modified by the options parameters listed in Table 13.3. This negotiation can be complex and arduous and may take many seconds. The frequently used shortcut is the special command IAC,DO,TERMINAL TYPE whereby one end of the connection suggests that a manufacturer's real terminal type is used.

If negotiation fails, the terminal can still interact with the remote host, but only enjoy the facilities of the NVT, which will only give line-by-line operation. The basis of negotiation is through the request for the remote end to use a feature, for example:

IAC, DO, ECHO

Table 13.2 Telnet commands.

Code	Decimal value	Explanation
SE	240	End of subnegotiation
NOP	241	No operation
DM	242	Data Mark
BRK	243	Break
IP	244	Interrupt Process; send an interrupt to the remote process
AO	245	Abort Output; clears all pending output until the next command prompt.
AYT	246	Are You There; requests the remote end to return some evidence that it is still there
EC	247	Erase Character; erase characters to the left
EL	248	Erase Line; erase the current line of data.
GA	249	Go Ahead; a half-duplex mode of operation required for terminals that can only transmit or receive at any one time
SB	250	Start subnegotiation
WILL	251	WILL negotiation command
WON'T	252	WON'T negotiation command
DO	253	DO negotiation command
DON'T	254	DON'T negotiation command
IAC	255	Interpret as command (the following)

which is 'I want you to echo', to which the response could be,

IAC, WILL, ECHO

which is 'I will echo' or,

IAC, WON'T, ECHO

'I won't echo'. If the request is negative the originator is now unable to change from local echo mode to remote echo mode. Once a feature has been refused, forcing the requester to take responsibility, it cannot be renegotiated.

The other way negotiation can go is with the 'I want to do' something or

IAC, WILL, ECHO

This is indicating 'I want to echo'. The response could be:

IAC, DO, ECHO

which is, 'OK go ahead and echo' or

IAC, DON'T, ECHO

which is 'Don't echo'.

Through these simple negotiation commands that are special character sequences placed in the data stream, Telnet is able to

Table 13.3 Telnet options.

Telnet options	Code	Explanation
Transmit binary	0	Ignore control codes in data
Echo	1	Character echoing
RCP	2	Reconnect option
Suppress-go-ahead	3	Suppress the half duplex go ahead function
NAMS	4	Negotiate Approximate Message Size
STATUS	5	View status of Telnet options
Timing-mark	6	Used to help on problems with type ahead
RCTE	7	Used with long echo delay circuits
NAOL	8	Negotiate output line width
NAOP	9	Negotiate page output size
NAOCRD	10	Used with NAOL and NAOP
NAOHTS	11	Negotiate horizontal tabstops
NAOHTD	12	Horizontal tabstop definition
NAOFFD	13	Form feed disposition option
NAOVTS	14	Vertical tabstop option
NAOVTD	15	Vertical tabstop disposition
NAOLFD	16	Linefeed disposition
EXTEND-ASCII	17	Extended ASCII option
LOGOUT	18	Logout option
BM	19	Byte Macro option
DET	20	Telnet Data Entry Terminal
SUPDUP	21	SUPDUP display controls
SUPDUP-OUTPUT	22	Used with SUPDUP
SEND-LOCATION	23	Send location id to Telnet server
TERMINAL-TYPE	24	Terminal type option
END-OF-RECORD	25	To alter the end of record character
TUID	26	User identification
OUTMRK	27	Output mark
EXOPL	255	To allow for more options...

negotiate for a level of service, or maybe just control when echoing or some other feature is turned on or off. There are several other features for which Telnet has reserved command codes (Table 13.2).

Some options require further levels of negotiation or **subnegotiation**. Subnegotiation is required for a particular activity when parameters must be agreed, for example when screen sizes must be agreed. It is performed by the normal process of agreeing on an option through the DO or WILL command that is acknowledged with WILL or DO respectively. Then one end of the connection will send IAC,SB followed by the relevant parameters and then the SE command, such as

IAC, DO, STATUS
IAC, WILL, STATUS

⋮

some delay

⋮

One host may later ask for the current Telnet status of the other with:

IAC, SB, STATUS, SEND, IAC, SE

The other host replies 'My status is' as follows:

IAC SB STATUS IS
WILL ECHO
DO SUPPRESS-GO-AHEAD
WILL STATUS
DO STATUS
IAC SE

Negotiation happens mainly at the start of a connection, and in most cases is very rapid through the IAC,DO,TERMINAL TYPE, although further subnegotiation may occur at any time through the life of the connection. Apart from handling negotiation and these special characters, Telnet sends user data in both directions between workstation and host. This data is passed to the normal terminal operating system environment.

Telnet security

An important feature of Telnet is the level of security it provides. A user connecting to a host using Telnet will be vetted in the same way as any other interactive user. So logging in normally requires a user id and password.

One feature of operating systems is that, by default, users connecting across a network are prevented from logging in as a **privileged user**. Privileged use can be further restricted to a single directly attached console port. Often this means that somebody attempting to log in as a privileged user using Telnet will be disconnected immediately. This, of course, is a security feature to make it more difficult to gain illegal access to the operating system features of a host.

Telnet carries user information including login ids and passwords in TCP segments without encryption. Access to network cables and to monitoring equipment may be a security issue in some environments.

Telnet protocol traces

Appendix H shows actual traces taken from an operational network using the Telnet protocol. In that example, we show Ethernet frames in hexadecimal without the preamble or the CRC. The table beneath the frame gives a breakdown of the fields in the frame and their values. For a further explanation of the format of these examples, see Appendix F.

Table 13.4 Listing a directory.

Operating system	Directory command
VMS	dir
DOS	dir
Windows 3	(Click on folder)
UNIX	ls
Finder (Macintosh)	(Double click on folder)

This example shows a user (system) logging in to a host. The frames are generated by the user typing their userid and the replies and acknowledgements to this. Notice the Telnet negotiation in certain frames and messages coming back from the host.

File transfer protocol

It is common to wish to transfer files between different types of computers, but to do this a number of problems need to be dealt with. Moving the data is straightforward, but what happens when it arrives? The major problems are that computers store data in different formats, their operating systems use different commands for similar functions and they have different security restrictions to prevent unauthorized access to programs and data. These considerations apply to data files; they do not begin to address the differences between executable files in two environments (nor does FTP or any other file transfer system).

FTP was designed to provide a service for applications that want to move files between networked computers. It provides the basic application layer services needed to move files; it does *not* define the interface[†] to a user, so a true user application is required to provide the interface between the user and FTP. Although you invariably type 'FTP' to perform file transfer, you are invoking an interface program as well as the relevant FTP software.

Like a terminal service, a file transfer service must not introduce errors. FTP requires a reliable communications service, so it uses the TCP transport service.

The main function of FTP is to reduce or remove the incompatibilities between the handling of files in different operating systems. For example, if you connect to a remote computer, your first requirement might be to list all the files in a directory. The commands to do this differ for different operating systems (Table 13.4).

Listing a directory is part of file management. As well as file transfer, FTP must provide basic file management functions in a standard way. When a user on one computer operating system is communicating

---

[†]Again, such is the relationship between UNIX and TCP/IP that the standard UNIX user interface for FTP has been copied to other environments.

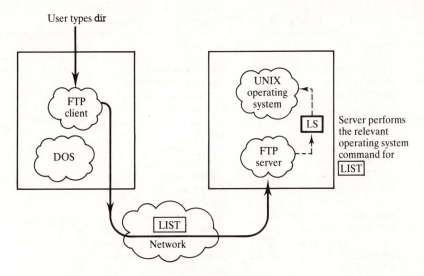

Figure 13.3 FTP command translation for a directory listing.

with a computer using a different operating system, the directory listing command requires translation. This is true for most other functions, such as change directory, login, create directory, delete file and so on.

A major facility of FTP is therefore to deal with the translation necessary to provide compatibility between different operating systems. The way FTP does this is through a set of defined **network standard commands**. A standard list of common functions is defined for FTP to ensure that, irrespective of the operating system, the command passed across the network is always the same.

Figure 13.3 shows conceptually how FTP deals with this translation. In this example, an MS-DOS user is communicating with a UNIX operating system. The MS-DOS system user wishes to see a list of all files in the directory on the remote computer. On an MS-DOS-based PC, the user would instinctively use the dir command, the normal command to display a directory with MS-DOS. The FTP client converts this request into an FTP command which is LIST. LIST is the standard FTP command from an FTP client to an FTP server to request a directory listing. When the server software receives this command, it performs the necessary UNIX commands to get a directory listing and then returns the output to the client.

Table 13.5 shows a list of the standard FTP commands. These commands are the actual ASCII uppercase characters sent across the network in the data field of TCP segments. In practice, they can be seen in text with a network analyser as they are transmitted. This can be a powerful aid to resolving incompatibilities between implementations.

The list of commands in Table 13.5 is not complete, but these are the most common provided by most implementations. Knowing these

Table 13.5 FTP client/server commands.

Command	Description
USER (userid)<cr,lf>	User ID to be logged in
PASS (password)<cr,lf>	The user's password
ACCT<cr,lf>	Account information
CWD (directory)<cr,lf>	Change working directory
CDUP<cr,lf>	Change to parent directory
QUIT<cr,lf>	Logout
PORT(socket)<cr,lf>	Define the socket to be used
TYPE type<cr,lf>	Type definition
RETR(filename)<cr,lf>	Retrieve a file
STOR(filename)<cr,lf>	Send a file
DELE(filename)<cr,lf>	Delete the file
RMD(directory name)<cr,lf>	Delete the directory
MKD(directory name)<cr,lf>	Create the directory
LIST(directory name)<cr,lf>	A directory listing for users
NLST(directory name)<cr,lf>	A directory listing for programs
STAT<cr,lf>	Status
HELP<cr,lf>	List of these commands available on server

commands is of no direct value to a user; they are only used by the FTP client and server software to communicate with each other. But these command names are sometimes visible to the user as FTP implementations will display them if tracing or debugging is switched on. Again, the value in knowing the commands comes in resolving system incompatibilities.

The FTP server has its own way of responding to these commands. Its responses come in two parts:

(Numeric value)(Response string)

For example:

230 User logged in, proceed

The FTP server sends these commands back to an FTP client. The number and the string always go together and mean the same thing. The numeric value is for use by the FTP client or by an application program controlling the client. The string can be displayed without further processing for human consumption. Common responses are:

220   Service ready
331   User name OK, need password
230   User logged in, proceed
150   File status OK, about to open data connection
226   Closing data connection
200   Command OK
550   Access denied

User prompts	User types	FTP client>	<FTP server
$	ftp oz		
			220 Service ready
Enter user name:	me	USER me	
			331 User name OK, need password
Enter password:	blob	PASS blob	
			230 User logged in, proceed
ftp>	dir	PORT (socket)	
			200 Command OK
		LIST	
			150 Opening data connection for (LIST) (socket)
<<<<Directory listing is transferred to the user over the new socket>>>>			
			226 Closing data connection
ftp>			

Figure 13.4 Typical set of FTP transactions.

Figure 13.4 follows through a typical FTP transaction showing the prompt to the user, the commands the user types, the commands the FTP client sends to the FTP server and the responses back from the FTP server.

Notice that the `dir` command did not immediately produce a LIST command; first a PORT command was issued. This is because FTP uses separate logical connections, one for control and another for data. This is why FTP server has two well-known ports, 21 for control and 20 for data transfer. When any request is made to transfer information in either direction, a control message is sent to port 21 and a separate logical connection is built for data transfer to port 20. The response to a `dir` command returns data, so the client first has to tell the server to which socket to send the data response and it should not be the command port on the client. When a multiple file transfer is performed, a new logical data transfer connection using a new client port is created and closed for each file transferred.

Using FTP

The FTP definition details the commands used between the FTP client and FTP server software; it does not define the commands the users see. Although there is a general consensus of which FTP commands are used, there can be significant variations between different manufacturers' user interface presentations of FTP. Normally the commands given to the user are a combination of commands they would see on their local operating system and equivalent UNIX commands.

Table 13.6 Typical FTP user commands.

Command	Usage
user	Login a new user
dir	Display a directory listing
ls	Display a directory listing
pwd	Display which directory we are looking at
cd	Change directory
get	Get or receive a file
put	Send a file
mget	Get multiple files
mput	Put multiple files
send	Send a file
receive	Get or receive a file
binary	Switch to binary
text	Switch to text
?	Help
!	Switch to local operating system without closing FTP
rmdir	Delete directory
open	Make a connection
quit	Close the connection
status	Show the status of the connection
remotehelp	Show the FTP commands implemented on the server

A common mistake by new users is to believe that the commands they use when in FTP are from the local operating system, indeed to believe that they are at the operating system prompt rather than within an application program called ftp. Though commands in the FTP client software look like commands to the operating system, quite often their syntax is just sufficiently different to cause annoyance when you are familiar with using a command in a certain way. For example, in DOS

```
cd\tcpbk\msword
```

(without spaces) is valid. While the same command is used in ftp, in some implementations a space must be included:

```
cd \tcpbk\msword
```

Common FTP commands

Looking at the commands in Table 13.6, you will notice several commands have the same function, for example, get and receive. It is common for a number of the commands to be represented in the form they would be for different operating systems (ls, dir). This makes it easier to use any implementation of ftp without completely relearning the commands. But once again differences in exact syntax cause frustration.

Unlike a normal OS command line, in FTP multiple operations with **wildcards** (use of * to mean 'any') have their own commands. When trying to transfer all files ending with the extension .doc, the normal reaction is to try

```
get *.doc
```

This will fail because the get command does not support wildcards. The commands to use for multiple actions are those beginning with m, which stands for multiple, for example mget, mdelete.

The FTP network standard commands do not directly support multiple file operations. The m user commands have to take special action to provide it. Normally, an m command will perform a directory listing, unbeknown to the user, to get a list of files. Then it builds up the whole task with individual specific file actions on that list. These m commands often refuse to treat the * in the way your favourite operating system does. Files with extensions may be ignored with a single *; files without extensions may be ignored when using *.*; the * may not be accepted when you expect it to be.

The remotehelp command is another good command for causing confusion. One might expect it to provide help with accessing the remote system. In practice, it provides a list of the FTP network standard commands that are available on the FTP server (STOR, RETR, USER) and of course the end user has no interest in these! They are important for checking compatibility between different manufacturers' FTP implementations.

FTP file conversions

The commonest mistake newcomers to FTP make is with its file conversion capabilities. By default, FTP assumes you are transferring text files between computers. Text files are represented in a standard format during transmission and are converted to and from this format by the sending and receiving hosts. One conversion function ensures that the file has the correct end-of-line sequences, so it remains revisable as it is transferred from one operating system to another, as shown in Figure 13.5. FTP on an IBM host will also convert between ASCII and EBCDIC, if required.

This is fine so long as the file you are moving is text and not a binary data file or an executable file (sometimes also called an image file in FTP). FTP cannot tell the difference between different types of files, so unless the user tells FTP to operate in binary mode, it will transfer a binary file and do its best to translate it as it would a text file suitable for editing and displaying on the destination host. It adds end-of-line characters, carriage return and line feed, (or just newline) in what it thinks are suitable places. This normally has the effect of making binary files unusable! If the file transferred is executable and has been put

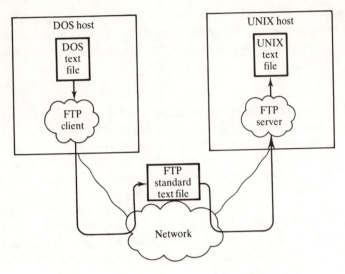

Figure 13.5 Text conversion in an FTP system.

through this treatment, it will most likely cause a computer to hang or give unusual error messages when run!

If a binary file is to be transferred using FTP, the FTP user command `binary` should be issued before the `put` or `get` commands are used. Of course, binary mode can be used to transfer text files, but if this is done and the destination operating system is different from the source operating system, it is most likely that the files will no longer be in revisable form on the destination system or the text formatting will be unusual.

Improving FTP

For the interface as just described, the FTP user must learn relatively obscure commands. It is a text-based interface from the early 1980s similar to the native interface to DOS or UNIX. It is a difficult interface for those who are not computer specialists, and even for those who are, it can be awkward due to the subtle differences in syntax of some commands and the differences between FTP implementations. For the average commercial user, this form of FTP is too cumbersome and one would expect it to be hidden by a front-end application program that interfaces to the file transfer facilities of the FTP application layer services.

With the growing use of graphical interfaces, as on the Apple Macintosh and with Windows or Presentation Manager for the PC, some recent TCP implementations are becoming easier to work with, as the syntactical issues which cause most user difficulty are hidden effectively.

FTP traces

Appendix I shows actual traces taken from an operational network using FTP. In that example, we show Ethernet frames in hexadecimal without the preamble or the CRC. The table beneath the frame gives a breakdown of the fields in the frame and their values. For a further explanation of the format of these examples, see Appendix F.

That example shows a user (system) logging in to a host. The frames are FTP requesting and transferring the user id, password, conducting port negotiation and preparing to transfer a directory listing.

Simple mail transfer protocol

For many years, the desire to use electronic mail has been strong. It can provide a quicker turn around than traditional mail and it can be used on most computer systems. Mail systems can be augmented to provide friendly services such as sending mail to groups of users, allowing word processors to transmit their files automatically, sending documents with the mail as attachments or handling registered mail so it is possible to know if and when the recipient has read an item.

The mail application layer in TCP/IP has undoubtedly helped in the development of the TCP/IP system itself by allowing information and ideas to be transferred freely throughout the Internet as draft RFCs.

SMTP is a service to allow mail packages to communicate with one another between different computers. As the name implies, it is a simple protocol. It operates in a similar way to FTP. The client sends ASCII-based commands to the server and the server responds with numeric and text responses as shown in Figure 13.6. Remember, such commands are intended for use between the SMTP client and server, not for end users.

As a moment's thought will show, mail has to be reliable, so SMTP uses TCP as its transport using well-known port 25.

The requests and responses shown in Figure 13.6 are carried in the data field of TCP, in ASCII, so a LAN analyser is able to display these transactions quite easily. Most mail systems have a debug option to help analyse problems. It allows the transactions to be viewed as they transfer between client and server .

Figure 13.7 shows a typical SMTP transaction. Notice that SMTP uses domain names (see Chapter 14) to identify hosts, and simply adds a user's name from the domain name of the host using the @ symbol. So Maggie@Training.edu is Maggie on host training.edu. It is also possible to use IP addresses instead of domain names if necessary. SMTP has to get the IP address of the remote host (from the domain name system or a hosts file) so it can deliver the mail.

Client commands (minimum implementation)

Command	*Explanation*
HELO<Training>	A connection request from system training
MAIL FROM:<JIM@Training.edu>	From Jim on system training
RCPT TO:<Kevin@Sales.com>	Send to Kevin on system sales
DATA	The text DATA follows terminated by <cr,lf>.<cr.lf>
QUIT	Terminate this connection
RSET	Abort the connection
NOOP	No operation

Server responses (subset)

250 OK
251 User not local; will forward to <wherever>
550 Requested action not taken: mailbox unavailable
354 Start mail input; end with <cr,lf>. <cr.lf>
500 Syntax Error

Figure 13.6   SMTP commands and responses.

Using SMTP

A user will not normally see the commands just considered. The user will be operating behind a manufacturer's user interface program, designed to make the service easier to use. Behind the scenes, the user interface program will be generating client commands and handling responses from the server.

Mail servers do not instantly attempt to deliver mail messages but check to see if there are any available at regular intervals, typically about 30 minutes. At this time a mail system will check its mail directories to see if there is outgoing information to send or received information to deliver to individual users. It will then perform the actions necessary to deliver it. Figure 13.8 shows an example of a front end used with SMTP.

From client	**From server**
	220 Training.edu service Ready
MAIL FROM:<JIM@Training.edu>	
	250 OK
RCPT TO:<Kevin@Sales>	
	250 OK
DATA	
	354 Start mail input; end with <cr,lf>. <cr.lf>

This is the actual data that will be transmitted from JIM on the training system to Kevin on the sales systems.

	250 OK
QUIT	
	250 OK

Figure 13.7   Typical SMTP transaction.

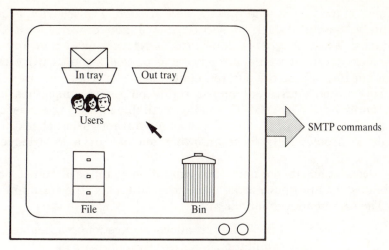

Figure 13.8 A front end used with SMTP.

At first sight, these actions might seem similar to the International Standard X.400 (Plattner *et al*, 1991) or MOTIS mail system. But there are some very important differences. X.400 distributes mail across a network of store and forward message switches. The unit of transmission between switches is the complete mail message. Although SMTP can use store and forward gateways, it normally delivers mail directly from originator user host to each recipient user host across a reliable TCP/IP connection. The unit of transmission is the TCP segment, not the message. For a single large message, SMTP should deliver faster. On the other hand, in X.400 the network of mail switches can expand and optimize the distribution list; the source need deliver the message to the network only once. With SMTP the source mail system must deliver the message to each receiving host across a separate TCP connection. The receiving host will create multiple copies for all recipients on its machine (on receipt of multiple RCPT commands).

It is possible to drive SMTP manually through a terminal connection as it accepts straight ASCII-based commands as shown above. This is not a recommendation, but an indication of how simple it is to communicate with the SMTP server protocol. It might have a diagnostic use for those perverse enough to try it.

R commands

The r commands (remote) are commonly supplied with TCP/IP implementations. These commands were intended as a simple mechanism for establishing connections between computers of the same type (UNIX), and were on a network where users were trusted. The security, or more accurately, potential lack of security, is a key concern with these commands. When they were developed, it was assumed that any user with access to them would already have passed some security check on another host. Since the environment was one of trust, the user could then be granted equivalent access rights on remote machines using the r commands. With TCP/IP readily available on PCs these assumptions are far from true. A DOS PC does no authorization check and is difficult to protect fully from unauthorized use by a knowledgeable person.

r commands do not have the negotiation facilities of Telnet, so the remote host has to know, or be configured to accept, the terminal type used. The common r commands are:

rlogin	Like Telnet, it allows connection to a remote computer
rsh	Allows a command to be executed on a remote computer
rexec	Allows a command to be executed on a remote computer
rcp	Allows files to be copied between remote computers

rlogin provides a terminal connection service similar to Telnet. On PCs, it therefore requires terminal emulation software to communicate with the remote host. In a situation where a terminal is connected directly to one host and its users connect to a remote host, the remote host must support that type of terminal for successful operation, as no negotiation is performed.

Compared to Telnet or FTP services, user validation on r commands is minimal. Furthermore, it is impossible to be definite about the way validation works with r commands. To access a host using the r commands normally only requires an IP address and user name to be in one of two files on the remote host, either in .rhosts or in rhosts.equiv. This varies between implementations, so you have to study the manufacturer's literature to be sure. Often you find that these commands are not protected at all or are almost impossible to get to work.

So, rlogin allows a user to access information on a remote machine. When connecting to a remote machine as the rlogin client, the client will issue the user's name and IP address or node name to the rlogin server when the connection is attempted. The rlogin server checks the supplied information against the entries in the .rhosts and rhosts.equiv file for that user. If there is a match, then access is allowed, if not, then access is denied. On PC implementations one of the options is to include the user id in a configuration file. This saves the user from typing it each time they log in. It also effectively dispenses with one small security feature.

Using r commands

In a trusted environment, the user can simply make a connection to a remote host by typing `rlogin hostname`. There is no need for logging in, and where the terminal type is the same there is no need to configure terminal types, so connection is rapid and users can quickly switch between systems at will. It is ideal for a development or maintenance environment where resources are on many machines. But there are few large commercial networks which can afford to be so open. Usually, security is important and terminal types vary, so the security and negotiation functions of Telnet become essential.

None the less, these command can be useful for system managers and other trustworthy system maintainers: `rsh` allows them to initiate commands on a remote computer without having to log in . `rexec` and `rcp` operate in the same fashion . `rcp` copies files between two machines. The initiator may be at a third machine that is neither the source nor destination of the transfer.

The issue is that putting any IP addresses and user names into the two key files lowers the defences against anyone with the knowledge to load `r` commands onto a PC and to configure it with a correct user id. Some PC implementations ask the user for a password locally before running an `r` command, but of course this password is contained in a file on the local PC and therefore will not defeat the knowledgeable attacker. Many suppliers' manuals recommend that PC IP addresses are not put in the key security files and that `r` commands are not available to PC users.

The latest versions of UNIX have new security features which prevent activities by networked users. It is possible to indicate a degree of trust of a particular user id and IP address. This will help reduce some of the problems with `r` commands. But in the end it depends not on the availability of advanced security features, but on understanding and applying the features to your environment through careful planning and system configuration.

Trivial file transfer protocol

The **Trivial File Transfer Protocol** (TFTP), as its name suggests, is a basic protocol. It was designed to be a small, easy-to-implement program. Because of this it lacks most of the features found in FTP and normally operates over UDP, the unreliable service. It must therefore carry out its own error correction. TFTP is seldom used directly by users as a service, but is more often used by machines for downloading programs and files. It cannot list directories and rarely has any provision for effective user authentication.

Authentication is usually performed through files on the destination host which normally need have only the IP address of the client

Table 13.7 Types of TFTP message.

Opcode	Command
1	Read request (RRQ)
2	Write request (WRQ)
3	Acknowledgement (ACK)
4	Data (DATA)
5	Error (ERROR)

machine and perhaps a user id. These files are usually .rhosts or rhosts.equiv, the same as used for the r commands but this is implementation dependent.

As TFTP does not use TCP, it has to manage its own error correction. For this, it uses a simple positive acknowledge protocol with time-out. If a datagram gets lost, the sender will time-out and try again. Normally datagrams contain exactly 512 octets. If the data is less than 512 octets, it is considered to be the last datagram for that file and so indicates that the transmission of the file is complete. The protocol uses its own block numbering scheme at the application layer above UDP. A block number starting at 1 is incremented for each block transmitted to identify if any are dropped. Major errors will cause TFTP connections to fail. An error is reported through the transmission of an error message. There are five types of TFTP message, shown in Table 13.7

The initial request is made to the well-known port 69 for TFTP, but the server will return a new port which subsequent transactions will use. Figure 13.9 shows an example of a TFTP transaction and the error message. The format of the read and write request are the same and the mode field is used to distinguish between the different types of file that can be transferred. The options this field can take are NETASCII, BINARY or MAIL. These options are transferred as words in ASCII terminated by a null.

Using TFTP

TFTP is not normally used for user-oriented file transfer as its facilities are too basic and its authentication mechanisms are, at best, suspect. It is often recommended that if TFTP is the only way, the user first accesses the remote host using Telnet. Once the access is approved by Telnet security, the user then uses the TFTP client on that remote system to connect back to their own originating host, before transferring files. This eliminates the need for a TFTP server on the remote host (Figure 13.10a). Unless automated behind some sort of front end, this type of convoluted communications activity is incomprehensible to the casual commercial computer user.

The major use for TFTP is as a bootstrap protocol. As it has small memory requirements and works with UDP, it can easily be configured

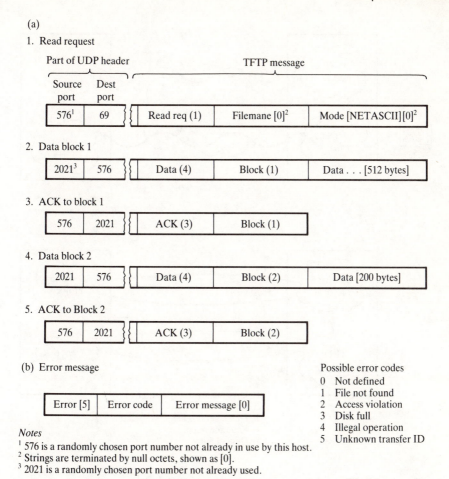

Figure 13.9 TFTP transactions, also showing the port numbers used in the UDP header.

into PROMs and installed on LAN cards. When a node is powered on or initialized the TFTP protocol will automatically connect to a server and download programs from that server. These programs could include a full TCP/IP protocol stack for other operations. Examples of these are shown in Figure 13.10(b).

Boot protocol

BOOTP was originally created for loading diskless computers. It has been designed to obtain all the information required for a computer to become fully operational on a TCP/IP network.

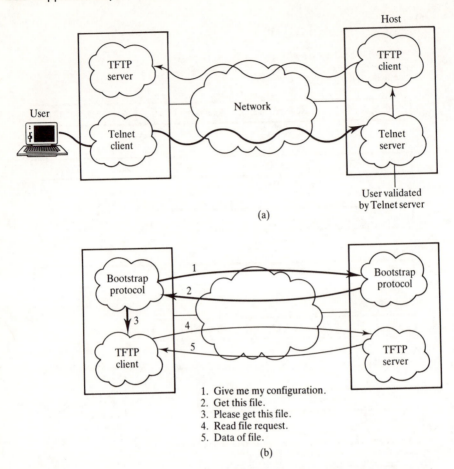

Figure 13.10 (a) Recommended usage of TFTP for improved security, and (b) TFTP with a bootstrap protocol.

A diskless node may not be able to store its IP address, or the programs which make up its sophisticated operating system, or the TCP/IP network code. BOOTP allows such a node to broadcast requests onto a network and obtain the information required from a BOOTP server. A BOOTP server is a computer that listens for incoming BOOTP requests and generates responses from a database of configurations for the BOOTP clients on that network.

The BOOTP header is shown in Figure 13.11. These headers are sent in UDP datagrams from port 68 on the client to port 67 on a server. Each has a number of fields that, in the request, can show what information the client already knows, but primarily they are filled in by a server based on information in its database. The database file is usually called bootptab (in UNIX systems).

Op	HTYPE	HLEN	Hops
Transaction id			
Seconds		Unused	
Client IP address			
Your IP address			
Server IP address			
Gateway IP address			
Client hardware address (16 octets)			
Server host name (64 octets)			
Boot file name (128 octets)			
Vendor specific (64 octets)			

Figure 13.11   Format of the BOOTP datagram.

On power up, the only information a diskless computer has regarding the network is often limited to the MAC address of its LAN card, as this is held in non-volatile memory. As a BOOTP client, it will transmit a BOOTP message onto the network with the MAC address field filled in. It may also fill in generic information such as the type of operating system it is to load (UNIX, DOS or OS/2 for example), perhaps chosen by a user from a displayed menu.

A BOOTP server that receives such a request will check in its database looking for a match of the MAC address from the request datagram. It should find at least an IP address which will be returned to the client computer. As can be seen in Figure 13.11, there are other very useful fields that can be used in the BOOTP message to configure the client more fully.

The fields used in the BOOTP datagram are:

- *Operation – 1 octet*   message opcode / message type: 1 = BOOT REQUEST, 2 = BOOTREPLY.

- *HTYPE – 1 octet*   Used to identify the network type (1 = 10 Mbps Ethernet).

- *HLEN – 1 octet*   Length of hardware addresses (6 for 10 Mbps Ethernet).

- *HOPS – 1 octet*   Optionally used by gateways in cross-gateway booting.

- *Transaction ID – 4 octets*   Used to match this boot request with the responses it generates.

- *Seconds – 2 octets*   Filled in by the client; seconds elapsed since client started trying to boot.

- *Unused – 2 octets*   Unused.

- *Client IP address – 4 octets*   Filled in by client in bootrequest if known.

- *Your IP address – 4 octets*   Your (client) IP address; filled in by server if client does not know its own address (client address was 0).

- *Server IP address – 4 octets*   Returned in bootreply by server.

- *Gateway IP address – 4 octets*   Used in optional cross-gateway booting.

- *Client hardware address – 16 octets*   Filled in by client.

- *Server host name – 64 octets*   Optional server host name as a null terminated string.

- *Boot file name – 128 octets*   Boot file name as a null terminated string; in bootrequest, a 'generic' name such as UNIX or DOS to specify OS type for the reply (or null). Fully qualified directory-pathname on the server in bootreply.

- *Vendor-specific – 64 octets*   Optional vendor-specific area, for example could be hardware type/serial number on request, or 'capability'/remote file system handle on reply. This information may be set aside for use by a third-phase bootstrap or kernel.

The vendor-specific field, as one would expect, was intended for use for vendors' special requirements to enhance their own products, but it soon became evident that these fields could be used for more general information useful for any diskless client. A suggested use for these fields has now been standardized by RFC 1084.

The format of the vendor-specific field is that it starts with a 'magic cookie', which identifies the format of the fields follow. If the format is to the standard defined in RFC1084, the cookie is 99.130.83.99 (dotted decimal notation). Apart from any padding and end tags, this is followed by a number of fields that each have a one-octet tag field, a one-octet length field, and a many-octet value field. Table 13.8 shows the common fields available.

When a computer is initialized and needs to send a BOOTP datagram, it will have no idea of the IP address of BOOTP servers or the IP address of the network it is connected to, so it has no idea of the IP broadcast address on that network either. To get around this problem, a special address, 255.255.255.255, is used as the destination IP address. 0.0.0.0 is used as the source. In principle, this indicates that this datagram is destined for all hosts on all networks, but this address on TCP/IP systems has a special meaning: 'broadcast on the local cable (I do not

Table 13.8   Common fields.

Name	Tag	Data	Description
Pad field	0	None	Used only for padding
Subnet mask field	1	4	Specifies the net and local subnet mask
Time offset field	2	4	Specifies the time offset of the local subnet in seconds from coordinated universal time (UTC); signed 32-bit integer
Gateway field	3	N octets	Specifies the IP addresses of $N/4$ gateways
Time server field	4	N octets	Specifies the IP addresses of $N/4$ time servers
IEN-116 name server field	5	N octets	Specifies the IP addresses of $N/4$ name servers
Domain name server field	6	N octets	Specifies the IP addresses of $N/4$ domain name servers
Log server field	7	N octets	Specifies the IP addresses of $N/4$ MIT-LCS UDP log server
Cookie/quote server field	8	N octets	Specifies the IP addresses of $N/4$ quote-of-the-day servers
LPR server field	9	N octets	Specifies the IP addresses of $N/4$ Berkeley 4BSD printer servers
Impress server field	10	N octets	Specifies the IP addresses of $N/4$ Impress servers
RLP server field	11	N octets	Specifies the IP addresses of $N/4$ resource location protocol servers
Hostname	12	N bytes of host name	Specifies the name of the client
Boot file size	13	2	A two-octet value (in network order) specifying the number of 512 octet blocks in the default boot file
Reserved fields	128–254	Undefined	Specifies additional site-specific information, to be interpreted on an implementation-specific basis
End field	255	None	Specifies end of usable data in the vendor information area. The rest of this field should be filled with PAD

know my network number)', so the BOOTP datagram is broadcast on the local cabling system by the LAN hardware.

This mechanism is fine provided the BOOTP server is located within that broadcast area. If it is in another area, across one or more routers, these routers must recognize the broadcast IP address and choose whether or not to forward the BOOTP requests to all their connected networks. It is suggested in the BOOTP RFCs that routers which support the passing of BOOTP datagrams can be configured to define which individual networks they will forward them to, and that they should wait for a number of requests to be made before doing so. By waiting, they would then only relay these broadcasts if a local BOOTP server did not satisfy the request. The seconds field in the BOOTP header can assist with this decision as it indicates how long the client has been attempting to boot.

One of the options when configuring a router port is whether IP broadcasts will be relayed on that port and what address is to be recognized as broadcast[†].

Another dilemma with BOOTP is: how does a server respond to the client? The server cannot use the client's IP address as a destination for, in the most general case[‡], the client does not yet know its IP address so the client will not respond to ARP requests. The server will already know the MAC address of the client as it is the MAC source address in the BOOTP request datagram, but not all systems allow programs to modify their ARP cache directly. To overcome these problems, it is common for the server response to be a broadcast back to the client if no IP address is given in the request, but if the client does know its IP address the response will be directly to that address, assuming that ARP will work. (The client must have enough software to run ARP.)

Since BOOTP uses UDP, BOOTP clients must add the reliability of getting the message to the BOOTP server. They will set a time-out and retransmit if that time-out matures.

Using BOOTP

These days, BOOTP is not used just for diskless workstations, but also for providing centralized control of IP addresses. It allows IP addresses to be managed from a single database and standard software configurations to be used even though the workstation may have disks.

System managers can define a standard software configuration that can be implemented on all systems without even having to configure an IP address on each workstation. The one key fact to obtain during installation is the physical (MAC) address of the LAN card for each installed system. This is the key to correct distribution of all other information. By this method, workstations can learn everything from their IP address to their default router, additional routers, domain name, host name, location of domain name servers and time servers.

Of course, the other use of BOOTP is for diskless workstations. In this case BOOTP is significant because it can allocate not just IP addresses for a node, but also the IP address of common hosts, routers and the name of program files to be downloaded. BOOTP does not download files; it will supply just the server IP address and the name of a file to be downloaded. TFTP is often used to download files indicated by BOOTP.

BOOTP can operate over routers if they support the special broadcast as discussed in the previous section. Consideration should be given to the amount of router traffic this will generate.

[†]Some early systems used 0.0.0.0 as the destination broadcast address. Continued use of this address is not encouraged.

[‡]It is possible for a computer to use BOOTP for information other than its IP address, in which case it could well already know its IP address.

Line printer services

As well as access to hosts for terminal services and file transfer, remote printing is a common requirement. This is especially true in the world of PC networking, where most users who have a PC will wish to print documents. In the past, it has been too expensive to supply them all with high-quality printers. Line Printer Services (LPS) allows these users to access printers controlled by a central resource, that is, a computer that has printers either directly or remotely connected to it, and that can handle the functions necessary to share printers or plotters.

LPS allows print output to be redirected from one computer to print queues on another. This enables print to be delivered where most appropriate, and makes best use of shared resources. LPS consists of two main processes: LPR, the client, and LPD, the server. LPD accepts print sent to it through LPR and places the output into a print queue, ready for printing on the machine running LPD.

The LPR/LPD protocol uses TCP as its transport. It has a basic format shown in Figure 13.12. The first byte defines the function of the command and the next field defines the target print queue with its name terminated by an ASCII line feed character, $^L{}_F$. Some functions have extra fields where necessary.

The well-known port number for the LPD is 515 (0x0203). The LPR client must use source ports between 721 (0x02CF) and 731 (0x02DB).

Using LPS

The biggest problem with LPS is configuring the relevant files correctly. LPS provides a number of useful standard utilities:

Command	*Action*
Client	
lpr	Assign output to queue
lpq	Display a queue
lprm	Remove output from queue
Server	
lpc	Control queue

The LPD listens for incoming connections on port 515; once one is received, it analyses the request, then verifies that the host from which the user is connecting is acceptable and that the user has authority to print, and checks that the requested print queue exits.

LPR can be used in a number of ways, but the most common and the default is that the user just types

```
lpr filename
```

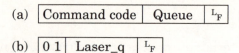

(a) | Command code | Queue | ^L_F |

(b) | 0 1 | Laser_q | ^L_F |

Figure 13.12 (a) LPS command format with (b) example of print any
waiting jobs command.

This causes `filename` to be printed on a remote default queue, but a
queue can be explicitly defined, such as:

```
lpr -Pqueue1@oz memo.txt
```

This command would print the file `memo.txt` through a queue called
`queue1` on host `oz`.

The LPS protocol

As with most TCP/IP application layer services, LPS has a simple protocol that is used to control the necessary printing functions. The basic
format of these commands is a one-octet command code followed by the
queue name and terminated with the ASCII Line Feed character (^L_F) (see
Figure 13.12).

Basic commands are listed in Table 13.9.

To print a file, the LPS client (LPR) sends a 'receive a printer job'
command to the LPS server (LPD) and then uses one of the subcommands
(Table 13.10) to indicate the operation to be handled.

If the 'receive control file' option is used, the details of a file that
handles a set of special control commands are passed so that file is transferred to LPD. LPD will then perform those actions on the print file that
follows. If the subcommand defines 'receive data file', the size and name of
the print file are given. This name takes the form 'dfA' followed by a three-
digit job number and then the host name of the originator, for example:

```
dfA003percy
```

Table 13.9 Basic LPS commands.

Command code	Function
01	Print any waiting jobs
02	Receive a printer job
03	Send queue status (short)
04	Send queue status (long)
05	Remove jobs

Table 13.10 LPS subcommands.

Sub-command code	Function
01	Abort job
02	Receive control file
03	Receive data file

Control filenames use the same format but start with cfA, for example

```
cfA005percy
```

Commands are acknowledged by a one-octet response from LPD. A value of zero indicates the command was accepted. Any other value indicates a failure of some kind.

A typical LPS print sequence is shown in Figure 13.13. A file called sometext.doc is to be printed from host gandalf on to host integv.

Using LPR

In simple configurations, LPR is easy to use once it is set up. A user prints documents as normal, the software handles the rest. The print output is sent from the application across the network and put into a spool file for the relevant printer queue on the target host operating as the LPD server. Once the spool file is completed, that is, all the document to be printed has been received, the print manager on the target host will select the spool file and send it to the relevant print device. As with most spooling systems, nothing may come out on the printer until the whole print job has been completed. This can lead to inordinate delays for large print tasks.

Some systems allow control files that will manage the way data is printed on the remote printer to be sent to the host.

NetBIOS

Before describing the relationship between NetBIOS and TCP/IP, we will review how NetBIOS was developed and what it means for networks today. To assist with this explanation, we will consider the normal BIOS (Basic Input/Output System) that is used in IBM PCs and compatibles.

The BIOS in a PC is intended to provide a standard interface to hardware, such that the type of hardware supplied in the machine becomes irrelevant. The BIOS handles commands to send and receive information from the disks, keyboard, communication ports and screens. It provides a level of independence from their specific physical attributes

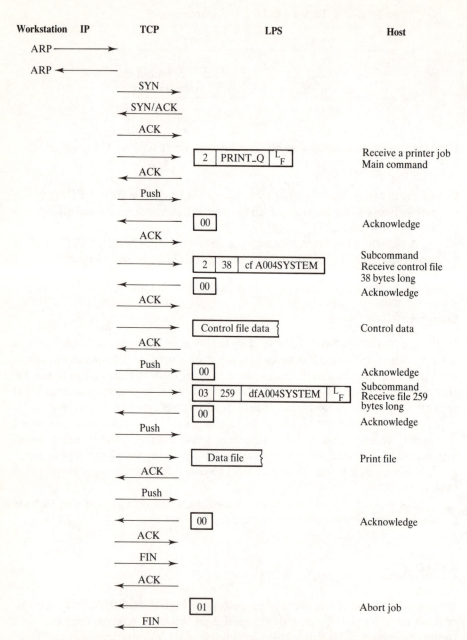

Figure 13.13 LPS transaction between hosts gandalf and integv.

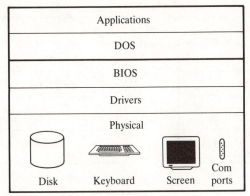

Com ports = Communication ports

Figure 13.14 PC architecture.

and establishes a standard set of commands for programs and programmers (Figure 13.14).

The BIOS has no concept of files – that is the function of the operating system that uses it – it just sends information to the relevant devices. This isolates programmers from the detail of the hardware – the screen, keyboard layout, and disk formats – of a particular machine implementation. It allows simple transportation of programs to different hardware platforms, compatibles and clones, without the need for exactly the same make and format of hardware. Applications become independent of (peripheral) hardware; they become BIOS dependent, but this has proved to be far more stable.

NetBIOS is an interface developed by IBM and Sytek Inc. (now part of Hughes LAN Systems) for the original IBM PC Network. It allows application programs to communicate with the underlying network protocols and hardware. NetBIOS is best thought of as an interface for naming and accessing resources in a LAN structure. It is equivalent to the BIOS in IBM's computer architecture.

When IBM and Sytek designed the network hardware for the IBM PC Network (circa 1984), they defined a similar interface to BIOS but to suit the networking environment. They called it the Network BIOS or NetBIOS (Figure 13.15). NetBIOS provided an interface to the Sytek network hardware and protocols, irrespective of their details. A major difference between the functions of BIOS and of NetBIOS is that before you can read and write information from network devices, you must connect to them first. NetBIOS supports the ability to open connections, read and write data, and close connections.

Above NetBIOS was a layer called the session layer. This equates to a Network Operating System (NOS), and manages access to resources

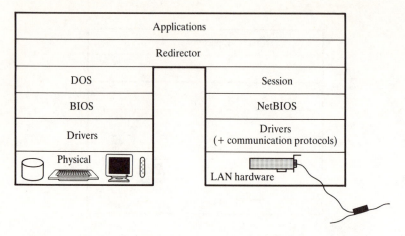

Figure 13.15 Architecture of a PC showing BIOS and NetBIOS.

on the network just as the local operating system, DOS for example, manages local resources.

Above the session layer and DOS is a layer called the redirector that chooses whether resources are local or across the network. It isolates applications from the network and local hardware and, in principle, the applications cannot tell the difference between data stored on a network and on local hardware. In machines which are also servers, it intercepts requests from remote clients and directs them to its local hardware without the local application being aware of it.

This allowed resource sharing of local area networking to become as transparent as it is today, introducing the concept of the **virtual drive**. A virtual drive appears no different to a local drive but is, in fact, on a remote machine and is potentially shared among many users.

The most common NetBIOS commands illustrate the functionality provided by this interface. The commands are in four groups:

(1) *General commands*

Reset   Reset the adapter: initializes the adapter to make it ready for use.

Cancel   Allows a command that has been issued but not serviced to be cancelled.

Adapter status   Provides a list of statistics and some configuration of the adapter card.

Unlink   Used when performing remote program load to disconnect from the initial server.

(2) *Name support*

Add name   Register a node's name on the network.

Add group name   Register a group name on the network.

Delete name   Remove a name from the network.

(3) *Session support*

Call	Make a connection.
Listen	Listen for a message.
Hang up	Close a connection.
Send	Send data.
Chain send	Send multiple buffers of data.
Receive	Data from a specific session.
Receive any	Data.
Session status	The status of a session.

(4) *Datagram support*

Send datagram	Send a datagram.
Send broadcast datagram	To all devices on a network.
Receive datagram	Wait for a datagram.
Receive broadcast datagram	Wait for a datagram from any device on the network.

The commands are accessed through software interrupts in the same way as normal DOS and BIOS functions. It is these commands and naming conventions that remain standard across all implementations of NetBIOS. The details of the original Sytek and IBM implementation are today largely irrelevant. What a DOS application must see is the correct interface to the network through the DOS software interrupt structure, and the correct blocks of information in memory to generate each command and interpret the responses. How that information is carried across the network is not important to the application, another advantage of a layered architecture.

But NetBIOS is more than just an interface. To perform the commands does also require a protocol to carry the commands so that the remote node can understand what is intended. When this protocol was based on the Sytek network protocols, it was proprietary. Other manufacturers produced emulations of the NetBIOS interface on their own hardware but using their own protocols. This allowed applications which could interface to the IBM PC Network to run over any manufacturer's NetBIOS. Because the protocols that carried the NetBIOS commands were different, different vendors' NetBIOS products could not interoperate.

Now it should be clearer how NetBIOS and TCP/IP are related. NetBIOS is the standard interface, naming convention and command structure as seen by DOS applications. TCP/IP is one way of carrying that structure between participating workstations.

NetBIOS and TCP/IP

The commercial success of TCP/IP protocols has encouraged its use as a common single network protocol replacing proprietary protocols. The management advantages of one protocol are self-evident. As PC networks grew to such a significant market, there was a need to provide the NetBIOS interface over TCP/IP. The interested bodies cooperated to define how the NetBIOS interface should operate over TCP/IP. Because there is a defined standard, then every vendor's implementation of NetBIOS on a TCP/IP network has a strong possibility of being compatible.

There are two RFCs, 1001 and 1002, which define the implementation of NetBIOS over TCP/IP. The first describes how NetBIOS node names are handled and the second describes the protocol.

NetBIOS allows users to define names for their computers. To ensure that the name is unique, NetBIOS broadcasts it onto a network at startup. If no other node indicates in a reply that it has registered that same name, then the originator can assume it is unique. When operating over TCP/IP, these names must be 'resolved' to IP addresses since all TCP/IP communication depends on the IP address; to make a connection to another NetBIOS node, a broadcast is sent out to discover the IP address of the remote node with the specified NetBIOS name.

This requirement to broadcast packets *throughout* a network, to check to see if your name is unique or to discover an IP address, is not practical in a large Internet. Potentially it could create a large number of broadcasts, so an alternative mechanism was required. The solution was to allow NetBIOS names to be associated with the domain name scheme (see Chapter 14) used with TCP/IP. The NetBIOS name is considered as a standard host name within one domain, so the test to see if a name is unique is then only relevant within a specific domain and not throughout the Internet.

If we have a NetBIOS server called 'lemming', this name would be concatenated with the domain name for our area. For example, in brewery.integralis.com.uk, the full name of the server would be:

```
lemming.brewery.integralis.com.uk
```

This domain name and NetBIOS name are often referred to as the **scope**. The test to see if a name is unique is now only performed with machines that are located in the same domain, brewery. integralis.com.uk.

NetBIOS servers

To complicate matters, when operating NetBIOS over TCP/IP, there are three different types of NetBIOS nodes. They are B nodes, P nodes and M nodes. B (or broadcast) nodes can only operate within a broadcast area, as they use broadcasts to discover other nodes and to register themselves to the network. P nodes communicate using directed datagrams and TCP; they need the services of a NetBIOS Name Server (NBNS) or a NetBIOS

Datagram Distribution Server (NBDD). M nodes are a mix of B node and P node operation. They use NBNS and NBDD servers but can still function within a broadcast area if servers are not used or not available.

An NBNS is modelled as closely as possible on the standard domain name server, but, to support a NetBIOS service, a number of additional functions are necessary:

- dynamic addition of entries
- dynamic update of entries
- support for group entities
- support for entry time-to-live and messages to refresh its value
- new entry attributes

NetBIOS nodes normally register their names when they are first activated. This means a name server must be able to add entries to its tables dynamically. Standard TCP/IP domain name servers use fixed tables that are configured by network managers.

An NBDD operates in environments that do not support broadcasting and multicasting. It holds a list of all nodes within the same NetBIOS scope, together with their IP addresses. It has the ability to communicate with them all directly for name registration and lookup. A node will communicate directly with an NBDD to register its name rather than use broadcast. Thus only unicast messages are required with this type of server, but the end node must know the IP address of the NBDD. As reducing broadcast traffic is always a useful aim, using NBDD even in a broadcast environment could have performance advantages.

B nodes perform name registration and name discovery by broadcasting claim requests in the broadcast domain, P nodes by using an NBDD, and M nodes by first broadcasting and then using an NBNS. Names registered in an NBNS have a time-to-live value after which time they are flushed from the database or the NBNS will first perform a name challenge to see if the node is still using that name. If it is still active, the time-to-live timer will be reset.

NetBIOS name encoding

To map NetBIOS names into domain name server compatible form, two levels of encoding are performed. NetBIOS names are normally 16 octets long. Even if the name seen by the user is shorter, it is filled out with spaces[†] when passed across the network protocol. NetBIOS names are case sensitive so 'a' does not equal 'A'. Standard TCP/IP domain names are not case sensitive, so 'a'='A'. One of the reasons for encoding NetBIOS

[†]White space or ASCII character 0x20.

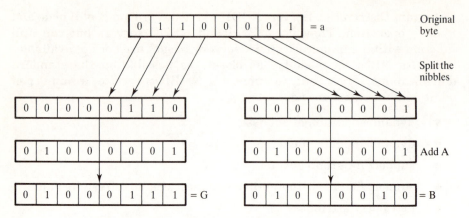

Figure 13.16 First level encoding for NetBIOS names.

names is, therefore, to prevent clashes and ensure that they remain case sensitive. The encoding technique splits each octet into 4 bit quantities and adds them to ASCII character 'A', hexadecimal 0x41. This creates two uppercase ASCII characters from each character of the NetBIOS name, so a NetBIOS name now becomes 32 octets long. Figure 13.16 gives an example of this encoding showing that lowercase 'a' becomes two uppercase characters 'G' and 'B'.

The name 'Server' in domain integralis.com.uk would be encoded as the string:

```
FDGFHCHGGFHCCACACACACACACACACACA.INTEGRALIS.COM.UK
```

Second-level encoding is exactly the same as for normal domain name system names and is explained in Chapter 14. In effect, the above name would then be encoded as:

```
32FDGFHCHGGFHCCACACACACACACACACACA10INTEGRALIS3COM2UK0
```

Keep-alive packets

Another feature of NetBIOS systems is their use of the **keep-alive-packet**. This is a packet request-and-reply sequence to check that a connection is still functional when no data is flowing. Again, in an Internet, the background traffic this would generate is wasteful of capacity, so the standard allows **keep-alive-packets** to be disabled.

RFC 1002 defines a well-known port for NetBIOS name services which is 137 for both TCP and UDP services. For TCP session services, NetBIOS uses port 139 and UDP datagrams services port 138. The maximum datagram length is 576 octets.

Using NetBIOS

NetBIOS provides a standard interface to LAN cards, allowing peer-to-peer connections to be established between machines. Although this interface was developed for the IBM PC, NetBIOS can now be found on mini- and mainframe computers as well. This allows mini- and mainframes to participate as file and print servers in what was originally a DOS PC domain. The term 'PC Network' has become obsolete. It is now a generic term for sharing data among any type of machine including PCs; it is more appropriate to talk today about Network Operating Systems (NOSs).

The NetBIOS interface is available with most NOSs. Microsoft LAN Manager and Microsoft Networks systems (MSNET) use NetBIOS. It is also available for Novell NetWare. NetBIOS can run over many networks, XNS, TCP/IP, IPX and X.25, so it has become a powerful tool for system integration. NetBIOS provides the 'interoperation' aspects of the internetworking equation. Two systems can, of course, only communicate if they are using the same interconnection methods, that is, the same network protocols to carry the NetBIOS commands.

A number of parameters can be set to improve operation. These are: session retry count (default 4), session time-out (30 seconds default) and keep-alive time-out (60 seconds default). In some systems keep-alive packets can be turned off altogether. With keep-alive packets enabled, the protocols detect network errors quicker than without, but the traffic they generate is not desirable over WAN connections.

Sockets library

When exploring TCP/IP literature one will often see reference to a **sockets library**. A sockets library is a set of programmer's tools for simplifying the development of applications over the TCP or UDP transport layer services. At a high level, it provides procedures or functions to create programs that will talk to application level services such as FTP, Telnet and TFTP; at the lower level, it provides access to the raw services of UDP or TCP which may just be used to develop a bespoke service. Some of the dangers of isolating programmers from the network quite so effectively were discussed in Chapter 7. Some faults and performance problems that occur in operational systems are due to programmers who did not appreciate the impact on the network of certain simple techniques available through the sockets interface.

The **socket** is the programmer's identifier for a communications path. In many programming environments, input/output devices are treated as generic objects that can be written to and/or read from. In UNIX systems the reference to such an object is a file descriptor, even though the object may be a printer or communications port; in the sockets environment this file descriptor equates to a socket.

The programmer uses sockets to refer to a remote application layer entity: if the program is not going to use existing servers, the developer must choose port numbers that have not been allocated to an existing application. The programmer can decide which transport service to use, TCP or UDP. With some implementations it is possible to generate and receive packets at any layer of the protocol stack[†], where an existing protocol would put too much restriction on the application.

The difference between reading and writing to a socket as compared to a local file descriptor is that the software has to establish a relationship with the remote node across the communications network. Once this relationship is established, reading and writing is identical to working with local objects.

Using sockets

For someone with programming experience, the basic principles of working with a sockets library are straightforward.

Getting a socket identifier

Initially the program must choose the type of service that it will use and acquire a unique socket reference for the remote resource. The command for this could be:

```
result=socket(AF,type,protocol);
```

The `result` of this function call will be the unique reference value for the `socket`. `AF` refers to the protocol family. There are various options, but the normal one with TCP/IP systems is `AF_INET`. The `type` field chooses the network interface and has the following options:

```
SOCK_STREAM
SOCK_DGRAM
SOCK_RAW
```

Setting the type field to be `SOCK_STREAM` configures the socket to operate over TCP, so the programmer has selected a reliable stream connection. Selecting `SOCK_DGRAM` selects the services of UDP. `SOCK_RAW` is referred to as the Do-It-Yourself (DIY) interface. With this type, a low-level interface below that of the TCP/IP transport layers is accessed, either IP or datalink. Whether it is IP or datalink depends on further options and who wrote the sockets library! This is a DIY interface so programmers will have to implement their own protocols to provide the services usually supplied by higher layers.

[†]The Do-It-Yourself (DIY) interface.

The protocol field is an extension of the protocol family that is required for some protocols. It is generally not required with TCP/IP systems.

Establishing a relationship

The next command depends on whether the program is a client or a server. A server program has to select which local port to attach itself to using the bind command, whereas TCP-based client software would need to establish a connection to a remote host using the connect command:

```
Server   bind(socket,localaddr,addrlen)
Client   connect(socket,dataaddr,addrlen)
```

The fields localaddr and dataaddr are pointers to some memory which defines, among other things, the port the application listens on, in the case of a server, and the port to connect to, in the case of a client.

Writing and reading

Once these relationships have been established and a connection has taken place, you can read and write from the socket as necessary using the commands:

```
write(socket,buffer,length)
read(socket,buffer,length)
```

In these commands buffer is the area which contains the data to be sent or an area to place data received. The length field indicates the length of the data to be sent or read.

Closing

When all the data has been sent and received the socket should be closed. This is simply performed by the command:

```
close(socket)
```

These six commands are the basis for all programs using the sockets interface. There are many more useful utilities to obtain information about addresses and to deal with data conversion, as well as libraries that perform typical FTP, TFTP and Telnet functions.

Figure 13.17 shows the basic steps required to act as a server or a client. The server creates the socket, binds a local IP address and port to that socket and then is ready to read and write from it. Once finished it closes the socket. For the client, again it first opens the socket, then connects to the remote IP address and port number, reads and writes as necessary and again closes the socket when finished.

Basic server commands

```
result=socket(AF,type,protocl)
bind(socket,localaddr,addrlen)
   write(socket,buffer,length)
   read(socket,buffer,length)
close(socket)
```

Basic client commands

```
result=socket(AF,type,protocl)
connect(socket,dataaddr,addrlen)
   write(socket,buffer,length)
   read(socket,buffer,length)
close(socket)
```

Figure 13.17 Basic commands required to create client and server programs using a sockets interface.

This is but a simple description of sockets programming. There are far more sophisticated facilities to help the programmer develop reliable effective programs. Servers must be capable of supporting multiple clients simultaneously.

A complete example

The following example is a 'C' code program used to demonstrate the basics of sockets programming. The server program uses UDP, selected in the socket procedure as SOCK_DGRAM, to broadcast the message Hello World contained in a buffer to the network. The client program is designed to receive these messages and indicate their sizes. The significant lines have been emboldened so they can be picked out more easily. The remaining lines are the definition of variables and error testing in case any step fails. As with most programs, handling errors is a major part of the task.

This example does not use TCP so no connections need be established. Each end binds to an address and port; the server transmits on its port; the client receives on its own port. Note that this program uses broadcast and the send routine loops as quickly as possible. The number of broadcasts it will generate would have a catastrophic impact on an operational network.

Server program

```
#include <4bsddefs.h>
#include <sys/socket.h>
#include <netinet/in.h>
main()
```

```
{
  int sock;
  struct sockaddr saddr;
  char *buffer;
  int flags = 0;
  int len;
  char opt = 1;
/* Set the socket up to be Internet and */
/* using datagrams */
  if((sock = socket(AF_INET, SOCK_DGRAM, 0)) <0)
  {
    perror("Open Socket Failed");
    exit(0);
  }
/* Set the socket options to use broadcast */
  setsockopt(sock, SOL_SOCKET, SO_BROADCAST, &opt,
  size of(opt));
    memset((char *)&saddr, '\0', sizeof(struct sock-
    addr));
    saddr.sa_family = AF_INET;
    saddr.sa_data[0] = htons(900);
    saddr.sa_data[2] = INADDR_ANY;
/* Bind the socket to a local address */
/* and port */
  if(bind(sock, &saddr, sizeof(struct sockaddr)) < 0)
  {
  perror("Bind Failed");
  exit(0);
  }
/* set the buffer to the data to be sent */
  buffer = "Hello World";
  while(!kbhit())
  {
    if((len = sendto(sock, buffer, strlen(buffer),
    flags, &saddr, sizeof(struct sockaddr))) < 0)
  {
  perror("Sendto Failed");
  exit(0);
  }
  }
close(sock);
  }
```

Client program

```c
#include <4bsddefs.h>
#include <sys\socket.h>
#include <netinet\in.h>

main()
{
  int sock;
  struct sockaddr saddr;
  unsigned char buffer[512];
  int flags = 0;
  int saddr_len;
  int len;

/* Set the socket up to be Internet and */
/* using datagrams */

  if((sock = socket(AF_INET, SOCK_DGRAM, 0)) < 0)
  {
      perror("Open Socket Failed");
      exit(0);
  }

  memset((char *)&saddr, '\0', sizeof(struct sockaddr));
  saddr.sa_family = AF_INET;
  saddr.sa_data[0] = htons(900);
  saddr.sa_data[2] = INADDR_ANY;

/* Bind the socket to listen on port 900 */

  if(bind(sock, &saddr, sizeof(struct sockaddr)) < 0)
  {
    perror("Bind Failed");
    exit(0);
  }

  while(!kbhit()) /* loop until a key is struck */
  {
    saddr_len = sizeof(struct sockaddr);

/* Receive data from the socket */

    if((len = recvfrom(sock, buffer, sizeof(buffer),
       flags, &saddr, &saddr_len)) < 0)
    {
      perror("Recv Failed");
      exit(0);
    }
    buffer[len] = '\0';
```

```
    printf("Message is : %s Length is : %d\n",
      buffer, len);
  }

  close(sock);
}
```

To those not familiar with C programming, this may look complex, but the key is in the few bold lines. This is a simple program made to look complicated by the level of error testing performed around each command. A few moments' study will indicate how logical the process of communication through the sockets library is.

X protocol

With the recent demand for 'windows' applications – applications which operate through a Graphical User Interface (GUI) – a standard programming interface that provides compatibility between different hardware systems is a useful addition to the application layer. To meet this requirement the X Window System is outlined in RFC 1013 and hence may be thought of as an 'open' standard, though it is developed by MIT (see Chapter 6). Full details of all the protocols are available from the X Window Consortium at MIT.

The operation of X Window System is not tied to any particular protocol but has so far been predominantly used with UNIX and hence on TCP/IP, so X Window has become associated with TCP/IP. The X Window System definition considers a program to consist of client and server modules that can be located on the same machine or on different machines across a network. The definition of how the client and server programs intercommunicate is defined by a protocol call the **X Protocol**.

X Window System goes a long way to providing computers with standards for accessing applications on different computing architectures. This is because it is much more involved in the representation of data to computer users than earlier techniques; it provides a standard interface between the true user interface and the remote software that drives that user interface. Using X Window System a user can access, in a standard way, any application that generates the X protocol as output, irrespective of what hardware or operating system that application is running on.

When discussing X Window, one must be careful with the terms 'server' and 'client'. Here the server is a program that controls the display of information to users; the client is an application that generates that information (Figure 13.18). X terminals are specific devices that are intelligent workstations dedicated to the task of being an X Window server. As the name suggests, X Window System is based on a windowed GUI environment where the mouse and menus are important additions to the keyboard in providing the user interface. These are all associated with the X server.

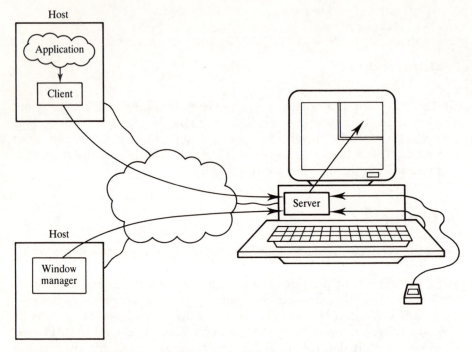

Figure 13.18 X Window System architecture.

In a client/server architecture, the server normally only responds to client requests. Within the X Window environment, mouse movements and keystrokes are reported to the client through **event commands**.

X Window System is becoming an important vehicle for cross-platform compatibility. This is because any application that can operate as an X client can be used by an X server irrespective of what computers or operating system they may be using. What is required is a common network connection and protocol such as TCP/IP.

The X protocol is a complete definition of functions that support the mouse, keyboard input, drawing windows, boxes, lines, circles, in fact anything to do with displaying pictures and text in windows on a screen. The protocol uses TCP as a reliable stream transport. It opens a separate port for each window starting with port 6000 and adding 1 for each subsequent window. There are four different types of message used by the X protocol: requests, replies, errors and events.

In its basic form, every event is passed across the network between server and client. Moving a mouse on an X Window display can generate a stream of network traffic. Such activity is only practical in a truly local environment, preferably on the same LAN cable. Recent changes to the X Window definition are aimed at changing the split between server and client activities; this will allocate more screen processing to the server and reduce the traffic between devices to levels acceptable over other types of link.

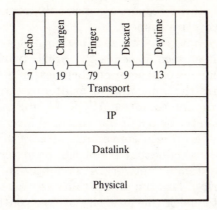

Figure 13.19 Architecture of the miscellaneous services.

Miscellaneous services

TCP/IP normally provides a number of services at the application layer which can be very useful for node and network diagnostics. These services are selected through the well-known port numbers which differentiate them. The most common and useful are listed in Table 13.11.

Figure 13.19 shows the architecture of these services. As the services themselves are server software, they will reply to any incoming client requests on their respective ports.

A remote client that connects into the **echo** service will have data it sends returned or echoed back. This provides an excellent confidence test at a higher level than ping, the ICMP echo. Ping only indicates that a node exists and that its IP layer is operational. The application layer echo moves beyond the IP layer through TCP or UDP to the application layer, stopping just short of end-user applications, and therefore testing through all layers of the protocol stack. Use of ping and then this service can help differentiate between failure either of an application or at a particular point in the protocol stack; if the client is able to get a response from echo but cannot access the end-user application, the application is

Table 13.11 Port numbers of miscellaneous services.

Service	Port number (decimal)
Echo	7
Chargen	19
Finger	79
Discard	9
Daytime	13

likely to be at fault; if the response comes only from ping, the transport and application layers are suspect.

Chargen is what is known as a 'barber-pole' test. When a connection is made to this service, it sends the ASCII printable character set continuously, sliding one character on each new line. This test was originally used to ensure that mechanical printers were working correctly, that they could print the complete ASCII set and support flow control. Today, this test can still be useful for checking a connection is functioning correctly by generating a continuous stream of traffic. With some hosts, a very high level of output traffic can be generated, so it can be a way of loading a system or network. It is not a test to run in a normal operational network unless the aim is to measure user tolerance! It can also still be used to check the integrity of flow control, to measure the throughput achieved on a particular route and to investigate the effects of altering the TCP/IP performance parameters of window and maximum segment sizes.

The **finger** service is intended to allow one person to determine the full details about another user from their user id. If someone is connected to a host remotely across a network, you can only see their user id, not their full name. User ids can be cryptic. The finger utility will request the full name and details of any user as furnished by the security access files in the user's own host. In most host security systems, a manager gives the full name and sometimes other details about a user against their user id; finger accesses this information. This is designed to allow a system manager, for example, to obtain the telephone number, room number and location of a remote user.

The **discard** utility is a bottomless pit for information, a 'null' destination. It allows information sent to a host to be completely ignored and discarded. This can be a useful way of checking the performance of networks and protocol stacks without producing significant load on a host's operating system. It can potentially differentiate between communications delays and host delays.

The **daytime** service returns the time and day in ASCII format so it can be read by programs or users. There are a number of other time-related services that provide the date and time in varying formats. These can be used to synchronize the time and date automatically on all computers in a network. This is a particularly useful function when mail systems are involved; mail sent by systems that have an incorrect date can cause administrative headaches in some operational environments.

Using debugging and measurement services

These services can be accessed by specially written programs (the sockets library) or connected to directly using Telnet. Telnet normally connects to server software by addressing its communications to port 23, but in many implementations of Telnet there is a command line option that allows the user to define the destination port number to be used. Any port number can be supplied and therefore Telnet can access any service. The possibility of a useful exchange with the server depends on the application layer protocol that server uses. Since many of the services just described send ASCII data streams, they can be usefully accessed for testing purposes via Telnet. There is an issue of performance and security. A network manager does not necessarily wish to encourage general computer users from using Telnet into well-known, but random, ports. There may be no general way of preventing this.

These tools might also be used through an application program. Some of these services require arguments to be passed to them. This is certainly easier from a specially constructed application. A service such as synchronizing the clocks on different computers is certainly better dealt with by an application.

How these miscellaneous services can be used is considered further in Chapter 18.

Relevant RFCs

General topics

1123 Requirements for Internet hosts – application and support
1173 Responsibilities of host and network managers: a summary of the 'oral tradition' of the Internet

Telnet and SUPDUP

698 Telnet extended ASCII option
726 Remote controlled transmission and echoing Telnet option
727 Telnet logout option
730 Extensible field addressing
732 Telnet data entry terminal option
734 SUPDUP protocol
735 Revised Telnet byte macro option
736 Telnet SUPDUP option
746 SUPDUP graphics extension
747 Recent extensions to the SUPDUP protocol
748 Telnet randomly-lose option
749 Telnet SUPDUP-output option
779 Telnet send-location option
818 Remote user Telnet service
854 Telnet protocol specification
855 Telnet option specifications
856 Telnet binary transmission

857 Telnet echo option
858 Telnet suppress go ahead option
859 Telnet status option
860 Telnet timing mark option
861 Telnet extended options: list option
885 Telnet end of record option
927 TACACS user identification Telnet option
933 Output marking Telnet option
946 Telnet terminal location number option
1041 Telnet 3270 regime option
1043 Telnet data entry terminal option: DODIIS implementation
1073 Telnet window size option
1079 Telnet terminal speed option
1080 Telnet remote flow control option
1091 Telnet terminal-type option
1096 Telnet X display location option
1143 Q method of implementing Telnet option negotiation
1184 Telnet linemode option
1205 5250 Telnet interface

FTP and TFTP

737 FTP extension: XSEN
775 Directory oriented FTP commands
783 TFTP protocol (revision 2)
743 FTP extension: XRSQ/XRCP
959 File transfer protocol

Mail

720 Address specification syntax for network mail
821 Simple mail transfer protocol
822 Standard for the format of ARPA Internet text messages
974 Mail routing and the domain system
976 UUCP mail interchange format standard
987 Mapping between X.400 and RFC 822
1026 Addendum to RFC 987: (mapping between X.400 and RFC-822)
1056 PCMAIL: a distributed mail system for personal computers
1090 SMTP on X.25
1137 Mapping between full RFC 822 and RFC 822 with restricted encoding (updates RFC 976)
1138 Mapping between X.400(1988)/ISO 10021 and RFC 822 (updates RFC 822, RFC 987, RFC 1026; updated by RFC 1148)
1148 Mapping between X.400(1988)/ISO 10021 and RFC 822
1211 Problems with the maintenance of large mailing lists

Bootstrapping

NetBIOS

X Window System

Miscellaneous services

Summary

In this chapter we have considered all the most common services provided by a TCP/IP system at the application layer other than NFS (ONC) – see Chapter 15.

First we considered the architecture of these services. The key fact is that client and server software is required for all of them; client must talk to server. Two clients cannot communicate. In the PC environment, it is sometimes not sensible to provide server software as a DOS PC is not a multitasking system; it can only deal with one application at a time.

There are other application services available for TCP/IP systems, but their operation is most likely to be similar to one of those described in this chapter.

14

Working with names

People prefer to use names instead of numbering schemes to refer to computers. This becomes even more marked on systems that are large and complex. A well-defined name structure, which is easy for users to understand, will help them remember and formulate names as necessary, thus helping the non-technician feel more at ease with the technology. There are two ways this can be done with TCP/IP systems: through a personal file on each computer or through centrally managed services. This chapter considers the operation of such systems. It introduces:

- The hosts file
- Domain name servers
- Domain name structure
- The domain name protocol
- Network information services

So far we have considered connecting to remote computers using their IP addresses. This is fine for computers as they can handle numbers far more efficiently than names, but those of us who have difficulty remembering complex numbering schemes find it easier to use simple names, for example SUN, VAX, IBM. These days we tend to find more adventurous names for our systems, such as Gandalf, Oz, Pooh, Eyore, Tiga – amusing names that are not only easy to remember, but make complex technology more approachable by the use of humour. In some situations, we may choose a more formal reference relating to the function of the computer.

However you may wish to approach naming and the management of names, as discussed in previous chapters, properly administered they can be extremely beneficial for the management and acceptability of computing systems.

TCP/IP uses a number of mechanisms to convert names to IP addresses. The most basic is the hosts file; another is the Domain Name System. NFS systems can use the Network Information Services (NIS). We will look at each of these in turn.

The hosts file

TCP/IP systems normally have a file called hosts that can be used to allow application services to request connections by using names instead of IP addresses. As shown in Figure 14.1, this file contains a simple list of IP addresses and the names that relate to them. Each address can have several names, usually a formal name and a number of less formal nicknames or aliases.

The problem with this type of system is that it can be difficult to control in a large network, where naming decisions cannot be left to individual users. In large networks, decentralized or distributed control of such facilities can be beneficial, but with an individual hosts file on each

```
; hosts file
;
;IP address      name            alias
;
127.0.0.0        Loopback        me        thisone
128.128.32.1     oz              zo
128.128.32.2     Gandalf         gandy     wizard
128.128.32.4     Pinball         pin
128.128.32.5     PC1             pc1
192.1.5.70       Extra.long.com  extra
```

Figure 14.1 Example of a hosts file.

and every computer, it becomes impossible to maintain a consistent set of names on all machines. Users will configure different names for the same hosts making it awkward for somebody else to use that computer system; or if IP addresses are added or changed on the network, every hosts file must be updated. Often the only way to do this is to visit each machine unless provision is made for automation of such processes.

With some systems the use of hosts files can be slow as their software is not particularly good at searching through a file to obtain the required mapping.

It is possible to manage hosts files by ensuring that a master version is kept on a central computer and that all other computers download that file at regular intervals. This mechanism is practical in small to medium systems, but for large systems, where responsibility needs to be devolved, it becomes difficult.

Figure 14.1 shows the layout of a hosts file giving IP addresses, names and a number of aliases used to refer to hosts. Any line starting with ';' is for comment only, to make the file more readable. Each machine is described on a separate line beginning with its IP address and followed by a list of names which all refer to that one IP address. This name list normally begins with a formal name and is followed by less formal aliases. Anywhere users would normally type an IP address to establish connection with a host, they can type an alias or a name. For example:

```
telnet 128.128.32.2<enter>
telnet Gandalf<enter>
telnet wizard<enter>
telnet gandy<enter>
```

are all requests to use Telnet to access the same computer.

When connected to a large Internet it is likely that more complex names are in use, so aliases can be convenient in allowing a short or preferred name to be used locally instead. Figure 14.1 gives an example with IP address 192.1.5.70. Instead of typing the full name a user can type 'extra' to refer to the host.

The domain name system

So important is this central control of names in a general computing service that the IAB has produced a standard for the domain name system, DNS. A domain name allows a computer that is registered to the Internet to be uniquely identified by that name wherever it may be in the world. The second major function of the domain name system is to translate those names into the corresponding unique IP address, since all TCP/IP communications depends on knowing the IP address. The reverse translation is also possible.

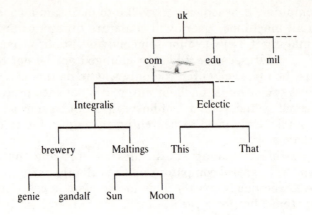

Host Domain names:

1. genie . brewery . Integralis . com . uk
2. gandalf . brewery . Integralis . com . uk
3. Sun . Maltings . Integralis . com . uk
4. Moon . Maltings . Integralis . com . uk
5. This . Eclectic . com . uk
6. That . Eclectic . com . uk

Figure 14.2 The domain name structure.

While these are the main functions of the DNS, it has a more general use. The standard allows the DNS to identify the types of applications that are available on a particular machine (well-known services), to identify gateways to networks and to show which machines are capable of mail relay and to which network. These are some of the functions required from a more general directory service.

To work with names, a general structure has to be defined. Any system where responsibility is devolved to successively lower levels of the structure is 'hierarchical'. The domain name system is hierarchical and uses separate components in a complete name to identify the different levels of management. Like other hierarchical systems, this one can be drawn as an inverted tree, with the trunk (or root as it is more often called) identifying the top level of management, and then spanning out into branches, twigs and leaves that point finally to an individual computer by name (see Figure 14.2).

The existing accepted structure of domain names is based upon that first produced by the Internet community. The system is a flexible and comprehensive scheme that allows two basic structures to be used; one is organizational, the other geographic. Most organizations in the USA elected to use the organizational approach and not the geographic, whereas the rest of the world tends to combine the geographic and organizational approaches.

Domain name	Explanation
COM	Commercial organizations
EDU	Educational organizations
GOV	Government organizations
MIL	Military groups
NET	Major network support centres
ORG	Other organizations
INT	International organizations
Country code	Non USA organizations

Figure 14.3 Internet top level domain references.

Under the root are seven top-level references which are organizational as shown in Figure 14.3. The geographic approach uses country codes. Originally, countries were supposed to use their international telephone dialling code as an identifier but this has not happened. Instead, a two-letter abbreviation of the country name is used, as defined in ISO 3166. Some of these are listed in Figure 14.4. Many non-US connections to the Internet have adopted a second tier of domains that closely matches the organization classification used at the top level of the Internet.

Notice that there is a top-level domain for international organizations (INT) that do not fall into the other classifications. The only entry under this at present is NATO, which one would expect to be more suited to the MIL domain.

Choosing a domain name scheme

A large company that does not wish to connect to the Internet[†] can design its own naming structure to match its organization. It need not follow these Internet conventions. The technology of the DNS is independent of the actual names used at each level, as long as a consistent hierarchy is defined. There is the usual dilemma as to whether the domain name system should be purely geographic or purely organizational. Since the IP addressing scheme has a tendency to become geographic for efficient routing, making the DNS purely organizational might give additional

---

[†]The authors recommend that the issue as to whether a network will attach to the Internet or not is considered very carefully before addressing and name schemes are put into effect. Changing them at a later date can be very costly.

Country code	Country name	Additional information
AU	Australia	Sometimes OZ.AU or just OZ
BE	Belgium	
CA	Canada	Some Canadian systems use US conventions
CH	Switzerland	
DE	Germany	
DK	Denmark	
ES	Spain	
FI	Finland	
FR	France	
GR	Greece	
IT	Italy	
JP	Japan	
KW	Kuwait	
NL	The Netherlands	
NO	Norway	
NZ	New Zealand	
SE	Sweden	
US	United States of America	A second tier was defined which specified the state the host was in, e.g. CA.US for a host in California

Figure 14.4   Some domain name system country codes.

flexibility. It is important that the scheme matches the organization as closely as possible, so that the names are easily recognizable; if the existing labels or abbreviations for company sites and divisions are adopted, employees will already be familiar with them.

When written down, a fully qualified host name or fully qualified domain name consists of the host or node name followed by all the domain components in ascending order of authority as shown in the example below. The name ends with the root of the system. Each component is separated by dots, or periods. A naming scheme designed for an international company might be:

node.site.department.division.company.org.country

for example:

gandalf.theale.development.integralis.co.uk

which translates to the machine called Gandalf at the Theale site of the development division of the company called Integralis which is a commercial company co[†] in the UK. Names are often all in lower case.

A smaller national company could use a simpler structure:

> *node.department.site*

for example:

> *gandalf.development.theale*

Note that there is a difference in the way these two examples have chosen to use the geographic component *site*. In the international company, the department is considered more important than the site; in the national company, the site is more important than the department. If staff move frequently between sites, it may be better to leave the site component out of the structure altogether. Sometimes the topmost level may be the company domain, such as:

> *node.department.geography.company*

for example:

> *gandalf.development.uk.integralis*

Within a particular domain, it is only necessary to specify enough of the name to identify the computer uniquely. The higher level domain information is automatically appended by the software making the request. As the machine you wish to specify gets further away in the organizational structure from your own management domain, it is likely that the fully-qualified domain name will be required to identify it. How much of a name is required to resolve an IP address depends on the abilities of the software on the client. These range from those that require the full domain name all the time to those that will append a list of pre-defined strings in an attempt to find a match.

This hierarchical structure devolves responsibility to local managers but maintains sufficient control at the centre. Consider the example:

> *node.site.department.division.country.company*

The parent company would define the country abbreviations to be used, while within a country the relevant authorities would define the divisions, who would in turn define the departments who would then allocate host or node names. Each fully-qualified name is assured of being unique while the local users have names that suit their requirements. As it is highly likely they will mainly need to access local systems, the names will be short. But if they do need to access an external system the full description is available and more easily understood than a meaningless numeric (IP) address.

[†]For some countries, including the UK, the abbreviation 'co' is used for commercial and 'ac' is used for the academic community rather than the US equivalents of 'com' and 'edu'. The definition of domain names is further confused by the existence of an earlier scheme for the UK Joint Academic NETwork (JANET), where the most significant component is on the left – uk.ac.umist.cs.

Reverse address mapping

In certain circumstances it is beneficial to be able to perform inverse mappings, that is, find the domain name of a host from its IP address. This type of mechanism can be used to discover the IP address of gateways to a particular network. As IP addresses are not strictly geographic in their structure this can be difficult. To help manage this problem a special domain has been defined, IN-ADDR, standing for inverse (IN) address (ADDR). This domain is treated as the root of names that are based upon the IP address of hosts and networks so that a name can be formulated to discover hosts on a particular network. Examples of such names could be:

    52.0.2.10.IN_ADDR.ARPA
    10.IN_ADDR.ARPA
    2.3.194.IN_ADDR.ARPA

The addresses in these names are shown in reverse. 52.0.2.10.IN.ADDR.ARPA refers to IP address 10.2.0.52, host 2.0.52 on network 10, the ARPANET. 10.IN-ADDR.ARPA refers to the ARPANET itself. 2.3.194. IN-ADDR.ARPA refers to network 194.3.2.

An IN_ADDR.ARPA database would look something like the following:

10.IN_ADDR.ARPA	PTR	IN	MILNET-GW-.ISI.ARPA
10.IN_ADDR.ARPA	PTR	IN	GW.MIT.ARPA
18.IN_ADDR.ARPA	PTR	IN	GW.MIT.ARPA
26.IN_ADDR.ARPA	PTR	IN	MILNET-GW-.ISI.ARPA
22.0.2.10.IN_ADDR.ARPA	PTR	IN	MILNET-GW-.ISI.ARPA
103.0.0.26.IN_ADDR.ARPA	PTR	IN	MILNET-GW-.ISI.ARPA
77.0.0.10.IN_ADDR.ARPA	PTR	IN	GW.MIT.ARPA
4.0.10.18.IN_ADDR.ARPA	PTR	IN	GW.MIT.ARPA

Through use of this system it is possible to determine the names of gateways that connect to a particular network, first from their network reference to get their full domain names and then from these domain names to get the corresponding IP address.

The gateway MILNET-GW.ISI.ARPA appears in the table a number of times. As 10.IN_ADDR.ARPA and 26.IN_ADDR.ARPA it appears as a gateway connecting networks 10 and 26 together. It then appears with its full address on each network.

This structure allows a computer to request all devices that connect to the domain name 10.IN_ADDR.ARPA; the response will show the devices that connect to network 10:

10.IN_ADDR.ARPA	PTR	IN	MILNET-GW-.ISI.ARPA
10.IN_ADDR.ARPA	PTR	IN	GW.MIT.ARPA

It is also possible to find a machine's domain name from a test for its IP address, e.g. what is the domain name of IP address 10.0.0.77, or 77.0.0.10.IN-ADDR.ARPA?

Domain name servers

A domain name system is implemented through the interaction of two components, the name resolver and the name server. The resolver is client software on a user's computer that queries domain name servers, normally to translate domain names into IP addresses. The domain name server is a program that accesses a database of domain and host names and their associated IP addresses from which it answers queries from resolvers. The database must be defined by the manager of the domain.

It is normal to have two operational servers – a primary, and a secondary as a backup for the first. Those who connect to, and provide services on, the Internet must undertake to run two servers to ensure that one can always be available to answer name queries. Workstations and hosts should have the IP addresses of primary and secondary name servers configured at installation, so their resolver software knows where to call.

One factor which will influence the design of a naming structure is that there must be a server with authority for each subdomain in the name hierarchy. These could be handled by a single name server running on one machine.

The set of domains that a domain name server controls is referred to as a **zone**. A zone is a group of connected domain names within the hierarchy. It is possible for a zone to contain only a single domain. Whether a zone contains a single or multiple domain is dependent on the management requirements for each domain.

If a server is unable to answer a name query (because the name is controlled by a higher authority or is in a different branch of the name tree), either it will answer the query with the name and IP address of a server which is better able to provide the true answer or it will attempt to obtain the full answer on behalf of the requester. This latter process is known as **recursion**.

It is more common to use recursion than to provide the originator with an alternative name server. Assuming a system is correctly configured and working, a properly formatted request will always receive a response. The two most likely reasons that a request is not answered successfully are either that the domain name of a host was typed incorrectly or that the host is not registered in the appropriate domain name server's database.

Root servers are located at the top of the domain name structure and are used to tie together the organizational and geographic name servers. Domain name servers use root servers as the starting place to discover name-to-address mappings outside their own domain. Root servers can work their way down the domain name tree in order to resolve a name completely. If a name server cannot answer a query from a resolver it will pass the query to a root server if recursion is allowed.

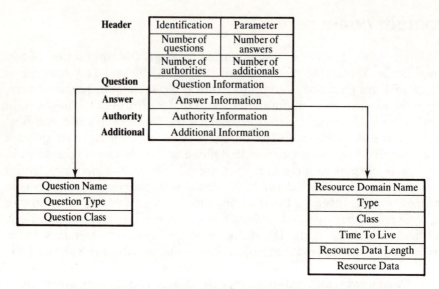

Figure 14.5   Format of the domain name server message.

Domain name server authority

A primary domain name server is given authority over a domain. Having authority over a domain requires it to hold the master database which has the names and IP addresses of nodes in that domain. Domain name servers normally keep a copy of answers they receive from other domains so repeat queries can be avoided. This speeds up responses and reduces network traffic.

To improve their performance, on start-up some host systems will query their domain name server to build their own mapping of IP addresses to names. A concern with this procedure is that this local database could become outdated as remote systems change. Any such system that caches domain names must also purge that information and reload it at intervals defined by the domain name server. This also applies to remote responses which are cached by the non-authoritative servers discussed above. The time limit is set in seconds and can be up to three years, but values of a day (86 400 seconds) or a week (604 800 seconds) are more common.

Domain name protocol

The domain name message format is complex. It is divided into five sections which consist of the header, question, answer, authority and additional information sections, see Figure 14.5. The header includes a 16-bit parameter field, each bit of which is used as a flag, see Figure 14.6.

Bit	Meaning
0	Operation: 0 = Query 1 = Response
1-4	Query type: 0 = Standard 1 = Inverse 2 = Obsolete 3 = Obsolete
5	1 = Answer authoritative
6	1 = Message is truncated
7	1 = Recursion is desired
8	1 = Recursion is available
9–11	Reserved
12–15	Response type 0 = No error 1 = Format error in query 2 = Server failure 3 = Name does not exist

Figure 14.6 The parameter field of the domain name server message.

The same format is used for requests as responses, but in some situations sections may be empty.

The best way of describing the operation of this system is to go through an example. We will start with a query for a host with a domain name of:

    oz.integralis.co.uk

from a host called `genie` in the domain `brewery.integralis.com.uk` with an IP address of 128.128.1.77:

    genie.brewery.integralis.co.uk

For this example, a request which cannot be answered immediately goes to `genie`'s local DNS and it is referred up the tree to the root server, which in this case is:

    integralis.co.uk

The flow of messages exchanged is shown in Figure 14.7. The initial request from the resolver in host `genie` is shown in Figure 14.8.

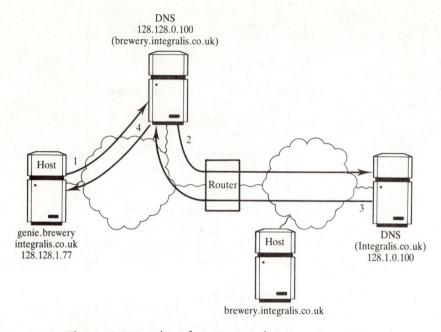

Figure 14.7 Flow of messages in domain name request.

The initial request was sent to domain name server 128.128.0.100 (`brewery.integralis.co.uk`) from host 128.128.1.77 (Figure 14.8). In this case, the domain name server did not have any reference to the host requested. As the host indicated that recursion was allowed, the domain name server of domain `brewery integralis.co.uk` repeated the request to the root server for the domain `integralis.co.uk`, shown in Figure 14.9. As host `oz` is within that domain, the name ser-ver `brewery.integralis.co.uk` has authority over it and therefore should have the address of `oz` in its database.

Mac Header >		
IP Header >		
IP addresses	Destination = 128.128.0.100	Source = 128.128.1.77
DNS Header >	Identification = 4	Parameter = Query + Recursion
	Number of questions = 1	Number of answers = 0
	Number of authorities = 0	Number of additionals = 0
	Name = oz.integralis.co.uk Type = HOST Class = IN	

Figure 14.8 Initial DNS request.

Mac Header >		
IP Header >		
IP addresses	Destination = 128.128.128.100	Source = 128.128.0.100
DNS Header >	Identification = 2	Parameter = Query
	Number of questions = 1	Number of answers = 0
	Number of authorities = 0	Number of additionals = 0
Question	Name = oz.integralis.co.uk Type = HOST Class = IN	

Figure 14.9   DNS message from 128.128.0.100 to its root
DNS 128.128.128.100.

When domain name server 128.128.128.100 (integralis.co.uk) receives the request from 128.128.0.100 (brewery.integralis.co.uk), it checks through its database and finds the answer, so it formulates and sends its reply, shown in Figure 14.10.

In its reply to brewery.integralis.co.uk (Figure 14.11), integralis.com.uk indicates that the answer field is used (number of answers=1) and puts the result in the answer field. It also gives the length of time this answer can be cached for (20 864 seconds or approximately 5 hours 48 minutes). Also notice that it does not put the name of the resource in the answer field but sets a pointer to the name in the question field to save space.

Mac Header >		
IP Header >		
IP addresses	Destination = 128.128.0.100	Source = 128.128.128.100
DNS Header >	Identification = 2	Parameter = Response authoritative Recursion available
	Number of questions = 1	Number of answers = 0
	Number of authorities = 0	Number of additionals = 0
Question	Name = oz.integralis.co.uk Type = HOST Class = IN	
Answer	name = (Pointer to name in Question section) type = HOST class = IN TTL = (20 864 seconds) Length = 4 Answer = 128.128.128.98	

Figure 14.10   DNS reply from integralis.co.uk to
brewery.integralis.co.uk.

Mac Header >		
IP Header >		
IP addresses	Destination = 128.128.1.77	Source = 128.128.0.100
DNS Header >	Identification = 4	Parameter = Response authoritative Recursion desired
	Number of questions = 1	Number of answers = 1
	Number of authorities = 0	Number of additionals = 0
Question	Name = oz.integralis.co.uk Type = HOST Class = IN	
Answer	name = (Pointer to name in Question section) type = HOST class = IN TTL = (20 864 seconds) Length = 4 Answer = 128.128.128.98	

Figure 14.11   DNS reply from the brewery.integralis.co.uk to the host
genie.brewery.integralis.co.uk.

To help reduce the size of DNS datagrams, domain names are encoded. The encoding is fairly simple – a length field followed by each domain reference or host name. In fact space is only saved if multiple domain names are used in the same datagram. The complete domain name is terminated by a zero length field or null (Figure 14.12). To conserve space when multiple answers that have common name areas are returned, pointers that point back to the common point of the domain name are allowed.

In Figure 14.12, the name oz.integralis.co.uk is the first domain name in the field, but the name gandalf.brewery. integralis.co.uk is sent as well. The lengths are shown in hexadecimal and the offset within the datagram is shown at the side to help with the example. The pointer at offset 57 has both its top bits set to 1, indicating that the rest of this octet and the following octet, a total of 14 bits, are to be used as a pointer. Once the two top bits are removed from the pointer, which is 0xD7, we are left with 0x17 which indicates the

Offset:

20	0x02	o	z	0x0A	i	n	t	e
28	g	r	a	l	i	s	0x02	c
36	o	0x02	u	k	0x00	0x07	g	a
44	n	d	a	l	f	0x07	b	r
52	e	w	e	r	y	0xD7		

Figure 14.12   Encoding of domain names.

offset this pointer is referring to, which is decimal 23. Offset 23 points to the length field of the continuation used by `gandalf.brewery` to concatenate it with `integralis.co.uk`. Octet 40 is null or zero to indicate the end of the name.

Unlike most instances in the TCP/IP protocol suite, the name fields do not have to be padded out to a 32-bit boundary, because the length fields passed with these names measure name lengths in octets, not 32-bit words. As in this example, names are not always going to end on a 32-bit boundary.

Using domain name services

A domain name server is an application program on a computer running TCP/IP network software. DNS does not have to run on a dedicated machine. Only in the largest systems will there be a lot of requests to the domain name server, so the processing overheads of this application are not normally high; a domain name server program can operate as a background task on a multitasking operating system such as UNIX. UNIX is usually supplied with DNS software called the name daemon, `named`.

If the domain name service is employed, user service will be dependent on it. Reducing the dependence on individual hosts files is a good reason to use DNS. It is important that there is at least one other domain name server acting as backup. If the domain name server is not available for any reason, workstations and hosts will not be able to resolve IP addresses and connect to services. This is especially important to machines that do not store name-to-address mappings.

Most TCP/IP implementations allow the IP addresses of two name servers, the primary and secondary, to be configured.

Types of name server

There are four types of name server: primary, secondary, caching and slave.

The **primary server** has the master database of names and IP addresses for its domain. It has authority over the mappings in its database. It enables this database when it first starts up.

A **secondary server** has the same database as its associated primary server and acts as a backup for the primary server. It will copy the database from the primary server at regular intervals and respond to requests from hosts in the same way as the primary server. As hosts are added or moved, it should only be necessary to make changes to the primary server in a domain. If the primary server fails, it will be the clients that switch to the secondary server based on their configuration for primary and secondary name servers.

A **caching server** does not have a database of mappings between IP addresses and names at start-up, but knows of primary and secondary servers that can supply such information if required. In large installations, this server is used to take some of the processing overhead away from primary and secondary servers.

A **slave server** operates in a similar way to a caching server. The slave server stores the addresses of primary and secondary servers. It is not as sophisticated as any of the other servers and can only be used with recursive operation – it cannot communicate with any servers other than those defined in its list. If a server was non-recursive and returned a response telling of another server that should be contacted to resolve a name, the slave server would fail.

Configuring domain name systems

The main objective of this section is to give some aid to understanding the configuration of a practical domain name server. The detail for a specific product may differ and the manufacturer's documentation should always be consulted.

The decisions to be made when setting up this service are more organizational than technical. The most important decisions in setting up a domain name service are the appropriate organizational structure and the names to be used for hosts. It is important that the hierarchy is easily understood by the system users and that the names and their meanings are easily remembered. Once the scheme has been planned, it has to be configured into the machines that will operate as name servers.

The basic steps necessary are:

- Gather the mappings between names and IP addresses you wish to control from this server.

- Determine how many servers you will use and whether you wish to use primary, secondary, caching or slave servers. In most situations a primary and secondary should be sufficient.

- If in a sub domain, the IP addresses of the root servers are required.

- If not connected to the Internet you may have to configure your own root servers.

- Configure the database file.

- Configure the end user hosts and workstations to have the addresses of primary and secondary domain name servers, either directly or using BOOTP extensions.

When working with domain name server files, the character 'period' ('.') should be observed and used with great care. Firstly, a period on its own is used to indicate the root or top level domain. More seriously, if there is no '.' on the end of a domain name, the existing domain is appended to

```
;
;        boot file
;
;type           domain                    Source file or host
domain      integralis.co.uk.
primary     integralis.co.uk.                named.db
primary     23.128.IN-ADDR.ARPA.             named.rev
primary     0.0.0.127.IN-ADDR.ARPA.          named.local
cache       .                                named.ca
```

Figure 14.13   Example boot file.

that name and it is possible to unintentionally create a name that is incorrect. When a domain name server is first set up, it is advisable to run the software with the debug option set, to check that names and addresses have been entered as intended and are being resolved correctly.

Different implementations of TCP/IP domain name services use different files for configuration but most are similar to those used with Berkeley Internet Name Domain Server, commonly known as BIND. BIND is distributed with 4.3BSD UNIX. the examples in this section are based around the BIND configuration.

Generally, there are five files that should be configured:

- boot file
- hosts database file
- cache file
- reverse database file
- loopback file

The significance and configuration of each of these is as follows.

Boot file

The boot file is the first to consider. This tells the server where to find, and what to do with, the different database files that it needs for its operation. There are normally four different database files that a server can use. Figure 14.13 shows an example boot file. As with some other examples of TCP/IP control files, any line starting with ';' is for comment only, to make the file more readable.

In Figure 14.13, the domain is defined as integralis.co.uk which the server will add to names it receives that do not have a period '.' in them, assuming them to be part of this domain. The main database file for integralis.co.uk. is in the file named.db. This is the primary server for the domain 23.128.IN-ADDR.ARPA which uses file named.rev

```
;
;          Database File
;
;
;                 addr- entry-
;name     ttl    class type  server
;
@                IN    SOA   integv.integralis.co.uk. root.integv (
                                   1        ; serial
                                   3600     ; Refresh
                                   600      ; Retry
                                   3600000  ; Expire
                                   86400 )  ; Minimum
                 IN    NS    integv.integralis.co.uk.
localhost        IN    A     127.0.0.1
integv           IN    A     128.128.16.99
issws            IN    A     128.128.16.98
gandalf          IN    A     128.128.16.100
merlin           IN    A     128.128.16.200
mac      360000  IN    A     128.128.16.112
```

Figure 14.14 Example database file.

to list the reverse lookup database. The loopback file, `named.local`, is also present. Here a cache file is also defined called `named.ca`.

Database files

The main database file is the database of the hosts in the domain over which this server has authority. This is the name-to-IP address mapping of nodes within the domain of this server.

At first sight, the syntax of the database file may not be self-evident. Figure 14.14 shows the definition for a domain. When a name-to-IP address mapping is requested within a particular authority, the domain name server software will look in this database for the name and, if found, return the matching IP address.

The file begins with comment lines starting with ';'. One of these lines gives the headings of the five fields that may occur on each line in the main body of the file:

```
;                 addr- entry-
;name    ttl     class type  server
```

In this file, only four of the fields are used except for the entry for `mac`.

The meanings of these fields are as follows:

- *name*   The machine name to be described by this record. If this field is '@', it is a shorthand for the current domain for this domain name server.

- *ttl (Time to Live)*   The time, in seconds, after which information must be refreshed for this record if the record was copied to another DNS. Not used by this DNS, as it is authoritative and is the master record.

  The ttl is always a number and since no number is present after the domain field, it is clear that the ttl for this record is the default value.

- *address class*   The address class of this entry, IN. A record for a machine which is Internet compatible.

- *entry type*   Possible values are: A, NS, SOA, MX, HINFO, WKS, CNAME.

  In this first record, the entry type is SOA, start of authority which indicates that there follows a complete description and set of DNS records for the domain name server which is the authority for the domain in the domain field of this record. (The database could contain the records for more than one domain managed by this machine, within the same zone.)

- *server*   The content depends on the entry type. It may be an IP address or a domain name.

The start of authority record   The start of authority record contains additional fields that describe the validity of this DNS information. Some of this information is used by secondary and caching servers to ensure that their information is current.

`integv.integralis.co.uk.` is the full domain name to which this SOA record refers. Note that it ends in a period '.' to indicate this is a full name.

`root.integv` is the name of the mailbox to which DNS related messages should be sent. This is the person responsible for this system. Normally, as with other SMTP mail boxes, this would be `root@integv` but the DNS specification says that in this position the @ should be replaced by a period '.'

Since `root.integv` does not end in period '.' it is considered as part of the local domain and expanded to `root.integv.integralis.co.uk.`

Inside parentheses are values describing the validity of this DNS information. In this file, their use is indicated by comments (;).

- *serial*   A 16-bit serial number which starts at 1 and indicates the version of the database information. It may wrap through 65 535 to 0.

This must be changed by the system manager manually each time a modified DNS database is put on-line. It indicates to secondary servers copying this database that their information is out of date.

- *refresh*   A 32-bit number, which is the time interval in seconds at which those servers copying this database should refresh their copy. In this example the value is 3600 or one hour.

- *retry*   A 32-bit number, which is the time interval in seconds at which those servers failing to refresh this database should retry the refresh (10 minutes).

- *expire*   A 32-bit number, which is the upper limit on time (in seconds) at which the zone is no longer authoritative (1000 hours).

- *minimum*   The minimum ttl field which should be exported with any resource record sent in response to an enquiry to this DNS (unless one is defined specifically with the record) (24 hours).

While these figures are chosen for use on the Internet, it is unusual to change these values in most operational systems.

The next part of the file is the detail of the database, showing the names and IP addresses within the authority. IN indicates the address is an Internet IP address.

The following are some valid values for the entry-type field:

- *A*   A host IP address record.
    What follows is the IP address of the host named in the name field.

- *NS*   An entry for a name server.
    In an SOA record this is a repetition of the domain name immediately after SOA.

- *MX*   A mail exchange record.
    Indicates that the host acts as a mail forwarder. When an SMTP mailer tries to deliver mail to a host, it will request the MX records to determine which mail routes there are to that host. It then attempts to deliver the mail to the mail forwarders in the order of preference for the destination host.

- *HINFO*   A host info record.
    Contains useful information about the host such as machine type, operating system and serial number.

```
;
;          cache file
;
;                                    addr-    entry-
;name                        ttl     class    type     server
integralis.co.uk.           999999   IN       NS       oz.brewery.
                                                        integralis.co.uk.
                            999999   IN       NS       as.isi.edu.
                            999999   IN       NS       ns.us.co.uk.
;
;
oz.brewery.integralis.co.uk 999999   IN       A        128.128.16.100
as.isi.edu.uk.              999999   IN       A        26.3.0.103
ns.us.co.uk.                999999   IN       A        194.3.5.2
```

Figure 14.15 Example cache file.

- *WKS*   Well-known service record.
                     Gives the address, protocol and service
                     provided by a machine, for example:

  128.128.32.5   Telnet   FTP

- *CNAME*   A canonical name.
                     A nickname for a host

These fields allow extra useful management information to be stored in the DNS database: aliases, mail exchange information, details of services provided and of host hardware and operating system. All these details can be obtained from the domain name server by a remote host. Detailed information on these fields and how to configure them should be obtained from manufacturer's documentation.

Cache file

The cache file is loaded into domain name server memory when the server starts. It contains information which must be immediately available to the server and normally identifies the servers which have authority over this server's domain. It may also indicate the addresses of root domain name servers.

The cache file shown in Figure 14.15 shows the domain name server for this domain and the address of a root server which will be loaded into the database cache so the domain name server can call them directly without having to search for them. Note that some of these entries have their own ttl. The domain name server should contact the root server to determine that the root server information is current and then ignore what it initially loaded into the cache.

```
;
;                        named.rev file
;
;                        Reverse Mappings for network 128.128
;
128.128.IN_ADDR.ARPA.    IN   SOA  integv.integralis.
                                   root.integv.integralis.co.uk. (
                                   1   ; serial
                                   3600        ; Refresh
                                   600 ; Retry
                                   3600000     ; Expire
                                   86400 )     ; Minimum
                         IN   NS   integv.integralis.co.uk.
;
;
99.16                    IN   PTR  integv.integralis.co.uk.
98.16                    IN   PTR  issws.integralis.co.uk.
100.16                   IN   PTR  gandalf.integralis.co.uk.
200.16                   IN   PTR  merlin.integralis.co.uk.
112.16                   IN   PTR  mac.integralis.co.uk.
```

Figure 14.16   Example reverse mappings file.

Reverse mapping

The second database file is for reverse mappings. Like the main database file, this file contains names and IP addresses, but it is intended to allow domain names to be found from IP addresses (Figure 14.16).

Loopback file

The last file is a loopback file which holds the loopback address used by the host (Figure 14.17).

```
;
;     named.local file
;
;     Local Mappings for loopback 127
;
@     IN      SOA       integv.integralis.uk.com. root.integv(
                                   1        ; serial
                                   3600     ; Refresh
                                   600      ; Retry
                                   3600000; Expire
                                   86400 ); Minimum
           IN      NS             integv.integralis.co.uk.
127.0.0.0  IN      PTR            localhost
```

Figure 14.17   Example loopback file.

Hosts files and the DNS

The hosts file can still exist alongside DNS. When a workstation is asked to connect to something that has the wrong format for an IP address, it assumes this to be a name. There is no conflict between DNS and the hosts file; names are always assumed to be local in the first instance. It searches the hosts file first. Only if the name cannot be found there will it make a request to a DNS.

The message 'Unable to resolve host name' could be the result of a mis-typed IP address, a missing or invalid hosts file, no domain name server entry in the workstation configuration or a failed DNS or DNS search. Hopefully, systems will give more clues, but alas it is not always so.

The use of the period '.' is important in the significance of a name. If a name string typed on a command line does not end in period '.', the host will append a predefined string to that name. There is normally a file that allows a string to be defined which is appended to names that do not end with a period '.'. Thus, from `genie.brewery.integralis.co.uk.` one would expect the string configured to be that of the domain this machine is in which would be 'brewery.integralis.co.uk.'.

Typing the request:

```
telnet wizard
```

would most probably cause a resolver to attempt to correct to `wizard.brewery.integralis.co.uk`. If the intention was to access `wizard.maltings.integralis.co.uk`, the command should be

```
telnet wizard.maltings.integralis.co.uk.
```

with a period on the end. If the period is omitted then the command will expand to:

```
telnet wizard.maltings.integralis.co.uk.brewery.
       integralis.co.uk
```

which is not the intention. Some systems may allow the minimum statement:

```
telnet wizard.maltings.
```

NIS

Open Network Computing (ONC) systems (more commonly known as the Network File System (NFS)) can use a service known as Network Information Services (NIS) to allow name-to-IP-address resolution. This system is described in Chapter 15 in more detail.

Summary

A good naming scheme will make it easier for users to remember the names of the hosts they select. Use of the domain name system can simplify life for users, particularly in a large network, by making host addressing easier than having to rely on IP addresses. DNS provides for central control over names and IP addresses and removes the need for individual hosts files. It allows control to be applied in a distributed way, and where it can be most effective in local sites and divisions.

The domain name protocol is quite complex syntactically but its operation is straightforward. A host, given a name, asks the server for a name-to-address translation. If a name server does not have that translation, it asks a server with higher authority than itself. This request will eventually be honoured, providing the name is correctly formed.

The configuration for the basic operation of domain name server can be quite awkward in all but the simplest of configurations, but once the core of information is in place, adding extra nodes into the databases is easy.

In a large network use of a domain name server instead of using a local hosts file makes it easier to manage addresses and to achieve consistency across a large user population. It allows changes to be accomplished centrally.

For participation in the Internet it is essential that you use domain name servers so that you can advertise your services to others and you can access Internet services.

15

The network file system

The Network File System (NFS) is a network operating system that provides transparent connections between networked computers, allowing files and directories on remote computers to appear local. Of all TCP/IP applications, this transparent interface makes NFS easiest to use once configured correctly.

NFS facilities and services are often not well understood or appreciated. If used correctly, they can provide a sophisticated and effective network system that hides the complexity of networking in a heterogeneous environment from the users. In this chapter we discuss some of those facilities with the intent of overcoming some of this unfamiliarity, covering:

- NFS
- XDR
- RPC
- Portmapper
- mountd
- Lockd
- Network information services
- Automounter
- PC-NFS
- Showmount
- Rpcinfo

As with TCP/IP, the term 'NFS' refers to a complete family of products, although Sun Microsystems Inc., the developers of NFS, prefer to call it **Open Network Computing** (ONC). Sun Microsystems released the specifications of some of the components of NFS into the public domain as RFCs and it has become an integral part of the TCP/IP protocol suite.

A number of manufacturers have produced versions of NFS which operate on their systems, so it is now available on most computers, from PCs to large mainframes, in some form. NFS provides an excellent way of transparently connecting PCs, mini- and mainframe computer systems together; it allows files to be stored centrally, shared among communities of mixed computers and supports remote printing. In essence, NFS provides virtual disk drive connections between computers. A remote file system can appear as an extension to your own local file system. Many people can access the same file systems and share data.

Sun Microsystems Inc. extended this UNIX service to allow PCs to access their computers using NFS through a product called PC-NFS, since when NFS and PC-NFS have become available on most computing platforms. Unlike other TCP/IP applications, NFS users need no specific training in using this system. When NFS is properly configured, users merely believe they have acquired additional disk capacity and printers.

So NFS provides a resource-sharing network system with similar features to Novell NetWare or LAN Manager from Microsoft. The major difference is that NFS bases the major part of its functionality on the native operating system available on the server hosts. As it need not add its own security and disk access mechanisms, it may appear less functional than these proprietary systems; in fact it has many of the same features but uses the security and multiuser facilities of UNIX or DEC's VMS or IBM's VM or MVS. This is just as powerful, if not more so, as a PC network operating system.

NFS architecture

NFS is usually implemented over the TCP/IP protocol suite but is not exclusive to it. The architecture is shown in Figure 15.1.

There are three layers: RPC, which defines the format of messages used by remote procedure calls; XDR, the eXternal Data Representation is a consistent representation of data between different machine architectures; and NFS, the Network File System, is an application layer interface for file transfer, access and management. This adds another three upper layers to the transport layer of the TCP/IP model, making a seven-layer model similar to the OSI reference model. In fact, the functionality of the layers maps quite closely to the OSI functionality available in the equivalent layers.

Sun Microsystems also produced a number of utilities that work with NFS to provide a seamless network system. These are also discussed in this chapter.

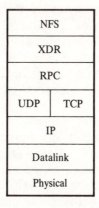

Figure 15.1   NFS architecture.

The operation of NFS is based on a **stateless relationship** between a client and a server. A stateless system never declares that there is any kind of fixed relationship between the two communicating computers; they pass transactions between each other. A datagram protocol is appropriate for such a system, so NFS uses UDP rather than TCP. Other components within the NFS family can use either TCP or UDP.

Being stateless allows clients to manage server failure easily. Only the client need have knowledge of what it is trying to do and where in the sequence of events it has reached. Because there are no connections to close, the client merely retries requests while waiting for a response. Once the server is operational again, clients can carry on where they left off. In a state-oriented system, if a server fails, connections to it fail and have to be re-established when the server recovers. If both machines are aware of the state, they must resynchronize, so that the client starts again from the relevant position.

As NFS often uses UDP and fixed retransmission time-outs, it performs best over LANs with a low and consistent delay and where the number of datagrams lost is small. Depending on the network characteristics and application requirements, NFS may not operate satisfactorily over all WAN paths. Some suppliers have adapted the NFS standards to use TCP transport, which is intended to provide reliable, high-performance connections over wide area links. While filling an important role, these products are not yet widely available.

Remote procedure calls

Remote procedure call (or client/server) technology is becoming increasingly popular as a way of realizing distributed computing. Distributed computing is, in turn, popular as it allows the processing power of all computers on a network to be harnessed to the greatest effect. Until distributed applications became available, resource-sharing networks primarily allowed disks and peripherals to be shared; distributed computing also allows the processing power of a computer to be shared with other machines on the network. The computers on a network can then be viewed as a single powerful computer with a network-wide operating system.

The best programming practice normally requires that a 'good' program is structured in self-contained procedures or functions; each procedure handles a specific task, such as 'display this message', 'get some data' or 'calculate this equation'. Often such procedures are common to many programs; if shared on a network, they could be useful to many different applications. Also, the local machine may not be the most appropriate place to perform a certain procedure. There may be other machines on the network optimized for that task. Distributed computing systems allow the best processor for the task to be identified and used.

Another strength of distributed computing is its ability to reduce the amount of data transferred across a network, especially where databases are concerned. Instead of transferring the entire database to each user's computer where some database sort or extraction would take place, the tasks are performed on the computer that holds the database. Only the requests (database queries) and their results are transmitted across the network. This changes the processing power required in different machines. The server is no longer just acting as a file server; like a traditional mainframe or minicomputer, it is an 'application server' and performs a significant proportion of the user's processing activities. The client machine becomes a sophisticated display station. The advantage is that the network is not saturated with unnecessary data traffic.

An example RPC

Figure 15.2 represents a program which gets two values (A and B), adds them together and displays the results on a screen. There is a 'main' routine that calls the individual procedures: first get the data, then perform the calculation and then display the results.

If we look at the operation of our program in a little more detail, we realize that the data required in the calculations is obtained by another computer, 128.1.0.22. Our program running on our PC, 128.1.0.1, has to make connections to 128.1.0.22 to retrieve the data each time it is required. Many other users on the network require the same data and the same calculations to be performed. Also, there is a computer on the network that would be far more efficient at calculating this result[†].

[†]In this example, we are only considering the trivial case of the addition of two numbers. It is assumed that in reality the calculation to be performed is a more complex operation.

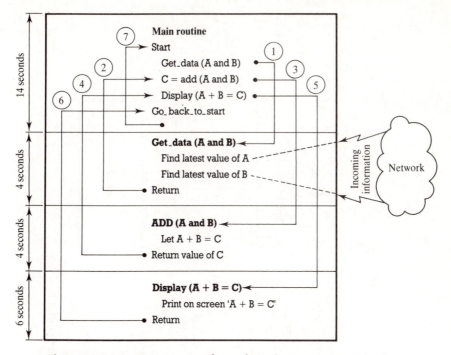

Figure 15.2 Diagrammatic form of simple program to add values.

As many users have the same needs, it makes sense to provide this calculation service as a utility, open to all computers on the network. It should run on a computer that can best perform it, from both a time and a cost perspective. The alternative is that the program runs on every PC. This is very costly due to the inordinate amounts of time it can take; while the computing time of a PC may be thought of as 'free', any unnecessary waste of users' time has an identifiable cost.

Traditional resource-sharing systems send large portions of data files in response to a simple request. It would also be beneficial to reduce the quantity of data passed to these many users, and allow programs to request specific items when necessary with a simple datagram call.

In our example (Figure 15.3), the data is on machine 128.1.0.22 and 128.1.0.5 is to be used for the calculations. So the whole program is to be distributed across the network with the procedure get_data on computer 128.1.0.22 and procedure add on computer 128.1.0.5. The main routine which coordinates the operation and displays the information is on PC 128.1.0.1.

The program on PC 128.1.0.1 will first send a request to 128.1.0.22 to get the numbers, then send them to 128.1.0.5 for adding and then display the result to the user on the PC's screen. By reducing the data volume and sharing a very powerful computer for the calculation, the

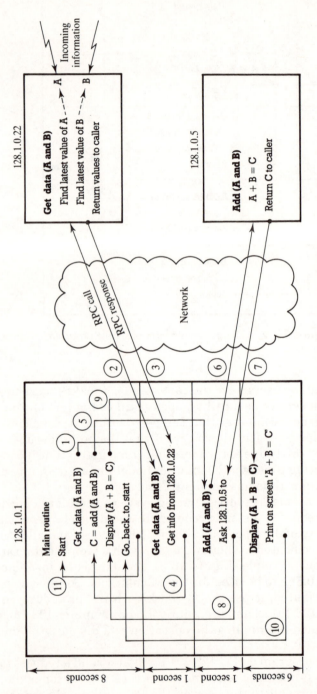

Figure 15.3 A simple distributed application.

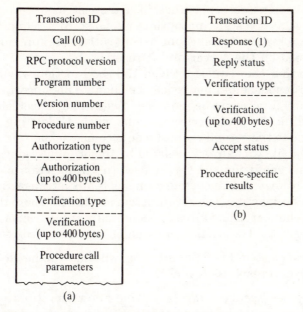

Figure 15.4 (a) RPC request and (b) RPC response headers.

time taken to execute the whole task may be reduced. In the example it has been reduced from 14 to 8 seconds (but then this example is hypothetical only).

The needs of a transparent networking system can be viewed in the same way. Many procedures are best performed by servers on the network, rather than performing all the work on the client. The principle is: distribute the functions to where they can be performed most efficiently and effectively. By using RPC technology, the operation of the system overall can be rationalized; rather than passing large amounts of data around the network, just pass the results required.

The RPC specification

The RPC request protocol header is shown in Figure 15.4. The RPC definition describes how remote procedures are accessed and how they should respond. It defines the structure of the protocol headers.

- *Transaction id*   This is used to identify requests uniquely and prevent them from being processed more than once. This is especially important, as RPC normally operates over UDP, so reliability is not assured. RPC must employ its own time-out, retry and check for duplicate requests.

A client does not know if a request has been performed unless it receives an appropriate response. If a request does not receive a response, the client assumes that the function was not performed on the server and it resends the request. Equally, it may be that the request arrived and the function was performed but the response did not reach the client. This uncertainty could cause any function to be requested twice. That uncertainty would cause difficulty with certain actions, such as deleting a file; the response to the second request would come back as 'file not found' since the file was already deleted by the original request. To prevent this confusion the server uses the transaction id. A server normally keeps a transaction cache (actually a transaction history file) to check for duplicate transaction ids. It will ignore the request from a client if it has already seen a particular transaction id. A client uses the transaction id to match responses with its request.

- *Call/response*   This field indicates whether the header is a call, value 0, or a response, value 1.

- *RPC protocol version number*   This allows multiple versions of RPC programs to be supported on a network. A server is able to respond to a request based upon the version of the request. For the NFS program, version 2 should currently be used.

- *Program number*   This number identifies the particular RPC program to be accessed on a server. For example:

Program	Number
Portmapper	100000
rstatd	100001
ruserd	100002
NFS	100003
NIS	100004
mountd	100005
walld	100008
sprayd	100012
rexd	100017
lockd	100021

- *Program version*   This number allows multiple versions of RPC programs to be supported on a network. A server is able to deal with a request based upon the version of the request. This simplifies upgrades and maintaining backwards compatibility.

- *Procedure number*   Programs are normally composed of a number of different procedures. The procedure number defines which procedure within the program is required. For example, two of the NFS procedures are: 9 – create a file, and 10 – delete a file. A fuller list is given later.

- *Authorization information* This consists of two fields, the **credentials** and the **verification**. The credentials are used for authorizing the client to perform the action requested. RPC does not specify exactly how authentication should be performed, but version 2 suggests four types: none, UNIX, short and DES encrypted.

    With UNIX authentication, the credentials field may contain:

    UNIX machine name
    user id (UID)
    group id (GID)
    an array of groups to which that user belongs

- *Authorization verification* In UNIX authentication, verification is not used. With DES-encrypted authentication, the verification field can contain a DES conversation key, encrypted using a Diffie–Hellman 192-bit public key encryption process.

- *Procedure call parameters* Any parameters required for the procedure call.

RPC defines the format of the header used to perform procedures on a server computer and is itself defined in XDR format.

External data representation

One of the problems with attempting to provide transparent networking in a heterogeneous computing environment is dealing with the representation of data, or, as it is called in OSI, presentation. Different computer operating systems and hardware have different ways of expressing information. How are values such as integers and negative numbers represented, and which bit is most significant, the first or the last?[†] A negative number can be represented with a **sign bit** or in **twos complement**. A computer that uses twos complement would misinterpret a value sent from another computer using sign-bit representation. Every type of numeric value or text character needs to be defined in a common way, to ensure that when they reach a remote machine, they arrive at an application in a form that retains the original meaning.

In OSI, the presentation layer protocols are explicit; each value exchanged has fields which define its type and size[‡]. In XDR the meaning is implicit; the format is predefined and there is no variation from the definition. A program communicating with a remote procedure using XDR must know what type of data to expect and so make provision for that. In an OSI system, each value is labelled with its type and size. While this is

---

[†] The different bit significance definitions used on computers are often referred to as 'little endian', least significant bit first, and 'big endian', most significant bit first.

[‡] The format for presentation is defined by ASN.1 and BER, described in Chapter 17.

more flexible, it also has potentially far more overhead, but the type of data exchanged can be understood unambiguously by any node receiving it.

XDR defines data in multiples of four bytes (32 bits). If the value to be represented does not fit exactly into a multiple of four bytes, the value is padded out with zeros. Some of the types of data defined are:

Type	Description
Integer	A value between $-2\,147\,483\,648$ and $2\,147\,483\,647$
Unsigned integer	A value between 0 and $4\,294\,967\,295$
Enumeration	Similar to integer but for constants
Boolean	True or false
Floating Point	A 'real' or floating-point value, for example 2.496
String	A string of characters
Arrays	Combinations of various types

XDR is a definition of how data should be formed before being transmitted over a network. An NFS client formats data based on XDR so an NFS server will translate data into the form understood by the local computer's operating system.

The services of NFS

NFS defines the top layer of the ONC architecture, which is an application layer interface. It maps remote file resources across the network so they appear as a file system to the local host computer. The network and networking issues are completely hidden from any application on that computer.

The services provided by this application layer are file system access and management (Table 15.1). Those familiar with the operations normally available on any file system may notice the absence of any open or close functions in this table. This is a consequence of a stateless system. NFS does not open files; it merely uses read and write to access areas of a file.

The NFS procedures shown in Table 15.1 are all accessed through program number 100003 and the procedure numbers used in the RPC header identify the specific procedure required of NFS.

Portmapper

Every program on a server needs to have a different UDP (or TCP) port number. ONC is comprised of a number of separate programs and requires several different ports. To reserve fixed well-known ports for the whole ONC family would be difficult to manage. Some of the numbers selected might already be used by other applications in some environments. This would complicate management as manual changes would

Table 15.1 NFS procedures and procedure numbers.

NFS procedure	Procedure number	Description
null	0	Do no work, just return a response
getattr	1	Get file attributes
setattr	2	Set file attributes
getroot	3	Obsolete
lookup	4	Get file handle and attributes
readlink	5	Read from symbolic link
read	6	Read a defined number of bytes from a named file
cache	7	Write to cache
write	8	Write a defined number of bytes from a named file
create	9	Create a file
delete	10	Delete a file
rename	11	Rename a file
link	12	Link to a file
symlink	13	Create a symbolic link to a file
mkdir	14	Make a directory
rmdir	15	Remove a directory
readdir	16	Get a directory listing
statfsres	17	Get file system attributes

have to be made for some machines at installation time and a consistent set of port numbers would not be available across all machines.

ONC programs use a process known as the **portmapper**. When an RPC process starts up, it obtains a free port number by some local means and then it registers itself and its port number with the portmapper process. When a program wishes to access a procedure on another computer, it uses the portmapper procedure on that machine. Portmapper is an RPC process that is always on well-known port 111. Using the portmapper procedure call, an application can find the port on which a particular program number has registered itself. The portmapper replies to the originator, giving the port number, so the originator is then able to send direct to the relevant port. This could be compared to the ARP process[†] or domain name server, but it is dealing with port numbers instead of IP addresses, MAC addresses or domain names.

In Figure 15.5, the NFS client wishes to communicate with NIS to make a request, but first it must discover the port number NIS is using on host 128.1.0.9. When NIS started on the host, it registered its port number with the portmapper. When 128.1.0.1 sends its request to the portmapper for the port number of NIS , the response indicates mountd

---

[†]Analogies should not be taken too far. This request is not broadcast, it is to a specific server and it is a request about another process. Domain name server is a closer analogy.

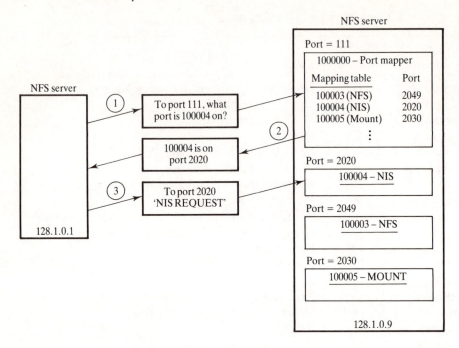

Figure 15.5 Portmapper process.

is on port 2020. 128.1.0.1 can then make its call direct through port 2020.

mountd

As with other UNIX programs ending in 'd', **mountd** is the mount daemon in UNIX systems, although other operating systems will tend to use
the same name. mount is the command used on UNIX systems to make a
file system available, very much like typing a: or c: under DOS. mountd
is the server program for remote mount requests. As NFS is supposed to
provide a transparent service to the user, the same mount command is
used to establish connections with a remote system. The mount command is
modified slightly to cater for NFS; there is a command line option for this.

As NFS is a stateless system, it does not create a connection
between the client and server when mounting a file system. To establish
a relationship between the client and a particular area of disk on the
server, mount must have a reference to the appropriate directory; this
directory reference is usually provided by a numerical value known as a
file handle. When a remote file system is mounted through the mount
command, the mount client uses an RPC request to access the particular
file system to which the mount server (mountd) returns an appropriate
file handle.

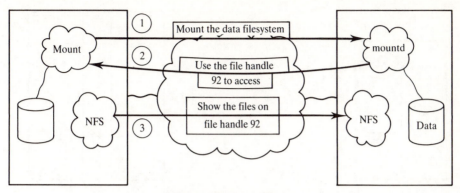

Figure 15.6   Mount.

Although it is stateless, mountd logs which clients have requested a mount of the file system. This helps with network management when there is some need to close the system or make other changes. But the record of clients is complicated by the stateless nature of the system. In the situation where a client using mountd fails, it will still remain logged in the mountd list. If a client does fail, when it restarts, it sends an 'unmount' message to all servers to ensure that outstanding requests are no longer valid.

In Figure 15.6, the client uses the `mount` command to access the file system on the remote host. mountd returns the file handle (92) for the appropriate file system, so NFS can now use that reference to access that disk or directory.

PC-NFS

Using PCs in the NFS environment has a particular problem, that of user validation. The user of a PC is rarely authenticated in any administrative way; anybody using a PC has access to all programs on it. If the PC programs in turn give access to services on networked hosts, it can compromise the security of those hosts unless the possibility has been considered and suitable security measures added.

Users on mini- and mainframe computers are usually validated for access to that computer. They are given individual user identification, passwords and perhaps account numbers that establish their rights to access certain areas of a system. The rights are often handled through a User IDentification number (UID) and Group IDentification number (GID). When users attempt to use a directory system or file, their UIDs and GIDs are checked for the relevant access rights. If such users attempt to access a remote system using NFS, their credentials on the original system, that is UID and GID, can be vetted for access on the other.

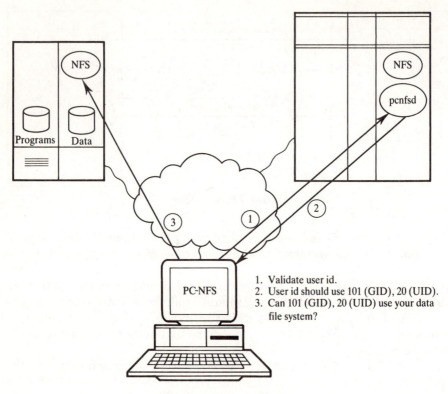

1. Validate user id.
2. User id should use 101 (GID), 20 (UID).
3. Can 101 (GID), 20 (UID) use your data file system?

Figure 15.7 PC-NFS.

To allow PC users to access files on minis and mainframes, some method of authentication is required. For PC users of NFS, this is provided by a program called pcnfsd, which is a host-based RPC service. This process runs on a mini- or mainframe and allows a system manager to define access rights for users of PCs. It asks for user identification and passwords from PC users before they are allowed to access any computers on a network. When a PC makes a request for connection, pcnfsd returns a UID and GID for that user to use when making a request to access remote file systems. This causes a PC user to be validated by a host like any other user. Of course for PC users to use pcnfsd they need to be managed by a host or NIS as with any other user.

Thus the pcnfsd is critical to the operation of PCs using NFS. It validates a user on that PC and controls their access to all other server computers within a network.

Figure 15.7 depicts the relationship between a PC using PC-NFS and pcnfsd. The address of the pcnfsd has to be programmed into the PC at installation. The PC first requests from the pcnfsd that the user id and password given at the login prompt be validated. If that user id is known to the computer operating pcnfsd and a valid password is given, pcnfsd will return a UID and GID. The PC can then use the UID and GID to access services on other hosts. In effect, the PC user is considered as a user of the computer that runs pcnfsd and has to be registered by the system manager as a user of that computer.

PC-NFS security

Security can be an issue with PC-NFS systems where there could be an attempted break-in across the network. The user id and password have to be transmitted across the network to the pcnfsd to be validated. As there is only rudimentary encoding[†] of this information, it is possible, given access to the encoding details, to decipher the user id and password from a network analyser trace. To combat this problem, there is a modified system based upon DES encryption, but this is not yet widely available.

The source code for the pcnfsd is widely available. Combined with other lax security, this could present an opportunity to those with ill intentions.

Network information services

When many computers are connected together using NFS, access rights to the files on those computers must be carefully managed. In a large network this will be complex. To simplify this, Sun Microsystems developed a system called Yellow Pages. This has since been renamed **Network Information Services** (NIS). Unlike RPC, XDR and NFS, the NIS specification is not published as an RFC. It is not a communications specification.

NIS is another RPC-based program service which is often available with NFS implementations. For file management purposes, NIS effectively treats the whole group of computers and network as a single logical computer. Access to all file services on all computers can be determined through a common access control database. The NIS database can be managed from any point in the network. This allows for a single point of control; instead of having to set up each user in every access control database on every computer that they wish to access, they can be configured just once in one central database.

NIS consists of a master database with slaves that can come into operation should the master fail. The slave servers are updated by the master to ensure concurrency throughout the system. Most of the files used by NIS are the standard access files used in a UNIX system, such as /etc/passwd, the password file and /etc/hosts, the hosts file. Because of

---

[†]To put this into perspective, this is many times better than Telnet and FTP where user ids and passwords are transmitted in a readable 'clear text' format over a network.

this, NIS can be used in place of domain name servers, if all hosts use NIS to provide a common hosts file. This is an application that takes advantage of operating within a distributed computing environment.

When used on non-UNIX computers, suitable translation has to be performed to map the access control operation into the new computing system. This is a particular problem with PCs since they have no file access control.

NFS in operation

The biggest problem we have found with NFS is that some people have difficulty in understanding the mechanism for setting access rights to relevant directories and files on a server's disk. Once the access rights are established, NFS operation is largely trouble-free and transparent to users.

One of the major limitations of NFS relates to file formats. When moving data from one operating system to another, NFS does not translate files to suit the operating system of the destination machine. The files remain in the format of the operating system that generated them. When files are sent to a computer with a different operating system, it is possible that text files will not be in revisable format on the destination machine. Word processors on that machine will not be able to manipulate the file reliably. For example, the DOS text file format terminates each line with carriage return, line feed (0x0d0a). UNIX terminates a line with line feed only (0x0a). If the same file was examined with a DOS utility and then with a UNIX command, the output would appear in a different way. To overcome this problem, it is normal for NFS implementations to supply conversion programs to translate files from one form to another before they are revised. These are named to show the conversion performed, for example:

Action	Command name
UNIX to DOS	`unix2dos`
DOS to UNIX	`dos2unix`
VMS to UNIX	`vms2unix`
UNIX to VMS	`unix2vms`

Apart from the file format, file attributes are likely to differ as well. The DOS attributes define whether a file can be written to or only read from. If a file can be immediately read in DOS (it is not 'hidden' or 'system'), it can be executed, if it is an executable file. In UNIX, a file has more complex attributes that define three separate levels of access, and files that are executable are explicitly defined that way. Another difference is that, in a UNIX system, files have owners, but in DOS there is expected to be only one user at a time, so there is no concept of an owner. DEC VMS has four categories for file protection: system, owner, group and world. Each category may have a combination of read, write, execute and delete authority for the file. An access control list can disable access by individuals within a group.

A third issue is that of **name mapping**. It is common for different systems to have different limitations in the formation of file names. For example, DOS allows a name to be up to eight characters in length with an optional extension of three characters after a period (.). With many UNIX NFS servers, there can be up to 255 characters with any number of periods in the name. Names are case sensitive in some systems but not in others. Some NFS DOS client implementations will automatically convert long file names in a consistent way, but file names can, in any event, cause some difficulty on a network with mixed operating systems. The safe, but laborious, approach to preventing difficulty in accessing files is to define a common file-naming scheme which is acceptable across all hosts.

NFS datagrams

NFS always tries to send a UDP datagram of 8192 octets. This is of little consequence if the total transaction has less than 8192 octets of data. What happens at the datalink frame level depends on the LAN used, but most LANs support a maximum data unit of less than 8192. On Ethernet, with its maximum size of 1500 octets, this will cause six IP fragments or frames to be transmitted. Where the network is reliable, this provides very efficient transfer. But, if frames are lost or corrupted, the complete 8192 byte datagram will be retransmitted by the higher level protocol, as the loss of a single fragment causes all fragments to be retransmitted. In this case it may be desirable to modify NFS to use a lower NFS MTU.

General issues

Lock manager

Early versions of NFS, prior to SUN OS 3.0[†], did not provide file sharing of any kind, so users accessing the same file would potentially suffer the problem of multiple and inconsistent updates. The multiple update problem has existed since the beginning of multiuser systems. The basic problem is that if more than one user accesses the same file at the same time, they are all working on different copies of the original file. Programs normally load working copies of files from disk into RAM, so whichever file is saved last, back from RAM to disk, becomes the updated copy on disk. Changes made by the user who first saved the file will be overwritten by the second and subsequent file saves; any changes made by the intermediate users who save early on will also be lost.

[†]The early versions of file sharing were faulty. The problem is solved in SUN OS 3.2

To manage the problem of multiuser access, file systems use file and record locking. **File locking** prevents more than one user from writing to a file at the same time[†]. **Record locking** allows more than one user to write to the same file at the same time but restricts their updates to individual records within that file; this is commonly used with databases where access is to records rather than to the complete database.

An RPC program called the **lock daemon** or **lockd** manages record and file locking for an NFS system on a host. lockd allows files and areas of files to be locked on an NFS server to help prevent multiple updates. A major problem with lockd is that on some systems, it only provides advisory locking, that is, it does not prevent the file or areas of a file from being changed, but advises which files or areas are currently locked. For a networked system to function correctly with advisory locking, all devices using one host must consult the lockd and reliably check the lock status of files or records before writing to them. In advisory locking, if a procedure chooses to ignore the lockd and write anyway, the file could be corrupted. The alternative to advisory locking is mandatory locking, where only the procedure which locked the file or file area can perform a write. Whether lockd gives advisory or mandatory locking depends on the operating system which is supporting it.

With PC-NFS the requirement to use lockd is optional. If any single PC on a network is not configured to use lockd, that PC will not check for locks and hence can access files that others may be using, potentially corrupting the information in the file.

Another concern with lockd is what happens if the server or the client fails. This is a stateless system, but once a client locks an area or all of a file, it constitutes a 'state'. If a client fails when using a server with lockd, lockd will keep the relevant areas of files locked for the client even after it has failed. When the client becomes operational again it should send calls to ensure that all files, or files areas it had locked, are freed. If the server with lockd fails, it will not normally restore the locks on recovery, so computers using it will have difficulty with their applications when the server returns.

Printing

NFS allows PCs to redirect their print output to the NFS server. This allows centralized printers to be shared among many users as with any other network operating system. However, like any other network operating system, shared printing raises certain issues that need to be considered before it will operate reliably or satisfactorily.

[†]Ideally, it allows only one user to open a file with 'write access'. Any number may open it for read access provided they can tolerate the possibility that it is already out of date as someone is updating it. This assumes a file system which has the concept of opening for read and write. NFS does not.

For shared printing, print output is sent to a print queue as a spool file. The spool file holds the print until the printer is free, after which it can be sent to the printer and removed from the queue. It is handling of these spool files that causes some difficulty. In spooled systems, to ensure that the printer can be used continuously, the print queue is processed in the order in which spool files are closed, not in the order in which they are opened. Short print tasks will emerge before long tasks which were started earlier.

One of the major problems with printing on a PC network is the result of the way certain older applications for DOS were written. When sending print to a printer, these applications assumed that the printer was physically connected to the port on the machine. In these circumstances any character sent to the printer would be printed immediately.

Some of the older PC applications do not send an end-of-file or perform any other action that signals to the operating system that printing is complete. This end-of-file is needed to close the print spool file output so that printing can commence. The end-of-file does not matter if a printer is directly connected, for when these applications were written they were the only applications on the PC. Now that the output is going to a spool file, if the file is not explicitly closed, it will not be printed. This problem is often easy to detect. When the application is closed and the DOS prompt reappears, suddenly files are printed. On closure of the application, the print redirector recognizes that the application must have finished printing and it automatically closes the output port. This in turn closes the spool file so it is printed.

Most network printing systems provide a number of ways to handle this. One possibility is a **hot key**. PC-NFS provides a hot key; when the user thinks the printing is finished they use the **hot key sequence** which causes the spool file to be closed and hence the file to be printed. This could cause a problem if the user misjudges the situation, so a more automatic method is preferable.

Such a method is the **inactivity timer**. This timer tests for inactivity on a spool file; if no data has been written to it for a specified amount of time, usually of the order of 20 to 60 seconds, the spooler program assumes that the print job is completed, and so closes the spool file. This works well in some circumstances but not all. As applications have become more complex, and printing has changed from just text to include bit-mapped graphics, the processing time to generate such print has become longer. If the spooler time-out is not long enough and there is a pause in output, the spool file will be closed and printed. The rest of the output becomes a new document and may well be delayed by other documents in the queue. Graphics and desktop-publishing packages that print text and complex drawings are particularly problematic. It can take considerable time to generate a 300 dpi A4 laser print of a drawing, so with a time-out that is too short, pictures or pictures and text intended for a single page may end up split across several sheets of paper.

One answer is to set long time-out values (60 seconds). This causes its own problems as a long time-out causes the spool file always to wait that time before printing. Even short files, single pages for example, take a long time to print, waiting for the time-out to mature. The safest solution is to dispose of mid-1980s applications and upgrade to newer versions that are network aware.

Another area of difficulty with NFS print comes from applications that allow users to escape to DOS without closing the application. If they use the EXIT command to return to the applications from DOS, this can cause the print port to be closed, hence closing the spool file and possibly delivering print before it is completed.

Sometimes there is difficulty with the standard print commands as well, so replacement commands such as netprint are provided as an alternative. It is usually recommended that the network print commands are used in place of standard print commands, as they will be more reliable and make more efficient use of the system.

Spooling is designed to allow many users to share one peripheral. When peripherals were slow and the time to produce the spool file (the time to create the print) was short, it could free the user's application for other activities even though the print had not been completed. In a networked environment, it is important to consider whether spooling is occurring more than once. When printing complex graphics output or the software-based fonts of Windows 3.1, the spool file may be many megabytes; the requirement to complete the spool file before anything is sent to the printer could delay any output for periods of minutes or hours if the application is wrongly configured. This was discussed in Chapter 7.

Automounter

Another server provided with later versions of SUN OS is the **automounter**. This system allows communications to be established with servers dynamically as and when required. The client does not have to mount many file systems permanently. When a utility or application attempts to use an area of a file system controlled by the automounter, it then attempts to make the necessary mount at that time; after a period of inactivity it will unmount the file system.

NFS testing

NFSping

NFS provides its own version of ping for testing that a server is available. **NFSping** is a client RPC command that attempts to get a response from the NFS server program on a host specified on the command line. If it does, it returns a message that tells the user that NFS is available.

```
c:>rpcinfo -p integv
[program,      version,      protocol,    port ]:
100003,        2,     17,           2049
100004,        2,     17,           1027
100004,        2,     6,            1029
100004,        1,     17,           1027
100004,        1,     6,            1029
100012,        1,     17,           1050
100005,        1,     17,           1051
```

Figure 15.8   rpcinfo command.

nfsping is an RPC request to the 'null routine' of the normal NFS program. The NFS program returns the data sent, and the response can be timed by the client.

rpcinfo

The utility rpcinfo shows the program number and versions of RPC programs running on a host. This is a useful way to determine that all ONC services are available and working on a particular host.

> rpcinfo   −u (over UDP)
> −t (over TCP)
> −p (by program number)

The command:

> rpcinfo   −u integv mountd

tells if the mountd program is operational on integv.

The example shown in Figure 15.8 shows the RPC services available on host integv. Program 100003 is NFS, version 2 running over UDP (protocol 17) on port 2049. Also shown is NIS, program number 100004 that has both version 1 and 2 running both on UDP (protocol 17) and TCP (protocol 6). 100012 is sprayd and 10005 is mountd.

Showmount

As shown in Figure 15.9, the showmount command, run on the client, lists those parts of the file system that are available for mounting and the user ids at the server machine that are allowed to mount those directories.

```
c:>showmount gandalf
Export list for gandalf
/usr/user1      user1
/usr/guest      everyone
/usr/test       everyone
/               root
```

Figure 15.9   Example of showmount.

nfsstat

This is the NFS equivalent to the `netstat` utility used with IP. It provides breakdown statistics of the number and type of RPC calls to NFS for server and client (Figure 15.10).

`Calls` shows the total number of RPC calls made to the server or from the client as appropriate, `badcalls` the number of errors, `nullrecv` an empty call, `badlen` a wrong length call and `xdrcall` a problem in comprehending the content of the call. The rest of the values break the calls down into specific types.

spray

This is a test that can be used to check the integrity of an NFS system. The destination host must have an operational sprayd, the **spray daemon**. As its name might suggest, spray sends consecutive RPC spray requests without waiting for responses. It can be used to determine if a server can support the maximum data rate the client can achieve.

This test can generate very high numbers of datagrams on a network, particularly from a high-performance workstation or server. It is important not to leave this test running on an operational network for more than a few seconds, especially if network loading is already high. It can interfere with the correct operation of other services.

Client RPC						
calls	badcalls	retrans	badxid	timeout	wait	newcred
63	0	0	N/A	N/A	N/A	N/A
Client NFS						
calls	badcalls	ndget	ndsleep			
63						
null	getattn	setattn	root	lookup	readlink	read
0 0%	3 4%	0 0%	0 0%	15 24%	0 0%	0 0%
wrcache	write	create	remove	rename	link	symlink
0 0%	40 63%	0 0%	0 0%	0 0%	0 0%	0 0%
mkdir	rmdir	readdir	fsstat			
0 0%	0 0%	0 0%	5 8%			

Figure 15.10   Example of nfsstat.

Configuring NFS security

Newcomers to NFS are frequently confused by the configuration of the databases NFS uses to control access. There are normally two database files: one file, usually called 'export', defines which parts of the server's directory system are available for access; the other file is for security and defines which users and machines are allowed access.

User access control is straightforward if the host systems use the same operating system. When they have different operating systems, there can be some difficulty in how to cross-map user ids from one host to the other. To access files on an NFS server, a valid user id is required on that server. A user connecting through NFS client software will have logged in to their local machine, but their login there will not relate to the user id required on the NFS server computer. To manage the mapping of user ids between the computers, a proxy database is used which relates the incoming user id to one that exists on the server. It is the mapping through this proxy database that often causes confusion and problems. One source of confusion is that there are two different items which are both loosely called 'user id'.

A computer user is allocated a unique alphanumeric user id which they type in reply to the logon prompt 'enter user id'. But a user on a VMS or UNIX operating system, for example, would also be referenced by the system through their UIC [group, member] or user id (UID)/group id (GID) pair of values. These are both *numerical* values. The VMS UIC member or UNIX UID is a number unique to each user and VMS UIC group or UNIX GID is used to collate users into groups. When you are assigned an alphanumeric user id on a UNIX host, the system manager also defines a UID and probably a GID, for example:

Claire	UID = 201	GID = 10
Katie	UID = 202	GID = 10

The two users, Katie and Claire, are both in the same group but have different user ids. NFS uses those numeric values of UID and GID to refer to a user rather than the alphanumeric user id or name.

A VMS host performs user id handling in a different way, so connecting between VMS and UNIX would require some conversion of the two security systems. Some systems map these names and group ids in very complex ways. Here we will use a more straightforward example. If Katie and Claire both need to access a VMS host using NFS, they require an account on the VMS host. The proxy database would define the mappings. Assume the two women are registered on the VMS host as Claire_unix and Katie_unix. The proxy database would be something like:

Claire_unix	UID = 201	GID = 10	host = unix
Katie_unix	UID = 202	GID = 10	host = *

This database structure is interpreted as defining that if a file access request is received on this host with a UID of 201 and GID 10, it would be assumed to be from Claire_unix and hence would have the access right of account Claire_unix on this host, but only if the requests came from a host called unix. A request with UID 202 and GID 10, on the other hand, would be checked against the access rights defined for Katie_unix and would be allowed from any host on the network. (Host = * is treated as a wildcard.)

The above explanation is not specific to any particular implementation; it is merely intended to highlight one of the major issues that has to be addressed when configuring an NFS system to operate effectively and securely across mixed vendor platforms.

This mapping problem becomes more acute for the **superuser** on a host. If the superuser (or **root** on UNIX) were to request remote access, in theory they could gain unrestricted access to the server host. This is likely to be unacceptable! It is common for a special setting to be defined for an incoming superuser which gives either restricted rights or no rights at all. If it was intended that superuser should have complete rights on a server, a suitable mapping could be devised, but fortunately this is not normally the default configuration.

The 'export' database defines which areas of a host will be made available to NFS clients. It lists the **export name** by which a file area will be known remotely and the hosts that are allowed access to that area. For example:

net_chess   /usr/games/chess   pawn, queen, king

This configuration allows the files in the directory /usr/games/chess to be made available to NFS clients as a file area called net_chess. The NFS client would mount with a command something like:

```
mount -t /games gandalf:net_chess
```

Whenever the client is working in the directory games, it would be connected to the host gandalf accessing the exported name net_chess which would be known to the server as directory /usr/games/chess. The NFS client would see /games as the root of the directory, not as a subdirectory.

Configuration issues

Most NFS implementations provide a number of adjustable parameters. How these parameters are set depends upon the implementation, but they cover the following factors. NFS version 4 dynamically alters some of the parameters to achieve better performance over wide area links.

Soft mount

A NFS connection normally is considered as a **hard mount**; if the connection to the server fails, the client continues to retry until it gets a response when the server becomes operational again. Setting the option to operate as a **soft mount** causes the connection to fail if a server fails. The NFS client software will return an error message to the application software if NFS has retransmitted a request a specified number of times without obtaining a response.

While most applications use the hard mount option, some may benefit from soft mount so that they can quickly revert to fallback servers if there is a server failure. The use of this option is service dependent.

Read maximum transfer size

This sets the maximum size of data that can be read from the server in one request. This prevents the client from requesting a datagram that is too large for some hardware or software component in the network, but decreases efficiency if set smaller than necessary. This value should be in increments of 1024 but less than 8192.

Some implementations of UDP allow the Maximum Datagram Size (MDS) that UDP will send to IP to be restricted. The MDS must be greater than the read maximum transfer size to allow for the headers of UDP and RPC.

Reducing the size of this parameter reduces the amount of memory required but also decreases performance.

Write maximum transfer size

The same as the read maximum transfer size but for write operations.

Time-out

This sets the time-out value for RPC retransmissions. It is often set to a value of about 700 ms. Too low a value will cause unnecessary retransmissions on a system that may already be overloaded as it is failing to respond. Balanced against this is the need for quick recovery after an occasional network error.

Time-out can only be chosen once the performance of a particular installation is understood. If soft mount is used, it should be set in conjunction with retransmissions (see below). A system manager should never consider changing time-out without careful consideration. A good maxim is that it should only ever be increased, not decreased. It would be appropriate to increase it if regular time-outs were occurring over a 'slow' wide area link. The temptation is to use a low value (down to perhaps 150–200 ms) if the client/server path involves no wide area connections, a fast response is essential and there is an unexpectedly high error rate on the LAN – but this is the wrong technical solution. The proper action is to correct the error so that the time-out never operates! The problem is that if it is server (or bridge) loading that is causing time-outs, repeating the request just adds to network and server load and will potentially cause network traffic to go unstable. The network fills up with retransmissions and the amount of useful work reduces to near zero. This is one cause of LAN 'meltdown' or the 'black hole' effect.

Retransmissions

This sets the number of successive retransmissions after a no response time-out on a soft mount connection. This value should be set along with time-out to suit the local conditions. The client will wait the time-out times the number of retransmissions before giving up and reporting a failure. Thus, one option is to keep the number of retransmissions small so the problem is reported as soon as possible. If the network is apt to lose datagrams, the retransmission count may be increased, but once again it would be far better to treat the disease (lost datagrams) and not the symptoms (error reports).

In most operational circumstances, retransmission counts range from 5 minimum to 25 maximum. The lower value reflects the fact that 5 successive retransmissions on a LAN should be quite exceptional, but 25 with a time-out of 700 ms gives a maximum of 15 seconds of network disruption. This could be due to the temporary failure or reinitialization of WAN equipment, or more likely some network operator changing a network cable. There should never be a need to set a higher retransmission value as this will tend to hide the underlying problem and is likely to exacerbate it. Instead, the real cause of the datagram loss should be solved.

Port

The default port number for NFS is 2049. It can be altered if necessary with the port option. Changing this value could allow different NFS server processes to operate on the same host identified by different port numbers. One could perhaps be for systems development staff, the other for the normal business production system.

If problems are experienced with PC-NFS that appear to relate to datagram sizes, it is possible that trailer encapsulation is being used. Trailer encapsulation can cause PC-NFS to fail if large frames are required.

Relevant RFCs

1014   XDR: External Data Representation standard
1057   RPC: Remote Procedure Call protocol specification (also covers
       portmapper)
1094   NFS: Network File System protocol specification (also covers
       mountd)

Summary

NFS provides a mechanism for connection between different computing systems which allows the remote disk and filing systems of a server to appear as extensions to the local filing system of the client. Access to a remote computer can be transparent to applications on a client computer. To provide transparency, the NFS architecture uses XDR to define the representation of information and RPC operation to carry the requests and responses of the NFS.

NFS can provide a resource-sharing networking system just like Novell NetWare or LAN Manager from Microsoft. The major difference is that NFS bases the major part of its functionality on the operating systems available on the hosts.

NFS is now available on most computers from PCs to large mainframes, so, combined with its transparent interface, it is currently the best vehicle for integrating different computing systems and architectures over TCP/IP.

Consideration must be given to file and record locking, the configuration of access rights, and the conversion of (text) file types between different systems.

16

Routing IP

As networks grow larger and more complex, it becomes more important to use routers to divide the network into manageable areas. As well as providing better control of traffic, routers often act as the political boundary between systems. Many companies are therefore interested in the management issues of routers and the technical issues of how they work. In this section, we will consider the technical principles of routing and how they are implemented in TCP/IP networks. Some of the managerial issues were covered in Chapter 5. Here we will cover:

- Principles of routing
- Router protocols
- Routing Information Protocol (RIP)
- The hello protocol
- The exterior gateway protocol
- Gated
- Open Shortest Path First (OSPF)
- IS–IS routing
- Border gateway protocol
- Using multiple routing protocols

Principles of routing

End systems and routers cooperate to make routing work. To consider the routing of TCP/IP, we must examine how routing works both in the end station and in the routers themselves.

Some of the design considerations and problems of routing TCP/IP have been further complicated by the confusion in terminology and in technology between bridges, routers, brouters and gateways. We have attempted to explain what these terms mean, how we use them and to use them consistently. Some authorities may disagree with our choice of terminology so be aware that these terms are still used differently by other bodies.

First of all, we will look at routing from the perspective of the end node and then move on to look at the network relays and the issues with routing and bridging. There are three major processes performed in a routing system:

(1) The end node needs to know how and when to communicate with a router.

(2) The router needs to know how to determine a suitable path to a remote network.

(3) The router on the destination network needs to know how to connect to the end node.

Routing is performed at layer 3 of the TCP/IP model, that is, at the network or IP layer. So, routing is transparent to the TCP and UDP layer. These layers have no concept of routing; they communicate end to end (Figure 16.1).

To allow routing to work, we have to apply the concept of networks having their own address or, in TCP/IP, a **network number**, sometimes referred to as a **network id**. Routing operates by recognizing that a particular network number relates to a specific area, like addressing of mail defines areas such as the United States of America, the United Kingdom or Germany. These countries are defined areas that a message could be routed to. The same technique is necessary for networks[†].

It is at this point that the differences between class A, B and C addressing schemes become significant. The significance is which of the 32 bits are dedicated to network number definition. It is this network number that end nodes and routers use to determine when and how to route datagrams to their destination. The basic routing rule of TCP/IP is:

[†]As discussed more fully in Chapter 5, the standard addressing scheme in TCP/IP is not hierarchical or geographic. IP network numbers really only identify organizations that are in control of a network rather than full geographic areas.

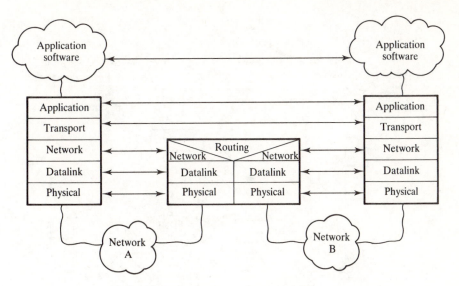

Figure 16.1 Routing model.

> Systems on different ports of a router must have different network numbers (or subnetwork numbers).

When discussing technology, it is always difficult to agree on standard definitions. Throughout this book we have used the terms 'network' and 'local area network' without giving strict definitions. It is now possible to give an answer to the question 'what is a LAN?'. If systems at either side of a router require different network numbers (Figure 16.2), we have just defined a dividing line between one LAN and another. Therefore, we could suggest that a single LAN consists of all the components that create a system up to a router, which includes cable, repeaters, bridges and software up to the network layer. Joining these LANs together becomes internetworking, for which TCP/IP was designed.

One of the confusing areas of TCP/IP is that what the industry now calls *routers*, systems which relay information at the network layer, have been referred to as *gateways* for many years. Today's terminology uses the term 'gateway' to mean a device that provides conversion between two incompatible systems at a high level (protocol conversion). Gateways in TCP/IP converted between dissimilar network technologies, so the term was not inappropriate. TCP/IP books and manufacturers' product literature still use the term 'gateway'. Today, when TCP/IP literature refers to a gateway, it is likely that a router is being discussed. We have chosen to use the term 'router' throughout, except when talking about the devices and protocols in the Internet.

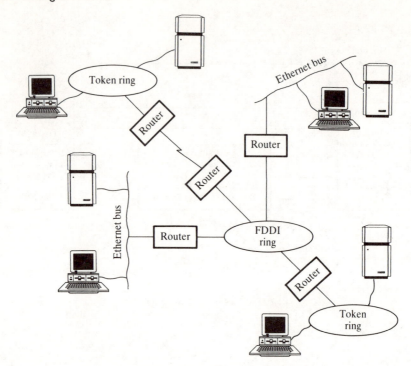

Figure 16.2 Routers connecting LANs.

Routing at the end node

For routing to work, an end node has to play its part. An end node has to decide whether a datagram it wishes to send is intended for the same network it is connected to, or for another. This, in principle, is quite a simple task. When asked to transmit an IP datagram, the IP layer first compares the network number portions of the source and destination IP addresses. If the network numbers are the same, the destination node must be on the same network. IP merely uses the ARP protocol, if it has not previously done so, to get the MAC address of the destination node. It then can send datagrams directly to that node. If the network numbers are different, then it is clear that the destination node is on a different network and the services of a router are required to relay this datagram. The end node now has to know how to transfer the datagram to a router. In most TCP/IP systems, the IP address of one router is configured into the software when it is set up, usually in a field referred to as the **default gateway**. (It would now be more appropriate for it to be called the default router, but that's all history!)

Having read the IP address of the default router from its configuration details, the end node sends the datagram to the router in the same way it would to any other IP device, by placing the MAC address of the router in the datalink frame. So the end node needs the MAC address of that router. It gets the MAC address, in the standard way, by broadcasting using the ARP protocol, if the address is not already in the ARP cache.

Three points emerge:

(1) Each router port has its own unique IP address on the IP network number to which that port connects.

(2) One router will be known by more than one IP address.

(3) One major function of this router IP address is that end systems can obtain the MAC address of the router by including the router's IP address in a standard ARP request.

It is also important to emphasize that the source and destination IP addresses in the datagram always refer to the two *end nodes* which are communicating. Only the MAC address of the router is used in the datagram; its IP address is only used to find that MAC address. To express this another way, MAC addresses are used in one-hop communication on the same LAN. IP addresses always describe the end-node-to-end-node communication, the original source and ultimate destination.

Once the end node sends the datagram with the router MAC address, it will be picked up by the MAC hardware of the router and passed up to its router IP layer. (Routers operate at the IP layer and hence run a full IP process.) The IP layer will realize that the destination address is not its own[†] and pass the datagram to the routing software, ready to be directed towards the relevant network.

Figure 16.3 summarizes the complete sequence of events for an end node wishing to send a datagram to a node located on a different network. It details the MAC and IP addressing of communication through a router. Note that, as stated above, the MAC addresses relate to the physical transportation between the *end node* and the *router*, and between the *router* and the *end node*, one-hop communication, whereas IP addressing relates to the end-to-end connection.

Node A (142.1.0.9) is about to make a connection with node B (30.0.0.1). First of all, the IP layer receives a datagram for node B. It compares the network address with its own, along with a subnet mask if necessary, and decides a router is required. It then decides to send the datagram to the router, but not knowing the MAC address of the router it has to perform ARP (frame 1) and gets an ARP response (frame 2). Node A now has the MAC address of the router so it sends the first frame, using the MAC address of the router with the IP address of node B.

When the router receives this datagram, it passes it to the IP layer on network 30.0.0.0 and realizes that it does not have the MAC address of node B, so it performs an ARP to get the MAC address (frame 4). It gets a response (frame 5) so it can then forward the datagram (frame 6) which

---

[†]Routers can act as end nodes for configuration and diagnostic messages.

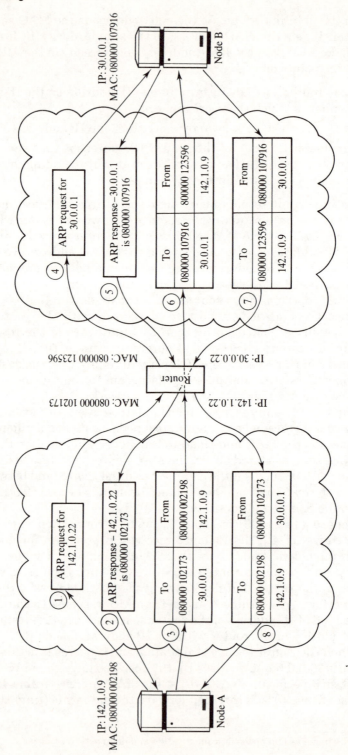

Figure 16.3 Routing at the end nodes.

is frame 3 with the MAC address changed to suit network 30.0.0.0. The response from node B is passed direct to the router (frame 7), as all of the MAC addresses have been learnt and the router passes the frame direct to node A (frame 8). From now on datagrams flow without the need for further ARP requests as the relevant addresses will be in the ARP caches.

In this simple example, there is only one router in the chain. In any chain of routers, the last router must direct the datagram to the destination end node. The process is the same: if it does not already know the mapping between the end node IP address and the MAC address (ARP cache), it uses the ARP protocol to obtain it. This is a standard procedure for the IP layer.

Note that ARP broadcasts do not travel through routers directly. In practice, one of the advantages of routers is their ability to block ARP broadcast traffic. In this example, ARP was required on both networks, so the broadcast was required at each end of the connection, giving the impression that the ARP request passed through the router. This is only the case if the end nodes have never communicated with the router. It is quite likely that a router will have discovered the address of a number of end nodes. Commonly used end nodes will be in many ARP caches, as they are operational for long periods of time. Routers will not have to keep relearning these MAC addresses.

The default gateway pitfall

A potential pitfall in networks that use routing is that some TCP/IP host implementations will not accept datagrams which come through a router from a different network, if they, themselves, are not configured with a **default router**. These datagrams will have a source IP address from a different network number. In principle, we would expect that data should be accepted irrespective of the network number in the source IP address, but this is not always the case. In a network where routing is to be used, some hosts, which themselves may not be initiating connections, still need to be aware of a default router before they will respond to incoming connections.

Routing between routers

Our previous example was a relatively simple routing scenario. We now consider more complex configurations.

If we extend our example network of Figure 16.3, this creates two further issues (Figure 16.4):

(1) How do the routers know how to route between two end networks?

(2) How does the end node choose between multiple routers?

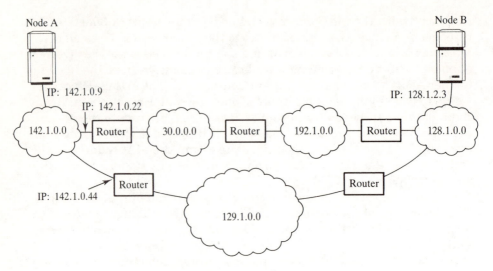

Figure 16.4   Routing between routers.

To solve the first problem, routers must learn about each other and the networks that are available. This can be done in two ways:

(1) By manually creating configuration tables in the router (routing tables). These tables list networks which exist, identified by network number and the IP address of the router that represents the next hop in the best route to that network.

(2) By using a protocol that allows the routers to discover each other and the networks they support.

Routers with both of the options are readily available, but it is more common for the routers to communicate with each other using a routing protocol rather than using fixed tables[†]. We will consider these protocols later.

How does an end node make use of more than one router if it can only be configured with the address of one default router? It only knows of that router, not of others that may be on the same network.

In many TCP/IP implementations, the default router is always the starting point. On trying to send datagrams to a new network, the end node will first send them to its default router. Standards state that if this router is aware that it does not hold the best route to the destination network, it will use the ICMP route-change request message to advise the end node to redirect the datagrams to a more appropriate router. On sending this message, the default router also forwards the first datagram that caused the redirect to the second router, which it suggested as a better route.

[†]Some organizations prefer to use manually configured tables as a security measure to control how networks can be accessed from each other. The most modern routing protocols address some of the security concerns that created this need.

If the host does not obey the redirect, the default router must continue to forward any datagrams received. Unfortunately, certain TCP/IP systems are known to take no notice of ICMP route-change requests, so every datagram from such a host for another network goes to the default router, which relays it to the 'best' path router, duplicating all the traffic for that conversation on the local LAN.

Secondary default routers

This dependence on a default router can affect system reliability. A workstation or host which can only identify one router is dependent on the availability of that router. This is fairly common with PC-based products. Even if multiple routers exist, when a default router fails it is possible that nodes configured for that router will not be able to send to other networks. The default router is configured in the software of each end node and cannot easily be changed. Some PC systems get around this by allowing a **secondary default router** to be defined.

Eavesdropping

More powerful computers can be quite clever at dealing with this problem; they can listen for routing protocol adverts and from these can learn of routers that are available and of the networks these routers support. This technique is referred to as **eavesdropping**. Such a computer can send datagrams to the appropriate router without going to a default router. This idea works well so long as the routing protocols being used are those that the end nodes are listening for. One of the problems with TCP/IP routing is that there is not one, but many different routing protocols that can be used. In the recent past, most routers used a protocol called RIP and this protocol was fairly simple and standard. More sophisticated systems are now using the OSPF routing protocol. Most end nodes are not yet able to eavesdrop on this more complex protocol.

Routing architectures

There are a number of architectures that can be employed for routing. One is for all routers to know about all networks; another is for routers to know only about networks that are directly attached; yet another is for routing to be handled by a central controller. Different network architectures require different approaches.

The technique of all routers learning about all networks is fine in a small network, where the routing tables in each router would only be relatively small. In a large network, the size of tables and the amount of processing required become unacceptable and make for powerful and expensive routers.

In the second approach, where routers only know about locally attached networks, a datagram addressed to an unrecognized network number will be passed to all other routers in the hope that one of them can forward it successfully. This long-winded process can be extremely inefficient.

For a small commercial system with only tens of networks and belonging to a single company, routers that know about all networks would perform adequately and not be unduly expensive. Commercial networks have a way of growing. It is possible for such a system to require access to a large internet system, maybe a corporate backbone network. An architecture based on knowing all networks cannot grow indefinitely, so we need to deal with a mix of architectures. One possibility is a 'backbone' network that knows of all networks, combined with local systems that only need to know of local networks most of the time, but sometimes know of others in the corporate system. This type of structure can be handled by IP routing.

The routing architecture defined for the Internet deals with this problem by having two classes of routing, backbone routing and local, or autonomous system, routing. On the backbone system, all routers know about all networks. They can be dedicated to the task of backbone routing. Routers in individual autonomous system networks are configured to send datagrams to the backbone if the destination address is recognized as not being in the local system. This means that local routers only need to know of local networks and the default route to the backbone. This default route is usually known by the address 0.0.0.0. Through their routing protocol, routers will announce the route 0.0.0.0 as leading to the backbone connection. Any router receiving a datagram for a network they do not recognize will send it to the router which advertised the route to 0.0.0.0. As the backbone router knows all networks, when this datagram arrives it can decide whether it is for a valid network or merely has an incorrect destination IP address. In the latter case, it can be discarded immediately without having to travel through the network until its time to live reaches zero.

The research environment for which TCP/IP was designed was one in which many networks interconnected across large distances, so routing was important. However, many different 'standards' for routing have evolved over time, which has made the problem rather unruly.

Routing protocols

Having raised the subject of routing protocols, we now consider their function and the facilities of the most important ones.

So that routers can make sensible routing decisions, they need tables that indicate the addresses of networks that exist, how to get to them, and the 'cost' of each path. The basic function of a routing protocol is to 'advertise accessibility'[†] to networks so that each router in a network is able to determine the 'best' route from one network to another. We will consider the different ways that each routing protocol does this.

The important features of routing protocols were outlined in Chapter 5. A routing protocol should be designed to:

- Describe the cost of the best route in a number of different ways – the routing metrics.
- Allow multiple active routes between two networks.
- Propagate routing information accurately and avoid creating incorrect routes.
- Minimize the network traffic due to the routing protocol itself.
- Minimize the load on machines which are not performing routing.
- Avoid sudden peaks in network load after a route change.
- Scale well to large networks.
- Converge quickly on a single agreed topology throughout the network after a routing change.
- Avoid propagating routing faults over long distances.
- Have security features to prevent false advertisements.

For the Internet itself, a protocol called the Gateway to Gateway Protocol (GGP) was defined. This is supposed to be used only in the core network of the Internet, so we can ignore it. For 'private' networks that connect to the Internet, a routing protocol was required to exchange routing information about the autonomous system with the Internet gateways. This protocol is called the Exterior Gateway Protocol (EGP).

The other routing concept in the Internet is that of the Interior Gateway Protocol (IGP), which is any routing protocol used within an autonomous system, in other words within a single private management domain. Recently, it has become apparent that private networks or autonomous systems may wish to communicate directly. While EGP can be used as the routing protocol between them, it is not ideal; the Border Gateway Protocol (BGP) has been developed to meet the need for a better inter-autonomous system routing protocol (Figure 16.5).

The IGP never appears on the Internet so IGP describes a need and not the name of a defined protocol. Since most commercial networks operate like autonomous systems, though they may not be connected to the Internet, IGPs are the most interesting area for us. Unfortunately, it is in this area that, until recently, there has been a lack of adequate standardization.

The most common IGPs are Routing Information Protocol (RIP), Hello, Exterior Gateway Protocol (EGP) and the more recent Open

---

[†]Sometimes referred to in routing protocol literature as 'reachability'.

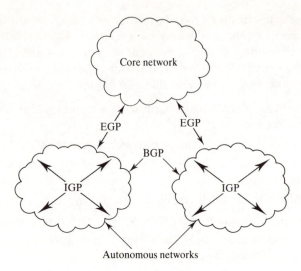

Figure 16.5   EGP/IGP/BGP architecture.

Shortest Path First (OSPF). While EGP was not designed as an IGP, it can be used internally as well as talking to the 'exterior'. It is fairly sophisticated in its implementation, and is sometimes used on LANs as an IGP wholly within private networks, so it is worth consideration.

We will now consider these routing protocols in more detail.

Routing information protocol

The major advantage of Routing Information Protocol (RIP) is its universal availability. RIP was supplied with BSD4.2 and hence has gained an undeserved reputation in TCP/IP circles as being *the* protocol to use. RIP is, however, only useful in small networks with a few routers.

RIP originates from the Xerox Network Systems protocol, XNS. In the TCP/IP world, RIP is more commonly known by the program name that implements the protocol which is **routed**, or **route daemon**.[†] Routed is very much based upon the original RIP definition, but has a more general network address format than is required just for routing IP.

By the requirements of today's larger corporate networks, RIP is very limited. Its only measure of performance of a route (metric) is **hop count**, the number of routers between that point and the destination network. For performance reasons, it limits the maximum number of hops to 15. It has no explicit support for subnetworking so it cannot support variable length subnet masks (see Chapter 4). It cannot utilize multiple

---

[†]The 'd' on the end of a program in UNIX systems usually refers to that program being a daemon, a program that uses little processing power until required for action.

active routes between two networks; a single route with the smallest number of hops is chosen even if a route with more hops uses higher speed circuits and has a lower delay. RIP does not respond quickly to network failures; it does not scale well and it can consume considerable circuit capacity when table updates occur. It uses Ethernet broadcasts for table updates. These are received by and interrupt every processor attached to the LAN even if they have no interest in routing. Long-lasting routing loops were a feature of the original implementation. Later changes to the code have ensured that routing loops are more quickly resolved but at the expense of the volume of RIP traffic.

This catalogue of disadvantages should have deterred most implementors of larger networks from taking RIP seriously; certainly network operators anticipating more than two to three hops between end systems and more than five to ten routers should consider more modern alternatives. To be more positive, because of the general availability of RIP, many hosts eavesdrop to learn about the presence of routers on their LAN and are not dependent on one default gateway. Upgrades have been carried out in different ways to overcome these limitations and RIP is available in all UNIX machines. In small networks with limited traffic, RIP will be perfectly satisfactory.

When using equipment from different vendors, it is possible that they may use different versions of RIP which may not be compatible. They may not function as expected.

How RIP works

RIP is simple in its approach, which is probably one reason why it is so popular. When a RIP router starts, it knows from configuration files which networks it has connected directly to it. It collects this information into a routing table and uses broadcast frames to send it out on each of those networks as advertisements of the networks it can reach. RIP uses UDP on well-known port 520 (0x208). Other routers on a network listen for RIP advertisements and add the network addresses found in the advert to their routing tables. When a router next advertises its table of connections, it will include the new networks found in adverts from other routers. In this way all of the network addresses in a system become known to all routers.

The table in a routed router will have the following fields for each network address:

Address	IP address of a network
Gateway	The neighbouring router with a path to that network
Interface	The physical interface to use to access the router
Metric	The number of hops to that network
Timer	Time since this entry was last updated

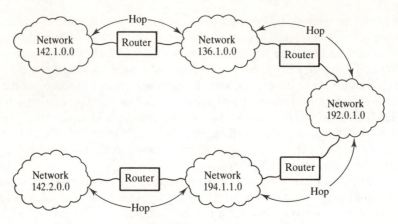

Figure 16.6   Hop count.

In their advertisements, routers indicate the cost of getting to networks in **hops**. A hop is defined as a passage through one router. So a path that goes through three routers is three hops away. As a network advertisement is passed from one interface to another, the cost of reaching each network is incremented by one. In this way, a router that finds multiple paths to a network can decide which is the best, based upon the number of hops; the path with the smallest hop count is considered the best. In Figure 16.6, network 142.2.0.0 is four hops away from network 142.1.0.0.

Early versions of RIP used a very simple advertising structure which sent a complete copy of the connectivity table it had assembled from adverts received on its network connections. This simple mechanism caused a phenomenon known as **slow convergence**. Slow convergence results in a significant delay in the discovery that a route or router to a network has failed. As changes can only be detected when adverts are made, which in TCP/IP is usually at 30 second intervals, it can take many minutes for all routers in a system to realize that the connection to a network has been lost. As mentioned earlier, the maximum hop count allowed for by RIP is 15. A hop count of 16 is considered an unreachable network. This limit is set to reduce the time it takes for a system to converge, that is, to reduce the time it takes all routers to agree a common view of the new network structure after they discover and adjust to network failures.

This limitation of 15 hops also reduces the amount of traffic generated by certain datagrams looping around in a system continuously if there are redundant paths. Each time an IP datagram passes through a router its Time To Live (TTL) field is decremented, supposedly by the amount of time in seconds that the router delays it. By today's standards if a router was delaying datagrams by even one second it would be considered extremely slow, but the standard says that TTL must be reduced by at least one at each router. Consequently TTL has effectively become a 'hop count'. If a router receives an IP datagram that has a TTL of 0, it will not pass it on, so a datagram that does loop around will only continue until its TTL field is decremented to 0.

RIP in operation

In Figure 16.7(a), there are two routers, A and B, connecting three networks 1, 2 and 3. After a short period of time all routers will have seen each other's adverts and therefore be in a stable state advertising all these networks. Consider what will happen if network 3 fails. Figure 16.7(b) shows the adverts that would be generated. Router B will realize that network 3 has failed. The next advert on network 2 could be from router A, indicating that it has a connection to network 3 that is 2 hops away, as shown in Figure 16.7(b). Router B accepts this advert and considers that a new path exists between router A and network 3, for A is advertising a route of 2 hops, less cost than a failed network. B sets the cost to network 3 as 3 hops and the direction as through router A. In router B's next advert (Figure 16.7c) it advertises this fact back to router A. In Figure 16.7(d), router A has just seen the only advert for network 3 from router B. This was greater than its own, so it has to increment its hop count to cater for the new cost, so it advertises network 3 as 4 hops away. This to-and-fro advertising of network 3 continues until the hop count reaches 15. At this time, it is recognized that all connections to network 3 have failed.

RIP adverts are usually transmitted at 30 second intervals, so the steps shown in Figure 16.7 are in 30 second increments. To reach step 15, when the routers agree what the true situation is, could take around seven minutes. This is the convergence time for RIP.

In an attempt to improve on the convergence time a number of amendments have been made to RIP. These are called **split horizon**, **reverse poison** and **triggered updates**. Split horizon helps reduce convergence times by stopping routers from advertising networks back in the direction they learnt about them. In Figure 16.8, with split horizon, network 2 only carries adverts for networks 1 and 3, none for itself. In this case, a failure on network 3 will mean that router B will not see an advert from router A suggesting another path to network 3. However, it would still take some time for router A to realize that it is no longer receiving adverts for network 3, discard the information for this network and consider the path to network 3 as failed. This reduces the possibility of routing loops but the convergence is still slow.

Reverse poison improves RIP performance by still advertising all networks back along the path from which the advert came, but always with the hop count set to the value 16, indicating the path is not usable. In the event of a network failure, router B will *still* see network 3 adver-

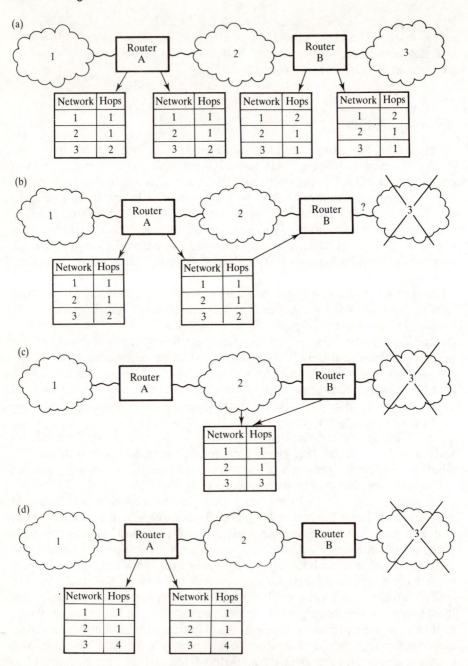

Figure 16.7 RIP in operation. (a) Stable. (b) Network 3 down. (c) Router B's next advert. (d) Router A sees router B's advert.

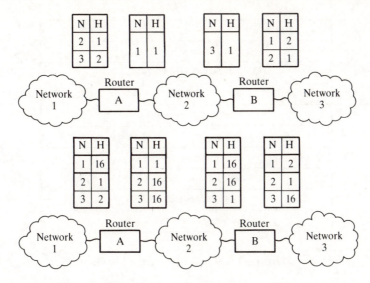

Figure 16.8 RIP advertising: (a) split horizon and (b) reverse poison.

tised by router A, but at a cost of 16, so it would ignore it. Again, this reduces the possibility of routing loops but the convergence is still slow.

Triggered updates significantly improve RIP's speed of convergence. With triggered updates, routers are allowed to send out an advert indicating that the cost of reaching a network has reached infinity (16!) as soon as it detects the problem, rather than having to wait for the next normal advertisement time. If all routers do this, convergence is fast, but at the expense of broadcast network traffic when any failure is detected. In a large RIP network, this traffic can become a serious concern with triggered updates.

There is a limitation on the size of RIP datagrams of 512 bytes (not including the IP and frame headers). If an advert cannot fit in a datagram of this size the router will generate more adverts to carry the remainder.

When purchasing RIP software, network managers should attempt to determine which modifications have been made to the implementations under consideration. Triggered updates will give the best performance provided the frequency of network and link failures is small and the volume of broadcast traffic is acceptable.

RIP format

Figure 16.9 shows the format of the RIP datagram. The fields are as follows:

- *Command – 8 bits*   A value of 1 denotes a request for routing information, 2 denotes a response. Usually a router will broadcast unsolicited response datagrams at 30 second intervals.

Command	Version	Reserved
Family of net 1		Net 1 address, octets 1–2
Net 1 address, octets 3–6		
Net 1 address, octets 7–10		
Net 1 address, octets 11–14		
Distance of network 1		
Family of net 2		Net 2 address, octets 1–2
Net 2 address, octets 3–6		
Net 2 address, octets 7–10		
Net 2 address, octets 11–14		
Distance of network 2		

⋮

Figure 16.9 RIP datagram format.

- *Version – 8 bits*   The protocol version number. This is used to help with compatibility between versions of RIP. A number of different versions exist.

- *Family of net 1 – 16 bits*   This field is supposed to be used to indicate the network protocol used on the networks being advertised, as RIP is not limited to any specific protocol. The address family for IP is 2.

- *Net 1 address – 112 bits*   This field is intended to be able to hold the network address of various different types of network and hence is much larger than the 32 bits needed for an IP address. It will normally be padded out with 0s. On TCP systems, the first 16 bits are left as 0 and then the IP address is inserted to be between 32-bit boundaries; the last 8 octets are also set to be 0.

- *Distance of net 1 – 32 bits*   The number of hops to reach the network listed in net 1 address.

Configuring RIP systems

Computers using RIP can usually be configured as active RIP routers or as RIP listeners. An active RIP router is a node that has two or more network interfaces and routes datagrams between them. A RIP listener is a device that listens for RIP information so that it can perform RIP routing for itself. This ensures that it can reach the most appropriate router when sending datagrams to other networks. This type of operation causes some processing overhead on the computer and its impact is dependent on the amount of RIP traffic on the network.

It is often possible to prevent RIP from using broadcast datagrams, by setting an option and defining the specific IP addresses of neighbouring routers it should communicate with directly. It then uses MAC-level unicasts. This requires manual intervention, but it can be worthwhile in reducing the number of broadcast datagrams on a network, always a useful achievement in larger networks.

Most systems have a command for the manual configuration of routing tables that allows router addresses and the cost of taking that route to be defined by the network manager. Where not all routers are using RIP, there is a need to be able to predefine in the RIP tables specific routes (default routes) for networks available through non-RIP routers and of which RIP routers would be unaware. When the RIP-based router realizes it must send datagrams to one of those networks, it will then send direct to the appropriate router. Such static manually configured routes cannot recover from link or router failure.

Another option with RIP systems is the definition of the default route. The default route is advertised as 0.0.0.0. It is used to define the path on which datagrams should be sent if their destination network address is unknown to the router. This option allows the default route to be defined for this router, with a specified hop count, and overrides messages about the default route advertised by other routers.

Some RIP implementations can be configured so that they will only accept routing information from known routers (defined by their IP address). This is a security feature. It prevents false adverts from unauthorized routers from diverting data through other equipment and phantom networks that claim to have the shortest route. If false paths are advertised, connectivity with a network can be lost as datagrams are sent the wrong path.

Hello

Hello is a protocol used in the Distributed Computer Network (DCN) which was based on an implementation of PDP11-based software called the fuzzball. Hello, unlike RIP, was designed to measure the delay to a network (a delay metric) instead of the number of hops (a distance metric), when considering the path cost. This is eminently more sensible because it allows the best path to be chosen based on a most important factor to end users – response time. Hello will always attempt to use the path with best response.

However, hello is limited as a general routing protocol by its implementation. Each host must actively participate in the routing function and has to hold tables indicating connections to all other hosts. Hello is limited to handling no more than 256 hosts as each host is given a unique address called a host id. This is derived from the host's IP address. Another problem with hello is that the tables it uses have to be con-

Net name	
Net(2)	Net(1)
Index	Net(3)
Hops	Gateway ID
Leader	

Figure 16.10 Hello networks table.

figured manually. Once configured, hello sends datagrams which determine the delay to each host, also considering multiple paths.

Each host holds two tables; a network address table and a host table. The network table is fixed at configuration time, indicating the gateway host to use to access another network. The host table is updated by the arrival of hello messages from other hosts. The network table format is shown in Figure 16.10 and has the following fields:

- *Net name*   A reference name for the network.
- *Net 1/2/3*   The octets of the network address.
- *Index*   An index into the routing matrix used by GGP or EGP and not used by hello.
- *Hops*   The number of hops to this network.
- *Gateway id*   The host id of the gateway host to this network.
- *Gateway leader*   A field used by EGP to carry the leader.

The host table entry for each host id is shown in Figure 16.11. The host which is being referred to by the table is indicated by a 'records' position within the table, the first record being Host ID 1. The fields are:

- *Name*   A name for reference.
- *TTL*   A time-out set by a host to indicate how long to wait after not receiving hello updates before declaring a host is down.
- *Port id*   The port ID of the network process on the remote host.
- *Delay*   The delay in milliseconds to the host.
- *Offset*   An estimate of the clock time in the remote host.
- *Local leader*   Information used to construct the local leader of outgoing datagrams if necessary.
- *Update time stamp*   The time when this entry was last updated.

All of the fields in the host table entry are updated by the hello datagrams. The hello datagrams indicate the time it takes to reach each host.

Name	
TTL	Port id
Delay	
Offset	
Local leader	
Update	
time stamp	

Figure 16.11 Hello host table.

The hosts are not explicitly defined in the datagram format, as the relative position of the information in the datagram implicitly defines which fields refer to which hosts.

Hello times the responses between nodes and keeps a table with respect to each one. Routing adverts would relate to the delay to reach a machine and the estimated clock time in that machine so that an approximation of the delay to a node could be calculated.

The hello datagram is shown in Figure 16.12. The important fields are the delay and offset fields. Delay is the delay in milliseconds to a host.

Fixed area	Checksum	
	Date	
	Time	
	Timestamp	
	Offset	Hosts(n)
Host area	Delay host 0	
	Offset host 0	
	$\vdots$	
	Delay host $n - 1$	
	Offset host $n - 1$	

Figure 16.12 Hello datagram.

Hello works by calculating the difference between the network time (the time of day in milliseconds since midnight) as advertised by a host in its hellos and the time at which the message arrives. To get a better estimate of delay, an estimate called offset is also kept for each remote host. Offset is the estimated difference between the clock time in the remote and local hosts. It is used by a host to correct the timing estimate of delay.

Periodically, all hosts using hello send a hello message to their neighbours on each link common to them. These hellos are used to calculate which is the best performance route at any particular time. As each node has an estimate of the time in each remote node, it is able to calculate how long it took for the datagram to reach it.

The protocol uses a threshold time when updating the host delay fields to prevent route hopping. This happens if a route through a network suddenly is recognized as a better performance route so all nodes switch to that route; it therefore becomes congested and the old route lightly loaded, so every connection switches back to the old route. Without a threshold time the operational route could hop back and forth.

Hello was never designed to operate on large networks but, with networks of fewer than 256 hosts, it is a dynamic routing protocol, choosing the best path based on performance and catering for multiple paths. It is used on some research systems today, but is not widely used on commercial networks.

Configuring hello systems

Hello systems have similar options to RIP. They can be set only to listen for hello datagrams and not participate in the dissemination of hello information, and they can have a default route.

The default route for hello is *not* 0.0.0.0. It is 10.0.0.0, which is the network address of the ARPAnet, the original core network of the Internet. This option could cause difficulty on networks that are not attached to the ARPAnet.

Exterior gateway protocol

The Exterior Gateway Protocol (EGP) was designed as the mechanism for an autonomous system to tell the core gateways of the Internet about networks it wanted to advertise. EGP can be used as an IGP. By using EGP for the interior routing protocol, an autonomous system which is connected to the Internet need only run one protocol in its routers.

EGP is a reasonably sophisticated protocol with 10 message types that are used to establish connections with other EGP gateways and then pass network reachability information between them. EGP operates directly over IP using the IP protocol number of 8. The commands are:

Type	Function
Request	Request connection with a neighbouring router
Confirm	Confirm connection with a neighbouring router
Refuse	Refuse connection with a neighbouring router
Cease	Request disconnection from a neighbouring router
Cease-ack	Acknowledge disconnection from a neighbouring router
Hello	Check neighbouring router is still active
I-H-U	Acknowledge to hello (I-Heard-You)
Poll	Request a routing table update
Update	A network routing table update
Error	An error report

The basic format of these messages is the same, as shown in Figure 16.13. Some messages have additional fields where necessary.

When a router using EGP is initialized, it first starts by requesting a connection with a known neighbouring EGP router, using the request command. It could get three possible responses to this, plus a possibility of no response at all. The replies could be:

Command (type-code)	Possible responses (type-code)
Request (3-0)	Confirm (3-1)
	Refuse (3-2)
	Error (8-0)

In the connection request the router indicates the frequency at which it would like to receive hello and poll commands. Typical values would be hello every 30 seconds and a poll for update every 2 minutes. Once the connection has been confirmed, the router clears all its tables and starts to receive and/or transmit hello and poll commands. The message sent then would be:

Command (type-code)	Possible responses (type-code)
Hello (5-0)	I-H-U (5-1)
	Error (8-0)
Poll (2-0)	Update (1-0)
	Error (8-0)

Version	Type	Code	Status
Checksum		Autonomous System Number	
Sequence number			

Figure 16.13 Basic format of EGP.

Version	Type (1)	Code (0)	Status
Checksum		Autonomous system number	
Sequence number		Internal gateways	Exterior gateways
IP source network			

Gateway A IP address (without net portion)
Num. distances

Distance A_1	Nets at A_1
Network 1 at distance A_1	
Network 2 at distance A_1	

$\vdots$

Distance A_n	Nets at A_n
Network 1 at distance A_n	
Network 2 at distance A_n	

$\vdots$

Gateway N IP address (without net portion)
Num. distances

Distance N_1	Nets at N_1
Network 1 at distance N_1	
Network 2 at distance N_1	

$\vdots$

Last network at last distance for gateway N

Figure 16.14 EGP routing information datagram.

Lastly is the `cease` command, which is used to break the connection between two routers. This command is:

Command (type-code)	*Possible responses (type-code)*
Cease (3-3)	Cease-Ack (3-4)
	Error (8-0)

As can be seen from the set of commands, EGP is an active protocol (as opposed to the more passive approach of RIP) in which routers positively check that their neighbours are still accessible and request updates to their routing tables. Figure 16.14 shows the routing information datagram of EGP. The type field is 1, for routing update, and the code field should always be 0. The status field can have one of the following values:

Status	*Meaning*
0	Intermediate
1	Up
2	Down
128	Unsolicited message bit

The remaining fields are described below. The terminology can seem quite complex but, in general, the format is a table of entries, where each entry consists of a counter or number that describes the number of sub-entries that follow. While not very readable to people, it is easy to write software to decode such a table.

- *Autonomous system number* This is an assigned number to identify the autonomous system to which this datagram refers. If a registered autonomous system number has been obtained from the Internet Registry (see Chapter 3), it should be used here.

- *Sequence number* To synchronize requests with responses.

- *Internal gateways* The number of gateways within the autonomous system to which this datagram (advert) refers.

- *External gateways* The number of external gateways to which this datagram (advert) refers.

- *Gateway IP address* The address of the gateway which can route datagrams to the list of networks following

- *Num. distances* The number of distances: this refers to the number of groups of networks at different hop counts which will be described in this advert. Each group will have a different hop count from the gateway in the gateway IP address field (but each network address in the group will have the same hop count).

- *Distance* The number of hops required to reach each of the network addresses in this group.

- *Networks at distance* The number of networks in this particular group which are at a distance given by the previous distance field.

- *Network addresses* A list of IP addresses of the networks that are the number of hops away given in the distance field and hence can be reached by the gateway in the gateway IP address.

This will be followed by entries referring to other gateways by starting again with another gateway IP address and repeating the structure until the total number of gateways in the internal gateways and external gateways fields has been described.

Configuring EGP systems

EGP systems can be more complex to configure than RIP and hello because it is a more complex protocol. EGP expects to have an autonomous system number, a value that must be obtained from the Network Information Center if you connect to the Internet. If you never intend to connect to the Internet, you can put your own value in this field.

EGP must know the addresses of peer gateways. It has to have a least one other gateway to exchange EGP information with.

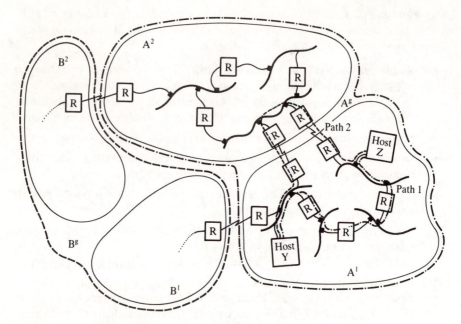

Figure 16.15 Controlling data flows in domains.

Gated

Routers that support RIP, hello and EGP are now common. In recent years, a router has become a dedicated device, a specific product that connects networks. With TCP/IP systems, ordinary application hosts (minicomputers) have been able to do routing for many years. The hosts that perform routing have multiple communication interfaces connected to several physical networks. They run routing protocols to route between these networks as necessary.

Over time, a program was developed to run these routing protocols. Called **gated** (standing for gate daemon), it supports all three common routing protocols – RIP, hello and EGP – and allows them to be configured for each interface port individually. It also provides extra functions for the management of traffic through a network. The system manager can control traffic flow and secure nodes or networks from outside access.

To control traffic flow with gated, costs are allocated to certain routes to coerce traffic to remain within a defined management domain. Figure 16.15 explains this more clearly. It shows six different management domains:

A^1	Company A site 1
A^2	Company A site 2
A^g	The whole company A
B^1	Company A site 1
B^2	Company A site 2
B^g	The whole company B

Within a site, domain A[1] for example, a number of routers may exist, probably controlling different subnetworks. For redundancy, there may be alternative paths between sites. In the figure, two separate paths are shown between hosts Z and Y, one having a hop count of 2, the other a hop count of 3. If we consider the hop count method for determining the best route, the lowest cost path goes outside the domain A[1]. This causes traffic to leave domain A[1] on an external router just to get back to a host within the same site. This is a management nightmare; internal traffic could well be taking a lower performance path and tying up expensive resources intended for intersite traffic.

Gated brings this traffic back under management control by biasing the cost of crossing a domain boundary. For example, we can define the cross-boundary connection as having a cost equivalent to 100 hops. Now path 2 will have a cost of 202 (100 + 100 + 1 + 1), whereas path 1 will still have a cost of 3, and will now be the preferred path.

The same applies to the intercompany connections, but, if we only treated them the same as a cross-domain link and allocated them a cost of 100, paths could be chosen that traversed company B's network between two devices in company A. In some countries, these traffic flows could infringe local telecommunications regulations. Again, to prevent this, we can define the cost of going across a company domain as being 200, for example. This high minimum cost of going across a boundary between two organizations would make it always less expensive to remain within the company private network or to use the company's own external lines, and not someone else's lines.

In the complete system, all networks will be available to all others, but the management of path costs will keep the traffic within the required domains. This mechanism can, of course, be extended to have more domains, if necessary. With eight bits we can define a cost of up to 256. The minimum cost allocated to crossing a domain boundary must always be greater than the sum of the costs for staying within the domain.

Configuring gated systems

Because gated supports RIP, hello and EGP, it should be able to set the options that you would find with each of these protocols. It also has a number of facilities to decide which protocols are used on which interfaces.

As described above, gated normally allows interface metrics to be set to bias the cost of using a certain interface when crossing domains. In some implementations, it is possible to modify the hop count contained in incoming RIP datagrams. This allows the network manager to bias the cost of RIP routes rather than use a true hop count.

Gated usually allows the network manager to choose which networks or hosts are advertised or not advertised, which provides a degree of security within a system. Gated systems, as they handle multiple routing protocols, tend to store their metrics internally in milliseconds. This allows the granularity of hello to be preserved. RIP hop count metrics will be mapped onto this mechanism.

Open shortest path first

Open Shortest Path First (OSPF) was developed in 1989–90 in the classic TCP/IP manner, by a specialist engineering group set up to produce a specification for a scalable IGP that would fully satisfy the routing protocol requirements for large private networks (an IGP for large ASs). The design aims for OSPF recognized the limitations of existing protocols.

One of the more recent requirements of the IAB is that new Internet standards must be specified so completely and rigorously, and written so clearly, that different designers can implement the standard successfully with no other source of information. To prove the standard, at least two totally independent implementations must be tested together, any anomalies resolved and necessary clarifications added to the standard. OSPF has completed this testing phase successfully.

In OSPF, 'open' is used to mean 'openly published and not controlled by a single manufacturer'. Shortest path first, also called the Dijkstra Algorithm, refers to the calculation which determines the best path. OSPF is not, today, an IEEE or ISO standard, but it does share many of the ideas and techniques which were developed for the OSI IS–IS routing protocol used for the OSI Connectionless Network Protocol (CLNP). Only the ideas are similar; OSPF and IS–IS cannot (directly) interwork.

OSPF is what is known as a **link state vector protocol**, as opposed to RIP and EGP which are **distance vector protocols**. A link state vector protocol is one which considers the status of connections to a network, taking into account performance aspects other than hop count (the distance), when making routing decisions.

OSPF uses IP. It has been defined as protocol number 89. It is important, though not essential, that routing information is not discarded. OSPF uses small datagrams that do not need fragmentation, for in using fragmentation, any single lost fragment would necessitate resending the complete larger datagram. Small datagrams reduce the throughput capabilities of the protocol but if one datagram is lost, only that one must be resent. In any case, OSPF is designed to produce as little traffic as possible.

OSPF terminology

OSPF is a routing protocol for use with an autonomous system, a private network under one overall management control. In OSPF parlance, an **area** is part of that autonomous system which is considered a self-contained routing domain. This could be one or more IP network addresses and could cover a few or many subnetwork addresses. Administration of routing within an area could be devolved to a particular body, so an area is firstly a management definition of a region within which an identifiable authority has control. But because an area is self-contained, it also has technical advantages as routing detail need not pass outside the area.

OSPF divides routing into three levels: **intra-area**, within area, **inter-area**, between areas, and **autonomous system external routes**. Areas communicate with each other through inter-area routers which themselves attach to a single backbone network that carries all inter-area traffic. There can only be one backbone and it must be contiguous. OSPF can 'import' external routes from other routing protocols, convert them to OSPF representations and re-advertise them within the autonomous system.

To assist the system manager with configuring the backbone, **virtual links** can also be defined. These are treated as a direct point-to-point connection between two routers though physically there may be other routers in between. A fixed relationship is defined for traffic between the routers at either end of the virtual link.

Each intra-area router keeps its own topological database of the networks and other routers within the area it resides in. An inter-area router, connected to more than one area, will have separate topology databases for each area. Information regarding routing outside an area is considered as being only summary information and is not used to change routing within an area, so routing problems are contained in the area in which they occur and should not impact the routing databases elsewhere.

As with other router protocols, OSPF advertises reachability, but as it is a link state protocol, it does more than just indicate the hop count to different networks; it considers objects. An object can be a network or a router. In OSPF, the route adverts are called **Link State Advertisements** (LSAs). They contain information about known network addresses and the subnet mask that is used with each address. OSPF works with subnets and variable length subnet masks.

OSPF is designed to operate with point-to-point networks, broadcast networks and non-broadcast networks:

- A **point-to-point 'network'** is one that joins a single pair of routers, for example, a single point-to-point circuit.

- A **broadcast network** is one that can support many attached routers and can send a single message simultaneously to all attached devices. Examples are Ethernet or Token Ring LANs.

- A **non-broadcast network** is one in which there can be multiple destinations from a single interface but which does not allow broadcast, for example an X.25 packet switched data network.

The last two are examples of multi-access networks.

How OSPF works

When an OSPF router is initialized, it first uses its hello[†] protocol to establish connection with its neighbours. On point-to-point and non-broadcast networks, the addresses of these neighbour devices must be configured into the OSPF router. On a broadcast network, the router uses a well-known multicast IP address (224.0.0.5) as the destination in its hellos. All OSPF routers will recognize this address. It is one of those class D addresses which are reserved for multicast and experimental use and are not available for general IP comunications. This IP multicast is mapped in a standard way into IEEE 802.1 LAN multicast addresses.

On multi-access networks, broadcast and non-broadcast, the OSPF hello protocol is used to 'elect' a **Designated Router** (DR), which will be responsible for route advertising on behalf of all other routers on that network. Having a DR reduces the amount of traffic required to pass information back and forth between routers. A backup DR, which will take over should the DR fail, is also elected. We shall describe later how to control the priority with which routers take on these roles. Another class D multicast address, 224.0.0.6, is reserved as a destination address for DRs and backup DRs. Other routers use this multicast address to send messages to the master and backup DRs. Using multicast addresses allows multiple devices to receive the datagrams but without the problems of using broadcast frames.

Once the DRs are agreed, **adjacencies** are defined, that is, it is agreed which routers will communicate directly with each other. The path between two routers, be it logical or physical, is called **an adjacency**. This is fairly straightforward on point-to-point and virtual links, but it is more difficult on multi-access networks where all routers can hear each other. In this situation, the DR becomes the node that establishes adjacencies. In other words, the line of communication is restricted to being between the two DRs and the other routers. Non-DR routers do not communicate directly with each other. This allows information to be passed back and forth using unicast datagrams on non-broadcast networks and reserved multicast addresses on broadcast networks (such as IEEE LANs). This reduces the overall volume of routing traffic and its impact on other nodes on the network.

Figure 16.16 shows two multi-access networks, a LAN and an X.25 PDN. It is possible for all routers to communicate with each other, but to reduce traffic and simplify control of the system, in each case RT5 becomes the DR and RT6 the backup DR.

The adjacencies are then used to pass routing database information to all routers. In OSPF, these LSAs, generated by each router, indicate the state and cost of its interfaces and the adjacencies. LSAs always

---

[†]Hello has become a general term. This 'hello' is just one message the OSPF protocol can send and is not to be confused with the complete protocol, DCN hello, described previously in this chapter.

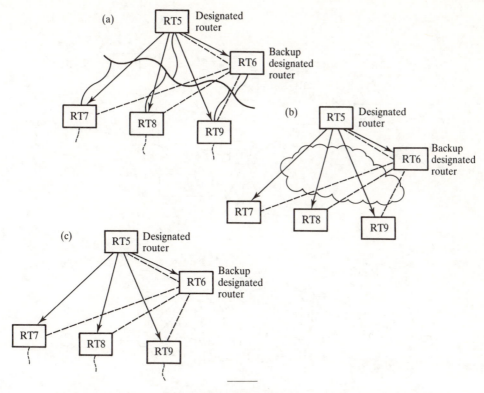

Figure 16.16 OSPF designated routers: (a) LAN, (b) X.25 PDN and (c) logical diagram.

flow to and from the DRs, never directly between DRs. Each router in an area will therefore build its routing database from information provided by the DRs. All routers in an area receive the LSAs and from this they build a topological database of the inter-connections throughout the area. From this database, and with itself as the 'root', each router builds a branching tree indicating connectivity to other networks. From the interface costs contained in the LSAs, it computes the cost of travelling each branch. Where two branches provide a connection to the same network, the higher cost path will not be used to carry traffic, unless the primary route fails. It will use the shortest path first, hence (O)SPF.

The cost of crossing each interface (for each TOS) must be decided and set up in the routers by the system manager. This gives the manager control of routing decisions within the network and hence allows traffic flow management.

Consider the more detailed example of Figure 16.17(a). The 10 networks in this system, N1–N10, use various cabling systems with different topologies and there are seven routers, RT1–RT7. A host, H1, is directly connected to RT6 using the Serial Line Internet Protocol (SLIP). The route to this directly connected host is advertised in OSPF as a host-

(a)

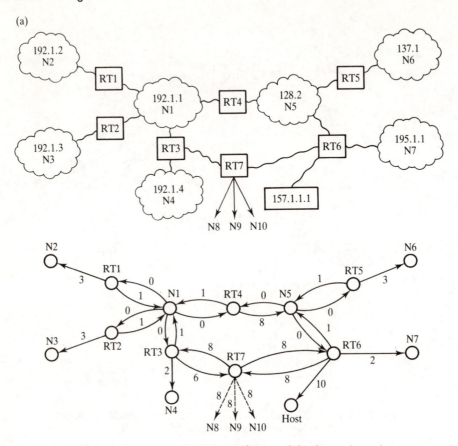

Figure 16.17 (a) OSPF topology and (b) directed graph.

specific route using the host's full IP address as a network address with a subnet mask of all 1s, or 0xFFFFFFFF. When a mask of all 1s is used, only one IP address, the host itself, can match that route. In OSPF, a default route can be advertised as any network address with a subnet mask of all 0s. Any IP address masked with all 0s, will produce a match.

Now we will look at the cost of paths connecting the different routers and networks. This is normally shown as a **directed graph**. Figure 16.17(b) shows the paths between each entity and the cost of going down that path. Note that the cost of going from a network to a router is always zero.

Next, we split the network shown in Figure 16.17(a) into two areas with some external networks from another autonomous system connected through RT7. As shown in Figure 16.18(a), RT4 now becomes an inter-area router and RT7 a backbone router, part of a backbone network.

If we now look at the area database for area 1, shown in Figure 16.18(b), we can see the cost of reaching every network. In this case we

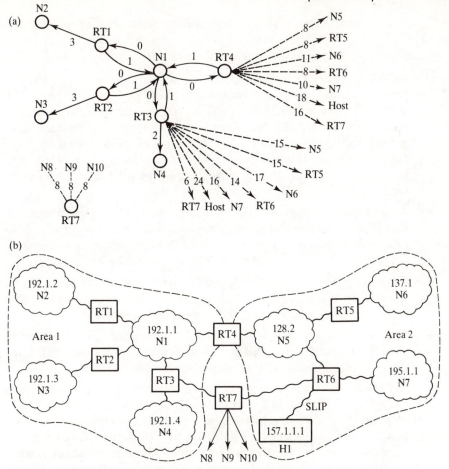

Figure 16.18 OSPF router network with two areas. (a) Area 1 database.
(b) Topology.

can see dual paths to certain objects, but they have different costs. If there were multiple paths with the same cost, OSPF would share datagrams among them (a useful improvement on other routing protocols). Note that RT7 is shown as a separate part of the database as it is not part of area 1. RT4 has two databases, one for area 1 and another for area 2.

Using OSPF

OSPF implementations are new and will undoubtedly continue to develop over the next few years. The definition of OSPF (RFC 1247) is thorough and it describes those parameters that need to be configured when installing an OSPF system. As with any node connection in an IP system, each network connection will need configuring with IP address and network mask and buffers.

The other important features required are:

- *Interface cost* This defines the cost of sending a datagram out across an interface of the router and is defined for each port. The cost units are arbitrarily chosen by the system manager with a range of 1 to 65 535. There can be a different cost for each TOS considered by the router, determining the route based on high throughput, low relay, high reliability and true cost (the DTRC bits of the TOS flags in the IP datagram). Not all router implementations provided TOS routing at first release.

- *Advertisement interval* Defined in seconds, this is the frequency at which LSAs are transmitted over an interface. Its value should be greater than the round trip delay across the interface concerned. A typical value for a local area network would be five seconds.

- *Transfer delay* This is supposed to be the estimated number of seconds it takes to send a link state update message across this interface. This would typically be one second for a LAN.

- *Router priority* This value is used to set which router becomes the DR on multi-access networks; the higher the value, the higher the likelihood of this router becoming the DR.

- *Hello interval* The length of time in seconds between router hello datagrams. The value for this should be the same for all routers attached to the same multi-access network. The smaller this value is set, the quicker network failures will be detected, but using a very low value will cause more traffic on the network. A recommended value for LANs is around 10 seconds but nearer 30 seconds for an X.25 PDN.

- *Router dead interval* The number of seconds from last seeing a router's hellos before declaring it has failed. This value should be the same for all routers on a multi-access network and should be a multiple of the hello interval, probably of the order of four. This would give a time of 40 seconds on a LAN or 2 minutes on an X.25 PDN. Since hellos are carried in IP datagrams and may occasionally be legitimately lost, this allows for up to three hellos to be missed.

- *Authentication key* This is the authentication value used to validate link state updates. Today's implementations provide at best a simple clear text password.

OSPF routers also need a unique **router identification** value. As each router already has at least two IP addresses, which themselves are unique in the network, it is suggested that the router identification is obtained by taking the smallest value IP address assigned to the router.

Routers within an area require an **area id**. This is a 32-bit number that must be greater than zero, as zero is reserved for the backbone area. Each router will require a list of all networks, and their subnet masks, used within its area.

While OSPF responds to complete failures of network links, it need not dynamically change the path costs entered by the system manager. These path costs must be carefully chosen during the network design phase and matched to the capacity and number of routes available so that the correct overall performance requirements for throughput, delay and resilience to failure are achieved.

The status of OSPF

OSPF has been implemented by a number of different manufacturers with 3Com, Cisco, Proteon, Wellfleet, and ACC participating in early interworking trials. Reports of these initial trials are enthusiastic about performance. Rerouting around link failures occurs in a few seconds in situations where RIP fails to repair paths at all. The routing traffic is a few per cent of that of RIP. Routing traffic grows at a much slower rate as the network expands.

The IAB has accepted that its design aims for an IGP (some of which we outlined above) and its requirements for acceptance of OSPF as an Internet standard have been met. In September 1991, it endorsed OSPF as *the* recommended IGP for future use in autonomous systems connected to the Internet, although the protocol has not yet advanced to full standard status. With the initial trials over during 1990 and 1991, and with this endorsement from the IAB, it is to be expected that an increasing number of router manufacturers will ship OSPF as the primary routing protocol for their IP router implementations.

OSPF gives a network manager unprecedented control over TCP/IP routing functions in an organization. All the issues concerning RIP are removed if OSPF is used:

- OSPF works with subnets and variable length subnet masks although the issues with variable length subnet masks have still to be fully resolved.
- Different metrics can be allocated to particular links so that OSPF can make routing decisions on the TOS bits of the IP datagram. These bits can select a path based on delay, or throughput, or the underlying probability of transmission errors (reliability) or monetary cost.
- Wide area point-to-point links between routers need not be identified with their own network number thus conserving valuable address space.
- OSPF divides a large network into different management areas.

- Details of routing within an area are not passed outside an area, which constrains the size and number of update messages, router processing power and memory requirements as networks grow.

- On IEEE LANs and Ethernet, updates are carried in multi-cast addressed frames rather than broadcast frames; the OSPF protocol is rejected by the network interface cards in application hosts, so unnecessary interrupts do not consume host processing power.

- OSPF has security features not present in previous TCP/IP routing protocols.

Some of the TOS features and authentication schemes are optional. When choosing a router supplier, it is important to verify that your required options are implemented in the way you expect.

In view of OSPF's range of features and the IAB endorsement, it would appear that it is a good choice for any organization intending to implement a TCP/IP router network.

Other routing protocols

The names of other routing protocols frequently appear in connection with TCP/IP routing. For completeness, the following paragraphs describe the main features of each without the technical detail required to manage them.

Integrated IS–IS

IS means 'intermediate system'. In OSI terms, an IS is a network layer relay component in the communication path between two end systems (or application hosts). In this context an IS is a router and IS–IS is the inter-mediate-system-to-intermediate-system routing protocol, standardized by the ISO OSI committees as IS10589[†], for use between routers[‡] with the OSI Connectionless Network Protocol (OSI CLNP). OSI CLNP is referred to as OSI's IP by TCP/IP users and there are many similarities: we prefer to think of OSI CLNP as 'IP with big addresses' – up to 160 bits rather than 32 bits.

IS–IS routing protocol was developed in the late 1980s in parallel with OSPF, and it shares most of the desirable features of a 'good' routing protocol. ISO OSI potentially has to solve the routing problems of

---

[†]DIS10589, a draft international standard at the time of writing.

[‡]Another OSI routing protocol, End System to Intermediate System (ES–IS) allows an end system to discover all routers available to it.

one global internet, based on OSI. The routing framework on which IS–IS is based divides into a four-level routing hierarchy of which IS–IS forms the lowest layer, equivalent to an IGP within IP. The Digital Equipment Corporation (DEC) has adopted OSI CLNP as one of the main protocols for its phase V implementation of DECnet. DEC has had a significant influence in the development and promotion of IS–IS protocols. In 1990, RFC 1195, which describes **integrated IS–IS**, was issued by the IS–IS working group of the IETF, Internet Engineering Task Force, a development arm of the IAB. The principal author of RFC 1195 is from Digital Equipment Corporation.

Integrated IS–IS is a modification of pure OSI IS–IS to allow a router to interpret and route either OSI CLNP datagrams or IP datagrams or both simultaneously. A router which uses such an integrated approach should be more efficient and require less memory, processing and network capacity for routing tables and routing table updates than a traditional multiprotocol router which regards each network protocol and its corresponding routing protocol as separate entities.

Integrated IS–IS supports IP subnetting, variable length subnet masks, TOS routing by mapping to the equivalent OSI quality-of-service routing and external routing. It also supports routing authentication (routing security). As in OSPF, networks may be divided into two levels with the detail of each level hidden from the other. Level 2 routers form a backbone supporting many level 1 areas; level 1 routers support collections of networks or subnetworks and route to an IP network or subnetwork.

Though many of the features are similar to OSPF, integrated IS–IS has not received the same support from other manufacturers, hence its development has not advanced as swiftly as OSPF. The IAB's endorsement of OSPF rather than integrated IS–IS may delay further progress. It is still possible that pressure from those using TCP/IP as a migration to full OSI may force greater support for integrated IS–IS by manufacturers other than DEC. If such a migration strategy is endorsed by the IAB for the internet, integrated IS–IS will have a significant role to play.

Border gateway protocol

The **Border Gateway Protocol** (BGP), is another 1990–91 addition to TCP/IP standards (RFC 1267). As its name suggests, the BGP is not an IGP. The BGP is designed as a more efficient and flexible alternative to the earlier EGP for routing between organizations – inter-autonomous system routing. BGP places no restrictions on the interconnections that can exist between autonomous systems. It allows a router to identify multiple routes between systems, to detect and avoid routing loops and to choose between multiple available routes.

BGP meets a need for **policy-based routing**. In recent years, the Internet has expanded beyond the expectations of the original creators. It was designed originally as a research vehicle for network protocols and the effects of sophisticated communications on organizations; it now supports the academic research of the US university and educational communities and the requirements of government. The core of the network is funded by the government. It is not a commercial carrier service and must not be used to carry commercial traffic. Around this core research network have sprung up a number of other commercial networks based on TCP/IP protocols, but selling information services. It is important that the core Internet does not begin to carry commercial traffic; that would infringe the rules, or the policy, under which it was established and operates. Other carriers will have limits on the types of traffic and the organizations for which they are prepared to transport data.

Controlling the type of traffic carried by considering origin and destination is one of the functions of this new type of routing. Policy-based routing is about enforcing routing decisions based on the use, or avoidance, of selected autonomous systems or network numbers as transit networks, or on acting as a transit network on behalf of other autonomous systems. With registration, these numbers indicate the nature of the communicating organization – educational, commercial, governmental, military, external to the USA, or another unclassified type.

RFCs for the BGP were first published in June 1989, with a later version, RFC 1267, in October 1991. The BGP allows routers to exchange details of routes between autonomous systems. The paths are described as a list of network and autonomous system numbers; since subnetworks describe a level of detail internal to an autonomous system, BGP does not describe subnetworks. Two communicating autonomous systems can make a 'policy' decision on whether to use and advertise a route incorporating particular network numbers. An autonomous system must only advertise routes which it is prepared to use. It must decide whether it is prepared to be a transit network (a carrier). BGP only specifies how path details are exchanged; how autonomous system managers derive a routing policy and how they configure that policy in routing software is outside the specification.

As with OSPF, there are several independent implementations of BGP in use on the Internet. Later versions of gated support BGP and this code is public domain.

A feature of BGP is its ability to detect and suppress routing loops. EGP, used previously to describe routes external to the autonomous system, could only have one connection to the core. BGP is more efficient than EGP in its use of bandwidth and processing power for, after an initial exchange of a complete routing table, only changes to that table and keep-alive messages are sent. EGP does not perform well in congested networks where packet loss occurs. BGP is more tolerant as routing information is retransmitted over a reliable TCP connection.

It is too early for BGP to be available in commercial products. From the technical descriptions, BGP would seem to have a role to play in the larger commercial network, for example in a multinational company where there were a number of centres of equivalent status each with their own TCP/IP systems. BGP could provide the right degree of autonomy for each 'autonomous system'.

Interior gateway routing protocol

The **Interior Gateway Routing Protocol** (IGRP) is a proprietary protocol developed by Cisco Systems for their multiprotocol routers. It is used with TCP/IP and other protocols that Cisco routers support. IGRP predates both OSPF and integrated IS–IS. It was designed to overcome the limitations of RIP in a multiprotocol environment and can use multiple paths simultaneously.

Using multiple routing protocols

A complex network is unlikely to use just a single routing protocol, though once a modern sophisticated protocol like OSPF is mastered, there are few technical reasons to introduce another IGP. Routers can operate more than one routing protocol, each performing updates on a single routing table simultaneously. They may use OSPF and RIP to communicate inside the autonomous system, and BGP and EGP to communicate outside the organization. Most combinations should operate correctly. Occasionally, the detail learnt about the same routes by two different methods may conflict and cause a routing 'black hole': IP datagrams reach a router which does not know of the destination network; its only option is to discard the data and inform the originator using the error protocol, ICMP. Black holes are more likely where manual routing tables are used to supplement dynamic routing.

Managing routing errors and network congestion

Even in a quite simple TCP/IP network, network implementors must set up procedures to detect and manage link, network, and equipment failures and performance problems. Because of the way a TCP/IP installation is structured, successful management will require technical cooperation across different management functions and organizations. The indication that some remedial action is required is the presence of certain types of ICMP error datagrams on a network.

When links and equipment fail, routes will change. During the time taken for the whole network to agree a new stable configuration, routers are likely to discard IP datagrams. When a router cannot forward

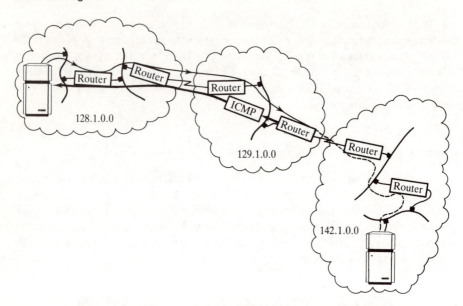

Figure 16.19   ICMP and multiple management domains.

a datagram, it should generate an ICMP destination-unreachable error message back to the source IP address of the discarded datagram.

In a complex network, this raises some organizational issues, for this error message will travel across several management responsibilities. It could originate from a router under one communications management control, addressed to a host system in another organization and level of management; it might well be caused by a failure in a network which is under yet another management control. The main problem is that the management function which has the physical network problem probably receives no notification because the failure is reported back along the route away from the source of the problem. It is the originating host that will receive an error message (Figure 16.19).

Similar considerations apply to the ICMP message, source quench, which is used to reduce router and network congestion. ICMP source quench must be accepted by all IP equipment. Routers generate source quench when they, or the links they serve, are overloaded and they are discarding datagrams as a result of this congestion. The effectiveness of source quench implementations varies widely. Network managers should monitor their networks for source quench on a regular basis. If they are occurring regularly during busy periods, then the network planners must investigate the implications for applications and attached equipment. Source quench indicates a lack of resources, which must be remedied before the rate of packet loss increases to a point where the network operation becomes unstable.

When a system receives an ICMP message, it records the fact in a set of counters for each ICMP message type. These counters can be read

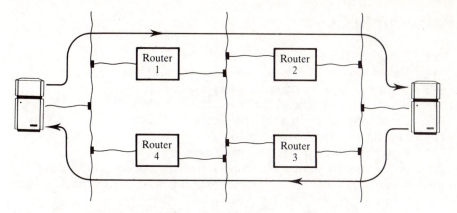

Figure 16.20   Asymmetric datagram transmission.

from the system console; in UNIX systems the command `netstat  -s` will list network statistics which include the ICMP messages. In recent implementations, the counters from network equipment can be read across the network with an SNMP management system; summary information can be collected and collated centrally. The detail is *not* recorded; neither the source address nor the time at which the ICMP error was received is available after the event. In general, the only way to see the detail is to trap ICMP error datagrams with a LAN analyser or remote monitor as they pass through the network.

Asymmetric and one-way transmission

A consequence of the flexibility of IP routing is that the path between two end systems need not be symmetric. In an internetwork with multiple paths between end systems and the routing protocols to take advantage of them, if a datagram travels between A and B through routers 1 and 2, in one direction, the response datagram may well travel back from B to A through routers 3 and 4 (Figure 16.20).

  Even where there is only one available path, it is possible for datagrams to pass from A to B successfully but not from B to A. This could occur if B has no default router, if it has an incorrect subnet mask, or if the subnet masks are incorrect on some of the router ports. Subnet masks are only used on outbound datagrams so it is possible for them to be correct in one direction of transmission and incorrect in the other. When the router compares the destination network number, it may decide it has no route to that network. It should generate an ICMP destination unreachable or route change request message.

  To determine where the fault lies requires a combination of good test equipment and methodical test techniques as discussed in Chapter 18.

Relevant RFCs

827 Exterior Gateway Protocol (EGP)
904 Exterior Gateway Protocol formal specification
1009 Requirements for Internet gateways
1058 Routing Information Protocol
1102 Policy routing in Internet protocols
1104 Models of policy-based routing
1124 Policy issues in interconnecting networks
1125 Policy requirements for inter-administrative domain routing
1126 Goals and functional requirements for inter-autonomous system routing
1136 Administrative domains and routing domains: a model for routing in the Internet
1195 Use of OSI IS–IS for routing in TCP/IP and dual environments
1245 OSPF protocol analysis
1246 Experience with the OSPF protocol
1247 OSPF version 2
1256 ICMP router discovery messages
1264 Internet Engineering Task Force Internet routing protocol standardization criteria
1265 BGP protocol analysis
1266 Experience with the BGP protocol
1267 Border gateway protocol 3 (BGP-3)
1268 Application of the border gateway protocol in the Internet.

Summary

In this section we have considered the principles of routing and the major protocols used on most commercial TCP/IP networks. Where a company is intending to work with anything but the smallest network, it is important to understand the mechanics of the routing protocols so that they can be selected and tuned to provide the best level of service.

The principles behind routing protocols are basically the same but protocols continue to be enhanced to handle more complex architectures efficiently and to be more responsive to network changes. Many of the earlier less sophisticated routing protocols are still in use today; it is important to appreciate their limitations.

The latest and most sophisticated routing protocol for use with TCP/IP systems is OSPF. This should be considered when purchasing new equipment. Not all the features of the protocol (TOS routing) are yet available in commercial equipment, but with the right market pressure this will change rapidly. OSPF requires careful network planning and implementation. Configuration of a large OSPF network will be quite complex due to the need to determine the appropriate costs for each port on the network so that available paths are used with optimum effectiveness.

Mixing multiple routing protocols on a network should be approached with caution as their interoperation may not be totally effective.

17

Simple network management protocol

In recent years, the Simple Network Management Protocol (SNMP) has become increasingly important. It has become the dominant mechanism for the distributed management of network equipment.

The most significant aspect of implementations of SNMP is the power they provide to monitor and control networks. SNMP's simplicity and effectiveness have positioned it as the vehicle for the development of increasingly sophisticated mechanisms for controlling network systems.

Topics covered in this chapter are:

- SNMP
- MIBs
- ASN.1/BER
- Use of SNMP

The history of SNMP is interesting for it reflects many of the differences between OSI and TCP/IP development. SNMP was originally defined for use with TCP/IP but was based on OSI definitions for network management. The term 'SNMP' is commonly used to refer to the complete set of components that are required to manage a network. To be correct, SNMP is only the protocol used to communicate management information between devices on a network; its definition does not cover all aspects of the system. In this chapter we will look at the other components that are used with SNMP, such as the Management Information Bases (MIBs).

The need for management systems

As networks become larger and more crucial to business success, the ability to keep that resource functioning becomes critical. Because large internetworks have been few and far between until recent years, there has not been sufficient demand to force the development of the tools required to manage a complex internetwork effectively. If only the biggest networks need these tools, with only one set for each, the market is not large enough to distribute the development costs. So they tend to be expensive. The available products only deal with single aspects of network management; they often do not provide an integrated approach. It is not until a number of organizations work together to agree a common standard that the total market for a single set of tools can become large enough to warrant development and therefore reduce the costs to where sophisticated management systems can become attractive to smaller network operators.

During the 1980s, networks changed from being terminal access networks to resource sharing networks consisting of PCs, minicomputers and mainframes all connected by cables and a network operating system. This is nothing less than a distributed computing system, with the internal communications paths of each computer replaced by the network. The overall function of this system is the basic tool of information technology and the network is the core of the whole system. Failure of the network can have a serious impact on a company.

The computing and communications vendors push the concepts of information technology hard: 'Use our computers and networks, because they help increase effectiveness and productivity'. Yet, with one or two notable exceptions, they have been slow to use this technology to help manage the network technology itself.

Network management is a classic information technology problem. Large amounts of detailed information are required to understand what is happening within the system so that necessary decisions can be made on how to control, adapt and grow the service. A potential issue is that a system may generate so much information in managing itself that it becomes self-perpetuating.

The development of management for TCP/IP

TCP/IP, like most communication systems, has lacked a set of integrated management tools suitable for looking after large systems. The main tools available to a manager using TCP/IP have been ping and netstat or their equivalents in non-UNIX environments. This is not to demean the power of ping and netstat, but they are simply not powerful enough for today's complex networks, particularly in environments where technical skills are at a premium. ISO committees had generated definitions of how network management should be structured; something similar was needed for TCP/IP systems.

Two separate groups have been working on management for TCP/IP. One group worked on SNMP and another on Common Management Information Services and Protocol Over TCP/IP (CMOT) (RFC 1095). CMOT uses the OSI standards Common Management Information Protocol (CMIP) and Common Management Information Services (CMIS) operating over TCP/IP communications protocols rather than OSI protocols. CMOT has very much taken a back seat in its acceptance, probably caused by the cost implications of implementing what is a more complex but more robust, and hence expensive, approach to network management. The SNMP committee based much of its work on that performed by the ISO committees on CMIP and CMIS, as far as this was practical; there was no point in replicating what had already been defined.

The SNMP was designed as closely as practical to the OSI model for management, but with a desire to produce a practical system that could economically be added to all nodes in a network. As a result, SNMP is a connectionless management system designed to operate over the UDP transport layer of TCP/IP. CMIP and CMIS (and hence CMOT) are based on connection-oriented systems.

One of the benefits of LANs is that every node connects to a common logical bus, so they can all be accessed, either for data or for management reasons from any point on that LAN. Until now, the general focus upon LAN development has been to provide interoperability, to get data flowing between various systems. Now that TCP/IP has achieved this, the next step is to keep it all working, to control and manage it.

Gathering management information

In the past, statistics on network performance have often only been available from analysers connected to single points on the network. The information from such a position does not represent an accurate view of the activity on the entire network unless in-depth studies of the protocols are made. This is technically complex, and rarely done, so the results can be misleading. One of the advantages of being able to access every node is that it can be queried on how well it believes the network is performing. This distributes the task of network analysis right to the periphery of the network. The general consensus of network performance will be developed from information direct from each node. The picture will be far more accurate. The main problem then is that there is so much information generated that it requires significant computing power and software sophistication to analyse the data and report appropriate exceptions or problems in a form network managers can easily recognize. One of the aims of a network management system is to make the statistics-gathering in each end system simple and to centralize the complex analysis. With a common protocol for delivering the statistics, manufacturers can concentrate on differentiating their products by the power of their analysis and display tools.

Most network management systems today are effective at collecting statistics, but there is still not enough assistance with analysing and interpreting the meaning of those statistics.

SNMP architecture

The basic architecture of SNMP is shown in Figure 17.1. As previously described, the architecture of SNMP includes more than just the protocols. It consists of the Management Information Base (MIB), for each component of the protocol stack and the simple network management protocol.

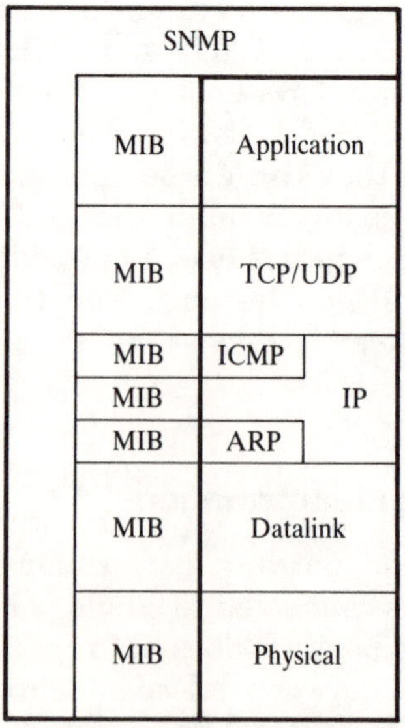

Figure 17.1 Simple network management architecture.

Information encoding

When information is passed between different computer architectures, the computers must agree on the representation of that information. Management systems have to agree on the meaning of management information as it is passed from computer to management system to prevent different computer architectures from misinterpreting it. SNMP has based the way it represents its data on two OSI standards: Abstract Syntax Notation 1 (ASN.1) and the Basic Encoding Rules (BER).

ASN.1 can be thought of as a strictly defined and 'highly typed' high-level computer language. Quantities to be described are defined in terms of primitive types like `integer` and `string`. Like any other high-level computer language, the results can be read and interpreted by both people and by machines. The ASN.1 language can be compiled into a sequence of octets (bits) using the BER. SNMP uses only a subset of ASN.1; normally the types `integer`, `octet string`, `object identifier`, `sequence` and `null`. It is possible for other application-wide types to be defined, but these must resolve into the primitive types.

BER deals with the same problem as XDR does for NFS (ONC), but BER is an explicit and unambiguous system – each value is clearly and explicitly defined. This makes it quite easy for a LAN analyser to decipher any information on the network that is encoded in BER. To do this with XDR would require knowledge of the structure of the information used by the application that generated it. In both cases, it is necessary to understand the context of the information to understand its meaning completely. But whereas XDR assumes that the device receiving the information understands what to expect, BER includes a label with the information indicating exactly what it is.

Most of the other TCP/IP application layers we discussed used ASCII strings to pass their commands across the network. The meaning of the information could be seen on any LAN analyser that shows ASCII data. As SNMP uses BER, it is more difficult to analyse than these other TCP/IP protocols; data passing across a network is encoded as apparently meaningless octets. To give a clearer understanding of SNMP messages[†] we must look a little deeper into BER.

The underlying form of BER is shown in Figure 17.2. All data encoded by BER has a type and length field preceding it. The type field indicates the construction of data being carried and the length field its size. This allows many different types of information to be carried and deciphered by the remote computer.

To give additional flexibility for other structures that may be required in the future, the type field has three subfields; bits 8 and 7 are used to denote the **tag class** (*cc*), bit 6 the **form** (*f*) and bits 5 to 1 the **tag number**. Tags can be extended beyond a single octet but this does not

---

[†]Sometimes referred to as Protocol Data Units (PDUs), an OSI term.

BER tag format

bits	8	7	6	5	4	3	2	1
	c	c	f	t	t	t	t	t

bit 8 7	Tag class	bit 6	Form	bits 5 4 3 2 1
0 0	Universal	0	primitive	Tag number
0 1	Application-wide	1	constructed	
1 0	Context-specific			
1 1	Private use			

Figure 17.2 BER tag definition.

change the concept and it is not necessary to describe the detail here. Some additional detail is given in Appendix J.

The length field is normally 1 octet long, but to describe long structures more than eight bits are needed. So, if bit 8 of the length field is 1, it denotes that the length field is more than one octet and that the remaining seven bits in the first octet actually denote the length of the length field, that is, these seven bits are a count of the number of following octets which are themselves the length field. A single octet length field can define data that has 127 octets, which will cover most cases for SNMP (Figure 17.3). For a detailed list of possible tags, see Appendix J.

Management information base

The Management Information Base (MIB) is a definition of the objects (quantities or fields) that should be provided on each managed node by the SNMP 'agent'. The management agent is the piece of software that responds to SNMP management requests from the central management station.

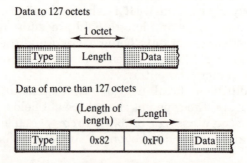

Figure 17.3 Length and extended length in BER.

The objects of the MIB are arranged in groups. Some groups relate to each layer or protocol in the protocol stack and some relate to the system as a whole. Many of the quantities are counters of events and are therefore an accumulation of the number of events seen since the counter was last zeroed – the number of frames sent and received categorized as unicast, multicast and broadcast would be one set of counters at the MAC layer. The details of 'when' and 'who' are not available after the event. Another MIB definition, RMON (Remote MONitor), describes how to access a remote device that will gather packets from a remote network to which it is attached, and return them to the management station for analysis. The remote monitor should retain the detail of the events, but the quantity of information available will be correspondingly larger.

These common definitions of the variables on each type of node in a network make gathering information on any device quite simple and independent of the manufacturer. Many manufacturers have created their own extensions to the standard MIBs to provide better function-ality with their own products. The protocol remains standard but the proprietary extensions make the management a little more complex. MIBs have been or are being defined for all (electronic) components of a network, from a repeater, through bridges and routers to hosts. They all contain elements of the protocol stack.

Because all of these systems follow the same MIB and protocol conventions, it is easy for management systems to use the standard and to provide cross-management of other vendors' products. Groups of manufacturers are now cooperating to exchange details of their pro-prietary MIB extensions which will allow complete management of each others' products.

Figure 17.4 shows the beginning of the Internet MIB II definition represented in ASN.1 syntax. This figure shows the basic object defini-tions that reference the individual groups of information that must be supported within managed equipment. These are: system, which identi-

```
mib            OBJECT IDENTIFIER ::= { mgmt 1 }

system         OBJECT IDENTIFIER ::= { mib 1 }
interfaces     OBJECT IDENTIFIER ::= { mib 2 }
at             OBJECT IDENTIFIER ::= { mib 3 }
ip             OBJECT IDENTIFIER ::= { mib 4 }
icmp           OBJECT IDENTIFIER ::= { mib 5 }
tcp            OBJECT IDENTIFIER ::= { mib 6 }
udp            OBJECT IDENTIFIER ::= { mib 7 }
egp            OBJECT IDENTIFIER ::= { mib 8 }
transmission   OBJECT IDENTIFIER ::= { mib 9 }
snmp           OBJECT IDENTIFIER ::= { mib 10}
```

Figure 17.4   MIB groups.

```
            - - the System group

    sysDescr OBJECT-TYPE
            SYNTAX   OCTET STRIN
            ACCESS   read-only
            STATUS   mandatory
            ::= { system 1 }

    sysObjectID OBJECT-TYPE
            SYNTAX   OBJECT IDENTIFIER
            ACCESS   read-only
            STATUS   mandatory
            ::= { system 2 }

    sysUpTime OBJECT-TYPE
            SYNTAX   TimeTicks
            ACCESS   read-only
            STATUS   mandatory
            ::= { system 3 }
```

Figure 17.5   The 'system' group of the Internet MIB II.

fies the product in use; `interfaces`, which details the network connections; and `at`, address translation. The rest detail facets of a particular protocol: `ip`, `icmp`, `tcp`, `udp` and `egp`.

Each of these groups has a varying number of further objects or fields defined within them. They describe a parameter relevant to that group. For example, within the `system` group is an object called the `sysDescr` or **system descriptor**. Figure 17.5 shows this definition in ASN.1 format. The system descriptor is a string object which identifies the name, hardware type, software operating system and network software. So retrieving this object from a node gives you a complete description of what type of system it is. From the ASN.1 definition, you can tell it is defined as an octet string – a string of 8 bit quantities. It is read only, so cannot be changed remotely and it is mandatory, so it must be provided on all implementations.

The third field is the `sysUpTime`, which indicates how long in hundredths of a second since this device was last reset in some way – (initialized or powered on).

The `sysObjectID` holds a vendor's authoritative identification. This is a definition of a registered identifier which is shown in dotted decimal notation and uniquely identifies a vendor's object groups and objects in their products.

The rules for the definition of the MIB descriptors are called the Structure of Management Information (SMI). This is based on OSI work for OSI management. Originally the MIB definitions were to be common between SNMP and CMIP, but they have now diverged.

Structure of an MIB

One function of these MIB definitions is to produce a sequence of numbers which will uniquely identify any management object in any management community, in this case the OSI or TCP/IP communities. These system object identifiers are derived from a hierarchical or tree structure starting at a root, which is unlabelled. Below that root are three 'main trunks' identifying the controlling organizations:

    0   CCITT
    1   ISO
    2   Joint-ISO-CCITT

There are further 'branches' beneath each of these. ISO has defined 'other international organizations' as being under a subtree number 3; one of these organizations is the US Department of Defense (DOD) as subtree number 6 off subtree 3 which is itself off the ISO trunk, 1. It is assumed that the DOD will define a further subtree of 1 for the Internet community. This generates a generic identifier for all TCP/IP management information of:

    1   . 3   . 6 . 1
    (ISO . Int org . dod . internet)

The next level of this definition is split four ways as:

    1   directory
    2   management
    3   experimental
    4   private

'Directory' is reserved for future use. 'Management' (mgmt) is used to identify objects which are defined in approved documents. So additions to the management tree will occur as new RFCs are approved that deal with management of specific Internet components. 'Experimental' is for temporary use with experimental systems and 'private'[†] is used to identify objects defined unilaterally for internal or private use. There is a subtree to 'private' defined for private extensions to the MIB system as:

    1   enterprises

[†]If a system moves from experimental or private to a fully accepted and generally available technique, it should move its definitions to one of the permanent branches of the MIB.

The result of this numbered tree is a sequence of numbers separated by periods (.) which define the path taken to a particular node on the management tree. Thus the object id:

1.3.6.1.4.1.42

could be used to refer to an individual manufacturer's extensions to the MIB of which:

1.3.6.1.4.1.42.1.1

could refer to a specific product as having a special MIB value.

A generic descriptor of 1.3.6.1.2.1.1.1 would refer specifically to the system descriptor (sysDescr); the numbers trace the values in the curly braces, { }, of the ASN.1 definition (see Figure 17.5).

BER encoding of MIB fields

When SNMP uses MIB fields, it refers to them through the object ids. In an SNMP datagram, the reference to the sysDescr would be 1.3.6.1.2.1.1.1. This would be expressed as a sequence of ASN.1 primitives and encoded using BER as:

0608 2B06 0102 0101 0100

The first octet defines the value as an **object identifier** (06), the second value is the length of the data (08) which is eight octets. With object identifiers, the first two octets can be combined in one octet. This will normally happen with SNMP values; they become 2B which translates back to 1 and 3. The following octets give the rest of the descriptor: 6.1.2.1.1.1. The 00 at the end is an octet to define which interface (referred to as an **instance**) on the computer this request relates to, if appropriate. If a computer has multiple interfaces, the instance used refers SNMP actions to the appropriate interface. On MIB fields where an instance is not appropriate, its value is set to 00. There can only be one sysDescr in a system, so the value of the 'instance octet' is always set to 00 with this object.

The object identifier shown would be followed by the value of the field in a response to an SNMP request or a null in the request itself. The BER type for null is 05, so an SNMP request is followed by 0500.

Consider another example of the use of the instance octet:

0608 2B06 0102 0102 0302

Tracing the tree, this refers to an object identifier (06) of length 8 on the tree 1.3.6.1.2 (the 'management' group of the DOD Internet). The next branch is mib (1) and the interfaces object (2) within that group. The next selector (3) refers to the interface type (ifType) field of which there could be more than one. So for a specific host, this identifier refers to iftype.2 on the computer specified. This should be its second interface

```
ifType OBJECT-TYPE
        SYNTAX   INTEGER {
                 other(1).-- none of the
                 following
                 regular1822(2),
                 hdh1822(3),
                 ddn-x25(4),
                 rfc877-x25(5),
                 ethernet-csmacd(6),
                 iso88023-csmacd(7),
                 iso88024-tokenBus(8),
                 iso88025-tokenRing(9),
                 iso88026-man(10),
                 starLan(11),
                 proteon-10MBit(12),
                 proteon-80MBit(13),
                 hyperchannel(14),
                 fddi(15),
                 lapb(16),
                 sdlc(17),
                 t1-carrier(18),
                 cept(19),
                 basicIsdn(20),
                 primaryIsdn(21),
                    -- proprietary serial
                    propPontToPointSerial(22)
                 }
        ACCESS   read-only
        STATUS   mandatory
        ::= { ifEntry 3 }
```

Figure 17.6 The ifType definition.

and will be one of the standard interface types of Figure 17.6. A common type in TCP/IP would be 6, ethernet-csmacd. More detailed examples are shown later in this chapter.

Figure 17.6 shows a portion of the MIB entries for the interface group showing possible interface types. The numbers against the specific types of interface would be returned in a response to indicate the interface type.

Figure 17.7 shows the beginning of the IP group from the Internet MIB II. The first field is the ipForwarding field which identifies whether this host acts as an IP router or just as a host. Notice the field ipDefault-TTL. This field is read-write, so a management system (with suitable access rights) can modify the TTL for the IP stack in this host. This therefore allows configuration changes to be performed remotely.

```
-- the IP group

ipForwarding OBJECT-TYPE
  SYNTAX  INTEGER {
    gateway(1), -- entity forwards datagrams
    host(2) -- entity does NOT forward datagrams
            ACCESS   read-only
            STATUS   mandatory
            ::= { ip 1 }
  ipDefaultTTL OBJECT-TYPE
            SYNTAX   INTEGER
            ACCESS   read-write
            STATUS   mandatory
            ::= { ip 2 }

  ipInReceives OBJECT-TYPE
            SYNTAX   Counter
            ACCESS   read-only
            STATUS   mandatory
            ::= { ip 3 }

  ipInHdrErrors OBJECT-TYPE
            SYNTAX   Counter
            ACCESS   read-only
            STATUS   mandatory
            ::= { ip 4 }
```

Figure 17.7 Part of the IP group from MIB II.

The protocol

The simple network management protocol provides a mechanism to access MIB objects so that they can be read and changed. It also allows a device to send unsolicited messages to an SNMP management station to indicate that some predefined condition has been met. The message types used to perform these functions are:

```
get-request
get-next-request
get-response
set-request
trap
```

They are referred to as Protocol Data Units (PDUs), as in OSI standards. The get-request PDU is used by an SNMP network management

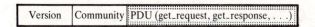

| Version | Community | PDU (get_request, get_response, . . .) |

Figure 17.8 SNMP message format.

station to obtain the value of a specific MIB variable from the SNMP management agent in a remote node. The `get-next-request` is similar to the `get-request`, except it allows MIB values to be received without defining them specifically. `get-next-request` is used where a table of variables, such as a routing table, exists. The client would not know the number of values in that table.

The `get-response` PDU is the answer from the management agent to `get-request` and `get-next-request`. The `set-request` is used by the management station to change MIB variables that can be altered in the management agent. One possibility is to set a trap for a defined event or condition detected by the management agent. When that condition occurs on the node, the agent sends a `trap` PDU to the management station. This message can be generated at any time, so a management station has to be listening for these continuously.

The `trap` messages use UDP well-known port number 162; other PDUs use port number 161. This allows `trap` messages to be handled independently of `get` and `set`.

The basic format of SNMP messages is shown in Figure 17.8. They all start with a version, which is 0 for version 1, followed by a **community** string. The community string defines a level of authentication which pertains to this message and hence determines whether it will have sufficient rights on a host to make changes or even read the information in the MIB.

The community string is followed by one or more PDUs which define the overall message encapsulated in this datagram. All PDUs, apart from the `trap` PDU, are the same. The format is shown in Figure 17.9. The normal PDUs start with a request id to help relate requests and responses; these messages are likely to use the UDP protocol and hence there is no reliability. The request id is followed by an error status field that is 0 if there is no error or:

1   The PDU is too big
2   No such name, that value does not exist
3   Bad value, that value is not suitable
4   Read only, the field cannot be altered
5   General error

The error index field can provide extra information relating to the error message. Last is the variable binding, which is an object identifier and a suitable field that can contain the value of that object variable. The variable field is provided in requests as well as responses but in a request it is set to a null value.

(a)

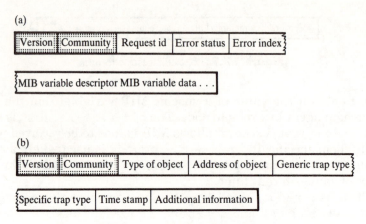

Figure 17.9 SNMP PDUs: (a) normal; (b) trap.

Figure 17.10 is an example of an SNMP `get-request` and its response. The exchange is represented in hexadecimal and then each of the fields is decoded and explained. The request is for the system-up-time on a node (objectdescr 1.3.6.1.2.1.1.3.0) and the resulting reply. The octets of the SNMP PDU have been split into their respective fields, although the order of transmission has been retained. The first octet of BER encoding is type, so the left-hand column contains the type, length and then value of the field. Notice the description starts by indicating that the whole structure is a sequence. Most of the constructs from then on are simple, apart from the PDU type, which is a context-specific construction, and the object identifier, which is an object id. As mentioned previously, an object identifier can be compressed; the first two bytes of the descriptor, which are 1 and 3, are encoded to become the value 2B. The remaining values are all in hexadecimal – 6.1.2.1.1.3.0 – indicating the system-up-time. This is then followed by a null field.

The response SNMP PDU is almost identical to the request; only the PDU type and the response value change. The PDU type changes to 2, encoded as A2, a context-specific construction, and the field following the descriptor that was null is now filled with the actual up-time, in one hundredths of a second since the device was re-initialized.

Using SNMP

SNMP has brought the potential of cost-effective network management even to small LANs. It has provided a generic mechanism by which different manufacturers' equipment can be monitored and controlled from a common management device. An SNMP management agent can now be added to most components on a LAN so that they can now be monitored and controlled by SNMP. Even a piece of cable can have a device

(a)

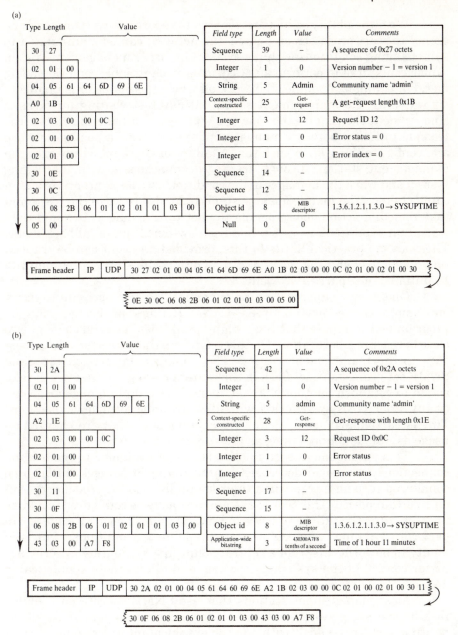

Figure 17.10 SNMP PDUs in BER encoding: (a) request and (b) response.

connected to it which will report its status, the status of the physical layer, to a management station. SNMP opens the door to higher level management of the network system, as both LAN and WAN components can be monitored and manipulated to increase effectiveness, reliability and security.

With the ability to instruct devices to report events (trap) and the ability to start processes on a node, the network can be manipulated to suit changing conditions within a system. In fact, a management system can be configured to perform any task on any identifiable condition being met. For example, imagine a network on which the manager is unable to sit watching the management screen all day just waiting for failures since some tasks require the manager's presence outside the office. It is feasible to link a network management system with a paging network and configure the system such that a failure of any kind will trigger the management station, through traps, to communicate with the paging system and warn the manager of the condition, so that appropriate action can be taken. The management system could also react to the traps and take remedial action before paging the network manager. It would then warn that a particular system had been switched into a fallback mode. There are no practical limits to this, provided an event can be trapped unambiguously and the reaction can be programmed into a computer to be initiated on a particular event.

One possible approach is the dynamic allocation of circuit capacity on remote connections between LANs. Routers or bridges can be programmed to report that their high-speed lines have reached, or are close to reaching, saturation. On this condition, they can send a trap message to the management station. The management station can send SNMP set-requests to set flags in the router or bridge so that it will take action to establish another channel, using ISDN, dial-up modems, X.25, or any other WAN system that will allow dynamic setup of connections. This is particularly useful with WAN connections that are charged on usage as well as connect time, as they are only used when required.

This management system can also be programmed to remove the connections when load decreases, as the router or bridges can also be configured to send a trap when their load falls below a predefined level for a certain period. This type of system can easily be configured to invoke fallback after the failure of a WAN link. Some bridges and routers can perform dynamic connections on predefined conditions, but the ability to perform this from a central point, in a standard way, provides better control of the system as a whole and allows more sophisticated decisions to be made.

Most management stations that use SNMP operate on a multi-tasking operating system within a windowed environment. This allows multiple tasks to be dealt with and the graphical interfaces make a complex system easier to view. Manufacturers also provide diagrammatic interfaces of the network with world maps that can be zoomed to pick out countries, towns, sites, buildings and the network segments and equipment within a building; even individual cards and ports within a piece of equipment can be examined. Today's management systems commonly represent errors as a red object on the display. To look at that object in more detail, the manager selects the object with a mouse pointer. The display zooms to the next level of the network hierarchy giving a more detailed view of the fault.

In any system of alarms, filtering out the most significant information is always an interesting design task. A problem with graphical management systems is how they react in the event of failure of a shared resource. This causes numerous error messages to be reported and can make it impossible for the manager to discern what component has failed due to the multitude of error reports presented on the screen. This problem is often handled by some type of artificial intelligence. The outcome is usually that the management system will best guess which device is causing the problem, show it as red, and show other failed components as some other less significant colour. The manager is drawn towards the element which is most likely to have failed; the problem is most likely to be identified quicker provided the diagnosis is not erroneous!

The processing demands on a management station at a time of serious failure is likely to be very high. These stations require a significant amount of processing power and not just to display colour graphics; a system that fails due to the high level of failure messages from the network will be no use at all when it is most required. Equally, a management system that is configured to generate a high level of unsolicited messages advising that the network is overloaded is perhaps not using its management systems to the best advantage.

While the features described are all based on the information provided by SNMP, such user functions are beyond the standardization process. It is up to the purchasers to decide what facilities are required in their management environment and to evaluate the competitive offerings. In view of the proprietary MIB extensions, it would be wise to check that all equipment which is to be managed is fully supported by the chosen management station.

Relevant RFCs

1052   IAB recommendations for the development of Internet network management
1155   Structure and identification of management information for TCP/IP-based Internets.
1156   Management information base for network management of TCP/IP-based Internets.
1157   Simple Network Management Protocol (SNMP)
1187   Bulk table retrieval with SNMP
1189   Common Management Information Services and Protocols for the Internet (CMOT and CMIP)
1212   Concise MIB definitions
1213   Management information base for network management of TCP/IP-based internets: MIB II

Summary

The requirements for network management are sure to expand significantly over the next few years, allowing networks, and even buildings, to be managed by standard management stations using the SNMP.

SNMP has paved the way for completely integrated management of networks. As the protocol itself is simple in its operation, the major activity has been agreeing the objects to be managed and their representation as the managed objects of an MIB. With many of these definitions in place, SNMP has been easy to include in products and already it is widely supported.

Most vendors of networking components are incorporating SNMP agents into products from repeaters to hosts. Some vendors have produced their own MIBs or extensions, but as these are defined in a standard fashion, it is technically easy to add support for all MIBs on any management station; copyright and royalty issues of proprietary MIB extensions might be more difficult to resolve.

MIBs will undoubtedly continue to grow and become more diverse as new products are introduced. As long as the existing definitions of ASN.1 are used and extended, a high level of compatibility is likely. Any device that has a defined MIB can be controlled by SNMP, so a natural extension is that standard machines will control building services such as air conditioning and any other building services that can benefit from centralized control. Once the standards are in place the technical problems are easily overcome. Organizational and managerial issues are more difficult to resolve as they involve the least standardized components – people.

18

Configuration and testing

This chapter brings together some of the configuration and testing issues covered in earlier chapters, with the aim of assisting with fault diagnosis. It also considers some of the standard tools that are available to ensure that TCP/IP systems are operating correctly.

In this chapter you will learn:

- A generic approach to testing TCP/IP systems
- Configuration issues
- More about debugging and measurement tools
- Common problems

In working with many different implementations of TCP/IP, we have found that product installation manuals rarely provide enough detail to understand fully how to configure all but the most rudimentary aspects of a system. This book is intended to provide the level of detail required to understand fully the ramifications of modifying parameters in a configuration setup, although we cannot expect to account for all the issues that may occur due to a particular vendor's implementation of TCP/IP.

Configuration

Configuration of a system can be easy or complex, depending on the way the product has been developed and which features the installer wishes to use. The more features and services that are used, the more complex the problem becomes. Often, systems are simply left at their default settings. This is usually of no consequence in small networks but it becomes important when a network grows. For example, many UNIX implementations of TCP/IP by default enable some services that are not necessary for most commercial installations. The effect of disabling such services varies from reducing the numbers of broadcast frames to preventing unauthorized access to a host.

With DOS-based PCs, the problem is simplified by the fact that they normally only run client services, and so the problem of other computers on the network gaining access is not usually a concern. On a computer using a multitasking operating system, it is worth while checking which features are enabled, before some TCP or host operating system expert on the network finds them first.

Minimum requirements

IP address

To get a workstation, host or router to function at a basic level is reasonably simple. The fundamental requirement for a node to work is that it has an IP address. It is important to ensure that the selected IP address matches the network address plan as described fully in Chapters 3 and 4.

Default gateway

If routing is to be used, a computer must be able to find a router. Either it should be configured with the IP address of a default gateway (router) or it must run a program that listens to the routing protocols on the network, to learn about routers for itself (eavesdropping). Some systems allow more than one 'default' gateway to be defined so that a backup is available. Of course, an eavesdropping host must listen to an operational routing protocol; there is no point in the host listening for RIP if the routers are only speaking OSPF.

On PCs, the default gateway is a parameter in the configuration setup when the software is installed. On more complex hosts routing tables may have to be configured manually if they are not eavesdropping. Commonly, the command `route add` allows routes to be added or removed and the costs of using those routes, expressed in hops, to be adjusted. Unless default gateways are defined, it is possible that, as well as not being able to make calls to other networks, a host will not accept incoming requests or calls from a node on another network. This is so unexpected that it can easily be overlooked.

Subnetwork mask

If subnetworks are used, it is important to set the correct mask every-where in the network. Variable masks are possible but must be used with care and with an understanding of how they are processed by routers. Initially, one value of mask should be used with one IP network number. In networks where the configuration is changed frequently, incorrect sub-net masks are a source of obscure routing problems and can in some instances cause broadcast storms.

Domain name server

If name servers are to be used, the node has to be configured with the IP address of the domain name server and secondary server for fallback purposes.

User id and host name

With some of the application services such as the `r` commands, a PC has to be configured with a host name and user id. The `r` protocol uses these fields to tell the destination host these user details so that the user does not need to enter them each time the command is used. Any user oper-ating the PC will be validated with the values stored in the PC. (Most hosts other than PCs will already know the user id and password as part of their configuration and user logon details anyway.)

More complex configuration

Configuration of TCP/IP systems to the level just described is straight-forward. Most products explain these items fairly well in their support-ing literature. The difficulty comes when a slightly more sophisticated configuration is required. Then, a manager's understanding of TCP/IP becomes important.

```
#   @(#)netd.cf      1.4 – 88/11/15
#
#   This is a configuration file for host-based
#   TCP/IP using the el ethernet interface
#


#   open control streams for transport protocols
tcp = "/dev/tcp"
udp = "/dev/udp"

#   open an IP stream for each transport protocol
ip_tcp = "/dev/ip" nsap 6      #   bind stream to TCP protocol id
ip_udp = "/dev/ip" nsap 17     #   bind stream to UDP protocol id

#   open ARP for ethernet use
arp    = "/dev/arp" lsap 0x800

#   open link level devices
el_arp = "/dev/el" lsap 0x806   #   stream for ARP messages
el_ip  = "/dev/el" lsap 0x800   #   stream for IP messages
loop   = "/dev/lo" lsap 0x800   #   stream for loopback driver

#   put it together
link ip_tcp under tcp
link ip_udp under udp

#   names must not assume a unit number so use as part of name
link loop under ip_tcp name "lo0"
link arp under ip_tcp name "el0"
link el_arp under arp type 0x101
link el_ip under arp type 0x1

#   initial configuration of interfaces
ifconfig "el0" gandalf up
ifconfig "lo0" localhost up
```

Figure 18.1   Format of netd.cf.

On many TCP/IP systems, whatever the computing platform, the files used to configure the system have standard names based upon those used in UNIX implementations. Where the names are different, it is usually easy to discern which aspects of configuration they relate to. The same file structures as UNIX are used, as the same configuration parameters have to be provided, determined by the RFCs that the software implements.

On UNIX systems important files for the basic operation of the TCP/IP protocols are:

/etc/netd.cf
/etc/inetd.conf
/etc/services

netd.cf

This file (Figure 18.1) enables all but the application layer services of the protocol stack. It is used to build (or bind) the components of the protocol stack together, and here the IP addresses, subnet masks and broadcast

```
#
#    Internet server configuration database
#        @(#)inetd.conf   1.2 – 88/11/11
#
ftp         stream    tcp    nowait    root    /etc/ftpd       ftpd
telnet      stream    tcp    nowait    root    /etc/telnetd    telnetd
shell       stream    tcp    nowait    root    /etc/rshd       rshd
login       stream    tcp    nowait    root    /etc/rlogind    rlogind
exec        stream    tcp    nowait    root    /etc/rexecd     rexecd
#    Run as user "uucp" if you don't want uucpd's wtmp entries.
#uucp       stream    tcp    nowait    root    /etc/uucpd      uucpd
finger      stream    tcp    nowait    bin     /etc/fingerd    fingerd
tftp        dgram     udp    wait      root    /etc/tftpd      tftpd
#comsat     dgram     udp    wait      root    /etc/comsat     comsat
#talk       dgram     udp    wait      root    /etc/talkd      talkd
ntalk       dgram     udp    wait      root    /etc/ntalkd     ntalkd
echo        stream    tcp    nowait    root    internal
discard     stream    tcp    nowait    root    internal
chargen     stream    tcp    nowait    root    internal
daytime     stream    tcp    nowait    root    internal
time        stream    tcp    nowait    root    internal
#echo       dgram     udp    wait      root    internal
#discard              dgram  udp       wait    root    internal
#chargen              dgram  udp       wait    root    internal
#daytime              dgram  udp       wait    root    internal
#time       dgram     udp    wait      root    internal
```

Figure 18.2   Format of inetd.conf.

addresses used by the network hardware are stored. A program, usually called ifconfig, performs the final binding of the parameters to the hardware. It is sometimes necessary to modify netd.cf file when multiple network interfaces are used.

inetd.conf

The file inetd.conf (Figure 18.2) is used to enable the application layer services. It shows the common name of the services and relates them to the executable programs that are activated to implement that service. This file should be modified to prevent services that are not required from being started. In case this service is required in future, it is normal to disable the service by adding a comment character (#) in front of the line which would start it, rather than delete the line completely and lose the correct format.

services

The services file (Figure 18.3) lists the well-known ports used by this host. This should include any in-house or specialist programs used on the host.

```
#
#    Network services, Internet style
#
echo            7/udp               ping
echo            7/tcp               ping
discard         9/udp               sink null
discard         9/tcp               sink null
systat          11/udp              users
systat          11/tcp              users
daytime         13/udp
daytime         13/tcp
netstat         15/tcp
quote           17/udp              text
quote           17/tcp              text
send            18/udp
send            18/tcp
chargen         19/udp              ttytst
chargen         19/tcp              ttytst
ftp-data        20/tcp
ftp             21/tcp
telnet          23/tcp
smtp            25/tcp              mail
time            37/udp              timserver
time            37/tcp              timserver
name            42/tcp              nameserver
whois           43/tcp              nicname
domain          53/tcp              nameserver       #  name-domain server
domain          53/udp              nameserver
mtp             57/tcp                               #  deprecated
bootp           67/udp                               #  boot program server
tftp            69/udp
finger          79/tcp
hostnames       101/tcp             hostname         #  usually from nic
pop2            109/tcp                              #  Post Office Protocol V2
pop3            110/tcp                              #  Post Office Protocol V3
sunrpc          111/tcp
sunrpc          111/udp
nntp            119/tcp             readnews untp    #  USENET News Transfer Protoc
snmp            161/udp
snmp-trap       162/udp             snmptrap
#
#    Host specific functions
#
tftp            69/udp
rje             77/tcp
finger          79/tcp
link            87/tcp              ttylink
supdup          95/tcp
ingreslock      1524/tcp
#
#    UNIX specific services
#
exec            512/tcp
login           513/tcp
shell           514/tcp             cmd              #  no passwords used
printer         515/tcp             spooler          #  experimental
efs             520/tcp                              #  for LucasFilm
courier         530/tcp             rpc              #  experimental
biff            512/udp             comsat
who             513/udp             whod
syslog          514/udp
talk            517/udp
route           520/udp             router routed    #  521 also
new-rwho        550/udp             new-who          #  experimental
rmonitor        560/udp             rmonitord        #  experimental
monitor         561/udp                              #  experimental
elcsd           704/udp                              #  errlog copy/server daemon
```

Figure 18.3   Format of services.

Domain name server

There are a number of files required for the operation of a domain name server. These are normally explained in sufficient detail in manufacturer literature as their syntax is so awkward, and causes so many problems in all but the simplest of configurations. There are usually four configuration files used by domain name systems:

named.boot	Indicates which files should be loaded on startup
named.db	This server's list of names (its authority)
named.rev	Used for reverse name lookup (IP to name)
named.ca	A list of names and IP addresses to be put into a cache

Further details on the use of these files were given in Chapter 14.

Debugging and measurement tools

Ping

Ping is the command that implements the ICMP echo functions. It is a useful confidence test if you can successfully 'ping' IP equipment. Most network connections that are identified with an IP address should reply to ping. The time to reply is usually given in milliseconds although the resolution may be limited to units of 10 or 20 ms.

In some implementations, ping gives access to the other features of the IP datagram header such as record route, timestamp, loose and strict source routing. Ping can then be used to gather statistics about network operation and test out the integrity and composition of a path to a remote node. It is usually possible to send different size datagrams to see if there is any limitation in the intervening network hardware. Ping normally reports on the response to each of its requests. Setting ping to operate continuously can be very useful for debugging a node that is failing to connect, as it provides a regular identifiable datagram which can be trapped on a protocol analyser.

But we must remember that ping only tests as far as the IP layer in the remote host, which may not be high enough in the TCP/IP stack to detect the fault. If ping works, it infers that all IP layers involved in the communication path are operational (Figure 18.4).

Most TCP/IP nodes have an address called 'local' or 'localhost' or 'me' or 'loopback' that is reserved for loopback testing. This can be used to check your own node with ping; executing 'ping loopback' or 'ping local' will test some of the local protocol stack and perhaps the network hardware. What 'pinging' your own node achieves is sometimes questionable, as the way it works varies from implementation to implementation. The best versions ping your machine all the way to the network hardware

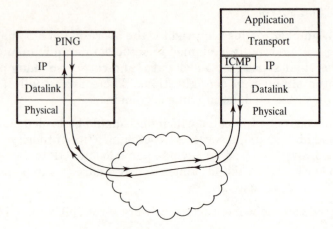

Figure 18.4   ICMP echo test (ping).

interface so the network card and the IP stack are tested. The poorer implementations of ping loopback, which unfortunately are most of them, only test down to the IP layer and back to the ICMP software. Yet other implementations allow the depth of testing to be specified, which is most useful. The problem for a network maintainer is that a negative result to 'ping loopback' indicates a fault but is rarely seen; a successful test is common but may not be of much value.

More detailed testing with ping is discussed later.

Standard services

There are many application layer services defined for use over the TCP/IP protocol stack. A number are of interest in this chapter as they are intended for use as diagnostic tools. These services are used to perform tests from other nodes on a network and are not particularly useful to the system where they reside. The most common application layer services are shown in Table 18.1.

Table 18.1   Standard services.

Service	Port number (decimal)	Function
Echo	7	Echoes character back to caller
Chargen	19	Sends the complete ASCII character set continuously
Finger	79	Discovers the real name of a user from their user identification
Discard	9	Receives information but does no work
Daytime	13	Gives the time and date.

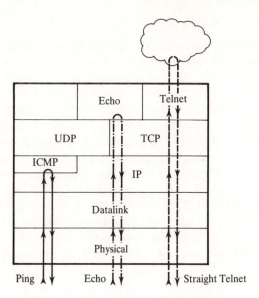

Figure 18.5   Ping, echo and O/S echo.

Echo is a service normally provided in the application layer that will return characters received from a remote TCP connection or in a UDP datagram. This may not seem very exciting, but it provides an excellent confidence test and checks more than ping can. Ping is capable of detecting that a node exists and its IP layer is operational; the application layer echo moves beyond the IP layer through TCP or UDP to the application layer, but stops short of an application. You may fail to connect to the application but get to echo; this indicates a fault with the application.

Figure 18.5 indicates the aspects of a protocol stack tested by the various echo mechanisms. ping checks the bottom three layers, application layer echo checks to the application layer and connection through Telnet to the operating system checks all but UDP.

These services can be accessed through special use of Telnet client software. By default, Telnet normally connects to its server software using port 23, but most implementations allow a command line option that lets the user specify an alternative port number. This allows you to connect directly to the port number of one of the services shown in Table 18.1 for testing. Another way these application layer services might be used is through an application. It would be fairly simple to write an application that would use the echo service at regular intervals to check a number of nodes to see they were available. Echo and chargen are the most useful programs for this type of testing. Chargen can be used to generate a load on a system and network, whereas echo tests that a connection is possible.

Netstat

Netstat, or a program of similar functionality to it, is provided on most TCP/IP products. The nearest equivalent commands on PC-based systems, which will only provide a subset of the information, may be called **status** or sometimes **inet**. To access these on a PC running DOS while a TCP/IP application is running, it will be necessary to leave the TCP/IP environment temporarily and run a copy of the DOS command processor, COMMAND.COM. This is called **shelling out to DOS** and usually involves typing the '!' character at the TCP/IP application command line. Different TCP/IP implementations will require slightly different actions. Having run the DOS command (status or inet) use EXIT to return from the DOS shell to TCP/IP.

On UNIX systems the usage or options available with a particular command can be determined by typing the command with -? as the option or sometimes without options altogether. For example

```
netstat -?<enter>
```

Whatever the name, this utility is the means of examining various aspects of the protocol stack to see how they are functioning. Netstat has some very useful diagnostic options for a TCP/IP stack on a host.

netstat -i

This option shows if the network drivers and interface cards are operational and how many good or errored frames they have seen. This is a useful confidence test. If the frames received value produced by netstat -i is increasing, it is likely that the drivers themselves are functioning. If, at the same time, the transmit counters are not increasing, the stack in that machine is having difficulty communicating with the drivers. If there are large numbers of errors then clearly there are problems either at the datalink level on the medium or with the drivers themselves.

netstat -r

This is usually the option for displaying the router tables. From this you can determine if the node is learning about routers on the internetwork and if it has a default gateway configured correctly.

netstat -a

Another netstat option allows the active server processes be viewed, showing that a server program is waiting for incoming connections. This option also shows connections established, indicating the IP address and port of the remote node. This option makes it clear what application level services are active on the host. If they are not in the netstat -a output, they are not active so users cannot connect to them. Of course the inverse is also true; if they are in the list, they are available to the network and this may show applications listening for connections that you would rather disable in the /etc/inetd.conf file.

Often, some of the utilities are shown by the port number they use, so a table of port numbers may be required to know what each utility is. There is a full list of port numbers in Appendix G but if there are locally developed applications, it is necessary to know their port numbers. Normally they will all be found in the /etc/services configuration file on the host computer.

Other netstat options

Two other useful options might be netstat -s, which gives the statistics of network operation and errors, similar to those reported by an SNMP management agent in a host, and netstat -m which lists buffer memory utilization. This will show whether a machine is correctly configured for the network tasks which have been processed, for it will indicate the number of buffers available and the average and maximum in use. It may also show any failure to provide a buffer when required.

There can be many more facilities than described here for netstat. The appropriate vendor's manuals should be consulted to ascertain the full functionality.

LAN analysers

For anybody who regularly deals with the installation of TCP/IP systems, it is almost mandatory to have open access to some kind of LAN analyser. Even for the most basic problems, a network LAN immediately allows you to detect whether there are any frames on the LAN and if a particular node is active. This does not always mean that a specialized expensive piece of test equipment must be purchased. Software such as etherfind or tcpdump, available on many UNIX implementations of TCP/IP, will monitor frames on the network and is adequate for a basic test. It is certainly better than no analyser at all.

There are also a number of low-cost analysers based on standard LAN interface cards and PCs. These may have limited performance and may not reliably record all traffic in a normal operational environment, only in simpler test installations. But a fast 386/486 PC with good video performance and a 16- or 32-bit interface card should be fast enough for the more lightly loaded system. In the busiest of networks, a specialist analyser with many megabytes of storage and the ability to capture frames for extended periods at high network loading is essential. The issue is that when looking for complex faults you must be able to trust the test equipment. If it is producing misleading results, you may waste a considerable amount of time chasing false leads.

If one of the more complex problems exists, an analyser is essential, along with the knowledge of how the protocol operates to the level covered in this book. With this book in hand and a properly functioning analyser, you should be able to solve most problems! For intractable problems, hiring a high-performance analyser for a week should be considered.

An analyser will show each phase of a connection as it is established, so failure at a certain point in the conversation between the computers can identify at what layer of the model difficulties start.

A significant benefit of using an analyser is that it can display ICMP datagrams. Even though ICMP datagrams are sent back to a specific computer to indicate some type of transmission problem, it is very rare for these events to be reported to the operator. As indicated in Chapters 11 and 16, the likely result is the incrementing of some ICMP statistics counter available to netstat or its equivalent. The detail is lost. The analyser can see all. The cause of many problems can be quickly identified from ICMP datagrams. Other than ICMP echo, which should only be generated by those testing for faults, most ICMP datagrams should occur infrequently. A useful starting point on a network in difficulty is to look for any ICMP datagrams and explain why they are occurring.

Debug

Many TCP/IP services can operate in a **debug** mode through a command option. This mode will provide a list of the steps the protocol goes through, either to the user's screen or to a file. The debug feature is only useful if the observer understands the function and detail of the protocol. It is rare for the output of a debug listing to be explained thoroughly by a manufacturer's documentation.

Most of the operations described by a debug utility are detailed in this book, so having got this far you are in a perfect position to understand a debug listing! Where the problem seems to occur within computer software and not on the network, knowing about system configuration and the relation to the protocol model will help track down the more difficult problems.

Finding faults

Fault-finding is costly in users' and maintainers' time. The best approach is to design the network and its management and installation procedures so that operational faults are rare.

A big mistake when starting to solve network problems is to rush around changing configuration values and pulling cables. This is inappropriate. For success, it is essential to approach the problem methodically and to take detailed notes of what was changed at every stage. Otherwise the situation becomes confused or the problem disappears and nobody is any wiser as to why.

One problem is the conflict in commerce between fault resolution and service restoration. The pressure is to restore service to a user so that business may continue, not to record the detailed symptoms of some system failure. If service restoration is the driving force, true fault resolution may never happen, and nothing is learnt from each event that would help prevent the problem in the future. When looking for faults, first think about the environment and any aspects about the problem that point clearly to the relevant area.

In recent years, some organizations have adopted a policy of remote fault diagnosis where, as far as is possible, faults are determined without visiting the equipment. Remote network management systems and tools may depend for their operation on the very network they are trying to diagnose. Where faults are intermittent and may be related to performance and system loading, it is prudent to remember that remote test systems may be affected by the fault conditions themselves. In some cases, the management traffic may itself be the extra loading that is causing the fault.

Approach

The initial approach to a problem with TCP/IP will be significantly different depending on whether the system has worked and then failed or if it has never worked at all. Here we will consider the 'never worked at all' scenario, as fault-finding on a system which has worked is a subset of the more general case. As there must be an infinite number of possibilities for system failure, we can only consider basic methods. The approach described is a mixture of remote and local testing. It can be adapted for remote testing as long as the previous caution about remote testing systems is observed.

The first step in fault-finding undoubtedly starts with 'it does not work'. If the local host is switched on, the operating system is running and the user can access the client program, the normal error message seen is something similar to 'host not found'. This message can be caused by anything from typing the wrong IP address to a major component of the network being faulty. The error messages given from most products are at best a rough indication of some problem. Rarely do they provide useful information for maintainers to guide them in the process of isolating the fault to a particular component.

The flowcharts in Figure 18.6 gives a guide to steps that can be taken to track down a problem in an IP system using netstat and ping. If these steps fail, it is time to get the analyser out and start tracing the problem based on the operation of the protocol.

The first part of the flowchart checks that the correct addresses are being used and that the node can talk to other machines on the network, thus proving its software and network connection is operational. If this proves to be the case, the other possibility is that there is a fault with the routing mechanism; either the default router (default gateway) has not been configured or there is something wrong with the routers themselves.

Flowchart 3 looks at the approach to using an analyser should use of flowcharts 1 and 2 fail. First it considers the basic operation of a TCP/IP connection (Figure 18.7). This sequence is the same even if routing is used. The only difference is that the ARP request will be for the MAC address of the router instead of the end node. If DNS is in use the ARP will be to find the DNS server. If the DNS server is on the same network it will ARP directly for it; if it is on another network the ARP will again be for the router.

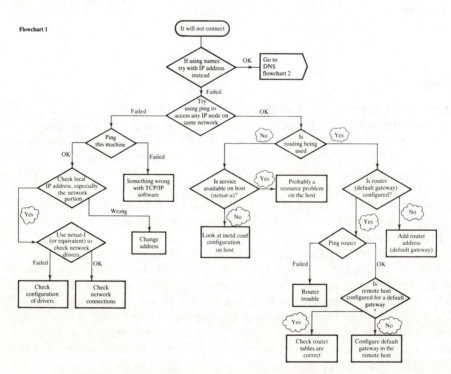

Figure 18.6   (a) Fault-finding flowchart.

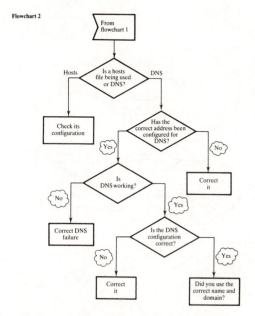

Figure 18.6 (b) Fault-finding flowchart.

Check the destination IP address is correct The best way to approach this test is to consider the steps the protocol goes through to establish a connection. Check if the address being used for the remote node is the correct IP address and that the IP address of this node is also correct.

Test local stack with Telnet or ping If a system fails to respond, start testing first with a service that is simple to use, such as Telnet or FTP, to establish what components in the network do operate. Telnet can be very useful for this on multitasking operating systems, as it is possible to Telnet to one's own IP address as a simple loopback test. This will not generate any network traffic. (This is not possible with a PC running DOS, as it is a 'client-only' implementation.)

Flowchart 3

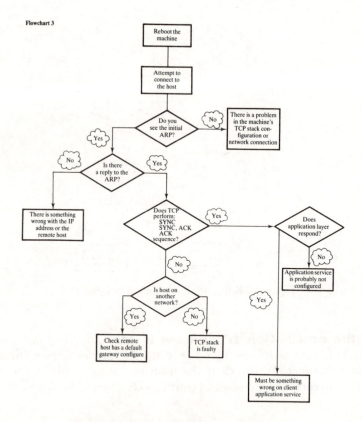

Figure 18.6 (c) Fault-finding flowchart.

Use netstat to check the datalink drivers are working If a local test works with Telnet or ping, you can be reasonably sure that the TCP/IP stack is all right. The next area to test is that the network drivers for the datalink are functioning. Problems often occur with network drivers, but there is very little diagnostic help in this area. The best mechanism available is netstat -i (status of the network interface) or its

Frame	Direction	IP layer	Transport layer	Application layer
1	→	ARP request		
2	←	ARP response		
3	→		TCP sync	
4	←		TCP sync, ack	
5	→		TCP ack	
6	↔			Application layer protocol
n	↔		⋮	⋮
$n+m$	↔			Application layer protocol
$l-2$	←		TCP fin	
$l-1$	→		TCP fin, ack	
l	←		TCP ack	

Figure 18.7   Basic operation of a TCP connection.

equivalent. With this command, you obtain information about the status of the interface; whether it is up (operational) or down (non-operational) or not available, that is, it does not appear in the netstat -i list of interfaces. In this case the software build is wrong or, due to a faulty configuration, the operating system has removed the driver. We discuss later how you might check the configuration.

Check that the IP address and subnet mask of the local host is correct   If netstat reports that the drivers are operational and local test worked, it is probable that the local computer and its network software is functional. Check then that the IP address and the network masks are correct[†]. If using names, instead temporarily use the IP address of the destination to verify that there is a path or whether there is a problem with the name to IP address resolution in local tables or through a domain name server.

If routing is being used check that the host knows of a gateway
First, try to connect to a local host to determine that communication is possible if no router is needed. Then make sure the node is configured with the correct IP address of the default gateway. If the destination network is on a different network number and no default gateway is configured, few products will give an explicit diagnostic message, even though the software must know exactly why it could not connect. It may

---

[†]Today most TCP/IP software uses subnet masks, even if subnetworking is not being used, by defining a default mask that matches the class of address being used.

report 'network unreachable' rather than 'host unreachable'. The former message normally indicates a problem with routing rather than a problem with the host, but the routing problem could be 'no default gateway'.

If routing is being used check that the distant node has a gateway configured   Even though your node may be able to send datagrams to a remote computer through routers, many implementations of TCP/IP will not respond if they themselves do not have a default gateway configured. (This problem is explained in more detail below.)

By now you should have a good idea where the problem lies if not exactly why it is happening. Keep reviewing the facts that you have collected to narrow your search.

Testing with ping

Since each port with an IP address should respond to ping, and that includes routers, ping can be used to test successively more remote points in a chain between two systems. By methodically working away from the source station, it is possible to determine the exact point at which communications fail. Each side of a router should be tested as it has a separate address. For this to be possible, maintainers must have a network diagram with all routers and their IP addresses marked on it.

While all TCP/IP equipment is *supposed* to implement ICMP and respond to ICMP echo, some hosts will refuse to respond to an unknown IP address, that is, an address which is not in the hosts file or some other security file. Equally, some cut-down versions used by management systems may not respond even though the equipment has an IP address. Knowing which of the equipment in your network will respond is part of the learning process of a network maintainer.

Ping can also be used to test a bridged network by pinging hosts at successively more remote points across the chain of bridges. Those bridges that are managed by SNMP or Telnet will have their own IP addresses for management. Some SNMP implementations and most Telnet implementations may respond to ping.

Some ping implementations by default send only one request and then exit; others send repeatedly without a further option being specified. Also, because they must first generate an ARP, some implementations of ping will fail the first time they send an echo request to a particular host. If you just type

```
ping 128.128.10.100
```

it may fail because only one request is generated; run it a second time and it will pass! Most ping implementations have options to specify how many times the host should be pinged, at what intervals, how long to wait for a reply and how much data to send.

A continuous ping test can produce four different results:

(1) *There is no response to ping at all*   First, is there an entry for the destination IP address in the ARP cache if the host had the same network number, or an entry for a router if it did not? This shows at least that ARP got a reply. If not, are there any entries in the ARP cache which would show the basic host hardware and drivers can transmit and receive frames? If not, either the IP address does not exist (some entries) or there is a cable or driver fault (no entries).

   Can anything else which is known to be operational ping this host? Can the host ping anything? Can it ping itself?

   The problem is that the gap between being able to ping loopback and being able to ping another machine is quite large. If the machine is being tested then reduce the test network to the simplest possible implementation with two machines directly connected. If it is on an operational network use an analyser to check whether it is transmitting any datagrams. Check the ARP cache to see whether the ARP, which works directly over the LAN interface, is working.

(2) *Ping works but replies are lost*   A small number of lost replies is possible on any datagram-based network, perhaps more so when wide area connections are involved, but if these losses are more than 2–3%, then there is a 'lost datagram' problem to be investigated, particularly if this only occurs when the network is busy.

   The fault will be:

   (a) transmission errors on WAN or LAN cables,

   (b) overloaded bridges or routers.

(3) *Every request is acknowledged and the echo time varies*   This is normal due to variations in host and network loading. If the variations in response time are wide and if they are regularly longer than 100 ms then the cause should be investigated, as such delays will make Telnet less acceptable to users and will have an impact on the performance of other applications, particularly those that use UDP. Likely causes are:

   (a) overloaded wide area links which are too slow for the traffic offered,

   (b) an overloaded host which is being pinged,

   (c) overloaded bridges or routers,

   (d) overloaded backbone LANs.

In the latter two cases, the problem is more likely to result in datagram loss as well as delay.

(4) *Every request is acknowledged and the echo time is reasonably constant* Congratulations, this is the best possible result and ping can tell you nothing more. Move on to more advanced tests.

Remember that ping is an ICMP message. ICMP error messages are never generated about problems with other ICMP messages. At some point in testing if routing errors are thought to be involved, application layer echo, port 7, should be used rather than ping, to see if an ICMP message results which can better pinpoint the problem.

Some common problems

Subnet masks

Check that your TCP/IP implementation automatically selects a suitable default subnet mask, even though subnetworking is not being used. If the implementation does not select a suitable subnet mask, it may not be possible to connect to all hosts dependent on the bits used in their IP address. We have seen systems that always select a 24-bit mask as default irrespective of their own IP address. This causes problems with class A and B addressing schemes, as part of the node address is considered as subnetwork bits.

IP addresses

A common fault is the incorrect use of IP addresses, which usually happens due to lack of understanding of the address structure[†]. It is common to see installations of minicomputers using the default class of address and network number that comes with the unit, usually the manufacturer's registered address. This could well be unsuitable for the network the host is operating on.

Routing

If the default gateway (router) has not been configured, it is common for software to 'hang' or return with a 'host not available' message, or sometimes a more helpful but not explicit 'network unreachable'.

A second problem is with hosts that eavesdrop on RIP. Using RIP is appropriate if routers on the system are also using RIP. If not, it is redundant and the host must have a default gateway configured so that it can find the router.

[†]This is explained in great detail in Chapters 3 and 4.

A third problem is if the destination computer does not have a default gateway configured. Some systems work because they can obtain the IP address of a router from the incoming datagram. But many systems cannot make use of this information and will not reply if they receive a request to start a TCP connection which comes from a network number different from their own and they do not have a default gateway configured.

Yet another problem occurs when the default gateway known to a node fails. It is likely that the node then cannot make connections to other networks even though there may be redundant paths. This is because the node relies on that one gateway being available. Some software only allows a single default gateway (router) to be defined.

Drivers

Many problems are related to software drivers for network hardware (LAN and WAN interface cards). Driver software rarely provides any assistance for fault diagnosis; there is no good indication whether it is operating or not, a particular problem with PCs.

The problem may manifest itself when the driver is loading, or the TCP/IP protocol may load, but the computer cannot send frames to the network; local ping works but remote ping does not. In this case a LAN analyser may show that datagrams are being sent on the network and responses are returning, but the protocol stack does not recognize the responses. This problem is usually caused by settings on the network hardware or in the drivers. Hardware settings may conflict with other settings in the computer, or with other cards, or the driver software may not have settings which match the hardware. Detection of this type of problem almost certainly needs a LAN analyser to be confident that this is what is happening.

On systems that have the netstat utility, netstat -i is useful. It shows that the drivers are active and the number of datagrams they receive and send. No change in the values of the counters provided by this utility on an active network, or no drivers being shown, gives a hint as to the problem. In UNIX systems check netd.cf to determine that ifconfig is binding the driver to the interface and if appropriate, use sysadm, the UNIX management utility, to check the match between hardware and driver software settings for interrupts, shared memory, DMA and I/O address. In the latter case be careful that you do not destroy the UNIX kernel!

If there are problems with the interrupt settings between software or hardware, the network software will have difficulty interrupting the main processor and so incoming information will be lost. If the input/output or DMA settings are incorrect, it will be output that is affected.

Buffers

Lack of buffers on a system will cause throughput to be slow for TCP connections or cause datagrams to be missed if UDP is used. While netstat -m is sometimes available to show buffer utilization, the only clear way of seeing this problem is through an analyser showing that the window sizes in the TCP segments frequently reduce to a low value or zero. Many systems provide a management function to increase the number of buffers available. This allows an improvement in performance, but at the expense of more memory for the protocol stack.

A common setting found on PCs is the low window threshold. This value can be set to limit the minimum size of buffer that will be announced after the buffers have been filled. This is done to prevent the 'silly window syndrome' which occurs when a node has filled its buffers, empties a few bytes, advertises a few bytes free, which become filled, empties a few bytes, advertises a few free and so on.... There is a very high overhead from TCP and IP headers in sending these few bytes each time. The minimum window threshold sets the point at which the window is re-advertised, so that a reasonable, significant size of frame can be sent.

Domain names

Problems with domain name systems are normally with the configuration of the databases in the domain name servers and the use of domain names themselves. One of the most common problems is with use of the dot (.) on a domain name. Leaving the dot off a name in the configuration files usually indicates that the default domain should be added to this name, which can result in a request for incorrect long domain names.

The second problem area is through not specifying enough of the domain name of a system for the address to be resolved, mainly when connecting between different domains.

Hosts file

The main problems with the hosts file are errors in configuring them, incorrect IP addresses or names typed incorrectly. Another area to be aware of is the difference between the name of a node and its aliases. Some software does not look for aliases when searching through the hosts file. Requesting a connection to the alias instead of the main name results in a 'host not known', or a similar message, perhaps a more helpful 'unable to resolve host name'.

Some PC software indicates the name and location of the file for 'hosts' in a configuration parameter, for example:

```
C:\TCPIP\hosts
```

If this path and file name is set wrongly, the software may be 'unable to resolve host name' rather than 'hosts file not found'.

Summary

In this chapter we have presented a few ideas on how fault-finding in TCP/IP systems should be approached and some of the unexpected and slightly obscure situations we have discovered in the field. Using this information as a basis, each system maintainer will quickly build upon this foundation and gradually determine what are the important diagnostic tools in his or her particular environment. Maintainers are also likely to end up with a list of surprises where particular implementations are 'rich in features' that the standards developers did not intend.

19

TCP/IP and the future

We have come to the end of the technical discussion of the TCP/IP protocol suite. In this the final chapter, we briefly look at some of the current discussion on the future of TCP/IP. We look at

- Pressures for change
- TCP/IP and OSI
- Changes to the architecture
- Future systems

The authors' experience is in technology and system management, not in predicting the future, though successful managers must usually attempt that too. So, this chapter is about some of the known limitations of the TCP/IP architecture and protocols, and the work that is under way to address them. It is not about prediction. Where the market for equipment moves depends on suppliers, their promotion budgets, having the right product at the right time and the desires of MIS managers.

TCP/IP is an eclectic technology. As new computing and communications requirements and techniques evolve at different levels of the communications model, TCP/IP can adapt the best techniques from developers in all computing and communications disciplines and, where necessary, develop its own new mechanisms.

While the 1980s has seen many successful proprietary mainframe, minicomputer and LAN operating systems, there is no doubt that TCP/IP has proved to be the most successful 'open' communications architecture. But the TCP/IP standards are under pressure. Fortunately the problems come from its very success, though this does not make them easier to solve; it merely increases the pressure on developers to provide rapid solutions. Like our motorway in Chapter 9, TCP/IP is suffering precisely because everyone is finding that a good transportation system gives people and organizations new options in how and where they operate. They all want to be part of this flexibility.

Pressures for change

The nature of the pressure for change is fourfold:

(1)   There is pressure on the implementation of the Internet itself, where the number of known hosts has been growing exponentially and is now climbing the steepest part of its growth curve. At present rates, it will reach some form of saturation quite quickly. There is a need to extend growth for a further five to ten years.

(2)   The registered address space, certainly for class B addresses, will be exhausted during 1993 or 1994.

(3)   The different levels of the protocols themselves are not totally satisfactory for some of the applications now being introduced.

(4)   The global nature of communications and the availability of TCP/IP equipment has resulted in thousands of private networks based on the technology. The need to communicate, not just within an organization but also between organizations for Electronic Data Interchange† (EDI) or for cooperative research, will require these systems to be interconnected. This currently requires proprietary relays if the addresses are not unique.

---

†Electronic or paperless trading – orders, acknowledgements, delivery notes, invoices and payments, and even catalogues, price lists, stock level and product specifications.

Those areas of stress are due primarily to limitations in:

- address space,
- routing flexibility in the current Internet implementation,
- policy routing and commercialization of the Internet,
- multiprotocol operation across the Internet,
- security,
- support for voice, video and image.

While it is not the responsibility of the IAB to resolve problems for private networks, some of the solutions for the problems of the Internet should be applicable to private commercial networks. Commercial users will certainly be interested in techniques of expanding the address space, and of support for the more demanding image and voice applications over newer high-speed networks.

TCP/IP and OSI

Since the mid-1980s many governments have voiced a desire to move to OSI protocols for government communications. OSI was designed with a worldwide internet in mind. OSI does not have some of the limitations of TCP/IP. For example, the address space is 160 bits[†]. In OSI, routing is based on a four-level hierarchy. Late in the day, OSI has had extensive security and management features incorporated into the architecture, more extensive than those in TCP/IP.

Indeed, the communications layers of OSI have undergone a significant change with the introduction of connectionless protocols as alternatives to the traditional wide area connection-oriented protocols of HDLC and X.25. At the datalink level of OSI there is now the connectionless LAN protocol, LLC1, and at network level the connectionless network protocol, IS8743. The datagram ES–IS and IS–IS routing protocols, which were developed in parallel with OSPF, operate in the connectionless environment. Connectionless alternatives for the OSI upper layers are also under development. The OSI connectionless network protocol is loosely referred to as the 'OSI Internet Protocol' by many.

One of the biggest test beds of these and other OSI protocols has been the Internet itself. The RFCs contain extensive information on coexistence and migration between the two systems and on testing the OSI higher layers across the TCP/IP internetwork.

[†]This suffers from the reverse problem to TCP/IP; the address space can never be exhausted. Using the standard adopted for the UK address space, every citizen could define their own unique computer network with around a million million IEEE 802.x LAN cards!

The view of some developers is that OSI solves the problems of TCP/IP; equally there is a view that it solves some of the issues but introduces problems in other areas which will be just as difficult to solve. Is it better to stay with and develop a system like TCP/IP which is mature and known, rather than move to OSI which is immature and unknown? Replacement of certain limited aspects of the TCP/IP model with OSI definitions effectively combining the two may well be the best path.

Certainly OSI and TCP/IP have cooperated and borrowed heavily on each other's developments in recent years. The extensive use of ASN.1 and BER in SNMP is just one example. It is likely that this cooperation will continue and expand. Development costs in times of recession must be shared.

Changes to the architecture

During 1991 and 1992, a number of RFCs have discussed the areas of concern in the current architecture, and possible changes to the Internet architecture and protocols which would overcome some of the known limitations. The following are of interest to the commercial user.

Addressing

There are two parallel initiatives for overcoming the problem of registered class B IP address exhaustion:

(1) In the short term, make more efficient use of the class 'C' address space by moving towards classless network addressing and routing, where any contiguous mask can be used to perform 'supernetting'. (An alternative early draft proposal describes C# (c-sharp) addressing, which is a less flexible form of supernetting.) This technique requires minimal change to host software, if change is necessary at all.

(2) In the longer term, of three to five years, introduce the OSI CLNP as an alternative to IP. This initiative is referred to as TCP and UDP with Big Addresses (TUBA). This will require major changes to host, router and DNS software

A further IETF draft discusses the implications of moving to CLNP for the network layer protocol. While there are many parallels between the two protocols, there are many important decisions that the IETF must make to ensure an equal level of service to IP.

These changes also aim to limit the increase in size of routing tables in the internet, in spite of individual network increases; controlled through a scheme referred to as route aggregation.

In parallel with this scheme, allocation of registered addresses are being devolved from the NIC to a number of service providers around the world, who will manage large blocks of the class C address space on behalf of the NIC/IAB. It is anticipated that the concept of address class will gradually disappear in favour of a classless network number, based on a network/mask pair of values. As previously described, this will involve changes to older routing protocols, and to the way hosts determine whether to route directly or via a router.

OSI CLNP already has a multilevel addressing and routing structure. One version of OSI addressing is based on ISO country codes. This was designed to minimize routing table size and to provide route aggregation.

Multiprotocol operation

There has been much greater recognition in the past few years, by all system developers, of the need to register and agree protocol identifiers at all levels. An example is the use of SNAP at the low level to ensure that all protocols can share the same media without interference. The same techniques are being adopted at the network layer with the use of registered Network Layer Protocol Identifiers (NLPIDs) in OSI, including the use of SNAP at the network layer to identify non-ISO protocols. This cooperation must continue, and some proprietary techniques which do cause interference will gradually be replaced.

Routing architecture

Changes to the use of the internet address space requires changes to the internet routing architecture. One possibility that is being examined is to use the OSI InterDomain Routing Protocol, the third level of the OSI routing hierarchy. (ES–IS and IS–IS are the first two levels.)

Security

Successful security is a complex issue that is dependent on many factors, of which the technology is just one component. It may not be the major factor. The IAB is examining security at four levels: datalink, net and subnet, host, and process and application.

The first requirement is to develop a security reference model for the Internet. In this area, OSI leads for it already has such a model.

Support for new applications

Apart from some recent use of the TOS bits to identify routing protocols, such as BGP which should use high reliability links, all IP datagrams are treated equally in the Internet.

Applications such as voice and video require a much more controlled throughput than existing computer data transmission systems. New standards are needed for traffic control in large Internets which will give guaranteed performance for some applications.

Data formats

Data formats in the Internet protocols are implicit. Knowing the application, the format of data is defined. While NFS provides XDR, this too has a restricted number of data types, and while XDR does indicate that the definitions of XDR objects in XDR 'source' could be passed between systems, this is not normally done.

The IETF has identified that there must be one standard data representation for the objects of more advanced applications, such as image, graphics, video, audio, display, and general data objects, such as integers, reals, strings and structures.

It remains to be seen whether the presentation methods of OSI which relate to many of these requirements will prove acceptable or too flexible and heavyweight to be useful.

Future systems

Future commercial computing applications and communications will be a closer blending of existing and future OSI and TCP/IP techniques. But this will only happen if OSI standards are seen as overcoming TCP/IP limitations or providing useful commercial facilities that are not available by other techniques. That means that OSI applications must start delivering an environment that is rich in function and is not available in any other way as an open standard.

Some of the areas that could be adapted are security, management, directory services (X.500), messaging (X.400), and EDI messaging (X.435). In particular, the newer OSI applications of virtual terminal protocol, which may have some advantages over Telnet for full-screen operation and the recently ratified Distributed Transaction Processing (DTP) standard, IS10026 could be adopted. Some of these standards will not be generally available in commercial products until the mid-1990s.

Fortunately, because of implementors' agreements and the decision by manufacturers to overcome the limitations of OSI standards and publish application program interface standards outside the OSI process,

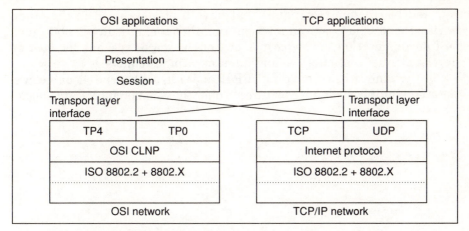

Figure 19.1 The flexibility of the transport layer interface.

migration from TCP/IP to OSI can be controlled and managed. The key is the standards such as the Transport Layer Interface from AT&T (AT&T TLI) and the eXtended Transport Layer Interface (XTLI), from the X Open Consortium.

While software stacks must be recompiled to interface to the new environment, these internal interfaces give the planning manager of the 1990s new flexibility in decoupling the networking components of planning from the application components. When combined with transport layer relays, TCP/IP and OSI environments may be mixed and matched (Figure 19.1).

Relevant RFCs

1287   Towards the future Internet architecture
1296   Internet growth (1981–1991)

Summary

This concludes our examination of the managerial and technological issues of TCP/IP. Despite some of the issues which exist with the TCP/IP protocol suite, it will remain the most successful and widely deployed 'open' network technology for many years to come.

In the coming years, the boundaries between open systems interconnection and TCP/IP will become blurred as the political and technical gap between the two technologies is bridged. Each will continue to borrow and learn from techniques that have been developed in the other environment. There is even a recognition that the difficulty of obtaining OSI documentation at low cost is one of the major reasons for lack of development of cost-effective and interoperating products.

Certainly, when comparing TCP/IP and OSI, neither one should eclipse the other, for they both have features to offer the commercial MIS manager.

PART III

Appendices

A

Contacting the Network Information Center

The Network Information Center (NIC) provides information services for the Internet community. It provides copies of RFCs and maintains the RFC library. It also provides the registration service for IP network numbers and Autonomous System numbers. The following are the full contact details for the new NIC in Chantilly, Virginia, USA. This took over the role from an earlier centre at SRI in California in October 1991. SRI has continued to act as a source of RFCs by electronic mail since that date.

Postal mail for the NIC should be addressed to:

Government Systems, Inc.
Attn: Network Information Center
14200 Park Meadow Drive
Suite 200
Chantilly, VA 22021

Telephone contacts are:

Voice: 1-703-802-4535
         1-800-365-3642[†] (1-800-365-DNIC)
Fax: 1-703-802-8376

Electronic mail is:

Email: NIC@NIC.DDN.MIL

Registration information should be addressed (electronically) to:

registrar@NIC.DDN.MIL

The help desk hours of operation are 7.00 a.m. to 7.00 p.m. eastern time.

[†]Toll-free numbers (800 numbers) are not usually available outside the USA and Canada.

B

Obtaining RFCs by electronic mail

For those who have mail access to the Internet, full information on obtaining RFCs by email or FTP is itself available by email. Such mail access is available from a number of commercial information systems. CompuServe (CIS) and Compulink (CIX) both provide a mail gateway, though they are by no means unique.

Up-to-date details of obtaining RFCs can be obtained by sending an email message to `rfc-info@ISI.EDU` with the message body `help:` `ways_to_get_rfcs`. For example:

```
Main: mail <enter>
Mail: to <enter>
To: rfc-info@ISI.EDU<enter>
Subject: getting rfcs<enter>
help: ways_to_get_rfcs<enter>
.<enter>
send/action:send <enter>
Sending..Memo 434371 sent
```

Rather than reproduce the document which is returned by this request, those who wish to retrieve RFCs will undoubtedly wish to test their procedures by retrieving full instructions for themselves! The mail message contains an up-to-date list of the sites which can supply RFCs and other Internet information by FTP and email. The format of the mail message is given for each server.

The following is the email dialogue to obtain the OSPF RFC 1247 and RFC 1294 (describing the use of frame relay) from the original NIC mail server at SRI California. RFCs are available in PostScript form by adding the suffix .ps to the name of the RFC file requested. If the ASCII text form is required, the suffix should be .txt. If no suffix is given .txt is usually assumed.

SRI NIC mail server

The SRI NIC server will provide RFC copies via email:

```
Main: mail <enter>
Mail: to <enter>
To:  mailserver@nisc.sri.com <enter>
subject:  <enter> (i.e. leave empty)
message: send rfc1247.txt<enter>
> send rfc1294.txt
> . <enter>
send/action:send <enter>
Sending..Memo 434372 sent
```

An index can be obtained:

```
Main: mail <enter>
Mail: to <enter>
To:  mailserver@nisc.sri.com <enter>
subject: <enter> (i.e. leave empty)
message: send rfc-index <enter>
.<enter>
send/action:send <enter>
Sending..Memo 434373 sent
```

By default, long documents are split into a number of mail messages. These pieces may arrive out of order. Some careful editing will be required to put the pieces back together. This is particularly so for PostScript documents where the precise format will affect the output of the printer dramatically.

Secondary sites

There are a number of sites around the world which hold copies of the RFCs from the USA. These are often in local academic establishments. Whether this information is available to commercial organizations varies from place to place. The following does not therefore identify a specific mail server but is included to show the variation in message format which may be encountered:

```
To: info-server@xxxx.ac.uk <enter>
subject: <enter>
message: request: rfc <enter>
topic: rfc#### <enter>
topic: rfc#### <enter>
request: end <enter>
.<enter>
```

```
send/action:send <enter>
Sending..Memo 434374 sent
```

If an incorrect entry is made, the mail server will normally return an error message with some helpful details of why the message could not be processed.

C

Useful RFCs

Many of the following are discussed in this book. Most of the applicable RFCs are available online in PostScript and Text format. See Chapter 6 and Appendix B for details on how to retrieve these. This list is based on the NIC's RFC index of May 1992.

1315   Management information base for frame relay DTEs. Brown, C.; Baker, F.; Carvalho, C. 1992 April; 19pp. (Format: TXT = 33 825 bytes)

1311   Introduction to the STD notes. Postel, J.B., ed. 1992 March; 5pp. (Format: TXT = 11 308 bytes)

1310   Internet standards process. Chapin, A.L. 1992 March; 23pp. (Format: TXT = 54 738 bytes)

1309   Technical overview of directory services using the X.500 protocol. Weider, C.; Reynolds, J.K.; Heker, S. 1992 March; 4pp. (Format: TXT = 35 694 bytes) (Also FYI 14)

1308   Executive introduction to directory services using the X.500 protocol. Weider, C.; Reynolds, J.K. 1992 March; 4pp. (Format: TXT = 9 392 bytes) (Also FYI 13)

1305   Network time protocol (version 3): specification, implementation, and analysis. Mills, D.L. 1992 March; 113pp. (Format: TXT = 307 085, tar.Z=815 759 bytes) (Obsoletes RFC 1119)

1302   Building a network information services infrastructure. Sitzler, D.D.; Smith, P.G.; Marine, A.N. 1992 February; 13pp. (Format: TXT = 29 135 bytes) (Also FYI 12)

1296   Internet growth (1981–1991). Lottor, M. 1992 January; 9pp. (Format: TXT = 20 103 bytes)

1294   Multiprotocol interconnect over frame relay. Bradley, T.; Brown, C.; Malis, A.G. 1992 January; 28pp. (Format: TXT = 54 992 bytes)

1293   Inverse address resolution protocol. Bradely, T.; Brown, C. 1992 January; 6pp. (Format: TXT = 11 368 bytes)

1292   Catalog of available X.500 implementations. Lang, R.; Wright, R. 1991 December; 103pp. (Format: TXT = 129 468 bytes) (Also FYI 11)

1288   Finger user information protocol. Zimmerman, D.P. 1991 December; 12pp. (Format: TXT = 25 161 bytes) (Obsoletes RFC 1196)

1287   Towards the future Internet architecture. Clark, D.D.; Chapin, L.A.; Cerf, V.G.; Braden, R.T.; Hobby, R. 1991 December; 29pp. (Format: TXT = 59 812 bytes)

1286   Definitions of managed objects for bridges. Decker, E.; Langille, P.; Rijsinghani, A.; McCloghrie, K. 1991 December; 40pp. (Format: TXT = 79 104 bytes)

1285   FDDI management information base. Case, J.D. 1992 January; 46pp. (Format: TXT = 99 747 bytes)

1284   Definitions of managed objects for the Ethernet-like interface types. Cook, J., ed. 1991 December; 21pp. (Format: TXT = 43 225 bytes)

1282   BSD rlogin. Kantor, B. 1991 December; 5pp. (Format: TXT = 10 704 bytes) (Obsoletes RFC 1258)

1281   Guidelines for the secure operations of the Internet. Pethia, R.D.; Crocker, S.D.; Fraser, B.Y. 1991 November; 10pp. (Format: TXT = 22 618 bytes)

1280   IAB official protocol standards. Postel, J.B., ed. 1992 March; 32pp. (Format: TXT = 70 458 bytes) (Obsoletes RFC 1250)

1279   X.500 and domains. HardcastleKille, S.E. 1991 November; 13pp. (Format: TXT = 26 669, PS = 170 029 bytes)

1276   Replication and distributed operations extensions to provide an Internet directory using X.500. HardcastleKille, S.E. 1991 November; 17pp. (Format: TXT = 33 731, PS = 217 170 bytes)

1275   Replication requirements to provide an Internet directory using X.500. HardcastleKille, S.E. 1991 November; 2pp. (Format: TXT = 4 616, PS = 83 736 bytes)

1274   COSINE and Internet X.500 schema. Kille, S.E.; Barker, P. 1991 November; 60pp. (Format: TXT = 92 827 bytes)

1271   Remote network monitoring management information base. Waldbusser, S. 1991 November; 81pp. (Format: TXT = 184 111 bytes)

1270   SNMP communications services. Kastenholz, F., ed. 1991 October; 11pp. (Format: TXT = 26 167 bytes)

1269   Definitions of managed objects for the border gateway protocol: version 3. Willis, S.; Burruss, J.W. 1991 October; 13pp. (Format: TXT = 25 717 bytes)

1268   Application of the border gateway protocol in the Internet. Rekhter, Y.; Gross, P., eds. 1991 October; 13pp. (Format: TXT = 31 102 bytes) (Obsoletes RFC 1164)

1267   Border gateway protocol 3 (BGP3). Lougheed, K.; Rekhter, Y. 1991 October; 35pp. (Format: TXT = 80 724 bytes) (Obsoletes RFC 1163)

1266   Experience with the BGP protocol. Rekhter, Y., ed. 1991 October; 9pp. (Format: TXT = 21 938 bytes)

1265   BGP protocol analysis. Rekhter, Y., ed. 1991 October; 8pp. (Format: TXT = 20 728 bytes)

1264   Internet Engineering Task Force Internet routing protocol standardization criteria. Hinden, R.M. 1991 October; 8pp. (Format: TXT = 17 016 bytes)

1261   Transition of NIC services. Williamson, S.; Nobile, L. 1991 September; 3pp. (Format: TXT = 4488 bytes)

1256   ICMP router discovery messages. Deering, S.E., ed. 1991 September; 19pp. (Format: TXT = 44 628 bytes)

1253   OSPF version 2: management information base. Baker, F.; Coltun, R. 1991 August; 42pp. (Format: TXT = 77 232 bytes) (Obsoletes RFC 1252)

1251   Who's who in the Internet: biographies of IAB, IESG and IRSG members. Matkin, G.S. 1991 August; 26pp. (Format: TXT = 72 721 bytes (Also FYI 9)

1247   OSPF version 2. Moy, J. 1991 July; 189pp. (Format: PS = 1 063 028, TXT = 443 917 bytes) (Obsoletes RFC 1131)

1246   Experience with the OSPF protocol. Moy, J., ed. 1991 July; 31pp. (Format: PS = 146 913, TXT = 72 180 bytes)

1245   OSPF protocol analysis. Moy, J., ed. 1991 July; 12pp. (Format: PS = 64 094, TXT = 27 492 bytes)

1244   Site security handbook. Holbrook, J.P.; Reynolds, J.K., eds. 1991 July; 101pp. (Format: TXT = 259 129 bytes) (Also FYI 8)

1243   Appletalk management information base. Waldbusser, S., ed. 1991 July; 29pp. (Format: TXT = 61 985 bytes)

1239   Reassignment of experimental MIBs to standard MIBs. Reynolds, J.K. 1991 June; 2pp. (Format: TXT = 3656 bytes) (Updates RFC 1229, RFC 1230, RFC 1231, RFC 1232, RFC 1233)

1234   Tunneling IPX traffic through IP networks. Provan, D. 1991 June; 6pp. (Format: TXT = 12 333 bytes)

1233   Definitions of managed objects for the DS3 interface type. Cox, T.A.; Tesink, K., eds. 1991 May; 23pp. (Format: TXT = 49 559 bytes) (Updated by RFC 1239)

1232   Definitions of managed objects for the DS1 interface type. Baker, F.; Kolb, C.P., eds. 1991 May; 28pp. (Format: TXT = 60 757 bytes) (Updated by RFC 1239)

1231   IEEE 802.5 Token Ring MIB. McCloghrie, K.; Fox, R.; Decker, E. 1991 May; 23pp. (Format: TXT = 53 542 bytes) (Updated by RFC 1239)

1228   SNMP-DPI: Simple Network Management Protocol Distributed Program Interface. Carpenter, G.; Wijnen, B. 1991 May; 50pp. (Format: TXT = 96 972 bytes)

1227   SNMP MUX protocol and MIB. Rose, M.T. 1991 May; 13pp. (Format: TXT = 25 868 bytes)

1220   Point-to-point protocol extensions for bridging. Baker, F., ed. 1991 April; 18pp. (Format: TXT = 38 165 bytes)

1219   On the assignment of subnet numbers. Tsuchiya, P.F. 1991 April; 13pp. (Format: TXT = 30 609 bytes)

1216   Gigabit network economics and paradigm shifts. Richard, P.; Kynikos, P. 1991 April 1; 4pp. (Format: TXT = 8 130 bytes)

1215   Convention for defining traps for use with the SNMP. Rose, M.T., ed. 1991 March; 9pp. (Format: TXT = 19 336 bytes)

1213   Management information base for network management of TCP/IP-based Internets: MIB-II. McCloghrie, K.; Rose, M.T., eds. 1991 March; 70pp. (Format: TXT = 146 080 bytes) (Obsoletes RFC 1158)

1212   Concise MIB definitions. Rose, M.T.; McCloghrie, K., eds. 1991 March; 19pp. (Format: TXT = 43 579 bytes)

1211   Problems with the maintenance of large mailing lists. Westine, A.; Postel, J.B. 1991 March; 54pp. (Format: TXT = 96 167 bytes)

1209   Transmission of IP datagrams over the SMDS Service. Piscitello, D.M.; Lawrence, J. 1991 March; 11pp. (Format: TXT = 25 280 bytes)

1208   Glossary of networking terms. Jacobsen, O.J.; Lynch, D.C. 1991 March; 18pp. (Format: TXT = 41 156 bytes)

1207   FYI on questions and answers: answers to commonly asked 'experienced Internet user' questions. Malkin, G.S.; Marine, A.N.; Reynolds, J.K. 1991 February; 15pp. (Format: TXT = 33 385 bytes) (Also FYI 7)

1206   FYI on questions and answers: answers to commonly asked 'new Internet user' questions. Malkin, G.S.; Marine, A.N. 1991 February; 32pp. (Format: TXT = 72 479 bytes) (Also FYI 4) (Obsoletes RFC 1177)

1205   5250 Telnet interface. Chmielewski, P. 1991 February; 12pp. (Format: TXT = 27 179 bytes)

1201   Transmitting IP traffic over ARCNET networks. Provan, D. 1991 February; 7pp. (Format: TXT = 16 959 bytes) (Obsoletes RFC 1051)

1198   FYI on the X Window system. Scheifler, R.W. 1991 January; 3pp. (Format: TXT = 3629 bytes) (Also FYI 6)

1197   Using ODA for translating multimedia information. Sherman, M. 1990 December; 2pp. (Format: TXT = 3620 bytes)

1195   Use of OSI IS–IS for routing in TCP/IP and dual environments. Callon, R.W. 1990 December; 65pp. (Format: PS = 381 799, TXT = 192 628 bytes)

1191   Path MTU discovery. Mogul, J.C.; Deering, S.E. 1990 November; 19pp. (Format: TXT = 47 936 bytes) (Obsoletes RFC 1063)

1189   Common Management Information Services and Protocols for the Internet (CMOT and CMIP). Warrier, U.S.; Besaw, L.; LaBarre, L.; Handspicker, B.D. 1990 October; 15pp. (Format: TXT = 32 928 bytes) (Obsoletes RFC 1095)

1188 Proposed standard for the transmission of IP datagrams over FDDI networks. Katz, D. 1990 October; 11pp. (Format: TXT = 22 424 bytes) (Obsoletes RFC 1103)

1187 Bulk table retrieval with the SNMP. Rose, M.T.; McCloghrie, K.; Davin, J.R. 1990 October; 12pp. (Format: TXT = 27 220 bytes)

1185 TCP extension for high-speed paths. Jacobson, V.; Braden, R.T.; Zhang, L. 1990 October; 21pp. (Format: TXT = 49 508 bytes)

1184 Telnet linemode option. Borman, D.A., ed. 1990 October; 23pp. (Format: TXT = 53 085 bytes) (Obsoletes RFC 1116)

1183 New DNS RR definitions. Everhart, C.F.; Mamakos, L.A.; Ullmann, R.; Mockapetris, P.V. 1990 October; 11pp. (Format: TXT = 23 788 bytes) (Updates RFC 1034, RFC 1035)

1180 TCP/IP tutorial. Socolofsky, T.J.; Kale, C.J. 1991 January; 28pp. (Format: TXT = 65 494 bytes)

1179 Line printer daemon protocol. McLaughlin, L. 1990 August; 14pp. (Format: TXT = 24 324 bytes)

1178 Choosing a name for your computer. Libes, D. 1990 August; 8pp. (Format: TXT = 18 472 bytes) (Also FYI 5)

1175 FYI on where to start: a bibliography of internetworking information. Bowers, K.L.; LaQuey, T.L.; Reynolds, J.K.; Roubicek, K.; Stahl, M.K.; Yuan, A. 1990 August; 42pp. (Format: TXT = 67 330 bytes) (Also FYI 3)

1174 IAB recommended policy on distributing Internet identifier assignment and IAB recommended policy change to Internet 'connected' status. Cerf, V.G. 1990 August; 9pp. (Format: TXT = 21 321 bytes)

1173 Responsibilities of host and network managers: a summary of the 'oral tradition' of the Internet. VanBokkelen, J. 1990 August; 5pp. (Format: TXT = 12 527 bytes)

1172 Point-to-Point Protocol (PPP) initial configuration options. Perkins, D.; Hobby, R. 1990 July; 38pp. (Format: TXT = 76 132 bytes)

1171 Point-to-point protocol for the transmission of multiprotocol datagrams over point-to-point links. Perkins, D. 1990 July; 48pp. (Format: TXT = 92 321 bytes) (Obsoletes RFC 1134)

1166 Internet numbers. Kirkpatrick, S.; Stahl, M.K.; Recker, M. 1990 July; 182pp. (Format: TXT = 566 778 bytes) (Obsoletes RFC 1117, RFC 1062, RFC 1020)

1160 Internet activities board. Cerf, V. 1990 May; 11pp. (Format: TXT = 28 182 bytes) (Obsoletes RFC 1120)

1157 Simple Network Management Protocol (SNMP). Case, J.D.; Fedor, M.; Schoffstall, M.L.; Davin, C. 1990 May; 36pp. (Format: TXT = 74 894 bytes) (Obsoletes RFC 1098)

1156 Management information base for network management of TCP/IP-based internets. McCloghrie, K.; Rose, M.T. 1990 May; 91pp. (Format: TXT = 138 781 bytes) (Obsoletes RFC 1066)

1155 Structure and identification of management information for TCP/IP-based internets. Rose, M.T.; McCloghrie, K. 1990 May; 22pp. (Format: TXT = 40 927 bytes) (Obsoletes RFC 1065)

1152 Workshop report: Internet research steering group workshop on very-high-speed networks. Partridge, C. 1990 April; 23pp. (Format: TXT = 64 003 bytes)

1151 Version 2 of the Reliable Data Protocol (RDP). Partridge, C.; Hinden, R.M. 1990 April; 4pp. (Format: TXT = 8293 bytes) (Updates RFC 908)

1150 FYI on FYI: Introduction to the FYI notes. Malkin, G.S.; Reynolds, J.K. 1990 March; 4pp. (Format: TXT = 7867 bytes) (Also FYI 1)

1149 Standard for the transmission of IP datagrams on avian carriers. Waitzman, D. 1990 April 1; 2pp. (Format: TXT = 3329 bytes)

1148 Mapping between X.400 (1988)/ISO 10021 and RFC 822. Kille, S.E. 1990 March; 94pp. (Format: TXT = 194 292 bytes) (Updates RFC 822, RFC 987, RFC 1026, RFC 1138)

1147 FYI on a network management tool catalog: tools for monitoring and debugging TCP/IP Internets and interconnected devices. Stine, R.H., ed. 1990 April; 126pp. (Format: TXT = 336 906, PS = 555 225 bytes) (Also FYI 2)

1146 TCP alternate checksum options. Zweig, J.; Partridge, C. 1990 March; 5pp. (Format: TXT = 10 955 bytes) (Obsoletes RFC 1145)

1144 Compressing TCP/IP headers for low-speed serial links. Jacobson, V. 1990 February; 43pp. (Format: TXT = 120 959, PS = 534 729 bytes)

1143 Q method of implementing Telnet option negotiation. Bernstein, D.J. 1990 February; 10pp. (Format: TXT = 23 331 bytes)

1138 Mapping between X.400 (1988)/ISO 10021 and RFC 822. Kille, S.E. 1989 December; 92pp. (Format: TXT = 191 029 bytes) (Updates RFC 822, RFC 987, RFC 1026; updated by RFC 1148)

1137 Mapping between full RFC 822 and RFC 822 with restricted encoding. Kille, S.E. 1989 December; 3pp. (Format: TXT = 6436 bytes) (Updates RFC 976)

1136 Administrative domains and routing domains: a model for routing in the Internet. Hares, S.; Katz, D. 1989 December; 10pp. Format: TXT = 22 158 bytes)

1135 Helminthiasis of the Internet. Reynolds, J.K. 1989 December; 33pp. (Format: TXT = 77 033 bytes)

1132 Standard for the transmission of 802.2 packets over IPX networks. McLaughlin, L.J. 1989 November; 4pp. (Format: TXT = 8128 bytes)

1129 Internet time synchronization: the network time protocol. Mills, D.L. 1989 October; 29pp. (Format: PS = 551 697 bytes)

1128 Measured performance of the network time protocol in the Internet system. Mills, D.L. 1989 October; 20pp. (Format: PS = 633 742 bytes)

1127 Perspective on the host requirements RFCs. Braden, R.T. 1989 October; 20pp. (Format: TXT = 41 267 bytes)

1126 Goals and functional requirements for interautonomous system routing. Little, M. 1989 October; 25pp. (Format: TXT = 62 725 bytes)

1125 Policy requirements for interadministrative domain routing. Estrin, D. 1989 November; 18pp. (Format: TXT = 55 248, PS = 282 123 bytes)

1124 Policy issues in interconnecting networks. Leiner, B.M. 1989 September; 54pp. (Format: PS = 31 5692 bytes)

1123 Requirements for Internet hosts – application and support. Braden, R.T., ed. 1989 October; 98pp. (Format: TXT = 245 503 bytes)

1122 Requirements for Internet hosts – communication layers. Braden, R.T., ed. 1989 October; 116pp. (Format: TXT = 295 992 bytes)

1118 Hitchhikers guide to the Internet. Krol, E. 1989 September; 24pp. (Format: TXT = 62 757 bytes)

1115 Privacy enhancement for Internet electronic mail: part III – algorithms, modes, and identifiers [Draft]. Linn, J. 1989 August; 8pp. (Format: TXT = 18 226 bytes)

1114 Privacy enhancement for Internet electronic mail: part II – certificate-based key management [Draft]. Kent, S.T.; Linn, J. 1989 August; 25pp. (Format: TXT = 69 661 bytes)

1113 Privacy enhancement for Internet electronic mail: part I – message encipherment and authentication procedures [Draft]. Linn, J. 1989 August; 34pp. (Format: TXT = 89 293 bytes) (Obsoletes RFC 989, RFC 1040)

1112 Host extensions for IP multicasting. Deering, S.E. 1989 August; 17pp. (Format: TXT = 39 904 bytes) (Obsoletes RFC 988, RFC 1054)

1111 Request for comments on request for comments: instructions to RFC authors. Postel, J.B. 1989 August; 6pp. (Format: TXT = 11 793 bytes) (Obsoletes RFC 825)

1110 Problem with the TCP big window option. McKenzie, A.M. 1989 August; 3pp. (Format: TXT = 5778 bytes)

1109 Report of the second ad hoc network management review group. Cerf, V.G.1989 August; 8pp. (Format: TXT = 20 642 bytes)

1107 Plan for Internet directory services. Sollins, K.R. 1989 July; 19pp. (Format: TXT = 51 773 bytes)

1106 TCP big window and NAK options. Fox, R. 1989 June; 13pp. (Format: TXT = 37 105 bytes)

1104 Models of policy-based routing. Braun, H.W. 1989 June; 10pp. (Format: TXT = 25 468 bytes)

1102 Policy routing in Internet protocols. Clark, D.D. 1989 May; 22pp. (Format: TXT = 59 664 bytes)

1101   DNS encoding of network names and other types. Mockapetris, P.V. 1989 April; 14pp. (Format: TXT = 28 677 bytes) (Updates RFC 1034, RFC 1035)

1099   Request for comments summary: RFC numbers 1000–1099. Reynolds, J.K. 1991 December; 22pp. (Format: TXT = 49 108 bytes)

1098   Simple Network Management Protocol (SNMP). Case, J.D.; Fedor, M.; Schoffstall, M.L.; Davin, C. 1989 April; 34pp. (Format: TXT = 71 563 bytes) (Obsoletes RFC 1067; obsoleted by RFC 1157)

1097   Telnet subliminal-message option. Miller, B. 1989 April 1; 3pp. (Format: TXT = 5490 bytes)

1096   Telnet X display location option. Marcy, G.A. 1989 March; 3pp. (Format: TXT = 4634 bytes)

1094   NFS: Network File System Protocol specification. Sun Microsystems, Inc. 1989 March; 27pp. (Format: TXT = 51 454 bytes)

1091   Telnet terminal-type option. VanBokkelen, J. 1989 February; 7pp. (Format: TXT = 13 439 bytes) (Obsoletes RFC 930)

1090   SMTP on X.25. Ullmann, R. 1989 February; 4pp. (Format: TXT = 6141 bytes)

1089   SNMP over Ethernet. Schoffstall, M.L.; Davin, C.; Fedor, M.; Case, J.D.1989 February; 3pp. (Format: TXT = 4458 bytes)

1088   Standard for the transmission of IP datagrams over NetBIOS networks. McLaughlin, L.J. 1989 February; 3pp. (Format: TXT = 5749 bytes)

1087   Ethics and the Internet. Defense Advanced Research Projects Agency, Internet Activities Board. 1989 January; 2pp. (Format: TXT = 4582 bytes)

1086   ISO-TP0 bridge between TCP and X.25. Onions, J.P.; Rose, M.T. 1988 December; 9pp. (Format: TXT = 19 934 bytes)

1085   ISO presentation services on top of TCP/IP-based Internets. Rose, M.T. 1988 December; 32pp. (Format: TXT = 64 643 bytes)

1084   BOOTP vendor information extensions. Reynolds, J.K. 1988 December; 8pp. (Format: TXT = 16 327 bytes) (Obsoletes RFC 1048)

1082   Post Office protocol: version 3: extended service offerings. Rose, M.T. 1988 November; 11pp. (Format: TXT = 25 423 bytes)

1080   Telnet remote flow control option. Hedrick, C.L. 1988 November; 4pp. (Format: TXT = 6688 bytes)

1079   Telnet terminal speed option. Hedrick, C.L. 1988 December; 3pp. (Format: TXT = 4942 bytes)

1078   TCP port service Multiplexer (TCPMUX). Lottor, M. 1988 November; 2pp. (Format: TXT = 3248 bytes)

1077   Critical issues in high bandwidth networking. Leiner, B.M., ed. 1988 November; 46pp. (Format: TXT = 116 464 bytes)

1076   HEMS monitoring and control language. Trewitt, G.; Partridge, C. 1988 November; 42pp. (Format: TXT = 98 774 bytes) (Obsoletes RFC 1023)

1075   Distance vector multicast routing protocol. Waitzman, D.; Partridge, C.; Deering, S.E. 1988 November; 24pp. (Format: TXT = 54 731 bytes)

1073   Telnet window size option. Waitzman, D. 1988 October; 4pp. (Format: TXT = 7639 bytes)

1072   TCP extensions for long-delay paths. Jacobson, V.; Braden, R.T. 1988 October; 16pp. (Format: TXT = 36000 bytes)

1067   Simple network management protocol. Case, J.D.; Fedor, M.; Schoffstall, M.L.; Davin, J. 1988 August; 33pp. (Format: TXT = 69 592 bytes) (Obsoleted by RFC 1098)

1060   Assigned numbers. Reynolds, J.K.; Postel, J.B. 1990 March; 86pp. (Format: TXT = 177 923 bytes) (Obsoletes RFC 1010)

1059   Network time protocol (version 1) specification and implementation. Mills, D.L. 1988 July; 58pp. (Format: TXT = 140 890 bytes) (Obsoleted by RFC 1119)

1058   Routing information protocol. Hedrick, C.L. 1988 June; 33pp. (Format: TXT = 93 285 bytes)

1057   RPC: Remote Procedure Call protocol specification: version 2. Sun Microsystems, Inc. 1988 June; 25pp. (Format: TXT = 52 462 bytes) (Obsoletes RFC 1050)

1056   PCMAIL: a distributed mail system for personal computers. Lambert, M.L. 1988 June; 38pp. (Format: TXT = 85 368 bytes) (Obsoletes RFC 993)

1055   Nonstandard for transmission of IP datagrams over serial lines: SLIP. Romkey, J.L. 1988 June; 6pp. (Format: TXT = 12 911 bytes)

1053   Telnet X.3 PAD option. Levy, S.; Jacobson, T. 1988 April; 21pp. (Format: TXT = 48 952 bytes)

1052   IAB recommendations for the development of Internet network management standards. Cerf, V.G. 1988 April; 14pp. (Format: TXT = 30 569 bytes)

1049   Content type header field for Internet messages. Sirbu, M.A. 1988 March; 8pp. (Format: TXT = 18 923 bytes)

1045   VMTP: Versatile Message Transaction Protocol: protocol specification. Cheriton, D.R. 1988 February; 123pp. (Format: TXT = 272 058 bytes)

1044   Internet protocol on network system's HYPERchannel: protocol specification. Hardwick, K.; Lekashman, J. 1988 February; 43pp. (Format: TXT = 103 241 bytes)

1043   Telnet data entry terminal option: DODIIS implementation. Yasuda, A.; Thompson, T. 1988 February; 26pp. (Format: TXT = 59 478 bytes) (Updates RFC 732)

1042   Standard for the transmission of IP datagrams over IEEE 802 networks. Postel, J.B.; Reynolds, J.K. 1988 February; 15pp. (Format: TXT = 35 201 bytes) (Obsoletes RFC 948)

1041 Telnet 3270 regime option. Rekhter, Y. 1988 January; 6pp. (Format: TXT = 11 608 bytes)

1039 DoD statement on open systems interconnection protocols. Latham, D. 1988 January; 3pp. (Format: TXT = 6194 bytes) (Obsoletes RFC 945)

1037 NFILE – a file access protocol. Greenberg, B.; Keene, S. 1987 December; 86pp. (Format: TXT = 197 312 bytes)

1036 Standard for interchange of USENET messages. Horton, M.R.; Adams, R. 1987 December; 19pp. (Format: TXT = 46 891 bytes) (Obsoletes RFC 850)

1035 Domain names – implementation and specification. Mockapetris, P.V. 1987 November; 55pp. (Format: TXT = 125 626 bytes) (Obsoletes RFC 973, RFC 882, RFC 883; Updated by RFC 1101, RFC 1183)

1034 Domain names – concepts and facilities. Mockapetris, P.V. 1987 November; 55pp. (Format: TXT = 129 180 bytes) (Obsoletes RFC 973, RFC 882, RFC 883; updated by RFC 1101, RFC 1183)

1033 Domain administrator's operations guide. Lottor, M. 1987 November; 22pp. (Format: TXT = 37 263 bytes)

1032 Domain administrator's guide. Stahl, M.K. 1987 November; 14pp. (Format: TXT = 29 454 bytes)

1027 Using ARP to implement transparent subnet gateways. Carl-Mitchell, S.; Quarterman, J.S. 1987 October; 8pp. (Format: TXT = 21 297 bytes)

1026 Addendum to RFC 987: (Mapping between X.400 and RFC-822). Kille, S.E. 1987 September; 4pp. (Format: TXT = 7117 bytes) (Updates RFC 987; updated by RFC 1138, RFC 1148)

1016 Something a host could do with source quench: the Source Quench Introduced Delay (SQuID). Prue, W.; Postel, J.B. 1987 July; 18pp. (Format: TXT = 47 922 bytes)

1015 Implementation plan for interagency research Internet. Leiner, B.M. 1987 July; 24pp. (Format: TXT = 63 159 bytes)

1014 XDR: External Data Representation standard. Sun Microsystems, Inc. 1987 June; 20pp. (Format: TXT = 39 316 bytes)

1013 X Window system protocol, version 11: alpha update April 1987. Scheifler, R.W. 1987 June; 101pp. (Format: TXT = 244 905 bytes)

1009 Requirements for Internet gateways. Braden, R.T.; Postel, J.B. 1987 June; 55pp. (Format: TXT = 128 173 bytes) (Obsoletes RFC 985)

1002 Protocol standard for a NetBIOS service on a TCP/UDP transport: detailed specifications. Defense Advanced Research Projects Agency, Internet Activities Board, End-to-End Services Task Force, NetBIOS Working Group. 1987 March; 85pp. (Format: TXT = 170 262 bytes)

1001   Protocol standard for a NetBIOS service on a TCP/UDP transport: concepts and methods. Defense Advanced Research Projects Agency, Internet Activities Board, End-to-End Services Task Force, NetBIOS Working Group. 1987 March; 68pp. (Format: TXT = 158 437 bytes)

1000   Request for comments reference guide. Reynolds, J.K.; Postel, J.B. 1987 August; 149pp. (Format: TXT = 323 960 bytes) (Obsoletes RFC 999)

987   Mapping between X.400 and RFC 822. Kille, S.E. 1986 June; 69pp. (Format: TXT = 127 540 bytes) (Updated by RFC 1026, RFC 1138, RFC 1148)

976   UUCP mail interchange format standard. Horton, M.R. 1986 February; 12pp. (Format: TXT = 26 814 bytes)

975   Autonomous confederations. Mills, D.L. 1986 February; 10pp. (Format: TXT = 28 010 bytes)

974   Mail routing and the domain system. Partridge, C. 1986 January; 7pp. (Format: TXT = 18 581 bytes)

962   TCP-4 prime. Padlipsky, M.A. 1985 November; 2pp. (Format: TXT = 2885 bytes)

959   File transfer protocol. Postel, J.B.; Reynolds, J.K. 1985 October; 69pp. (Format: TXT = 151 249 bytes) (Obsoletes RFC 765 [IEN 149])

957   Experiments in network clock synchronization. Mills, D.L. 1985 September; 27pp. (Format: TXT = 70 490 bytes)

956   Algorithms for synchronizing network clocks. Mills, D.L. 1985 September; 26pp. (Format: TXT = 68 868 bytes)

955   Towards a transport service for transaction processing applications. Braden, R.T. 1985 September; 10pp. (Format: TXT = 23 066 bytes)

954   NICNAME/WHOIS. Harrenstien, K.; Stahl, M.K.; Feinler, E.J. 1985 October; 4pp. (Format: TXT = 7623 bytes) (Obsoletes RFC 812)

953   Hostname server. Harrenstien, K.; Stahl, M.K.; Feinler, E.J. 1985 October; 5pp. (Format: TXT = 8588 bytes) (Obsoletes RFC 811)

951   Bootstrap protocol. Croft, W.J.; Gilmore, J. 1985 September; 12pp. (Format: TXT = 29 038 bytes)

950   Internet standard subnetting procedure. Mogul, J.C.; Postel, J.B. 1985 August; 18pp. (Format: TXT = 39 010 bytes) (Updates RFC 792)

949   FTP unique-named store command. Padlipsky, M.A. 1985 July; 2pp. (Format: TXT = 4130 bytes)

947   Multinetwork broadcasting within the Internet. Lebowitz, K.; Mankins, D. 1985 June; 5pp. (Format: TXT = 12 854 bytes)

946   Telnet terminal location number option. Nedved, R. 1985 May; 4pp. (Format: TXT = 6513 bytes)

941 Addendum to the network service definition covering network layer addressing. International Organization for Standardization. 1985 April; 34pp. (Format: TXT = 70 706 bytes)

940 Toward an Internet standard scheme for subnetting. Gateway Algorithms and Data Structures Task Force. 1985 April; 3pp. (Format: TXT = 7061 bytes)

936 Another Internet subnet addressing scheme. Karels, M.J. 1985 February; 4pp. (Format: TXT = 10 407 bytes)

933 Output marking Telnet option. Silverman, S. 1985 January; 4pp. (Format: TXT = 6943 bytes)

932 Subnetwork addressing scheme. Clark, D.D. 1985 January; 4pp. (Format: TXT = 9509 bytes)

931 Authentication server. St Johns, M. 1985 January; 4pp. (Format: TXT = 9259 bytes) (Obsoletes RFC 912)

927 TACACS user identification Telnet option. Anderson, B.A. 1984 December; 4pp. (Format: TXT = 5702 bytes)

925 Multi-LAN address resolution. Postel, J.B. 1984 October; 15pp. (Format: TXT = 31 992 bytes)

922 Broadcasting Internet datagrams in the presence of subnets. Mogul, J.C. 1984 October; 12pp. (Format: TXT = 24 832 bytes)

921 Domain name system implementation schedule – revised. Postel, J.B. 1984 October; 13pp. (Format: TXT = 24 059 bytes) (Updates RFC 897)

920 Domain requirements. Postel, J.B.; Reynolds, J.K. 1984 October; 14pp. (Format: TXT = 28 621 bytes)

919 Broadcasting Internet datagrams. Mogul, J.C. 1984 October; 8pp. (Format: TXT = 16 838 bytes)

917 Internet subnets. Mogul, J.C. 1984 October; 22pp. (Format: TXT = 48 326 bytes)

915 Network mail path service. Elvy, M.A.; Nedved, R. 1984 December; 11pp.(Format: TXT = 22 262 bytes)

914 Thinwire protocol for connecting personal computers to the Internet. Farber, D.J.; Delp, G.; Conte, T.M. 1984 September; 22pp. (Format: TXT = 58 586 bytes)

913 Simple file transfer protocol. Lottor, M. 1984 September; 15pp. (Format: TXT = 21 784 bytes)

912 Authentication service. St Johns, M. 1984 September; 3pp. (Format: TXT = 4715 bytes) (Obsoleted by RFC 931)

911 EGP gateway under Berkeley UNIX 4.2. Kirton, P. 1984 August 22; 22pp. (Format: TXT = 57 043 bytes)

910 Multimedia mail meeting notes. Forsdick, H.C. 1984 August; 11pp. (Format: TXT = 25 553 bytes)

908 Reliable data protocol. Velten, D.; Hinden, R.M.; Sax, J. 1984 July; 56pp. (Format: TXT = 101 185 bytes) (Updated by RFC 1151)

907   Host access protocol specification. Bolt Beranek and Newman, Inc. 1984 July; 75pp. (Format: TXT = 134 566 bytes) (Updated by RFC 1221)

906   Bootstrap loading using TFTP. Finlayson, R. 1984 June; 4pp. (Format: TXT = 10 329 bytes)

904   Exterior gateway protocol formal specification. Mills, D.L. 1984 April; 30pp. (Format: TXT = 65 226 bytes) (Updates RFC 827, RFC 888)

903   Reverse address resolution protocol. Finlayson, R.; Mann, T.; Mogul, J.C.; Theimer, M. 1984 June; 4pp. (Format: TXT = 9572 bytes)

896   Congestion control in IP/TCP internetworks. Nagle, J. 1984 January; 9pp. (Format: TXT = 27 294 bytes)

895   Standard for the transmission of IP datagrams over experimental Ethernet networks. Postel, J.B. 1984 April; 3pp. (Format: TXT = 5156 bytes)

894   Standard for the transmission of IP datagrams over Ethernet networks. Hornig, C. 1984 April; 3pp. (Format: TXT = 5868 bytes)

893   Trailer encapsulations. Leffler, S.; Karels, M.J. 1984 April; 3pp. (Format: TXT = 13 695 bytes)

885   Telnet end of record option. Postel, J.B. 1983 December; 2pp. (Format: TXT = 3346 bytes)

881   Domain names plan and schedule. Postel, J.B. 1983 November; 10pp. (Format: TXT = 24 070 bytes) (Updated by RFC 897)

879   TCP maximum segment size and related topics. Postel, J.B. 1983 November; 11pp. (Format: TXT = 22 662 bytes)

878   ARPANET 1822L host access protocol. Malis, A.G. 1983 December; 48pp. (Format: TXT = 77 784 bytes) (Obsoletes RFC 851)

877   Standard for the transmission of IP datagrams over public data networks. Korb, J.T. 1983 September; 2pp. (Format: TXT = 3385 bytes)

874   Critique of X.25. Padlipsky, M.A. 1982 September; 13pp. (Format: TXT = 37 259 bytes)

872   TCP-on-a-LAN. Padlipsky, M.A. 1982 September; 8pp. (Format: TXT = 22 994 bytes)

871   Perspective on the ARPANET reference model. Padlipsky, M.A. 1982 September; 25pp. (Format: TXT = 76 037 bytes)

869   Host monitoring protocol. Hinden, R.M. 1983 December; 70pp. (Format: TXT = 98 720 bytes)

868   Time protocol. Postel, J.B.; Harrenstien, K. 1983 May; 2pp. (Format: TXT = 3140 bytes)

867   Daytime protocol. Postel, J.B. 1983 May; 2pp. (Format: TXT = 2405 bytes)

866   Active users. Postel, J.B. 1983 May; 1pp. (Format: TXT = 2087 bytes)

865   Quote of the day protocol. Postel, J.B. 1983 May; 1pp. (Format: TXT = 1734 bytes)

864   Character generator protocol. Postel, J.B. 1983 May; 3pp. (Format: TXT = 7016 bytes)

863   Discard protocol. Postel, J.B. 1983 May; 1pp. (Format: TXT = 1297 bytes)

862   Echo protocol. Postel, J.B. 1983 May; 1pp. (Format: TXT = 1294 bytes)

861   Telnet extended options: list option. Postel, J.B.; Reynolds, J.K. 1983 May; 1pp. (Format: TXT = 3181 bytes) (Obsoletes NIC 16 239)

860   Telnet timing mark option. Postel, J.B.; Reynolds, J.K. 1983 May; 4pp. (Format: TXT = 8108 bytes) (Obsoletes NIC 16 238)

859   Telnet status option. Postel, J.B.; Reynolds, J.K. 1983 May; 3pp. (Format: TXT = 4443 bytes) (Obsoletes RFC 651)

858   Telnet suppress go ahead option. Postel, J.B.; Reynolds, J.K. 1983 May; 3pp. (Format: TXT = 3825 bytes) (Obsoletes NIC 15 392)

857   Telnet echo option. Postel, J.B.; Reynolds, J.K. 1983 May; 5pp. (Format: TXT = 11 143 bytes) (Obsoletes NIC 15 390)

856   Telnet binary transmission. Postel, J.B.; Reynolds, J.K. 1983 May; 4pp. (Format: TXT = 9192 bytes) (Obsoletes NIC 15 389)

855   Telnet option specifications. Postel, J.B.; Reynolds, J.K. 1983 May; 4pp. (Format: TXT = 6218 bytes) (Obsoletes NIC 18 640)

854   Telnet protocol specification. Postel, J.B.; Reynolds, J.K. 1983 May; 15pp. (Format: TXT = 39 371 bytes) (Obsoletes RFC 764, NIC 18 639)

827   Exterior Gateway Protocol (EGP). Rosen, E.C. 1982 October; 44pp. (Format: TXT = 68 436 bytes) (Updated by RFC 904)

826   Ethernet address resolution protocol: or converting network protocol addresses to 48 bit Ethernet address for transmission on Ethernet hardware. Plummer, D.C. 1982 November; 10pp. (Format: TXT = 22 026 bytes)

822   Standard for the format of ARPA Internet text messages. Crocker, D. 1982 August; 47pp. (Format: TXT = 109 200 bytes) (Obsoletes RFC 733; updated by RFC 1138, RFC 1148)

821   Simple mail transfer protocol. Postel, J.B. 1982 August; 58pp. (Format: TXT = 124 482 bytes) (Obsoletes RFC 788)

819   Domain naming convention for Internet user applications. Su, Z.; Postel, J.B. 1982 August; 18pp. (Format: TXT = 36 358 bytes)

818   Remote user Telnet service. Postel, J.B. 1982 November; 2pp. (Format: TXT = 3809 bytes)

817   Modularity and efficiency in protocol implementation. Clark, D.D. 1982 July; 26pp. (Format: TXT = 47 319 bytes)

816   Fault isolation and recovery. Clark, D.D. 1982 July; 12pp. (Format: TXT = 20 754 bytes)

815   IP datagram reassembly algorithms. Clark, D.D. 1982 July; 9pp. (Format: TXT = 15 028 bytes)

814   Name, addresses, ports, and routes. Clark, D.D. 1982 July; 14pp. (Format: TXT = 25 426 bytes)

813   Window and acknowledgement strategy in TCP. Clark, D.D. 1982 July; 22pp. (Format: TXT = 39 277 bytes)

793   Transmission control protocol. Postel, J.B. 1981 September; 85pp. (Format: TXT = 177 957 bytes)

792   Internet control message protocol. Postel, J.B. 1981 September; 21pp. (Format: TXT = 30 404 bytes) (Obsoletes RFC 777; updated by RFC 950)

791   Internet protocol. Postel, J.B. 1981 September; 45pp. (Format: TXT = 97 779 bytes) (Obsoletes RFC 760)

783   TFTP protocol (revision 2). Sollins, K.R. 1981 June; 18pp. (Format: TXT = 23 522 bytes) (Obsoletes IEN 133)

782   Virtual terminal management model. Nabielsky, J.; Skelton, A.P. 1981; 20pp. (Format: TXT = 44 887 bytes)

781   Specification of the Internet Protocol (IP) timestamp option. Su, Z. 1981 May; 2pp. (Format: TXT = 4100 bytes)

779   Telnet send-location option. Killian, E. 1981 April; 2pp. (Format: TXT = 2680 bytes)

775   Directory-oriented FTP commands. Mankins, D.; Franklin, D.; Owen, A.D. 1980 December; 6pp. (Format: TXT = 9822 bytes)

774   Internet protocol handbook: table of contents. Postel, J.B. 1980 October; 3pp. (Format: TXT = 3625 bytes) (Obsoletes RFC 766)

768   User datagram protocol. Postel, J.B. 1980 August 28; 3pp. (Format: TXT = 6069 bytes)

767   Structured format for transmission of multimedia documents. Postel, J.B. 1980 August; 33pp. (Format: TXT = 62 316 bytes)

761   DoD standard transmission control protocol. Postel, J.B. 1980 January; 84pp. (Format: TXT = 172 234 bytes)

760   DoD standard Internet protocol. Postel, J.B. 1980 January; 41pp. (Format: TXT = 84 214 bytes) (Obsoletes IEN 123; obsoleted by RFC 791, RFC 777)

759   Internet message protocol. Postel, J.B. 1980 August; 71pp. (Format: TXT = 127 948 bytes)

757   Suggested solution to the naming, addressing, and delivery problem for ARPANET message systems. Deutsch, D.P. 1979 September 10; 17pp. (Format: TXT = 36 773 bytes)

756   NIC name server – a datagram-based information utility. Pickens, J.R.; Feinler, E.J.; Mathis, J.E. 1979 July; 11pp. (Format: TXT = 24 172 bytes)

749   Telnet SUPDUP-output option. Greenberg, B. 1978 September 18; 4pp. (Format: TXT = 9160 bytes)

748   Telnet randomly-lose option. Crispin, M.R. 1978 April 1; 2pp. (Format: TXT = 2858 bytes)

747   Recent extensions to the SUPDUP protocol. Crispin, M.R. 1978 March; 3pp. (Format: TXT = 2928 bytes)

746   SUPDUP graphics extension. Stallman, R. 1978 March; 15pp. (Format: TXT = 31 081 bytes)

743   FTP extension: XRSQ/XRCP. Harrenstien, K. 1977 December; 8pp. (Format: TXT = 16 720 bytes)

742   Name/finger Protocol. Harrenstien, K. 1977 December; 7pp. (Format: TXT = 12 733 bytes) (Obsoleted by RFC 1194)

738   Time server. Harrenstien, K. 1977 October; 1pp. (Format: TXT = 1909 bytes)

737   FTP extension: XSEN. Harrenstien, K. 1977 October; 1pp. (Format: TXT = 2185 bytes)

736   Telnet SUPDUP option. Crispin, M.R. 1977 October; 2pp. (Format: TXT = 3200 bytes)

735   Revised Telnet byte macro option. Crocker, D.; Gumpertz, R.H. 1977 November; 5pp. (Format: TXT = 10 879 bytes) (Obsoletes RFC 729)

734   SUPDUP Protocol. Crispin, M.R. 1977 October; 14pp. (Format: TXT = 33 920 bytes)

732   Telnet data entry terminal option. Day, J.D. 1977 September; 30pp. (Format: TXT = 58 929 bytes) (Obsoletes RFC 731; updated by RFC 1043)

730   Extensible field addressing. Postel, J.B. 1977 May; 5pp. (Format: TXT = 9812 bytes)

728   Minor pitfall in the Telnet protocol. Day, J.D. 1977 April; 1pp, (Format: TXT = 2265 bytes)

727   Telnet logout option. Crispin, M.R. 1977 April; 3pp. (Format: TXT = 5850 bytes)

726   Remote controlled transmission and echoing Telnet option. Postel, J.B.; Crocker, D. 1977 March; 16pp. (Format: TXT = 39 594 bytes)

720   Address specification syntax for network mail. Crocker, D. 1976 August; 4pp. (Format: TXT = 6835 bytes)

698   Telnet extended ASCII option. Mock, T. 1975 July; 4pp. (Format: TXT = 5307 bytes)

D

Subnetting a class B address

This table shows, in a summarized form, all possible subnets for a single class B address to the point where there are 254 hosts per subnetwork. This is equivalent to subnetting the address to the same as a class C address. The table headings are as follows:

- *Subnet bits*   The number of additional bits which are added to the default class B subnet mask of 255.255.0.0.

- *Subnet mask*   The subnet mask which is the result of adding subnet bits to the default mask.

- *No of networks*   The number of usable networks which will result. This is two fewer than might be expected because of 'this network' reservation and the broadcast network.

- *No of hosts*   The maximum number of hosts on each subnetwork.

- *Net no.*   A designator to indicate the position in the sequence of networks (from 1 up to number of networks). This is purely for convenience in this table; it has no significance in TCP/IP conventions.

- *Net step*   The value in the third and fourth octets of the IP address which must be added to distinguish the successive networks.

- *Net id*   The IP address which identifies the network – a Host Id of all 0s.

- *First host*   The first usable host id on this network.

- *Last host*   The last usable host id on this network.

- *Local broadcast*   The address used to indicate (at the IP layer) a broadcast on this cable.

Subnet bits	Subnet mask	No. of networks	No. of hosts	Net no.	Net step	Net id	First host	Last host	Local broadcast
0	255.255.0.0	1	65534	0	0.0	XXX.YYY.0.0	XXX.YYY.0.1	XXX.YYY.255.254	XXX.YYY.255.255
1	255.255.128.0	0	32766	0*	128.0				
				1*					
2	255.255.192.0	2	16382	0*	64.0				
				1		XXX.YYY.64.0	XXX.YYY.64.1	XXX.YYY.127.254	XXX.YYY.127.255
				2		XXX.YYY.128.0	XXX.YYY.128.1	XXX.YYY.191.254	XXX.YYY.191.255
				3*					
3	255.255.224.0	6	8190	0*	32.0				
				1		XXX.YYY.32.0	XXX.YYY.32.1	XXX.YYY.63.254	XXX.YYY.63.255
				2		XXX.YYY.64.0			
				3		XXX.YYY.96.0			
				4		XXX.YYY.128.0	+32.0	+32.0	+32.0
				5		XXX.YYY.140.0			
				6		XXX.YYY.192.0	XXX.YYY.192.1	XXX.YYY.223.254	XXX.YYY.223.255
				7*					
4	255.255.240.0	14	4094	0*	16.0				
				1		XXX.YYY.16.0	XXX.YYY.16.1	XXX.YYY.31.254	XXX.YYY.31.255
				2		XXX.YYY.32.0	XXX.YYY.32.1	XXX.YYY.47.254	XXX.YYY.47.255
				.					
				.		+16.0	+16.0	+16.0	+16.0
				.					
				13		XXX.YYY.208.0	XXX.YYY.208.1	XXX.YYY.223.254	XXX.YYY.223.255
				14		XXX.YYY.224.0	XXX.YYY.224.1	XXX.YYY.239.254	XXX.YYY.239.255
				15*					

Subnet bits	Subnet mask	No. of networks	No. of hosts	Net no.	Net step	Net id	First host	Last host	Local broadcast
5	255.255.248.0	30	2046	0*	8.0				
				1		XXX.YYY.8.0	XXX.YYY.8.1	XXX.YYY.15.254	XXX.YYY.15.255
				.		+8.0	+8.0	+8.0	+8.0
				.					
				.					
				29					
				30		XXX.YYY.240.0	XXX.YYY.240.1	XXX.YYY.247.254	XXX.YYY.247.255
				31*		XXX.YYY.248.0	XXX.YYY.248.1	XXX.YYY.255.254	XXX.YYY.255.255
6	255.255.252.0	62	1022	0*	4.0				
				1		XXX.YYY.4.0	XXX.YYY.4.1	XXX.YYY.7.254	XXX.YYY.7.255
				.		+4.0	+4.0	+4.0	+4.0
				.					
				62		XXX.YYY.248.0	XXX.YYY.248.1	XXX.YYY.251.254	XXX.YYY.251.255
				63*					
7	255.255.254.0	126	510	0*	2.0				
				1		XXX.YYY.2.0	XXX.YYY.2.1	XXX.YYY.3.254	XXX.YYY.3.255
				.		+2.0	+2.0	+2.0	+2.0
				126		XXX.YYY.252.0	XXX.YYY.252.1	XXX.YYY.253.254	XXX.YYY.253.255
				127*					
8	255.255.255.0	254	254	0*	1.0				
				1		XXX.YYY.1.0	XXX.YYY.1.1	XXX.YYY.1.254	XXX.YYY.1.255
				.		+1.0	+1.0	+1.0	+1.0
				254		XXX.YYY.254.0	XXX.YYY.254.1	XXX.YYY.254.254	XXX.YYY.254.255
				255*					

Note: the first and last network number in each group are regarded as not usable because the first has a subnetwork id of 'all 0s', meaning 'this subnetwork' and the last has a subnet id of 'all 1s', meaning 'broadcast'.

E

Official IAB standard protocols

The following is a list of IAB official protocols, with their standard numbers and the RFCs which describe them. This was obtained from RFC 1311, 'RFC on STD RFCs', March 1992, written by Jon Postel, USC/Information Sciences Institute, on behalf of the Internet Activities Board.

STD	Protocol	Name	Status[†]	RFC
1		IAB official protocol standards	Req	1280
2		Assigned numbers	Req	1060
3		Host requirements	Req	1122, 1123
4		Gateway requirements	Req	1009
5	IP	Internet protocol as amended by:	Req	791
5		IP subnet extension	Req	950
5		IP broadcast datagrams	Req	919
5		IP broadcast datagrams with subnets	Req	922
5	ICMP	Internet control message protocol	Req	792
5	IGMP	Internet group multicast protocol	Rec	1112
6	UDP	User datagram protocol	Rec	768
7	TCP	Transmission control protocol	Rec	793
8	TELNET	Telnet protocol	Rec	854, 855
9	FTP	File transfer protocol	Rec	959
10	SMTP	Simple mail transfer protocol	Rec	821
11	MAIL	Format of electronic mail messages	Rec	822
11	CONTENT	Content type header field	Rec	1049
12	NTP	Network time protocol	Rec	1119
13	DOMAIN	Domain name system	Rec	1034, 1035
14	DNS-MX	Mail routing and the domain system	Rec	974
15	SNMP	Simple network management protocol	Rec	1157
16	SMI	Structure of management information	Rec	1155
17	MIB-II	Management information base-II	Rec	1213
18	EGP	Exterior gateway protocol	Rec	904
19	NETBIOS	NetBIOS service protocols	Ele	1001, 1002
20	ECHO	Echo protocol	Rec	862
21	DISCARD	Discard protocol	Ele	863

[†]See p.490 for an explanation of these abbreviations.

STD	Protocol	Name	Status	RFC
22	CHARGEN	Character generator protocol	Ele	864
23	QUOTE	Quote of the day protocol	Ele	865
24	USERS	Active users protocol	Ele	866
25	DAYTIME	Daytime protocol	Ele	867
26	TIME	Time server protocol	Ele	868

The Telnet options have their own standards numbers:

STD	Name	Telnet options	Option	Status	RFC
27	TOPT-BIN	Binary transmission	0	Rec	856
28	TOPT-ECHO	Echo	1	Rec	857
29	TOPT-SUPP	Suppress go ahead	3	Rec	858
30	TOPT-STAT	Status	5	Rec	859
31	TOPT-TIM	Timing mark	6	Rec	860
32	TOPT-EXTOP	Extended-options-list	255	Rec	861

The status field indicates whether the protocol is

Req   Required
Rec   Recommended
Ele   Elective

These describe the importance of the particular protocol or technique to implementations which connect to the Internet.

Protocol traces

This appendix describes more fully the format of the examples of protocol traces shown in the main chapters and appendices. These are examples of the TCP/IP protocol in action. Each network frame is shown in two formats:

(1) The complete frame in hexadecimal with ASCII representation (a hexadecimal dump) but without preamble or cyclic redundancy check.

(2) A breakdown of each layer of the protocol showing the fields and their values.

Here are a few examples to explain the format of these traces.

The first frame (frame 1) is the bit stream of the frame exactly as taken from an Ethernet network but shown in hexadecimal. All that is missing is the preamble and the CRC. In this example, the Ethernet header is shown shaded.

First is the destination address of the frame (FFFF FFFF FFFF), which is a broadcast, then the source address (02608C0AC49D) then the type field (0806). The type field value is that for ARP, so we know the Ethernet frame is carrying an ARP datagram, therefore the following information is an ARP header.

The dots and characters at the end of each line are an ASCII representation of the hexadecimal values. Dots are used when the ASCII representation of the hexadecimal value is not a printable character. If it is printable, it will be printed so we see some recognizable characters. When a frame is carrying user data, this data can be read in this part of the trace.

Frame 1

```
FFFF  FFFF  FFFF  0260  8C0A  C49D  0806  0001    .......`..D.....
0800  0604  0001  0260  8C0A  C49D  1E00  0001    .......`..D.....
0000  0000  0000  1E00  0063  0000  0000  0000    .........c......
0000  0000  0000  0000  0000  0000                ............
```

The following is a further breakdown of frame 1, decoding the hexadecimal values into the elements of the protocol. It deciphers the fields of frame 1 into something comprehensible. In this case, the datalink frame can clearly be identified, followed by the ARP header and the information encoded in it.

Datalink:	Dest MAC:	FFFFFFFFFFFF	Source MAC:	02608C 0AC49D	Type(Length):	0806
ARP:	Hardware:	0001	Protocol:	0800	HLEN:	06
	PLEN:	04	Operation:	01		
	Source IP:	30.0.0.1	Source MAC:	02608C 0AC49D		
	Dest IP:	30.0.0.99	Dest MAC:	000000000000		

Frame 2 is another example. This is an Ethernet frame (the first shaded part), carrying an IP datagram (unshaded), carrying a TCP segment (shaded), with FTP control messages (unshaded), between an FTP client and server. The message sent by the server can be seen to the right of the hexadecimal listing represented in ASCII (226 Closing data connection <cr,lf>).

Frame 2

```
0260  8C0A  C49D  AA00  0400  0104  0800  4500    .`...D.*.......E.
0046  0B6D  0000  3C06  36E2  1E00  0063  1E00    .F.m...6b...c..
0001  0015  1A57  1245  BC13  0000  17BA  5018    .....W.E....:P.
07DA  601B  0000  3232  3620  436C  6F73  696E    .Z`...226 Closin
6720  6461  7461  2063  6F6E  6E65  6374  696F    g data connectio
6E2E  0D0A                                        n...
```

The above frame is decoded in the following table to describe the functions and options being used:

Datalink:	Dest MAC:	02608C 0AC49D	Source MAC:	AA0004 000104	Type(Length):	0800
IP:	Version:	4	IHL:	5	Type of service:	00
	Length:	0046	ID:	0B6D	FLAGS:	0
	Offset:	0	Time to live:	3C60	Protocol:	06
	Checksum:	36E2	Source IP:	30.0.0.99	Dest IP:	30.0.0.1
TCP:	Source port:	FTP-Control	Dest port:	1A57	Sequence:	1245BC13
	Acknowledge:	000017BA	Offset:	5	Code:	18(psh,ack)
	Window:	07DA	Checksum:	601B		
Data:	226 Closing data connection...					

The frames used in normal examples will not be shaded. Shading is used here to identify the different levels of the protocol in the respective headers in the frame.

Sometimes a frame will be less than the minimum 64 octets required by Ethernet. Some characters will be left in the end fields of the frame and are in fact only fill characters. Where this occurs the fill information will not be translated.

For those who must diagnose more difficult faults on internetworked systems, having the equipment to display and decode information at this level is essential. Once the test equipment is acquired, the skills to use it effectively are just as important.

G

Well-known ports

Decimal	Keyword	Description
0	Reserved	
1	TCPMUX	TCP port service multiplexor
2–4	Unassigned	
5	RJE	Remote job entry
7	ECHO	Echo
9	DISCARD	Discard
11	USERS	Active users
13	DAYTIME	Daytime
15		Unassigned
17	QUOTE	Quote of the day
19	CHARGEN	Character generator
20	FTP-DATA	File transfer [default data]
21	FTP	File transfer [control]
23	TELNET	Telnet
25	SMTP	Simple mail transfer
27	NSW-FE	NSW user system FE
29	MSG-ICP	MSG ICP
31	MSG-AUTH	MSG authentication
33	DSP	Display support protocol
35		Any private printer server
37	TIME	Time
39	RLP	Resource location protocol
41	GRAPHICS	Graphics
42	NAMESERVER	Host name server
43	NICNAME	Who is
44	MPM-FLAGS	MPM flags protocol
45	MPM	Message processing module [recv]
46	MPM-SND	MPM [default send]
47	NI-FTP	NI FTP
49	LOGIN	Login host protocol
51	LA-MAINT	IMP logical address maintenance
53	DOMAIN	Domain name server
55	ISI-GL	ISI graphics language
57		Any private terminal access
59		Any private file service
61	NI-MAIL	NI MAIL

Decimal	Keyword	Description
63	VIA-FTP	VIA systems – FTP
65	TACACS-DS	TACACS-database service
67	BOOTPS	Bootstrap protocol server
68	BOOTPC	Bootstrap protocol client
69	TFTP	Trivial file transfer
71	NETRJS-1	Remote Job service
72	NETRJS-2	Remote Job service
73	NETRJS-3	Remote Job service
74	NETRJS-4	Remote Job service
75		Any private dial out service
77		Any private RJE service
79	FINGER	Finger
81	HOSTS2-NS	HOSTS2 name server
83	MIT-ML-DEV	MIT ML device
85	MIT-ML-DEV	MIT ML device
87		Any private terminal link
89	SU-MIT-TG	SU/MIT Telnet gateway
91	MIT-DOV	MIT Dover spooler
93	DCP l	Device control protocol
95	SUPDUP	SUPDUP
97	SWIFT-RVF	Swift remote virtual file protocol
98	TACNEWS	TAC news
99	METAGRAM	Metagram relay
101	HOSTNAME	NIC host name server
102	ISO-TSAP	ISO-TSAP
103	X400	X400
104	X400-SND	X400-SND
105	CSNET-NS	Mailbox name nameserver
107	RTELNET	Remote Telnet Service
109	POP2	Post Office protocol – Version 2
110	POP3	Post Office protocol – Version 3
111	SUNRPC	SUN remote procedure call
113	AUTH	Authentication service
115	SFTP	Simple file transfer protocol
117	UUCP-PATH	UUCP path service
119	NNTP	Network news transfer protocol
121	ERPC	Encore expedited remote proc. call
123	NTP	Network time protocol
125	LOCUS-MAP	Locus PC-interface net map server
127	LOCUS-CON	Locus PC-interface conn server
129	PWDGEN	Password generator protocol
130	CISCO-FNA	CISCO FNATIVE
131	CISCO-TNA	CISCO TNATIVE
132	CISCO-SYS	CISCO SYSMAINT
133	STATSRV	Statistics service
134	INGRES-NET	INGRES-NET service
135	LOC-SRV	Location service
136	PROFILE	PROFILE naming system
137	NETBIOS-NS	NETBIOS name service
138	NETBIOS-DGM	NETBIOS datagram service
139	NETBIOS-SSN	NETBIOS session service
140	EMFIS-DATA	EMFIS data service

Decimal	Keyword	Description
141	EMFIS-CNTL	EMFIS control service
142	BL-IDM	Britton-Lee IDM
143	IMAP2	Interim mail access protocol v2
144	NEWS	News
145	UAAC	UAAC protocol
146	ISO-TP0	ISO-TP0
147	ISO-IP	ISO-IP
148	CRONUS	CRONUS-SUPPORT
149	AED-512	AED 512 emulation service
150	SQL-NET	SQL-NET
151	HEMS	HEMS
152	BFTP	Background file transfer program
153	SGMP	SGMP
154	NETSC-PROD	NETSC
155	NETSC-DEV	NETSC
156	SQLSRV	SQL service
157	KNET-CMP	KNET/VM command/message protocol
158	PCMail-SRV	PCMail server
159	NSS-Routing	NSS-routing
160	SGMP-TRAPS	SGMP-TRAPS
161	SNMP	SNMP
162	SNMPTRAP	SNMPTRAP
163	CMIP-Manage	CMIP/TCP Manager
164	CMIP-Agent	CMIP/TCP Agent
165	XNS-Courier	Xerox courier
166	S-Net	Sirius Systems
167	NAMP	NAMP
168	RSVD	RSVD
169	SEND	SEND
170	Print-SRV	Network PostScript
171	Multiplex	Network Innovations Multiplex
172	CL/1	Network Innovations CL/1
173	Xyplex-MUX	Xyplex
174	MAILQ	MAILQ
175	VMNET	VMNET
176	GENRAD-MUX	GENRAD-MUX
177	XDMCP X	Display manager control protocol
178	NextStep	NextStep window server
179	BGP	Border gateway protocol
180	RIS	Intergraph
181	Unify	Unify
182	Unisys-Cam	Unisys-Cam
183	OCBinder	OCBinder
184	OCServer	OCServer
185	Remote-KIS	Remote-KIS
186	KIS	KIS protocol
187	ACI	Application communication interface
188	MUMPS	MUMPS
189	QFT	Queued file transport
190	GACP	Gateway access control protocol
191	Prospero	Prospero
192	OSU-NMS	OSU network monitoring system

Decimal	Keyword	Description
193	SRMP	Spider remote monitoring protocol
194	IRC	Internet relay chat protocol
195	DN6-NLM-AUD	DNSIX network level module audit
196	DN6-SMM-RED	DNSIX session mgt module audit red
197	DLS	Directory location service
198	DLS-Mon	Directory location service monitor
198–200	Unassigned	
201	AT-RMTP	AppleTalk routing maintenance
202	AT-NBP	AppleTalk name binding
203	AT-3	AppleTalk unused
204	AT-ECHO	AppleTalk echo
205	AT-5	AppleTalk unused
206	AT-ZIS	AppleTalk zone information
207	AT-7	AppleTalk unused
208	AT-8 AppleTalk	unused
209–223	Unassigned	
224–241	Reserved	
243	SUR-MEAS	Survey measurement
245	LINK	LINK
246	DSP3270	Display systems protocol
247–255	Reserved	

H

Telnet protocol traces

This appendix shows actual traces taken from an operational network using the Telnet protocol. In this example, we show Ethernet frames in hexadecimal without the preamble or the cyclic redundancy check. The table beneath the frame gives a breakdown of the fields in the frame and their values. For a further explanation of the format of these examples, see appendix F.

This example shows a user 'system' logging in to a host. The frames show the user typing the user id, and the replies and acknowledgements to this. Notice the Telnet negotiation in certain frames and messages coming back from the host.

Frame 1 (host welfare banner)

```
0260   8C0A   C49D   AA00   0400   0104   0800   4500      .`..D.*.......E.
004D   0B0E   0000   3C06   373A   1E00   0063   1E00      .M.....7:...c...
0001   0017   19CB   11E7   39BE   0000   3E39   5018      .....K.g9..9P...
0400   514F   0000   0A20   2020   2020   2020   2057      ..QO...        W
656C   636F   6D65   2074   6F20   5641   582F   564D      elcome to VAX/VM
5320   5635   2E33   2020   2020   0D                      S V5.3      .
```

Datalink:	Dest MAC:	02608C 0AC49D	Source MAC:	AA0004 000104	Type(Length):	0800
IP:	Version:	4	IHL:	5	Type of service:	00
	Length:	004D	ID:	0B0E	Flags:	0
	Offset:	0	Time to live:	60	Protocol:	06
	Checksum:	373A	Source IP:	30.0.0.99	Dest IP:	30.0.0.1
TCP:	Source port:	Telnet(0017)	Dest port:	19CB	Sequence:	11E739BE
	Acknowledge:	00003E39	Offset:	5	Code:	18(Ack,Push)
	Window:	0400	Checksum:	514F		
Data:	Welcome to VAX/VMS V5.3 <sp> <sp><sp><sp><cr>					

Frame 2 (<lf> <cr> from host)

```
0260   8C0A   C49D   AA00   0400   0104   0800   4500      .`..D.*.......E.
002A   0B0F   0000   3C06   375C   1E00   0063   1E00      .*.....7\...c...
0001   0017   19CB   11E7   39E3   0000   3E39   5018      .....K.g9c..9P..
0400   C174   0000   0A0D   0000   0000                    ..At........
```

Datalink:	Dest MAC:	02608C 0AC49D	Source MAC:	AA0004 000104	Type(Length):	0800
IP:	Version:	4	IHL:	5	Type of service:	00
	Length:	002A	ID:	0B0E	Flags:	0
	Offset:	0	Time to live:	3C(60)	Protocol:	06
	Checksum:	375C	Source IP:	30.0.0.99	Dest IP:	30.0.0.1
TCP:	Source port:	Telnet(0017)	Dest port:	19CB	Sequence:	11E739E3
	Acknowledge:	00003E39	Offset:	5	Code:	18(Ack,Push)
	Window:	0400	Checksum:	C174		
Data:	<lf><cr>					

Frame 3 (acknowledge)

```
AA00   0400   0104   0260   8C0A   C49D   0800   4500      *.......`..D...E.
0028   0004   0000   FF06   7F68   1E00   0001   1E00      .(.......h......
0063   19CB   0017   0000   3E39   11E7   39BB   5010      .c.K....9.g9;P..
0400   CBB3   0000   0000   0000   0000                    ..K3........
```

Datalink:	Dest MAC:	AA0004 000104	Source MAC:	02608C 0AC49D	Type(Length):	0800
IP:	Version:	4	IHL:	5	Type of service:	00
	Length:	0028	ID:	0004	Flags:	0
	Offset:	0	Time to live:	FF(255)	Protocol:	06
	Checksum:	7F68	Source IP:	30.0.0.1	Dest IP:	30.0.0.99
TCP:	Source port:	Telnet(0017)	Dest port:	19CB	Sequence:	00003E39
	Acknowledge:	11E739BB	Offset:	5	Code:	10(Ack)
	Window:	0400	Checksum:	CBB3		
Data:						

Frame 4 (use name prompt)

```
0260   8C0A   C49D   AA00   0400   0104   0800   4500      .`..D.*.......E.
0035   0B10   0000   3C06   3750   1E00   0063   1E00      .5.....7P...c..
0001   0017   19CB   11E7   39E5   0000   3E39   5018      .....K.g9e..9P.
0400   F496   0000   0A0D   0055   7365   726E   616D      ..t......Usernam
653A   20                                                  e:
```

Datalink:	Dest MAC:	02608C 0AC49D	Source MAC:	AA0004 000104	Type(Length):	0800
IP:	Version:	4	IHL:	5	Type of service:	00
	Length:	0035	ID:	0B10	Flags:	0
	Offset:	0	Time to live:	3C(60)	Protocol:	06
	Checksum:	3750	Source IP:	30.0.0.99	Dest IP:	30.0.0.1
TCP:	Source port:	Telnet(0017)	Dest port:	19CB	Sequence:	11E739E5
	Acknowledge:	00003E39	Offset:	5	Code:	18(Ack,Push)
	Window:	0400	Checksum:	F496		
Data:	<lf><cr>Username:<sp>					

Frame 5 (acknowledge)

```
AA00  0400  0104  0260  8C0A  C49D  0800  4500    *......`..D...E.
0028  0008  0000  FF06  7F64  1E00  0001  1E00    .(.......d......
0063  19CB  0017  \0000  3E39  11E7  39F2  5010    .c.K....9.g9rP.
0400  CB7C  0000                                  ..K|..
```

Datalink:	Dest MAC:	AA0004 000104	Source MAC:	02608C 0AC49D	Type(Length):	0800
IP:	Version:	4	IHL:	5	Type of service:	00
	Length:	0028	ID:	0004	Flags:	0
	Offset:	0	Time to live:	FF(255)	Protocol:	06
	Checksum:	7F64	Source IP:	30.0.0.1	Dest IP:	30.0.0.99
TCP:	Source port:	Telnet(0017)	Dest port:	19CB	Sequence:	00003E39
	Acknowledge:	11E739F2	Offset:	5	Code:	10(Ack)
	Window:	0400	Checksum:	CB7C		
Data:	:					

Frame 6 (Telnet negotiation)

```
AA00  0400  0104  0260  8C0A  C49D  0800  4500    *......`..D...E.
0031  0009  0000  FF06  7F5A  1E00  0001  1E00    .1.......Z......
0063  19CB  0017  0000  3E39  11E7  39F2  5018    .c.K....9.g9rP.
0400  B36D  0000  FFFD  03FF  FC03  FFFC  18       ..3m...}..|..|.
```

Datalink:	Dest MAC:	AA0004 000104	Source MAC:	02608C 0AC49D	Type(Length):	0800
IP:	Version:	4	IHL:	5	Type of service:	00
	Length:	0031	ID:	0009	Flags:	0
	Offset:	0	Time to live:	FF(255)	Protocol:	06
	Checksum:	7F5A	Source IP:	30.0.0.1	Dest IP:	30.0.0.99
TCP:	Source port:	Telnet(0017)	Dest port:	19CB	Sequence:	00003E39
	Acknowledge:	11E739F2	Offset:	5	Code:	18(Ack,Push)
	Window:	0400	Checksum:	B36D		
Data:	:	[Do Suppress Go-Ahead(FFFD03)][Won't Go-ahead(FFFC03)][Won't terminal type(FFFC18)]				

Frame 7 (acknowledge)

```
0260  8C0A  C49D  AA00  0400  0104  0800  4500    .`..D.*.......E.
0028  0B11  0000  3C06  375C  1E00  0063  1E00    .(.....7\...c..
0001  0017  19CB  11E7  39F2  0000  3E42  5010    .....K.g9r..BP.
0400  CB73  0000  0000  0000  0000                ..Ks........
```

Datalink:	Dest MAC:	02608C 0AC49D	Source MAC:	AA0004 000104	Type(Length):	0800
IP:	Version:	4	IHL:	5	Type of service:	00
	Length:	0028	ID:	0B11	Flags:	0
	Offset:	0	Time to live:	3C(60)	Protocol:	06
	Checksum:	375C	Source IP:	30.0.0.99	Dest IP:	30.0.0.1
TCP:	Source port:	Telnet(0017)	Dest port:	19CB	Sequence:	11E739F2
	Acknowledge:	00003E42	Offset:	5	Code:	10(Ack)
	Window:	0400	Checksum:	CB73		
Data:	:					

Frame 8 (acknowledge)

```
AA00  0400  0104  0260  8C0A  C49D  0800  4500    *......`..D...E.
0028  000B  0000  FF06  7F61  1E00  0001  1E00    .(.......a......
0063  19CB  0017  0000  3E42  11E7  39F2  5010    .c.K....B.g9rP.
0400  CB73  0000                                  ..Ks..
```

Datalink:	Dest MAC:	AA0004 000104	Source MAC:	02608C 0AC49D	Type(Length):	0800
IP:	Version:	4	IHL:	5	Type of service:	00
	Length:	0028	ID:	000B	Flags:	0
	Offset:	0	Time to live:	FF(255)	Protocol:	06
	Checksum:	7F61	Source IP:	30.0.0.1	Dest IP:	30.0.0.99
TCP:	Source port:	Telnet(0017)	Dest port:	19CB	Sequence:	00003E42
	Acknowledge:	11E739F2	Offset:	5	Code:	10(Ack)
	Window:	0400	Checksum:	CB73		
Data:	ahead					

Frame 9 ("s")

```
AA00  0400  0104  0260  8C0A  C49D  0800  4500    *......`..D...E.
0029  000C  0000  FF06  7F5F  1E00  0001  1E00    .)......._......
0063  19CB  0017  0000  3E42  11E7  39F2  5018    .c.K....B.g9rP.
0400  586A  0000  73                              ..Xj..s
```

Datalink:	Dest MAC:	AA0004 000104	Source MAC:	02608C 0AC49D	Type(Length):	0800
IP:	Version:	4	IHL:	5	Type of service:	00
	Length:	0029	ID:	000C	Flags:	0
	Offset:	0	Time to live:	FF(255)	Protocol:	06
	Checksum:	7F5F	Source IP:	30.0.0.1	Dest IP:	30.0.0.99
TCP:	Source port:	Telnet(0017)	Dest port:	19CB	Sequence:	00003E42
	Acknowledge:	11E739F2	Offset:	5	Code:	18(Ack,Psh)
	Window:	0400	Checksum:	586A		
Data:	s					

Frame 10 (acknowledge, negotiation and echo "S")

```
0260  8C0A  C49D  AA00  0400  0104  0800  4500    .`..D.*.......E.
002C  0B12  0000  3C06  3757  1E00  0063  1E00    .,.....7W...c..
0001  0017  19CB  11E7  39F2  0000  3E43  5018    .....K.g9r..CP.
0400  C814  0000  FFFE  0353  0000                ..H....~.S..
```

Datalink:	Dest MAC:	02608C 0AC49D	Source MAC:	AA0004 000104	Type(Length):	0800
IP:	Version:	4	IHL:	5	Type of service:	00
	Length:	002C	ID:	0B12	Flags:	0
	Offset:	0	Time to live:	3C(60)	Protocol:	06
	Checksum:	375C	Source IP:	30.0.0.99	Dest IP:	30.0.0.1
TCP:	Source port:	Telnet(0017)	Dest port:	19CB	Sequence:	11E739F2
	Acknowledge:	00003E43	Offset:	5	Code:	18(Ack,Push)
	Window:	0400	Checksum:	C814		
Data:	[Don't Suppres-go-ahead(FFFE03)] S					

Frame 11 (acknowledge)

```
AA00   0400   0104   0260   8C0A   C49D   0800   4500        *......`..D...E.
0028   000D   0000   FF06   7F5F   1E00   0001   1E00        .(......._.....
0063   19CB   0017   0000   3E43   11E7   39F6   5010        .c.K....C.g9vP.
0400   CB6E   0000                                           ..Kn..
```

Datalink:	Dest MAC:	AA0004 000104	Source MAC:	02608C 0AC49D	Type(Length):	0800
IP:	Version:	4	IHL:	5	Type of service:	00
	Length:	0028	ID:	000D	Flags:	0
	Offset:	0	Time to live:	255	Protocol:	06
	Checksum:	7F5F	Source IP:	30.0.0.1	Dest IP:	30.0.0.99
TCP:	Source port:	Telnet(0017)	Dest port:	19CB	Sequence:	00003E43
	Acknowledge:	11E739F6	Offset:	5	Code:	18(Ack,Psh)
	Window:	0400	Checksum:	CB6E		
Data:						

Frame 12 ("y')

```
AA00   0400   0104   0260   8C0A   C49D   0800   4500        *......`..D...E.
0029   000E   0000   FF06   7F5D   1E00   0001   1E00        .).......]......
0063   19CB   0017   0000   3E43   11E7   39F6   5018        .c.K....C.g9vP.
0400   5265   0000   79                                      ..Re..y
```

Datalink:	Dest MAC:	AA0004 000104	Source MAC:	02608C 0AC49D	Type(Length):	0800
IP:	Version:	4	IHL:	5	Type of service:	00
	Length:	0029	ID:	000E	Flags:	0
	Offset:	0	Time to live:	FF(255)	Protocol:	06
	Checksum:	7F5D	Source IP:	30.0.0.1	Dest IP:	30.0.0.99
TCP:	Source port:	Telnet(0017)	Dest port:	19CB	Sequence:	00003E43
	Acknowledge:	11E739F6	Offset:	5	Code:	18(Ack,Psh)
	Window:	0400	Checksum:	5265		
Data:	y					

Frame 13 (acknowledge and echo "Y")

```
0260   8C0A   C49D   AA00   0400   0104   0800   4500        .`..D.*.......E.
0029   0B13   0000   3C06   3759   1E00   0063   1E00        .).....7Y...c..
0001   0017   19CB   11E7   39F6   0000   3E44   5018        .....K.g9v..DP.
0400   7264   0000   5900   0000   0000                      ..rd..Y.....
```

Datalink:	Dest MAC:	02608C 0AC49D	Source MAC:	AA0004 000104	Type(Length):	0800
IP:	Version:	4	IHL:	5	Type of service:	00
	Length:	002C	ID:	0B13	Flags:	0
	Offset:	0	Time to live:	60	Protocol:	06
	Checksum:	3759	Source IP:	30.0.0.99	Dest IP:	30.0.0.1
TCP:	Source port:	Telnet(0017)	Dest port:	19CB	Sequence:	11E739F6
	Acknowledge:	00003E44	Offset:	5	Code:	18(Ack,Push)
	Window:	0400	Checksum:	7264		
Data:	Y					

Frame 14 (acknowledge)

```
AA00   0400   0104   0260   8C0A   C49D   0800   4500      *......`..D...E.
0028   000F   0000   FF06   7F5D   1E00   0001   1E00      .(.......]......
0063   19CB   0017   0000   3E44   11E7   39F7   5010      .c.K....D.g9wP.
0400   CB6C   0000                                         ..Kl.
```

Datalink:	Dest MAC:	AA0004 000104	Source MAC:	02608C 0AC49D	Type(Length):	0800
IP:	Version:	4	IHL:	5	Type of service:	00
	Length:	0028	ID:	000F	Flags:	0
	Offset:	0	Time to live:	FF(255)	Protocol:	06
	Checksum:	7F5D	Source IP:	30.0.0.1	Dest IP:	30.0.0.99
TCP:	Source port:	Telnet(0017)	Dest port:	19CB	Sequence:	00003E44
	Acknowledge:	11E739F7	Offset:	5	Code:	10(Ack)
	Window:	0400	Checksum:	CB6C		
Data:						

Frame 15 ("s")

```
AA00   0400   0104   0260   8C0A   C49D   0800   4500      *......`..D...E.
0029   0010   0000   FF06   7F5B   1E00   0001   1E00      .).......[......
0063   19CB   0017   0000   3E44   11E7   39F7   5018      .c.K....D.g9wP.
0400   5863   0000   7300                                  ..Xc..s
```

Datalink:	Dest MAC:	AA0004 000104	Source MAC:	02608C 0AC49D	Type(Length):	0800
IP:	Version:	4	IHL:	5	Type of service:	00
	Length:	0029	ID:	0010	Flags:	0
	Offset:	0	Time to live:	FF(255)	Protocol:	06
	Checksum:	7F5B	Source IP:	30.0.0.1	Dest IP:	30.0.0.99
TCP:	Source port:	Telnet(0017)	Dest port:	19CB	Sequence:	00003E44
	Acknowledge:	11E739F7	Offset:	5	Code:	18(Ack,Psh)
	Window:	0400	Checksum:	5863		
Data:	s					

Frame 16

```
0260   8C0A   C49D   AA00   0400   0104   0800   4500      .`..D.*.......E.
0029   0B14   0000   3C06   3758   1E00   0063   1E00      .).....7X...c..
0001   0017   19CB   11E7   39F7   0000   3E45   5018      .....K.g9w..EP.
0400   7862   0000   53                                    ..xb..S.....
```

Datalink:	Dest MAC:	02608C 0AC49D	Source MAC:	AA0004 000104	Type(Length):	0800
IP:	Version:	4	IHL:	5	Type of service:	00
	Length:	0029	ID:	0B14	Flags:	0
	Offset:	0	Time to live:	3C(60)	Protocol:	06
	Checksum:	3758	Source IP:	30.0.0.99	Dest IP:	30.0.0.1
TCP:	Source port:	Telnet((0017)	Dest port:	19CB	Sequence:	11E739F7
	Acknowledge:	00003E45	Offset:	5	Code:	18(Ack,Push)
	Window:	0400	Checksum:	7862		
Data:	S					

Frame 17 (acknowledge)

```
AA00   0400   0104   0260   8C0A   C49D   0800   4500      *......`..D...E.
0028   0011   0000   FF06   7F5B   1E00   0001   1E00      .(.......[......
0063   19CB   0017   0000   3E45   11E7   39F8   5010      .c.K....E.g9xP.
0400   CB6A   0000                                         ..Kj..
```

Datalink:	Dest MAC:	AA0004 000104	Source MAC:	02608C 0AC49D	Type(Length):	0800
IP:	Version:	4	IHL:	5	Type of service:	00
	Length:	0028	ID:	0011	Flags:	0
	Offset:	0	Time to live:	255	Protocol:	06
	Checksum:	7F5B	Source IP:	30.0.0.1	Dest IP:	30.0.0.99
TCP:	Source port:	Telnet(0017)	Dest port:	19CB	Sequence:	00003E45
	Acknowledge:	11E739F8	Offset:	5	Code:	10(Ack)
	Window:	0400	Checksum:	CB6A		
Data:						

Frame 18("t")

```
AA00   0400   0104   0260   8C0A   C49D   0800   4500      *......`..D...E.
0029   0012   0000   FF06   7F59   1E00   0001   1E00      .).......Y......
0063   19CB   0017   0000   3E45   11E7   39F8   5018      .c.K....E.g9xP.
0400   5761   0000   74                                    ..Wa..t
```

Datalink:	Dest MAC:	AA0004 000104	Source MAC:	02608C 0AC49D	Type(Length):	0800
IP:	Version:	4	IHL:	5	Type of service:	00
	Length:	0029	ID:	0012	Flags:	0
	Offset:	0	Time to live:	255	Protocol:	06
	Checksum:	7F59	Source IP:	30.0.0.1	Dest IP:	30.0.0.99
TCP:	Source port:	Telnet(0017)	Dest port:	19CB	Sequence:	00003E45
	Acknowledge:	11E739F8	Offset:	5	Code:	18(Ack,Psh)
	Window:	0400	Checksum:	5761		
Data:	t					

Frame 19 (acknowledge and echo "T")

```
0260   8C0A   C49D   AA00   0400   0104   0800   4500      .`..D.*.......E.
0029   0B15   0000   3C06   3757   1E00   0063   1E00      .).....7W...c..
0001   0017   19CB   11E7   39F8   0000   3E46   5018      .....K.g9x..FP.
0400   7760   0000   54                                    ..w`..T
```

Datalink:	Dest MAC:	02608C 0AC49D	Source MAC:	AA0004 000104	Type(Length):	0800
IP:	Version:	4	IHL:	5	Type of service:	00
	Length:	0029	ID:	0B15	Flags:	0
	Offset:	0	Time to live:	60	Protocol:	06
	Checksum:	3757	Source IP:	30.0.0.99	Dest IP:	30.0.0.1
TCP:	Source port:	Telnet(0017)	Dest port:	19CB	Sequence:	11E739F8
	Acknowledge:	00003E46	Offset:	5	Code:	18(Ack,Push)
	Window:	0400	Checksum:	7760		
Data:	T					

Frame 20 (acknowledge)

```
AA00   0400   0104   0260   8C0A   C49D   0800   4500      *......`..D...E.
0028   0013   0000   FF06   7F59   1E00   0001   1E00      .(.......Y......
0063   19CB   0017   0000   3E46   11E7   39F9   5010      .c.K....F.g9yP.
0400   CB68   0000                                         ..Kh..
```

Datalink:	Dest MAC:	AA0004 000104	Source MAC:	02608C 0AC49D	Type(Length):	0800
IP:	Version:	4	IHL:	5	Type of service:	00
	Length:	0028	ID:	0013	Flags:	0
	Offset:	0	Time to live:	FF(255)	Protocol:	06
	Checksum:	7F59	Source IP:	30.0.0.1	Dest IP:	30.0.0.99
TCP:	Source port:	Telnet((0017)	Dest port:	19CB	Sequence:	00003E46
	Acknowledge:	11E739F9	Offset:	5	Code:	18(Ack,Psh)
	Window:	0400	Checksum:	CB68		
Data:						

Frame 21 ("e")

```
AA00   0400   0104   0260   8C0A   C49D   0800   4500      *......`..D...E.
0029   0014   0000   FF06   7F57   1E00   0001   1E00      .).......W......
0063   19CB   0017   0000   3E46   11E7   39F9   5018      .c.K....F.g9yP.
0400   665F   0000   65                                    ..f_..e
```

Datalink:	Dest MAC:	AA0004 000104	Source MAC:	02608C 0AC49D	Type(Length):	0800
IP:	Version:	4	IHL:	5	Type of service:	00
	Length:	0029	ID:	0014	Flags:	0
	Offset:	0	Time to live:	FF(255)	Protocol:	06
	Checksum:	7F57	Source IP:	30.0.0.1	Dest IP:	30.0.0.99
TCP:	Source port:	Telnet(0017)	Dest port:	19CB	Sequence:	00003E46
	Acknowledge:	11E739F9	Offset:	5	Code:	18(Ack,Psh)
	Window:	0400	Checksum:	665F		
Data:	e					

Frame 22 (acknowledge and echo "E")

```
0260   8C0A   C49D   AA00   0400   0104   0800   4500      .`..D.*.......E.
0029   0B16   0000   3C06   3756   1E00   0063   1E00      .).....7V...c..
0001   0017   19CB   11E7   39F9   0000   3E47   5018      .....K.g9y..GP.
0400   865E   0000   45                                    ...^..E
```

Datalink:	Dest MAC:	02608C 0AC49D	Source MAC:	AA0004 000104	Type(Length):	0800
IP:	Version:	4	IHL:	5	Type of service:	00
	Length:	0029	ID:	0B16	Flags:	0
	Offset:	0	Time to live:	60	Protocol:	06
	Checksum:	3756	Source IP:	30.0.0.99	Dest IP:	30.0.0.1
TCP:	Source port:	Telnet(0017)	Dest port:	19CB	Sequence:	11E739F9
	Acknowledge:	00003E47	Offset:	5	Code:	18(Ack,Push)
	Window:	0400	Checksum:	865E		
Data:	E					

Frame 23 (acknowledge)

```
AA00  0400  0104  0260  8C0A  C49D  0800  4500    *......`..D...E.
0028  0015  0000  FF06  7F57  1E00  0001  1E00    .(.......W......
0063  19CB  0017  0000  3E47  11E7  39FA  5010    .c.K....G.g9zP.
0400  CB66  0000                                  ..Kf..
```

Datalink:	Dest MAC:	AA0004 000104	Source MAC:	02608C 0AC49D	Type(Length):	0800
IP:	Version:	4	IHL:	5	Type of service:	00
	Length:	0028	ID:	0015	Flags:	0
	Offset:	0	Time to live:	255	Protocol:	06
	Checksum:	7F57	Source IP:	30.0.0.1	Dest IP:	30.0.0.99
TCP:	Source port:	Telnet(0017)	Dest port:	19CB	Sequence:	00003E47
	Acknowledge:	11E739FA	Offset:	5	Code:	10(Ack)
	Window:	0400	Checksum:	CB66		
Data:						

Frame 24 (acknowledge)

```
0260  8C0A  C49D  AA00  0400  0104  0800  4500    .`..D.*.......E.
0028  0B17  0000  3C06  3756  1E00  0063  1E00    .(.....7V...c..
0001  0017  19CB  11E7  39FA  0000  3E47  5010    .....K.g9z..GP.
0800  C766  0000                                  ..Gf..
```

Datalink:	Dest MAC	02608C 0AC49D	Source MAC:	AA0004 000104	Type(Length):	0800
IP:	Version:	4	IHL:	5	Type of service:	00
	Length:	0028	ID:	0B17	Flags:	0
	Offset:	0	Time to live:	60	Protocol:	06
	Checksum:	3756	Source IP:	30.0.0.99	Dest IP:	30.0.0.1
TCP:	Source port:	Telnet(0017)	Dest port:	19CB	Sequence:	11E739FA
	Acknowledge:	00003E47	Offset:	5	Code:	10(Ack)
	Window:	0400	Checksum:	C766		
Data:						

Frame 25 ("m")

```
AA00  0400  0104  0260  8C0A  C49D  0800  4500    *......`..D...E.
0029  0016  0000  FF06  7F55  1E00  0001  1E00    .).......U......
0063  19CB  0017  0000  3E47  11E7  39FA  5018    .c.K....G.g9zP.
0400  5E5D  0000  6D                              ..^]..m
```

Datalink:	Dest MAC:	AA0004 000104	Source MAC:	02608C 0AC49D	Type(Length):	0800
IP:	Version:	4	IHL:	5	Type of service:	00
	Length:	0029	ID:	0016	Flags:	0
	Offset:	0	Time to live:	255	Protocol:	06
	Checksum:	7F55	Source IP:	30.0.0.1	Dest IP:	30.0.0.99
TCP:	Source port:	Telnet(0017)	Dest port:	19CB	Sequence:	00003E47
	Acknowledge:	11E739FA	Offset:	5	Code:	18(Ack,Psh)
	Window:	0400	Checksum:	5E5D		
Data:	m					

Frame 26 (acknowledge and echo "M")

```
0260  8C0A  C49D  AA00  0400  0104  0800  4500    .`..D.*.......E.
0029  0B18  0000  3C06  3754  1E00  0063  1E00    .).....7T...c..
0001  0017  19CB  11E7  39FA  0000  3E48  5018    .....K.g9z..HP.
0800  7A5C  0000  4D                              ..z\..M
```

Datalink:	Dest MAC:	02608C 0AC49D	Source MAC:	AA0004 000104	Type(Length):	0800
IP:	Version:	4	IHL:	5	Type of service:	00
	Length:	0029	ID:	0B18	Flags:	0
	Offset:	0	Time to live:	3C(60)	Protocol:	06
	Checksum:	3754	Source IP:	30.0.0.99	Dest IP:	30.0.0.1
TCP:	Source port:	Telnet(0017)	Dest port:	19CB	Sequence:	11E739FA
	Acknowledge:	00003E48	Offset:	5	Code:	18(Ack,Psh)
	Window:	0400	Checksum:	7A5C		
Data:	M					

Frame 27 (acknowledge)

```
AA00  0400  0104  0260  8C0A  C49D  0800  4500    *......`..D...E.
0028  0017  0000  FF06  7F55  1E00  0001  1E00    .(.......U......
0063  19CB  0017  0000  3E48  11E7  39FB  5010    .c.K....H.g9{P.
0400  CB64  0000                                  ..Kd..
```

Datalink:	Dest MAC:	AA0004 000104	Source MAC:	02608C 0AC49D	Type(Length):	0800
IP:	Version:	4	IHL:	5	Type of service:	00
	Length:	0028	ID:	0017	Flags:	0
	Offset:	0	Time to live:	FF(255)	Protocol:	06
	Checksum:	7F55	Source IP:	30.0.0.1	Dest IP:	30.0.0.99
TCP:	Source port:	Telnet(0017)	Dest port:	19CB	Sequence:	00003E42
	Acknowledge:	11E739F2	Offset:	5	Code:	10(Ack)
	Window:	0400	Checksum:	CB64		
Data:						

Frame 28 (password prompt)

```
0260  8C0A  C49D  AA00  0400  0104  0800  4500    .`..D.*.......E.
0034  0B1B  0000  3C06  3746  1E00  0063  1E00    .4.....7F...c..
0001  0017  19CB  11E7  39FD  0000  3E4A  5018    .....K.g9}..JP.
0800  D283  0000  0D00  5061  7373  776F  7264    ..R.....Password
3A20                                              :
```

Datalink:	Dest MAC:	02608C 0AC49D	Source MAC:	AA0004 000104	Type(Length):	0800
IP:	Version:	4	IHL:	5	Type of service:	00
	Length:	0034	ID:	0B1B	Flags:	0
	Offset:	0	Time to live:	3C(60)	Protocol:	06
	Checksum:	3746	Source IP:	30.0.0.99	Dest IP:	30.0.0.1
TCP:	Source port:	Telnet(0017)	Dest port:	19CB	Sequence:	11E739FD
	Acknowledge:	00003E4A	Offset:	5	Code:	18(Ack,Psh)
	Window:	0400	Checksum:	D283		
Data:	<cr>Password<sp>					

Frame 29 (acknowledge)

```
AA00  0400  0104  0260  8C0A  C49D  0800  4500    *......`..D...E.
0028  001D  0000  FF06  7F4F  1E00  0001  1E00    .(.......O......
0063  19CB  0017  0000  3E4A  11E7  3A09  5010    .c.K....J.g:.P.
0400  CB54  0000                                  ..KT..
```

Datalink:	Dest MAC:	AA0004 000104	Source MAC:	02608C 0AC49D	Type(Length):	0800
IP:	Version:	4	IHL:	5	Type of service:	00
	Length:	0028	ID:	001D	Flags:	0
	Offset:	0	Time to live:	FF(255)	Protocol:	06
	Checksum:	7F4F	Source IP:	30.0.0.1	Dest IP:	30.0.0.99
TCP:	Source port:	Telnet(0017)	Dest port:	19CB	Sequence:	00003E4A
	Acknowledge:	11E73A09	Offset:	5	Code:	18(Ack,Psh)
	Window:	0400	Checksum:	CB54		
Data:						

FTP traces

This trace shows part of an FTP session, showing the user login and a directory listing. Parts of the trace have been left out as they did not add any new information about the protocol interaction, which is of interest to us here (in the missing frames usually the two nodes were exchanging acknowledgements).

Note particularly the use of the ASCII commands and responses, the FTP control port used for those commands and the new data port opened for a transfer. Note also that this version of FTP requests an IP type of service of 'throughput' (THRPT) for data transfer.

All acknowledgement Ethernet frames are padded out with six octets to make the minimum Ethernet size frame of 64 octets. The four octets of frame check sequence (cyclic redundancy check) are not shown. This padding can first be seen clearly in frame 8.

Frame 1 (TCP "syn" and mss negotiation of 1024)

```
AA00  0400  0104  0260  8C0A  C49D  0800  4500     *......`..D...E.
002C  0075  0000  FF06  7EF3  1E00  0001  1E00     .,.u....~s......
0063  1A57  0015  0000  1732  11E7  4257  6002     .c.W.....2.gBW`.
0400  D39A  0000  0204  0400  0000                 ..S.........
```

Datalink:	Dest MAC:	AA0004 000104	Source MAC:	02608C 0AC49D	Type(Length):	0800
IP:	Version:	4	IHL:	5	Type of service:	00
	Length:	0044	ID:	0075	Flags:	0
	Offset:	0	Time to live:	FF(255)	Protocol:	06
	Checksum:	7EF3	Source IP:	30.0.0.1	Dest IP:	30.0.0.99
TCP:	Source port:	1A57	Dest port:	FTP-Control	Sequence:	00001732
	Acknowledge:	NONE	Offset:	6	Code:	02(syn)
	Window:	0400	Checksum:	D39A	Options:	MSS 1024
Data:	:					

Frame 2 (TCP "syn" and "ack" and mss negotiation of 1024)

```
0260  8C0A  C49D  AA00  0400  0104  0800  4500    .`..D.*.......E.
002C  0B56  0000  3C06  3713  1E00  0063  1E00    .,.V...7....c..
0001  0015  1A57  1245  B9C0  0000  1733  6012    .....W.E9@...3`.
0400  5BC2  0000  0204  0400  0000                ..[B........
```

Datalink:	Dest MAC:	02608C 0AC49D	Source MAC:	AA0004 000104	Type(Length):	0800
IP:	Version:	4	IHL:	5	Type of service:	00
	Length:	002C	ID:	0B56	Flags:	0
	Offset:	0	Time to live:	3C(60)	Protocol:	06
	Checksum:	3713	Source IP:	30.0.0.99	Dest IP:	30.0.0.1
TCP:	Source port:	FTP-Control	Dest port:	1A57	Sequence:	1245B9??
	Acknowledge:	000017??	Offset:	6	Code:	12(SYN,ACK)
	Window:	0400	Checksum:		Options:	mss1024
Data:						

Frame 3 (acknowledge)

```
AA00  0400  0104  0260  8C0A  C49D  0800  4500    *.......`..D...E.
0028  0076  0000  FF06  7EF6  1E00  0001  1E00    .(.v....~v......
0063  1A57  0015  0000  1733  1245  B9C1  5018    .c.W.....3.E9AP.
0400  71C3  0000  0001  0800  0604                ..qC.......
```

Datalink:	Dest MAC:	AA0004 000104	Source MAC:	02608C 0AC49D	Type(Length):	0800
IP:	Version:	4	IHL:	5	Type of service:	00
	Length:	0028	ID:	0076	Flags:	0
	Offset:	0	Time to live:	FF(255)	Protocol:	06
	Checksum:	7EF6	Source IP:	30.0.0.1	Dest IP:	30.0.0.99
TCP:	Source port:	1A57	Dest port:	FTP-Control	Sequence:	00001733
	Acknowledge:	1245B9C1	Offset:	5	Code:	18(psh,ack)
	Window:	0400	Checksum:	71C3		
Data:						

Frame 4 (FTP welcome banner)

```
0260  8C0A  C49D  AA00  0400  0104  0800  4500    .`..D.*.......E.
0099  0B57  0000  3C06  36A5  1E00  0063  1E00    ...W...6%...c..
0001  0015  1A57  1245  B9C1  0000  1733  5018    .....W.E9A...3P.
0400  82C8  0000  3232  302D  436F  6E6E  6563    ...H..220-Connec
7465  6420  746F  2046  5553  494F  4E20  4E65    ted to FUSION Ne
7477  6F72  6B20  536F  6674  7761  7265  2046    twork Software F
5450  2073  6572  7665  720D  0A32  3230  2040    TP server..220 @
2823  2920  5072  6F67  7261  6D20  5665  7273    (#) Program Vers
696F  6E3A  2039  2F31  2F38  3920  4020  3134    ion: 9/1/89 @ 14
3A34  303A  3030  202D  2D2D  2033  2E33  2E37    :40:00 --- 3.3.7
2040  2823  290D  0A                              @(#)..
```

Datalink:	Dest MAC:	02608C 0AC49D	Source MAC:	AA0004 000104	Type(Length):	0800
IP:	Version:	4	IHL:	5	Type of service:	00
	Length:	99	ID:	0B57	Flags:	0
	Offset:	0	Time to live:	3C(60)	Protocol:	06
	Checksum:	36A5	Source IP:	30.0.0.99	Dest IP:	30.0.0.1
TCP:	Source port:	FTP-Control	Dest port:	1A57	Sequence:	1245B9C1
	Acknowledge:	00001733	Offset:	5	Code:	
	Window:	0400	Checksum:	82C8		
Data:	220-Connected to FUSION Network Software FTP server..220 @(#)					
	Program Version: 9/1/89 @ 14:40:00 ---3.3.7@(#)<cr><lf>					

Connection established to FTP server

Frame 5 (acknowledge)

```
AA00   0400   0104   0260   8C0A   C49D   0800   4500        *......`..D...E.
0028   0077   0000   FF06   7EF5   1E00   0001   1E00        .(.w....~u......
0063   1A57   0015   0000   1733   1245   BA32   5010        .c.W.....3.E:2P.
0400   715A   0000   0001   0800   0604                      ..qZ........
```

Datalink:	Dest MAC:	AA0004 000104	Source MAC:	02608C 0AC49D	Type(Length):	0800
IP:	Version:	4	IHL:	5	Type of service:	00
	Length:		ID:		Flags:	0
	Offset:	0	Time to live:	FF(255)	Protocol:	06
	Checksum:		Source IP:	30.0.0.1	Dest IP:	30.0.0.99
TCP:	Source port:	1A57	Dest port:	FTP-Control	Sequence:	000017??
	Acknowledge:		Offset:	5	Code:	18(psh,ack)
	Window:	0400	Checksum:			
Data:						

Frame 6 (FTP user login command for user "system")

```
AA00   0400   0104   0260   8C0A   C49D   0800   4500        *......`..D...E.
0035   0078   0000   FF06   7EE7   1E00   0001   1E00        .5.x....~g......
0063   1A57   0015   0000   1733   1245   BA32   5018        .c.W.....3.E:2P.
0400   5146   0000   5553   4552   2073   7973   7465        ..QF..USER syste
6D0D   0A                                                    m..
```

Datalink:	Dest MAC:	AA0004 000104	Source MAC:	02608C 0AC49D	Type(Length):	0800
IP:	Version:	4	IHL:	5	Type of service:	00
	Length:	35	ID:	0078	Flags:	0
	Offset:	0	Time to live:	FF(255)	Protocol:	06
	Checksum:	7EE7	Source IP:	30.0.0.1	Dest IP:	30.0.0.99
TCP:	Source port:	1A57	Dest port:	FTP-Control	Sequence:	00001733
	Acknowledge:	1245BA32	Offset:	5	Code:	18(psh,ack)
	Window:	0400	Checksum:	5146		
Data:	USER system <cr><lf>					

Frame 7 (response from the FTP server)

```
0260   8C0A   C49D   AA00   0400   0104   0800   4500        .`..D.*.......E.
004C   0B58   0000   3C06   36F1   1E00   0063   1E00        .L.X...6q...c..
0001   0015   1A57   1245   BA32   0000   1740   5018        .....W.E:2...@P.
0400   C417   0000   3333   3120   5573   6572   206E        ..D...331 User n
616D   6520   6F6B   6179   2C20   6E65   6564   2070        ame okay, need p
6173   7377   6F72   642E   0D0A                             assword...
```

Datalink:	Dest MAC:	02608C 0AC49D	Source MAC:	AA0004 000104	Type(Length):	0800
IP:	Version:	4	IHL:	5	Type of service:	00
	Length:	004C	ID:	0B58	Flags:	0
	Offset:	0	Time to live:	3C(60)	Protocol:	06
	Checksum:	36F1	Source IP:	30.0.0.99	Dest IP:	30.0.0.1
TCP:	Source port:	FTP-Control	Dest port:	1A57	Sequence:	1245BA32
	Acknowledge:	00001740	Offset:	5	Code:	12(syn,psh)
	Window:	0400	Checksum:	C417		
Data:	331 User name okay, need password <cr><lf>					

Frame 8 (acknowledgement)

```
AA00  0400  0104  0260  8C0A  C49D  0800  4500    *......`..D...E.
0028  0079  0000  FF06  7EF3  1E00  0001  1E00    .(.y....~s......
0063  1A57  0015  0000  1740  1245  BA56  5010    .c.W.....@.E:VP.
0400  7129  0000  5553  4552  2073               ..q)..USER s
```

Datalink:	Dest MAC:	AA0004 000104	Source MAC:	02608C 0AC49D	Type(Length):	0800
IP:	Version:	4	IHL:	5	Type of service:	00
	Length:	28	ID:	0079	Flags:	0
	Offset:	0	Time to live:	FF(255)	Protocol:	06
	Checksum:	7EF3	Source IP:	30.0.0.1	Dest IP:	30.0.0.99
TCP:	Source port:	1A57	Dest port:	FTP-Control	Sequence:	00001740
	Acknowledge:	1245BA56	Offset:	5	Code:	10(ack)
	Window:	0400	Checksum:	7129		
Data:	:					

Note the padding 'USER s' in this acknowledgement frame. This is formed from random characters in the buffer from the last data frame sent by this machine.

Frame 9 (acknowledgement)

```
0260  8C0A  C49D  AA00  0400  0104  0800  4500    .`..D.*.......E.
0028  0B59  0000  3C06  3714  1E00  0063  1E00    .(.Y...7....c..
0001  0015  1A57  1245  BA56  0000  174D  5010    .....W.E:V...MP.
0400  711C  0000  0000  0000  0000               ..q.........
```

Datalink:	Dest MAC:	02608C 0AC49D	Source MAC:	AA0004 000104	Type(Length):	0800
IP:	Version:	4	IHL:	5	Type of service:	00
	Length:	0028	ID:	0B59	Flags:	0
	Offset:	0	Time to live:	3C(60)	Protocol:	06
	Checksum:	3714	Source IP:	30.0.0.99	Dest IP:	30.0.0.1
TCP:	Source port:	FTP-Control	Dest port:	1A57	Sequence:	1245BA56
	Acknowledge:	0000174D	Offset:	5	Code:	10(ACK)
	Window:	0400	Checksum:	711C		
Data:	:					

The password transmission has been omitted.

Frame 10 (acknowledgement)

```
AA00  0400  0104  0260  8C0A  C49D  0800  4500    *......`..D...E.
0028  007C  0000  FF06  7EF0  1E00  0001  1E00    .(.|....~p......
0063  1A57  0015  0000  174D  1245  BA56  5010    .c.W.....M.E:VP.
0400  711C  0000  5041  5353  2069               ..q...PASS i
```

Datalink:	Dest MAC:	AA0004 000104	Source MAC:	02608C 0AC49D	Type(Length):	0800
IP:	Version:	4	IHL:	5	Type of service:	00
	Length:	0028	ID:	007C	Flags:	0
	Offset:	0	Time to live:	FF(255)	Protocol:	06
	Checksum:	7EF0	Source IP:	30.0.0.1	Dest IP:	30.0.0.99
TCP:	Source port:	1A57	Dest port:	FTP-Control	Sequence:	0000174D
	Acknowledge:	1245BA56	Offset:	5	Code:	19(ack)
	Window:	0400	Checksum:	711C		
Data:	:					

Frame 11 (user logged in message to FTP client)

```
0260   8C0A   C49D   AA00   0400   0104   0800   4500      .`..D.*.......E.
0046   0B5A   0000   3C06   36F5   1E00   0063   1E00      .F.Z...6u...c..
0001   0015   1A57   1245   BA56   0000   174D   5018      .....W.E:V...MP.
0400   AC61   0000   3233   3020   5573   6572   206C      ..,a..230 User l
6F67   6765   6420   696E   2C20   7072   6F63   6565      ogged in, procee
642E   0D0A                                                d...
```

Datalink:	Dest MAC:	02608C 0AC49D	Source MAC:	AA0004 000104	Type(Length):	0800
IP:	Version:	4	IHL:	5	Type of service:	00
	Length:	0046	ID:	0B5A	Flags:	0
	Offset:	0	Time to live:	3C(60)	Protocol:	06
	Checksum:	36F5	Source IP:	30.0.0.99	Dest IP:	30.0.0.1
TCP:	Source port:	FTP-Control	Dest port:	1A57	Sequence:	1245BA56
	Acknowledge:	0000174D	Offset:	5	Code:	18(psh,ack)
	Window:	0400	Checksum:	AC61		
Data:	230 User logged in, proceed <cr><lf>					

Frame 12 (acknowledge)

```
AA00   0400   0104   0260   8C0A   C49D   0800   4500      *......`..D...E.
0028   007D   0000   FF06   7EEF   1E00   0001   1E00      .(.}....~o......
0063   1A57   0015   0000   174D   1245   BA74   5010      .c.W.....M.E:tP.
0400   70FE   0000   5041   5353   2069                    ..p~..PASS i
```

Datalink:	Dest MAC:	AA0004 000104	Source MAC:	02608C 0AC49D	Type(Length):	0800
IP:	Version:	4	IHL:	5	Type of service:	00
	Length:	28	ID:	007D	Flags:	0
	Offset:	0	Time to live:	FF(255)	Protocol:	06
	Checksum:	7EEF	Source IP:	30.0.0.1	Dest IP:	30.0.0.99
TCP:	Source port:	1A57	Dest port:	FTP-Control	Sequence:	0000174D
	Acknowledge:	1245BA74	Offset:	5	Code:	10(ack)
	Window:	0400	Checksum:	70FE		
Data:						

Frame 13 (FTP command CWD changes working directory on the server to 'user1')

```
AA00   0400   0104   0260   8C0A   C49D   0800   4500      *......`..D...E.
0033   008C   0000   FF06   7ED5   1E00   0001   1E00      .3......~U......
0063   1A57   0015   0000   1794   1245   BB8D   5018      .c.W.......E;.P.
0400   D220   0000   4357   4420   7573   6572   310D      ..R ..CWD user1.
0A                                                         
```

Datalink:	Dest MAC:	AA0004 000104	Source MAC:	02608C 0AC49D	Type(Length):	0800
IP:	Version:	4	IHL:	5	Type of service:	00
	Length:	33	ID:	008C	Flags:	0
	Offset:	0	Time to live:	FF(255)	Protocol:	06
	Checksum:	7ED5	Source IP:	30.0.0.1	Dest IP:	30.0.0.99
TCP:	Source port:	1A57	Dest port:	FTP-Control	Sequence:	00001794
	Acknowledge:	1245BB8D	Offset:	5	Code:	18(psh,ack)
	Window:	0400	Checksum:	D220		
Data:	CWD user1 <cr><lf>					

Frame 14 (response from FTP server)

```
0260  8C0A  C49D  AA00  0400  0104  0800  4500      .`..D.*.......E.
0061  0B66  0000  3C06  36CE  1E00  0063  1E00      .a.f...6N...c..
0001  0015  1A57  1245  BB8D  0000  179F  5018      .....W.E;.....P.
07F5  1FCD  0000  3235  3020  4469  7265  6374      .u.M..250 Direct
6F72  7920  6368  616E  6765  6420  746F  2022      ory changed to "
444B  4233  3030  3A5B  3030  3030  3030  2E47      DKB300:[000000.G
5545  5354  2E55  5345  5231  5D22  2E0D  0A        UEST.USER1"...
```

Datalink:	Dest MAC:	02608C 0AC49D	Source MAC:	AA0004 000104	Type(Length):	0800
IP:	Version:	4	IHL:	5	Type of service:	00
	Length:	0061	ID:	0B66	Flags:	0
	Offset:	0	Time to live:	3C(60)	Protocol:	06
	Checksum:	36CE	Source IP:	30.0.0.99	Dest IP:	30.0.0.1
TCP:	Source port:	FTP-Control	Dest port:	1A57	Sequence:	1245BB8D
	Acknowledge:	0000179F	Offset:	5	Code:	18(psh,ack)
	Window:	07F5	Checksum:	1FCD		
Data:	250 Directory changed to "DKB300:[000000.GUEST.USER1]"<cr><lf>					

Frame 15

```
AA00  0400  0104  0260  8C0A  C49D  0800  4500      *......`..D...E.
0028  008D  0000  FF06  7EDF  1E00  0001  1E00      .(......~_......
0063  1A57  0015  0000  179F  1245  BBC6  5010      .c.W.......E;FP.
0400  6F5A  0000  4357  4420  7573                  ..oZ..CWD us
```

Datalink:	Dest MAC:	AA0004 000104	Source MAC:	02608C 0AC49D	Type(Length):	0800
IP:	Version:	4	IHL:	5	Type of service:	00
	Length:	28	ID:	008D	Flags:	0
	Offset:	0	Time to live:	FF(255)	Protocol:	06
	Checksum:	7EDF	Source IP:	30.0.0.1	Dest IP:	30.0.0.99
TCP:	Source port:	1A57	Dest port:	FTP-Control	Sequence:	0000179F
	Acknowledge:	1245BBC6	Offset:	5	Code:	10(ack)
	Window:	0400	Checksum:	6F5A		
Data:						

Frame 16 (FTP client indicates the socket [ip address and port] the server should use to return the results of the following command)

```
AA00  0400  0104  0260  8C0A  C49D  0800  4500      *......`..D...E.
003D  008E  0000  FF06  7EC9  1E00  0001  1E00      .=......~I......
0063  1A57  0015  0000  179F  1245  BBC6  5018      .c.W.......E;FP.
0400  5044  0000  504F  5254  2033  302C  302C      ..PD..PORT 30,0,
302C  312C  3132  2C32  330D  0A                    0,1,12,23..
```

Datalink:	Dest MAC:	AA0004 000104	Source MAC:	02608C 0AC49D	Type(Length):	0800
IP:	Version:	4	IHL:	5	Type of service:	00
	Length:	003D	ID:	008E	Flags:	0
	Offset:	0	Time to live:	FF(255)	Protocol:	06
	Checksum:	7EC9	Source IP:	30.0.0.1	Dest IP:	30.0.0.99
TCP:	Source port:	1A57	Dest port:	FTP-Control	Sequence:	0000179F
	Acknowledge:	1245BBC6	Offset:	5	Code:	18(psh,ack)
	Window:	0400	Checksum:	5044		
Data:	PORT 30,0,0,1,12,23<cr><lf>					

Frame 17 (FTP server response)

```
0260  8C0A  C49D  AA00  0400  0104  0800  4500      .`..D.*.......E.
003B  0B67  0000  3C06  36F3  1E00  0063  1E00      .;.g...6s...c..
0001  0015  1A57  1245  BBC6  0000  17B4  5018      .....W.E;F...4P.
07E0  899C  0000  3230  3020  436F  6D6D  616E      .`....200 Comman
6420  6F6B  6179  2E0D  0A                          d okay...
```

Datalink:	Dest MAC:	02608C 0AC49D	Source MAC:	AA0004 000104	Type(Length):	0800
IP:	Version:	4	IHL:	5	Type of service:	00
	Length:	003B	ID:	0B67	Flags:	0
	Offset:	0	Time to live:	3C(60)	Protocol:	06
	Checksum:	36F3	Source IP:	30.0.0.99	Dest IP:	30.0.0.1
TCP:	Source port:	FTP-Control	Dest port:	1A57	Sequence:	1245BBC6
	Acknowledge:	000017B4	Offset:	5	Code:	18(psh,ack)
	Window:	07E0	Checksum:	899C		
Data:	200 Command okay <cr><lf>					

Frame 18 (acknowledgement)

```
AA00  0400  0104  0260  8C0A  C49D  0800  4500      *......`..D...E.
0028  008F  0000  FF06  7EDD  1E00  0001  1E00      .(......~]......
0063  1A57  0015  0000  17B4  1245  BBD9  5010      .c.W.....4.E;YP.
0400  6F32  0000  504F  5254  2033                  ..o2..PORT 3
```

Datalink:	Dest MAC:	AA0004 000104	Source MAC:	02608C 0AC49D	Type(Length):	0800
IP:	Version:	4	IHL:	5	Type of service:	00
	Length:	0028	ID:	008F	Flags:	0
	Offset:	0	Time to live:	FF(255)	Protocol:	06
	Checksum:	7EDD	Source IP:	30.0.0.1	Dest IP:	30.0.0.99
TCP:	Source port:	1A57	Dest port:	FTP-Control	Sequence:	000017B4
	Acknowledge:	1245BBD9	Offset:	5	Code:	10(ack)
	Window:	0400	Checksum:	6F32		
Data:						

Frame 19 (FTP client sends directory listing command LIST to FTP server)

```
AA00  0400  0104  0260  8C0A  C49D  0800  4500      *......`..D...E.
002E  0090  0000  FF06  7ED6  1E00  0001  1E00      ........~V......
0063  1A57  0015  0000  17B4  1245  BBD9  5018      .c.W.....4.E;YP.
0400  C27C  0000  4C49  5354  0D0A                  ..B|..LIST..
```

Datalink:	Dest MAC:	AA0004 000104	Source MAC:	02608C 0AC49D	Type(Length):	0800
IP:	Version:	4	IHL:	5	Type of service:	00
	Length:	002E	ID:	0090	Flags:	0
	Offset:	0	Time to live:	FF(255)	Protocol:	06
	Checksum:	7ED6	Source IP:	30.0.0.1	Dest IP:	30.0.0.99
TCP:	Source port:	1A57	Dest port:	FTP-Control	Sequence:	000017B4
	Acknowledge:	1245BBD9	Offset:	5	Code:	18(psh,ack)
	Window:	0400	Checksum:	C2C7		
Data:	LIST <cr><lf>					

Frame 20 (FTP server acknowledging the request to perform a LIST command and return the output to socket 30.0.0.1.12.23 [12.13 represents the port (12*256 + 13) 3095 in decimal, 0C17 in hexadecimal])

```
0260   8C0A   C49D   AA00   0400   0104   0800   4500      .`..D.*.......E.
0062   0B68   0000   3C06   36CB   1E00   0063   1E00      .b.h...6K...c..
0001   0015   1A57   1245   BBD9   0000   17BA   5018      .....W.E;Y...:P.
07DA   1E58   0000   3135   3020   4F70   656E   696E      .Z.X..150 Openin
6720   6461   7461   2063   6F6E   6E65   6374   696F      g data connectio
6E20   666F   7220   284C   4953   5420   2920   2833      n for (LIST ) (3
302E   302E   302E   312C   3330   3935   292E   0D0A      0.0.0.1,3095)...
```

Datalink:	Dest MAC:	02608C 0AC49D	Source MAC:	AA0004 000104	Type(Length):	0800
IP:	Version:	4	IHL:	5	Type of service:	00
	Length:	0062	ID:	0B68	Flags:	0
	Offset:	0	Time to live:	3C(60)	Protocol:	06
	Checksum:	36CB	Source IP:	30.0.0.99	Dest IP:	30.0.0.1
TCP:	Source port:	FTP-Control	Dest port:	1A57	Sequence:	1245B9D9
	Acknowledge:	000017BA	Offset:	5	Code:	18(psh,ack)
	Window:	0400	Checksum:			
Data:	150 Opening data connection for (LIST) (30.0.0.1,3095) <cr><lf>					

Insignificant frames left out

Frame 21 (FTP server starting a new connection to port 30.0.0.1.12.23 ready to transfer the data from the LIST command)

```
0260   8C0A   C49D   AA00   0400   0104   0800   4500      .`..D.*.......E.
002C   0B69   0000   3C06   3700   1E00   0063   1E00      .,.i...7....c..
0001   0014   0C17   180C   CAF6   0000   0000   6002      ........Jv....`.
0000   6CC1   0000   0204   0588   0000                    ..lA........
```

Datalink:	Dest MAC:	02608C 0AC49D	Source MAC:	AA0004 000104	Type(Length):	0800
IP:	Version:	4	IHL:	5	Type of service:	00
	Length:	002C	ID:	0B69	Flags:	0
	Offset:	0	Time to live:	3C(60)	Protocol:	06
	Checksum:	3700	Source IP:	30.0.0.99	Dest IP:	30.0.0.1
TCP:	Source port:	FTP-DATA	Dest port:	0C17	Sequence:	180CCAF6
	Acknowledge:	NONE	Offset:	6	Code:	02(SYN)
	Window:	0	Checksum:		options:	MSS 1416
Data:						

Frame 22 (acknowledge to 20)

```
AA00   0400   0104   0260   8C0A   C49D   0800   4500      *......`..D...E.
0028   0091   0000   FF06   7EDB   1E00   0001   1E00      .(.......~[......
0063   1A57   0015   0000   17BA   1245   BC13   5010      .c.W......:.E.P.
0400   6EF2   0000   0D00   0000   0000                    ..nr........
```

Datalink:	Dest MAC:	AA0004 000104	Source MAC:	02608C 0AC49D	Type(Length):	0800
IP:	Version:	4	IHL:	5	Type of service:	00
	Length:	0028	ID:	0091	Flags:	0
	Offset:	0	Time to live:	FF(255)	Protocol:	06
	Checksum:	7EDB	Source IP:	30.0.0.1	Dest IP:	30.0.0.99
TCP:	Source port:	1A57	Dest port:	FTP-Control	Sequence:	000017BA
	Acknowledge:	1245BC13	Offset:	5	Code:	10(ack)
	Window:	0400	Checksum:	6EF2		
Data:						

Frame 23 ("syn" and "ack" for new connection plus mss negotiation)

```
AA00  0400  0104  0260  8C0A  C49D  0800  4500     *......`..D...E.
002C  0092  0000  FF06  7ED6  1E00  0001  1E00     .,......~V......
0063  0C17  0014  0000  0A9E  180C  CAF7  6012     .c..........Jw`.
0400  5F9A  0000  0204  0400  4F70                 .._.......Op
```

Datalink:	Dest MAC:	AA0004 000104	Source MAC:	02608C 0AC49D	Type(Length):	0800
IP:	Version:	4	IHL:	5	Type of service:	00
	Length:	002C	ID:	0092	Flags:	0
	Offset:	0	Time to live:	255	Protocol:	06
	Checksum:	7ED6	Source IP:	30.0.0.1	Dest IP:	30.0.0.99
TCP:	Source port:	0C17	Dest port:	FTP-DATA	Sequence:	000017??
	Acknowledge:		Offset:	5	Code:	12(syn,ack)
	Window:	0400	Checksum:	5F9A	options:	MSS 1024
Data:						

Frame 24 (acknowledge)

```
0260  8C0A  C49D  AA00  0400  0104  0800  4500     .`..D.*.......E.
0028  0B6A  0000  3C06  3703  1E00  0063  1E00     .(.j...7...c..
0001  0014  0C17  180C  CAF7  0000  0A9F  5010     ........Jw....P.
0400  75A3  0000  0000  0000  0000                 ..u#.........
```

Datalink:	Dest MAC:	02608C 0AC49D	Source MAC:	AA0004 000104	Type(Length):	0800
IP:	Version:	4	IHL:	5	Type of service:	00
	Length:	0028	ID:	0B6A	Flags:	0
	Offset:	0	Time to live:	60	Protocol:	06
	Checksum:	3703	Source IP:	30.0.0.99	Dest IP:	30.0.0.1
TCP:	Source port:	FTP-DATA	Dest port:	0C17	Sequence:	180CCAF7
	Acknowledge:	00000A9F	Offset:	5	Code:	12(ACK)
	Window:	0400	Checksum:	75A3		
Data:						

Frame 25 (directory listing being transferred)

```
0260  8C0A  C49D  AA00  0400  0104  0800  4508     .`..D.*.......E.
0278  0B6B  0000  3C06  34AA  1E00  0063  1E00     .x.k...4*...c..
0001  0014  0C17  180C  CAF7  0000  0A9F  5018     ........Jw....P.
0400  8B59  0000  4654  5044  2E4C  4F47  3B32     ...Y..FTPD.LOG;2
2020  2020  2020  2020  2020  205B  5553  4552           [USER
315D  2020  2020  352F  3620  2020  2032  362D     1]    5/6    26-
```

Frame 25 continued on page 518

```
4155  472D  3139  3930  2031  353A  3534  2020      AUG-1990  15:54
2852  5745  442C  5257  4544  2C52  452C  290D      (RWED,RWED,RE,).
0A46  5450  442E  4C4F  473B  3120  2020  2020      .FTPD.LOG;1
2020  2020  2020  5B55  5345  5231  5D20  2020           [USER1]
2035  2F36  2020  2020  3236  2D41  5547  2D31      5/6    26-AUG-1
3939  3020  3135  3A35  3420  2028  5257  4544      990 15:54  (RWED
2C52  5745  442C  5245  2C29  0D0A  4753  532E      ,RWED,RE,)..GSS.
3B31  2020  2020  2020  2020  2020  2020  2020      ;1
205B  4755  4553  545D  2020  2020  302F  3133          [GUEST]    0/13
3737  2020  312D  4A55  4E2D  3139  3930  2031      77  1-JUN-1990 1
303A  3337  2020  2852  5744  2C52  5744  2C52      0:37   (RWD,RWD,R
5744  2C52  5744  290D  0A48  454C  4C4F  2E4D      WD,RWD)..HELLO.M
5347  3B31  2020  2020  2020  2020  2020  5B55      SG;1            [U
5345  5231  5D20  2020  2031  2F33  2020  2020      SER1]    1/3
3234  2D4A  554C  2D31  3939  3020  3039  3A31      24-JUL-1990 09:1
3120  2028  5257  4544  2C52  5745  442C  5245      1  (RWED,RWED,RE
2C29  0D0A  4D41  494C  2E4D  4149  3B31  2020      ,)..MAIL.MAI;1
2020  2020  2020  2020  205B  5553  4552  315D               [USER1]
2020  2033  302F  3330  2020  2032  342D  4A55          30/30    24-JU
4C2D  3139  3930  2031  343A  3334  2020  2852      L-1990 14:34   (R
572C  5257  2C2C  290D  0A4D  452E  3B31  2020      W,RW,,)..ME.;1
2020  2020  2020  2020  2020  2020  2020  5B55                    [U
5345  5231  5D20  2020  2031  2F33  2020  2020      SER1]    1/3
3234  2D4A  554C  2D31  3939  3020  3134  3A33      24-JUL-1990 14:3
3920  2028  5257  4544  2C52  5745  442C  5245      9  (RWED,RWED,RE
2C29  0D0A  5354  432E  3B31  2020  2020  2020      ,)..STC.;1
2020  2020  2020  2020  205B  4755  4553  545D               [GUEST]
2020  2033  382F  3435  2020  2033  312D  4D41          38/45    31-MA
592D  3139  3930  2031  393A  3334  2020  2852      Y-1990 19:34   (R
5744  2C52  5744  2C52  5744  2C52  5744  290D      WD,RWD,RWD,RWD).
0A54  454D  502E  434F  4D3B  3120  2020  2020      .TEMP.COM;1
2020  2020  2020  5B47  5545  5354  5D20  2020           [GUEST]
3137  2F31  3820  2020  2031  2D4A  554E  2D31      17/18    1-JUN-1
3939  3020  3130  3A33  3120  2028  522C  522C      990 10:31   (R,R,
522C  5229  0D0A                                    R,R)..
```

Datalink:	Dest MAC:	02608C 0AC49D	Source MAC:	AA0004 000104	Type(Length):	0800
IP:	Version:	4	IHL:	5	Type of service:	08(THRPT)
	Length:	0278	ID:	0B6B	Flags:	0
	Offset:	0	Time to live:	60	Protocol:	06
	Checksum:	34AA	Source IP:	30.0.0.99	Dest IP:	30.0.0.1
TCP:	Source port:	FTP-DATA	Dest port:	0C17	Sequence:	180CCAF7
	Acknowledge:	00000A9F	Offset:	5	Code:	18(psh,ack)
	Window:	0400	Checksum:	8B59		

Data:	FTPD.LOG;2		[USER1]	5/6	26-AUG-1990
	15:54	(RWED,RWED,RE,)..FTPD.LOG;1			[USER1]
	5/6		26-AUG-1990	15:54	(RWED,RWED,RE,)..GSS.;1
	[GUEST]		0/1377	1-JUN-1990	10:37
	(RWD,RWD,RWD,RWD)..HELLO.MSG;1				[USER1]
	1/3			24-JUL-1990	09:11
	(RWED,RWED,RE,)..MAIL.MAI;1				[USER1]
	30/30		24-JUL-1990	14:34	(RW,RW,,)..ME.;1
	[USER1]		1/3	24-JUL-1990	14:39
	(RWED,RWED,RE,)..STC.;1				[GUEST]
	38/45			31-MAY-1990	19:34
	(RWD,RWD,RWD,RWD)..TEMP.COM;1				[GUEST]
	17/18 1-JUN-1990 10:31 (R,R,R,R). <cr><lf>				

Frame 26 (acknowledgement)

```
AA00   0400   0104   0260   8C0A   C49D   0800   4500      *......`..D...E.
0028   0093   0000   FF06   7ED9   1E00   0001   1E00      .(.......~Y......
0063   0C17   0014   0000   0A9F   180C   CD47   5010      .c.........MGP.
0400   7353   0000   4F70   656E   696E                    ..sS..Openin
```

Datalink:	Dest MAC:	AA0004 000104	Source MAC:	02608C 0AC49D	Type(Length):	0800
IP:	Version:	4	IHL:	5	Type of service:	00
	Length:	0028	ID:	0093	Flags:	0
	Offset:	0	Time to live:	FF(255)	Protocol:	06
	Checksum:	7ED9	Source IP:	30.0.0.1	Dest IP:	30.0.0.99
TCP:	Source port:	1A57	Dest port:	FTP-DATA	Sequence:	00000A9F
	Acknowledge:	180CCD47	Offset:	5	Code:	10(ack)
	Window:	0400	Checksum:	7353		
Data:						

Frame 27 (more of the directory listing)

```
0260   8C0A   C49D   AA00   0400   0104   0800   4508      .`..D.*.......E.
0075   0B6C   0000   3C06   36AC   1E00   0063   1E00      .u.l...6,...c..
0001   0014   0C17   180C   CD47   0000   0A9F   5019      .......MG....P.
0001   1E46   0000   544F   5543   484F   5349   2E43      ...F..TOUCHOSI.C
4647   3B31   2020   2020   2020   205B   4755   4553      FG;1       [GUES
545D   2020   2020   362F   3920   2020   2020   312D      T]     6/9       1-
4A55   4E2D   3139   3930   2031   303A   3032   2020      JUN-1990 10:02
2852   5744   2C52   5744   2C52   5744   2C52   5744      (RWD,RWD,RWD,RWD
290D   0A                                                  )..
```

Datalink:	Dest MAC:	02608C 0AC49D	Source MAC:	AA0004 000104	Type(Length):	0800
IP:	Version:	4	IHL:	5	Type of service:	08(THRPT)
	Length:	0075	ID:	0B6C	Flags:	0
	Offset:	0	Time to live:	3C(60)	Protocol:	06
	Checksum:	36AC	Source IP:	30.0.0.99	Dest IP:	30.0.0.1
TCP:	Source port:	FTP-DATA	Dest port:	0C17	Sequence:	180CCD47
	Acknowledge:	00000A9F	Offset:	5	Code:	19(psh,fin,ack)
	Window:	0001	Checksum:	1E46		
Data:	TOUCHOSI.CFG;1		[GUEST]		6/9	1-JUN-1990
	10:02 (RWD,RWD,RWD,RWD) <cr><lf>					

Frame 28 (the data connection is finished with)

```
0260   8C0A   C49D   AA00   0400   0104   0800   4500      .`..D.*.......E.
0046   0B6D   0000   3C06   36E2   1E00   0063   1E00      .F.m...6b...c..
0001   0015   1A57   1245   BC13   0000   17BA   5018      .....W.E....:P.
07DA   601B   0000   3232   3620   436C   6F73   696E      .Z`...226 Closin
6720   6461   7461   2063   6F6E   6E65   6374   696F      g data connectio
6E2E   0D0A                                                n...
```

Datalink:	Dest MAC:	02608C 0AC49D	Source MAC:	AA0004 000104	Type(Length):	0800
IP:	Version:	4	IHL:	5	Type of service:	00
	Length:	0046	ID:	0B6D	Flags:	0
	Offset:	0	Time to live:	3C(60)	Protocol:	06
	Checksum:	36E2	Source IP:	30.0.0.99	Dest IP:	30.0.0.1
TCP:	Source port:	FTP-Control	Dest port:	1A57	Sequence:	1245BC13
	Acknowledge:	000017BA	Offset:	5	Code:	18(psh,ack)
	Window:	07DA	Checksum:	601B		
Data:	226 Closing data connection <cr><lf>					

Frame 29 (acknowledge, data connection)

```
AA00  0400  0104  0260  8C0A  C49D  0800  4500    *......`..D...E.
0028  0094  0000  FF06  7ED8  1E00  0001  1E00    .(.......~X......
0063  0C17  0014  0000  0A9F  180C  CD95  5010    .c.........M.P.
0400  7305  0000  0D00  0000  0000              ..s.........
```

Datalink:	Dest MAC:	AA0004 000104	Source MAC:	02608C 0AC49D	Type(Length):	0800
IP:	Version:	4	IHL:	5	Type of service:	00
	Length:	0028	ID:	0094	Flags:	0
	Offset:	0	Time to live:	FF(255)	Protocol:	06
	Checksum:	7ED8	Source IP:	30.0.0.1	Dest IP:	30.0.0.99
TCP:	Source port:	0C17	Dest port:	FTP-DATA	Sequence:	00000A9F
	Acknowledge:	180CCD95	Offset:	5	Code:	10(ack)
	Window:	0400	Checksum:	7305		
Data:	⋮					

Frame 30 (acknowledge control connection)

```
AA00  0400  0104  0260  8C0A  C49D  0800  4500    *......`..D...E.
0028  0095  0000  FF06  7ED7  1E00  0001  1E00    .(.......~W......
0063  1A57  0015  0000  17BA  1245  BC31  5010    .c.W.....:.EP.
0400  6ED4  0000  484F  5349  2E43              ..nT..HOSI.C
```

Datalink:	Dest MAC:	AA0004 000104	Source MAC:	02608C 0AC49D	Type(Length):	0800
IP:	Version:	4	IHL:	5	Type of service:	00
	Length:	0028	ID:	0095	Flags:	0
	Offset:	0	Time to live:	FF(255)	Protocol:	06
	Checksum:	7ED7	Source IP:	30.0.0.1	Dest IP:	30.0.0.99
TCP:	Source port:	1A57	Dest port:	FTP-Control	Sequence:	000017BA
	Acknowledge:	1245BC31	Offset:	5	Code:	10(ack)
	Window:	0400	Checksum:	6ED4		
Data:	⋮					

Frame 31 (data connection closing)

```
AA00  0400  0104  0260  8C0A  C49D  0800  4500    *......`..D...E.
0028  0096  0000  FF06  7ED6  1E00  0001  1E00    .(.......~V......
0063  0C17  0014  0000  0A9F  180C  CD95  5019    .c.........M.P.
0400  72FC  0000  436C  6F73  696E              ..r|..Closin
```

Datalink:	Dest MAC:	AA0004 000104	Source MAC:	02608C 0AC49D	Type(Length):	0800
IP:	Version:	4	IHL:	5	Type of service:	00
	Length:	0028	ID:	0096	Flags:	0
	Offset:	0	Time to live:	FF(255)	Protocol:	06
	Checksum:	7ED6	Source IP:	30.0.0.1	Dest IP:	30.0.0.99
TCP:	Source port:	0C17	Dest port:	FTP-DATA	Sequence:	00000A9F
	Acknowledge:	180CCD95	Offset:	5	Code:	19(psh,ack,fin)
	Window:	0400	Checksum:	72FC		
Data:	⋮					

J

ASN.1 and BER tag types

ASN.1 (Abstract Syntax Notation Number 1) is an international high-level language used with software which allows 'objects' to be defined and described in a standard way, based on a few fundamental types and values such as object identifiers, integers, Boolean, real numbers, strings, characters, sequences, sets and enumerated values. In network management these objects are used to refer to aspects of a communication system, such as a frame count serial number or software type and version, to an interface card and the error conditions it sees.

The Basic Encoding Rules (BER) describe how the ASN.1 language 'compiles' to a sequence of octets that unambiguously represents the description of the object and is what can be seen in protocol traces of SNMP. There are four classes of identifiers: universal, application, context specific and private. Of these, 'universal' is the class which will ensure that objects can be understood by everyone.

The first octet of any description contains the tag which classifies the object. The second (and perhaps later) octets give the length of the whole description. As discussed in Chapter 17, a tag consists of three components: the class, the form (a primitive/constructed flag) and the tag number within the class (Table J.1).

Table J.1 Tag components.

Name	Bits	Values	Meaning
Tag class	8,7	00	Universal
		01	Application wide
		10	Context specific
		11	Private use
Form	6	0	Primitive
		1	Constructed
Tag value	5,4,3,2,1	0–30	The value indicates the characteristics of the item

Table J.2   SNMP tags.

ASN.1 identifier	Class	P/C*	Number
Integer	Universal	P	2
Octet string	Universal	P	4
Object identifier	Universal	P	6
Sequence	Universal	C	16
Null	Universal	P	5

* P/C is primitive/constructed

The universal class of tags defines up to 30 basic types of items for which a single octet can act as a header. These basic types are predefined or reserved by ISO/CCITT. Further and indefinite extension beyond 30 types is possible as the tag with the value 31 is used to indicate that the following octets indicate a tag value bigger than 31. But this extension is not required for SNMP which uses only five simple types. One of these is **sequence**. By using sequence, more complex constructed types can be built.

The ASN.1 identifiers used by SNMP and their tags are listed in Table J.2. When these are encoded using the BER, the octet identifiers which result are those given in Table J.3.

An octet of Table J.3 will be the first octet of a sequence which describes one item and it will be followed by a single or multiple octet length field which indicates how many octets follow in this item. A single octet length, which can indicate a length up to 127, is normally all that is required for SNMP.

When SNMP is used to manage Internet equipment, the tag object identifier defines the item or object from the management information base (MIB) which is to be described. An MIB is a tree structure in which the branches and leaves identify objects and the parameters which are to be managed. The start of the tree for Internet MIB II is shown in Figure J.1. Each object can be described as a sequence of numbers. For human use these are written down in dotted notation, reading from the top of the tree. If we wish to refer to the ICMP protocol, the sequence would be:

1.3.6.1.2.1.5

Table J.3   Encoding SNMP basic identifiers.

ASN.1 identifier	Binary	Hex
Integer	00000010	2
Octet string	00000100	4
Object identifier	00000110	6
Sequence	00110000	30
Null	00000101	5

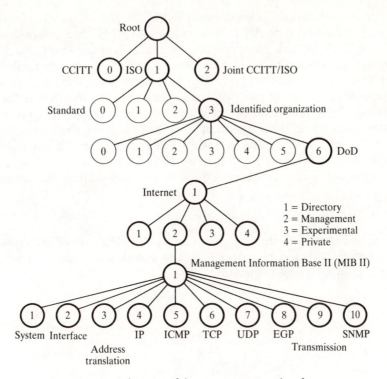

Figure J.1   The start of the Internet MIB II identifier tree.

We cannot give the whole MIB (RFC 1213), but we find the ICMP group contains items to access counters for all the major types of ICMP messages received, for example, destination unreachable (3), time exceeded (4), source quench (6) and redirect requests (7). So each of these would be referred to as:

> 1.3.6.1.2.1.5.3
> 1.3.6.1.2.1.5.4
> 1.3.6.1.2.1.5.6
> 1.3.6.1.2.1.5.7

Basic encoding rules

The Basic Encoding Rules (BER) describe how the identifiers of ASN.1 are carried on a network. When the numeric sequences produced above are transmitted across a network in SNMP, they are preceded by the tag for object identifier. The sequence of numbers

> 0607 2B06 0102 0105 07

can then be decoded as follows: From Table J.3, the value 06 is an object identifier. The next octet 07 indicates that seven further octets describe this object. Since the item 'object identifier' comes from the set of identifiers controlled by one of the international standards bodies, the next number identifies that body. But to save an octet, the next octet, 2B, is an encoded version of two numbers in the tree. As the root of the tree will always have few branches, this octet contains the first two numbers from the identifying dotted sequence. If these two numbers are X and Y then this octet has the value $(X * 40) + Y$. The hex value 2B is 43 decimal so in this case X is 1 and Y is 3 (giving $40 * 1 + 3 = 43$).

The complete decoded sequence is then expressed in dotted form as:

1.3.6.1.2.1.5.7

Looking at Figure J.1, this is object 7 in the ICMP group of Internet MIB II. As mentioned above, object 7 is the counter for received redirect requests (change route requests).

Index